Table of Contents

Foreword to Murder

In 1988, the world's foremost authority on *The Vatican and World Politics,*[1] Avro Manhattan, wrote, "*The lack of importance the United States gave to the election of a Pope after the death of pro-American Pius XII through the election of John Paul II has become paramount in the thinking of subversive elements in America. The lingering evidence is too striking to be ignored.*

Manhattan

The failure of the United States to influence the election of a pro-American Pope in 1963 was a lesson not to be repeated. The adverse consequence of that failure enormous, the price astronomical in terms of lost opportunity and the deployment of United States policies and billions spent in counteracting Paul VI's subversive operations.

Paul disseminated his pernicious and anti-American principles via encyclicals condemning the basic capitalistic tenets upon which the United States had been founded. He repeatedly condemned the imperialism of money and condemned private property claiming to give wealth and land to the poor was to give them God's province...

Paul's doctrine 'Liberation Theology'[2] *took on horrendous roots where the poor were collectively dominant in Latin America, the stability of which was severely threatened. When they reached Central America, military and undercover operations had to be undertaken by the United States to halt his revolution of the poor.*

Paul's doctrine 'Populorum Progressio'[3] *fueled the movement toward communism in Europe forcing American intervention in Italy where his ally Aldo Moro's 'Historic Compromise'*[4] *threatened to bring about a communist state—in the spring of 1978, Moro was*

4

MURDER IN THE VATICAN

"...by the grace of God."

Lucien Gregoire

Friend-Biographer John Paul I

Did his struggle for basic human rights

for born-out-of-wedlock children, the handicapped, women,

the remarried, homosexuals and the poor

cost him his life?

AuthorHouse ™
1663 Liberty Drive, Suite 200
Bloomington, IN 47403
www.authorhouse.com
Phone: 1-800-839-8640

First published by AuthorHouse 10/12/2010

ISBN: 978-1-4490-2305-8 (dj)   ISBN: 978-1-4490-2304-1 (sc)
ISBN: 978-1-4490-2306-5 (e-book)
Library of Congress Control Number: 2010914815

Printed in the USA and Milton Keynes UK

This book is printed on acid-free paper

Author contact: vatican@att.net 410 625 9741

Some kind words

"Yes, I remember him. He was all you say he was, and much more. My hope for a more just church and a better world died with him." Archbishop Bruce Simpson

"One Beautiful Life... explodes into a trail of death and destruction in the Roman Catholic Church." Howard Jason Smith, Boston Globe

"Like 'The Da Vinci Code,' it will enrage the devout and draw low marks from the Vatican pawns. Yet, unlike Brown, Gregoire has the proof." Dean Webster, historian

"In revealing the dark secret that must have haunted him all of his life, Gregoire forces the transformation of Christianity." Toby Johnson, White Crane Journal

2

kidnapped while enroute to the House of Representatives where he was about to move communist ministers into control of Parliament.

On the heels of the Moro murder, Paul's sudden and unexplained death was wrapped with subtle speculations and vague rumors. His deterioration had been so extremely unusual whispers concerning the acceleration of his demise circulated.

These suspicions were well justified when his death was met with delight in the United States, specifically the headquarters of the CIA and the Pentagon which had labeled him the 'pro-Communist Pope.'

Nevertheless, his providential death gave the CIA the opportunity to carry out its scheme—to force election of a pro-American Pope. The CIA joined factions inside and outside the Church backing the Opus Dei anti-Communist Polish Cardinal Wojtyla. When Albino Luciani, an avowed Marxist in every sense of the word, was elected, it struck a nerve of shattering proportions in the United States... "[5]

Immediately after the election of John Paul I, Chicago's Cardinal Cody, a CIA subversive agent, accompanied the disturbed Cardinal Wojtyla back to Krakow where they spent a week together.[6]

On his first day outside the Vatican walls, John Paul I greeted Carlo Argan, the communist Mayor of Rome, and held him in such an embrace one normally reserves for one's father.

His first executive order called for a review of the Church's finances including an accounting of the Church's worldwide assets in the interest of determining liquidity of dead assets. The image of children starving to death gnawed at the new Pope's conscience.[7]

His first audience with a foreign dignitary was with the youthful leader of the Russian Orthodox Church, Metropolitan Nikodim, at the time believed to be—and today known to have been—a KGB affiliate. *Right wing* factions in the United States suspected the Pope sought Soviet financial and arms assistance for his friend Oscar Romero who was struggling against American backed dictators in Central America. Yet, nothing came of the meeting as Nikodim fell dead at John Paul's feet after sipping coffee.[8]

The following week, Enrico Berlinguer, leader of the Italian Communist Party, showed up at the Papal Palace—perceived by the CIA as an attempt to resurrect the *Historic Compromise* which had been sidelined by the murder of Aldo Moro.[9]

On September 13[10] Cardinal Wojtyla flew back to Italy[10] where he spent a week with two bishops who shared the papal palace with the new pope—Agostino Casaroli and Giovanni Caprio. Men Wojtyla had just spent weeks with at the conclave which had elected Luciani.

In early September, it was no surprise appraisers showed up in the Vatican Museum as the new pope had threatened the hypocrisy of the Vatican treasures for years. The surprise came when a real estate outfit showed up on September 17th to survey the papal retreat at Castle Gandolfo—a resort of five sprawling palaces sitting on the Mediterranean—among the most valuable real estate in the world.

On September 20th came the most controversial statement of his brief papacy, *"Ubi Lenin, ibi Jerusalem." "Where Lenin is, there is Jerusalem,"* *Jerusalem* synonymous with *Paradise* in the Bible.[11]

A few days later, the *Bolshevik Pontiff* changed the theme of the upcoming Puebla Conference in Mexico from *Liberation Theology* to *Liberation of the Poor* and announced he, himself, would preside over it. The man who had once led the *revolution of the workers* which had given rise to the socialist movement in Italy would now lead the *revolution of the poor* in Central America. Whereas Paul had fed them faith, he would feed them food. In the United States *revolution of the poor* was then—and still is today—communism.[12]

On September 26, 1978, John Paul scheduled an all-day private audience for October 24th with The Scheuer Group, an American group that supported the 'pill'—necessary to end the driving force behind worldwide poverty and starvation—overpopulation.[13]

On September 27, 1978, the day before he was found dead, the most influential man in the western world threatened the United States and its capitalistic allies, *"It is the inalienable right of no man to accumulate wealth beyond the necessary while other men starve to death because they have nothing."*[14]

John Paul's last words to his long time ally in his struggle to rid the world of poverty, Cardinal Colombo, demonstrates the extreme confidence he had in accomplishing his lifelong dream, *"Sadly, Giovanni, when we have finally completed our work and everyone has enough; there will always be those who want too much."*[15]

The threat of communism in Europe and Central America had resurfaced. The perils of a swell of multi-Cubas driven by the will of the people loomed on the horizon in America's backyard. The dangers to the security of the United States had become real...

Author's note

The photo of Avro Manhattan was taken in November 1990 just two weeks before his death. It accompanied a leak that the renowned historian was in the process of writing a book linking the CIA to the deaths of Aldo Moro, Paul VI, John Paul and others.

Prime Minister Andreotti's disclosure in November 1990[16] of his involvement with the CIA and Operation Gladio in covert operations intended to terrorize the Italian population and turn its mindset against communism in the nineteen-seventies, together with Judge Casson's findings earlier the same year, gave great credence to what until then had been not much more than Manhattan's suspicions.

Murder in the Vatican is the book Avro Manhattan was writing when he met his sudden and unexplained death in December 1990.

1 Manhattan wrote his best seller *The Vatican in World Politics* in1949.

2 Paul's *Liberation Theology* in 1969 ignited a clergy-led revolution of the poor in Central America

3 Paul's *Populorum Progressio* in 1967 ignited the priest-worker movement in Italy which gave rise to the overwhelming success of the Communist and Socialist Parties in the polls

4On Paul's encouragement, Moro united his Christian Democratic Party (38.8%) with the Communist Party (34.4%) in the *'Historic Compromise'* giving the coalition overwhelming control of Italy.

5Avro Manhattan's *The Dollar and the Vatican* 1988 pgs 130-142, paraphrased by the author. Manhattan's observations are repeated in several of his books in the 1980s.

6 *Malopolska Silesia 7 Sep 78* . Cody, a friend of CIA Director William Colby and a frequent visitor to CIA headquarters is believed by most historians to have been a CIA subversive agent

7 To many observers John Paul's objective appeared to be to determine the liquidity of the Church's worldwide assets in the interests of liquidation to help the poor

8 See Chapter 16

9 *La Stampa* 14 Sep 78

10 *Genova Secolo XIX* 13 Sep 78

11Realizing his use of the word 'Lenin' might be misconstrued, he told his listeners what was going on in the Soviet Union at the time was not paradise. He corrected his statement *'Where a redistribution of wealth society is, there is paradise.'*

12 *L'Osservatore* 23 Sep 78

13 *Washington Post* 27 Sep 78

14 See film-clip of John Paul saying this on www.JohnPaul1.org

15 *Corriere della Sera* Milan 30 Sep 78. John Paul said this to his long time coconspirator in accomplishing a redistribution of wealth society—Cardinal Colombo of Milan—in a phone conversation just before the 33-day Pope retired for the last time. It expresses the extreme confidence the *Bolshevik Pontiff* had in accomplishing the platform of his papacy—to rid the world of poverty.

16 In 1990, former Prime Minister Andreotti presented a document *The Parallel SID* to the Italian Parliament in which he detailed his involvement with the CIA and Operation Gladio. The document was published in its entirety in the magazine *Panorama* December 1990

Photo Avro Manhattan – *Associated Press*

Preface to Murder

For those of us who remember him, I bring nothing new. Yet, for those of us who have allowed the Vatican's misrepresentations of what he was all about, who have allowed its falsehoods to distort his legacy, I bring a treasure trove of yesterday.

In the crypt beneath St. Peter's Basilica is a granite slab,

IOANNES PAVLVS P. P. I

Like its counterpart in Arlington across the pond, it, too, marks an unknown tomb, *The Tomb of the Unknown Pope.*

Not even his period of reign marks his place in time. The Church would rather his life remain a secret, *The Secret Life of John Paul I.*

The Missing Will

In the fall of 1978, I had scheduled a vacation to visit my friend Jack Champney in the Vatican. The nature of my visit would change when John Paul died. I would console Jack who had been so close to the Pope. A couple of days later, it would change again. Jack was killed by a hit- run driver and shipped back home.

Though I had suspicions at the time, I have no evidence to this day other than coincidence Jack's murder was linked to that of his long term friend and confidant, Albino Luciani.

Nevertheless, I kept my date. When John Paul II—the CIA-Opus Dei candidate—rose to the papacy, I grew concerned. I flew to the Veneto country where Luciani had spent his ministry.

I visited my friend Antonio Cunial, bishop of Vittorio Veneto. I hoped to secure some of Luciani's records that I might someday put them to print. He told me agents from the Vatican foreign minister's office had shown up the week before and had taken everything with them. I asked him why he had surrendered the records.

During his installation a pope undergoes intense legal counseling as his legal status changes dramatically when he becomes pope.[1] As part of these procedures, a pope is required to file his will with the Vatican. Often a new will is drafted. Yet, at the very least, a proviso is added to accommodate the change in legal position.

Although Cardinal Felici insisted he had filed the will together with an appropriate rider, the Vatican Clerk reported it lost in the Vatican offices. After Luciani's death, his lawyer in Venice was asked to send another copy of the original will to Rome. At first he complied. A few days later, he sent a message he had discovered Albino Luciani's will missing from his files; he would secure a copy from the Venice office. The next day, he sent another message—the will was missing from the City Clerk's files.

Bishop's Castle
Vitorrio Veneto

When confronted, Cunial called Luciani's lawyer and was told the will had provided his records pertaining to his ministries as a priest and as a bishop had been willed respectively to the Belluno and Vittorio Veneto dioceses. Yet, that it could not be found, he had no right to resist and surrendered the records.

He told me something else. There had been a break-in at the local newspaper and some of its archives stolen. This did not mean much to me as when he was a bishop most of the important things he did reached notoriety and were recorded in many newspapers.

This is why what I have to say about his twenty years as a bishop is so well documented: irrefutable references from Italian and world periodicals and other public records which survived the Vatican's attempt to annihilate the controversial life of Albino Luciani.

Yet, even newspapers can often be misleading depending on which side of the aisle they represent. For example, when he said, *"God is more our Mother than She is our Father,"* L'Osservatore Romano and other *right wing* newspapers did not report the incident at all while other *right wing* publications dropped the inference of the superiority of the fair sex: *"God is the Father, but also the Mother."*[2] Middle-of-the-road journals like *La Repubblica* may have come closer to what had actually been said: *"God is our Father, more so, our Mother."*[3] *Left wing* papers *La Stampa* and *Il Mondo* went so far as to speculate an imminent change in the Holy Trinity.[4]

Yet, as a common priest, Luciani was far less politicized. One could depend on the integrity of *Corriere delle Alpi* for those twenty years he spoke out on humane issues as a priest. I arrived in Belluno too late. Bishop Ducoli had given up Luciani's records on demand.

When I approached *Corriere delle Alpi*, I was told there had been a break-in a week earlier. Much later, I found out that the P2-

Opus Dei coalition had bought out this paper in the early seventies to seal archives of articles it had published of John XXIII.

As Patriarch of Venice, Roncalli (John) had been critical of the visionary saints. It was he who coined the phrase *'The Fatima Cult.'*

In 1955, when Pius claimed to have a vision of Christ, Roncalli was caught off guard the Pope was making up stories to lead the world into a third world war. He told a reporter, *"...If we are to have a true church it must be built on truth, not one built on myth."*[5]

Yet, what really made me realize what I was up against is a more recent incident in Vittorio Veneto with an aging seminary instructor. I asked what he knew of John and the visionary saints.

He told me he knew things which might be of interest to me— yet, all clergy in the Veneto country were required to run inquiries of both Roncalli and Luciani through Venice. He took my card.

A month later, I received an email describing Roncalli as a man who spent his life on his knees in adoration of plaster statues.

So, for Luciani's time as a child, as an outspoken seminarian and as a revolutionary priest, except for his more prominent stands on humane issues which reached notoriety, I rely primarily on my direct witness—my personal encounters with the man himself.

I recall each of them as if it was yesterday. I relished those times, as I witnessed this good man Luciani smiling, grinning, laughing, teasing, joking and then smiling some more.

He went into great detail and spoke hours on end of his days as a teenage troublemaker in the seminary at Feltre and I recount much of that here. He had less to say of his days in the major seminary at Belluno and as a young priest. Yet, he gave me enough to bridge the gap between his childhood and the time he became a bishop.

Except for his more controversial behavior in which he defied papal decrees and stirred the world press, we may never be able to reconstruct the true Luciani. We may never be able to come up with precisely what kind of pope he would have been.

Yet, we can try. Even if we fail to recreate the man he truly was; we will, at least, get closer to what a pope should be.

Some of what I speak of here is the record of my friend Jack's correspondence and the conversations he had with me. Only one of Jack's letters arrived during John Paul's papacy.

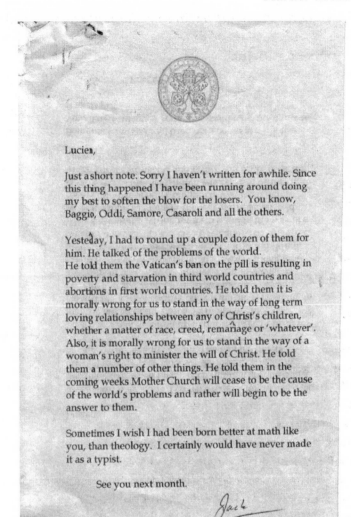

Lucien,

Just a short note. Sorry I haven't written for awhile. Since this thing happened I have been running around doing my best to soften the blow for the losers. You know, Baggio, Oddi, Samore, Casaroli and all the others.

Yesterday, I had to round up a couple dozen of them for him. He talked of the problems of the world.
He told them the Vatican's ban on the pill is resulting in poverty and starvation in third world countries and abortions in first world countries. He told them it is morally wrong for us to stand in the way of long term loving relationships between any of Christ's children, whether a matter of race, creed, remarriage or 'whatever'. Also, it is morally wrong for us to stand in the way of a woman's right to minister the will of Christ. He told them a number of other things. He told them in the coming weeks Mother Church will cease to be the cause of the world's problems and rather will begin to be the answer to them.

Sometimes I wish I had been born better at math like you, than theology. I certainly would have never made it as a typist.

See you next month.

Jack

1 One becomes a citizen of the Vatican when one becomes Pope. A pope's will must adhere to the laws of the Vatican and not any other country. Also, a pope yields certain rights of ownership, etc.
2 *Il Gazzettino 9* Sep 78. The Vatican held controlling interest in this Venice newspaper at the time
3 *La Repubblica* 7 Sep 78
4 *La Stampa* 7 Sep 78   *Il Mondo 8* Sep 78
5 *Messaggero Mestre* 29 Sep 55

Photo bishop's castle - *author photo*

Author's note: *Italicized* text is supported by public record. Unitalicized dialogue, though representative of what was actually said, is not supported by public record.

Important people in *Murder in the Vatican*

Cardinal Benelli, Archbishop of Florence. He was in the midst of lining up opposition in the College of Cardinals to block the ratification of the Prelature of Opus Dei when he met with his death.

George Bush, CIA Director. The author presents compelling evidence he and Cardinal Wojtyla (John Paul II) masterminded the Vatican bank scandal which cumulated in the Vatican-Contra Affair.

Roberto Calvi, President Banco Ambrosiano. Found hanging under a bridge—believed to have been lured to London by Opus Dei and P2 on the guise of a loan to get him out of his predicament.

Bishop Caprio, Treasurer of the Vatican bank. He handled the technicalities of the bank scandal transactions. One of three prelates who had access to John Paul the night he died; eventually promoted to the third most powerful position in the Church.

Bishop Casaroli, Foreign Minister. One of three prelates who had free access to John Paul the night he was murdered; promoted to Cardinal Secretary of State shortly after John Paul II took office.

Reverend Champney, the author's closest friend and at the same time one of John Paul's closest confidants; killed by a hit-run driver outside the Vatican the second day following the Pope's death.

Alois Estermann, Commander of the Swiss Guard. He, his wife and his alleged young lover Corporal Cedric Tornay were murdered in his Vatican apartment. Known to be the closest confidant of John Paul II, the author presents compelling evidence Estermann was the guard assigned to the post closest to John Paul I the night he died.

Cardinal Felici, Prefect Tribunal of the Apostolic Signatura. The Vatican's chief counsel was in the midst of investigating Opus Dei' involvement in the Vatican bank scandal when he dropped dead a few minutes after drinking wine in the consecration of the Mass.

Cardinal Filipiak, Archbishop of Gniezno. Archenemy of John Paul II who died mysteriously a day before the latter became Pope.

Licio Gelli, personal friend of Wojtyla, Bush and Casaroli and Grandmaster of the Masonic Lodge P2, the only killer organization which had a presence in the Vatican the night of John Paul's death.

John XXIII, He started the movement to transform the Church from what it had become—a symbol of wealth and pompous ritual and preferences—back to the Church for all Christ had intended.

Albino Luciani, John Paul I. The Vatican was caught by the press in a series of lies concerning his death that gave rise to rumors of foul play. When elected, he was billed as a moderate-liberal.

Paul Marcinkus, President of the IOR. Under John Paul II he got caught up in the Vatican bank scandal. Found dead a week after a court trying the Mafia for Calvi's murder attempted to extradite him.

Aldo Moro, leader of the Christian Democratic Party during the reign of Paul VI. He was kidnapped and murdered the morning he was to move communist members into control of Parliament.

Metropolitan Nikodim, Archbishop of Leningrad and youthful Marxist leader of the Orthodox Church fell dead at John Paul's feet after sipping coffee rumored to have been intended for the Pope.

Paul VI, Luciani was his handpicked successor and he stacked the College to that end. He died under mysterious circumstances.

Cardinal Ratzinger, after the assassination attempt of John Paul II, he was moved by Opus Dei to the Vatican to position him to step in if anything happened to John Paul II.

Cardinal Suenens, Archbishop of Brussels. This liberal leader died under circumstances similar to those of John Paul I, *'Sitting up reading a book, which book was clutched upright in his hands.'*

Cardinal Vagnozzi, Prefect of Economic Affairs. Found dead in his apartment when he was conducting an audit of the Vatican bank.

Cardinal Villot, Secretary of State. His sudden death followed closely those of Paul and John Paul. The Vatican bank scandal could not have taken place as long as he remained alive.

Cardinal Violardo, Paul VI's 'voice' in Italian Parliament and friend of Aldo Moro was found dead under a stairway in a remote corner of the Vatican bank on the same day Moro was kidnapped.

Cardinal Wojtyla, Archbishop of Krakow. He became John Paul II in the second conclave of 1978. A conservative, he brought an end to change in the Church begun by John XXIII and Paul VI. *Murder in the Vatican* answers the question how it was possible the same constituency of cardinals elected a liberal—Luciani—in one election and just a few weeks later elected a conservative—Wojtyla

Cardinal Yu Pin, Archbishop of Taiwan. He controlled eastern cardinal votes needed by Luciani to win the papacy—dropped dead at Paul's funeral. The press suspecting foul play demanded autopsy.

CIA Director George Bush - Paul VI - John Paul I - John Paul II - Benedict XVI

Chapter 1

The Murder of John Paul I

"Never be afraid to stand up for what is right, whether your adversary be your parent, your teacher, your peer, your politician, your preacher, your constitution, or even your God!"   Albino Luciani

He honors Susan B. Anthony and Lincoln for their courage to have set aside the tenth commandment which held women as mere property of men and protected the right of one man to enslave another

"Thou shalt not covet thy neighbor his property, his house, his wife, his slaves, his ox, his ass"

Thirty-three days into his papacy, the youngest pope to die in four hundred years and the only pope in the two-thousand year history of the Church whose death was unwitnessed was found dead in his bed.

At seven-thirty the morning of September 29, 1978 the Vatican issued the following, *"Pope John Paul died just before midnight last evening of myocardial infarction to the heart. He was discovered by his secretary Magee at six-thirty this morning who went to look for the Pope when he failed to show up for his morning chapel service... He was found sitting up in bed in his daytime clothes with the lamp on and his glasses on reading the 'Imitation of Christ' which book remained upright in his hands. Father Magee summoned Cardinal Jean Villot who performed the last rites... Villot tapped the Pope on the forehead three times. With no response, he removed the Fisherman's Ring from John Paul's finger and smashed it and one of the shortest pontifical reigns in history came to an end... "[2]*

Contradictions and rumors

The medical community did not delay a day. The Italian Medical Society issued the statement, *"...It is irresponsible for any doctor to infer myocardial infarction without autopsy in the case of one whose death was unwitnessed and had no history of heart disease."[3]*

There were a few contradictions in the release itself.

Villot had administered the last rites contradicted the Pope having died before midnight as it is canon law the soul leaves the body when rigor mortis sets in. No priest, much less a cardinal, would

15

administer the last rites to a cold corpse. Also, it was widely known John Paul had refused to order the Fisherman's Ring cast as a part of his intent to demolish the symbolic regency of the papacy.[4]

The embalmers told reporters, in his hands were notes written on the stationary of Vittorio Veneto. They also said they were picked up by a Vatican car shortly after five-thirty, an hour before the release said the body was found. In addition, they were told by Swiss Guards a nun had discovered the Pope. It was their opinion the Pope had not been dead for much more than an hour or two as it was a chilly morning and the windows were open and the body was still warm.[5]

The press interviewed the nun who had found the body.

The clock that should have rung and did not ring

Sister Vincenza said she routinely delivered coffee at four-thirty each morning. When she first knocked there was no answer. She waited a minute or so and knocked again, this time a bit louder. It was obvious the Pope was still in the bathroom.

She opened the door and entered the room intending to leave the tray on his nightstand. She knew he was up and about, as it was his rule to set his alarm clock for a few minutes before she delivered coffee in the event he overslept. If he was still sleeping, the alarm would be ringing loud enough to wake the dead. At least, that is what she thought. This meant, he had risen at his usual time of four and had completed his first task of each day—turned off the alarm.

The light was on. He was sitting up in bed in his daytime clothes reading papers held upright in his hands. She greeted him, *"Good morning."* He resembled a mime deeply involved in his reading.

It was not unusual for him, once dressed for the day, to be sitting in bed reading when she delivered coffee. Vincenza, who had served him for twelve years, had come to know this man as a jovial one, always smiling, often laughing and, at times, joking.

At first she thought it was a joke. Actually, she knew it was a joke. He was wearing his glasses. Though nearsighted and he required them to walk across the room, he did not require them to read. That is, he did not require them to read in private.

Yet, someone not close to him would think he required them to read because he usually wore them

16

when reading from the pulpit to allow him to view his audience.

She approached the bed, *"Please don't joke with me, Albino."* As she placed the tray on the stand she realized something was wrong.[6]

Her testimony confirmed that of the embalmers—he was holding papers and not a book. More importantly, he had been discovered dead shortly after four-thirty and not at six-thirty.

That the alarm clock should have rung and did not ring raised eyebrows of the Agatha Christie mystery buff. The Pope had turned it off or someone else who knew his practice had turned it off. Being electric, it would have been ringing when the nun was at the door.

Yet, when one investigates murder, one must consider not only the evidence that is there, but also the evidence which should be there, and is not there.

In the case of Hercule Poirot's *Hickory Dickory Dock* we have the footprints which should have been there and were not there. In the case of Sherlock Holmes' *Silver Blaze* we have the dog which should have barked and did not bark. In the case of the *Swiss Guard Murders* we have the commander's weapon which should have been there and was not there. In the case of the 33-day Pope, we have the alarm clock which should have rung and did not ring.

The listings of cardinals to be replaced

These contradictions of the nun and the embalmers gave birth to a rumor the notes held in the Pope's hands were listings of cardinals to be replaced; he was planning a shakeup of the Church's hierarchy—something that had been expected ever since he had been elected.

It was no secret Benelli would replace Villot as Secretary of State something both these cardinals looked forward to. Benelli had been the architect of Luciani's election and was more than qualified to head up the Church's administration. Villot was looking forward to living in Rome and teaching in the Gregorian University.

But who were the others? Why was there such concern?

Other than this, there was concern about only one job. Except for the incumbent who would lose his job, the others didn't mean much.

The Prefect of the Doctrine of the Congregation of the Faith—the chief theologian of the Church—dictates the morals of the Catholic world. It was rumored the archbishop of Utrecht Willebrands—an

17

advocate of contraception, married priests, ordained women and tolerance of homosexuality—would get the job.

This expectation was sound as the Curia post Willebrands held— President of the Secretariat for Christian Unity—interfaced directly with the Prefect position and was viewed as a stepping stone to it. Yet, there was more than just that.

On September 28, 1978 John Paul scheduled a synod of opposing *left* and *right* wing bishops to examine these same issues. He named Willebrands to chair the synod—the kind of assembly normally led by the Prefect of the Doctrine of the Congregation of the Faith.[7]

Poisoning

That the embalmers were roused from their sleep so early in the morning fired rumors of poisoning. It was the practice of the Mafia to embalm immediately after death to erase signs of arsenic when it was the instrument of murder. For this reason, it was illegal in Italy to embalm until twenty-four hours after death.

Of course, Italian law did not apply in the Vatican. Yet, it had been its practice to adhere to the law ever since it came into effect in 1946—embalming of popes had been delayed for twenty-four hours. This included Pius XII, John XXIII and—a month earlier—Paul VI.

In the case of John Paul, ANSA News—Italy's most reliable wire service—reported embalmers were roused at five in the morning, over an hour before the Vatican said the body had been found.[8]

There is the possibility one wanted to avoid a repetition of what had happened in the cases of Pius and Paul where skin discoloration and odor presented problems in the viewings. Yet, if this was true, why not summon the embalmers at a more reasonable time like eight o'clock which would have allowed more than ample time for the embalming before the first viewing in the St. Clementine Chapel at noon and would have avoided raising unnecessary suspicions.[9]

The bell cord

Most questionable of all, was something killed him so suddenly he was unable to reach for the bell cord which hung a whisker from his right shoulder, as this would have summoned in an instant the guard at the entrance to the corridor leading to the Pope's chambers. Also, he was not afforded the time to press one of the service buttons on the intercom just to his left which would have brought to his side any of five people who resided elsewhere in the palace that night.

John Paul also had the option of pressing an emergency button on the bedside console which would have activated a flashing light in the corridor just outside his quarters and buzzed the guard.

The Vatican newspaper reported an interesting coincidence. On the previous morning, maintenance workers happened to have tested the bell cord, something that had not been done for years as Pope Paul always used the intercom. The bell rang so loud those in the palace thought it to be a fire alarm and headed for the stairs.[10]

The time of death

The time of death is critical to the supposition the Pope died of natural causes. It is also critical to the supposition he was murdered.

As we will demonstrate clearly in what is to come, if he died before midnight—as the Vatican claimed—he could have died of natural causes. Yet, if he died in the early morning hours—as the embalmers claimed—the case for murder is almost certain.

If he died before midnight his light would have been on all night. Both the nun and the Vatican release were explicit the light was on. This is consistent with he would not be reading in the dark.

At the upper right hand corner of the palace, the papal bedroom overlooks St. Peter's Square. It is a focal point of tourists who roam the square into the wee hours of the morning. Those that hang their hat on the supposition the pope died before midnight depend on the chance not a tourist nor the police assigned to the square that night noticed the light was on all night. That the light was not on all night was widely reported in the press in the following days.[11]

Also, if the Pope had died just before midnight the previous day, why would he be dressed in his daytime clothes? If one decides to read oneself to sleep one first dons one's bedtime clothes.

On October 10, 1978 the Vatican issued a corrected release,

"While the death of John Paul came as a surprise, there was the fact the pope suffered from a serious low blood pressure condition

and was in poor health and frail throughout his brief papacy. Most recently, he had complained of swollen feet...

John Paul did not have in mind to make revolutionary changes in the Vatican hierarchy...

We wish to correct our statement it was the Pope's secretary Magee who discovered the body. The Pope was first discovered by the nun who delivered his coffee at the usual time. When she sensed something wrong she summoned Magee...

We wish to correct our statement the Pope was reading the 'Imitation of Christ.' This was a communications error. He was reviewing some notes. That he retained them upright in his hands in the midst of a massive heart attack is by the grace of God...

It is immaterial who found His Holiness. It is immaterial when he was found dead. It is immaterial when he died. All that is material is that he was found dead...   The Vatican"[12]

Effortil, low blood pressure and swollen feet

Reacting to the release, a Venice area newspaper published a photo of his physical exam of five months before his death which raised considerable question concerning the alleged heart attack.[13]

It showed him to be in extraordinary physical health. Pertaining to his arterial condition, his cholesterol count was at normal levels and his blood pressure was 106 over 65—considered low at the time when a 'normal' reading was considered to be 100 plus one's age—yet, today, an optimal reading for anyone particularly a man of 65.

It was this blood pressure reading which led to the rumor he had been taking Effortil—a low blood pressure medication. The rumor claimed digitalis had been added to the medicine. Some authors embellished the rumor claiming Cardinal Villot pocketed the bottle of Effortil from the nightstand to build a case against him.

More damaging to the claim of an arterial problem, his blood viscosity was normal and ultrasound tests of his legs, stomach area and carotid arteries showed no blockage at all. His doctor had made this a routine part of his twice-a-year physicals since the mid-sixties when the tests had reached some level of reliability.

The premier books on John Paul's mysterious death are David Yallop's *In God's Name* and John Cornwell's *A Thief in the Night*.

These accomplished journalists interviewed dozens of the same witnesses and came up with different conclusions. Yallop proved his case for murder and Cornwell proved his case for natural death.

One thing that has always puzzled me is that neither of these men interviewed Dr. Da Ros, the only material witness I talked to.

I find it especially strange Cornwell—a renowned journalist sent by a sitting Pontiff John Paul II—claims he repeatedly tried to talk to Da Ros, a devout Catholic, but was unable to get an interview.

Even stranger, he was unable to bring a third party witness to the table who could shed some light on what Dr. Da Ros had to say. When asked, his leading witness, the Pope's niece Lina Petri, tells Cornwell, *"Da Ros refuses to talk to me. He is extremely abrupt."*[15]

I was practically a 'nobody' at the time and had no problem enjoying a fine lunch and an afternoon with the doctor on the Lido. One is talking of the possibility of murder vs. natural causes here.

Dr. Da Ros was the most qualified man in the world to write a book about the nature of John Paul's death and come up with a logical answer. He had not only been Luciani's doctor for twenty years, he had been his closest friend in Venice. How could one go onto second base and so forth without first touching first base?

Nevertheless, when I visited the doctor in the fall of 1978, I was searching for Luciani's will and had no interest in his death. Yet, I did ask him if he agreed heart attack had been involved?

He laughed, "I agree with the whole of the medical community. Without autopsy, it is impossible to know what killed him. Yet, from what I knew of him, heart attack would bottom the list."[14]

He dispelled the rumor digitalis had been added to his Effortil.

Though Luciani's blood pressure ran a bit on the low side, it had never been a concern and Da Ros told me he had never prescribed Effortil or any other low blood pressure medication. Not news to me, as he had told the press this when queried about the rumor.[14]

Investigative reporters since—including Yallop and Cornwell—clearly established no prescription was issued John Paul by the Vatican pharmacy and no Vatican doctor had treated him for any condition during his papacy—eradicating the claim of swollen feet.[15]

Nevertheless, because it is the strongest of rumors we must put digitalis to 'sleep.' A large dose will induce violent vomiting and kill in a few minutes. A teaspoonful will take an hour or so to do the job. Blurred vision and hallucinations are followed by abdominal pain

21

and violent vomiting and often head pain ending in congestive heart failure. In any case, one is certain to empty one's stomach.

If digitalis was used to kill the Pope, it tells one something about the perpetrator. Only an imbecile would have employed digitalis as the degree of vomiting it precipitates would ring a bell in the least suspicious doctor. Not a very wise choice when there are hundreds of lethal toxins which would have done the job with far less visible evidence. Also, vomiting is inconsistent with the position the body was found and none of those brought to the room mentioned it.

Adding digitalis to Effortil was first used by Agatha Christie in her mysteries *Appointment with Death* and *The Secret of Chimneys* and some of her other works. The Christie' market exploded in the 1970s on the heels of the box office buster motion pictures *'Murder on the Orient Express'* (1974) and *'Death on the Nile'* (1978). Though no one knows who started the rumor, one knows its origin.

Dr. Da Ros was more concerned with the *'swollen feet'* in the 2nd Vatican release. Luciani had never suffered of swollen extremities. What's more Da Ros had visited John Paul a week before his death.

The medical community had demolished the idea of *'myocardial infarction'* in the 1st Vatican release. It made sense to Da Ros it had included *'swollen feet'* in its 2nd release to set the stage for what it would subsequently claim the pope died of *'pulmonary embolism.'* In this kind of embolism, the embolus usually originates in the legs.

One also has the conflicting rumors *'swollen feet'* vs. *'low blood pressure.'* Swollen feet can be symptomatic of high blood pressure, yet, is not symptomatic of low blood pressure. Medical dictionaries list scores of causes of swollen feet. Low blood pressure is not among them. Unlike symptoms of high blood pressure which are vague, symptoms of low blood pressure are exact: blurry vision, lack of concentration and train of thought, dizziness, confusion or fainting. Swollen extremities is not among them.[16]

Though he never told me outright, I came away with a feeling the doctor suspected foul play in his friend's death.

To me, this explains why he refused to talk to Cornwell in 1987. He knew Cornwell—as an envoy of John Paul II—was out to prove Luciani had died of natural causes. He knew if Cornwell interviewed him he would have to lie or he might not live to tell of it.

Regardless, his blood pressure—a bit low at the time—together with the viscosity and clear arterial readings of his physical all but

22

eradiate the possibility Luciani succumbed to arterial disease of any kind. Particularly when one considers what is known today—not known in 1978—low blood pressure is as surefire a prevention of myocardial infarction and pulmonary embolism as exists.[17]

His physical exam was consistent with his having climbed a peak in near record time at about the same time.[18] It was also consistent with his having not a hint of heart problems at any time in his life.

Because of the unexplained circumstances of his demise, his medical history has been scrutinized for the slightest sign of arterial problems in many of the world's medical journals to no avail.[19]

The missing will

Concerning his will, there are some things we know and other things we do not know. Among those things we know, Luciani wanted to be interred in a pine box inscribed, *"Christ picked me up from the Mud in the Street and gave me to you."* The box was to be displayed behind glass set into a side altar of a church in the Veneto country.[20] In death, he wanted to send a message of humility as he had in life. This would have exposed his corpse to autopsy.

We also know from his Venice attorney he had willed his papers to the respective dioceses he had served. The lack of a will, gave the Vatican unilateral authority to destroy records of anything he had said or done of a controversial nature. It also prevented his family from demanding autopsy or obtaining anything one might construe as DNA today other than what the Vatican choose to give them.

As a part of indoctrination, an incoming pope is counseled by the papal attorney—in John Paul's case, Pericle Felici. A pope's will is a part of the process. At the very least, a rider is attached to an existing will as the papacy dramatically changes one's legal position.

On becoming pope one becomes a citizen of the Sovereign State of the Vatican and the will must comply with its laws and not those of any other nation. Yet, there is much more than just that.

It is common for popes to include in their wills their reflections on the direction the Church should take. In this respect, a pope's will can be, as it has on occasion in the past, been interpreted as doctrine. This is not usually a problem as popes normally conform to doctrine. Yet, in John Paul's case one has to consider he may have struck at the fundamental canon of the Church.

Certainly, he must have known he was in danger. The path his papacy had taken in the short term had not only alarmed many of those in his own ranks but his enemies across the pond as well. He would have been an imbecile not to sense he might not live to attain the objectives he had worked all his life to achieve. He would have been a fool to have not set forth his intentions in his will should he not live to bring them to fruition. Nevertheless, we have come to the suppositions regarding his will—things we don't know.

Did his will strike at the central doctrine of the Roman Catholic Church: *Some kinds of people are better than others and are entitled to more*? Did he include in his will the most prolific testimony of his ministry: *"We have made of sex the greatest of sins, whereas it is nothing more than human nature and not a sin at all?"*[1]

Did he strike at the integral core of canon law that invades the privacy of bedrooms? Did he change the definition of morality in the Church from what is acceptable in the bedroom in the minds of a bunch of old men in the Curia who have never been in the bedroom, to what is humanely right or wrong? One will never know.

What one does know, there had existed at least nine copies of the will: one hardcopy and one on microfilm in his attorney's office in Venice, a hardcopy in the diocese office in Venice, one hardcopy and one on microfilm in the Venice City Clerk's Office, one hardcopy and another on microfilm in the Vatican Office, one with his brother Edoardo, and a hardcopy held by his secretary Lorenzi. All of these disappeared simultaneously from the face of the earth.

The slipper socks, spectacles and the lock of hair

Some questions were raised by the Luciani family. His sister-in-law sought to recover a pair of slipper socks she had knitted for him. She knew, as a boy, he had often gone barefoot in the Italian Alps; she wanted to make sure he had something to keep his feet warm. They were white satin and had his coat of arms embroidered in gold on them. They may have been used to wipe a tinge of blood a needle or even a creature might leave. Regardless, they vanished.[2]

Then there were his spectacles. Though they were found on the body, they disappeared. It could be someone close to him who knew he did not require them to read—not involved in the deed itself—had been a part of a conspiracy; realizing a mistake had been made

24

placing them on him, pocketed them for if they survived they would assay of foul play. Perhaps, they were just broken in the shuffle. [22]

One will never know.

A niece, in response to a request for a lock of hair, received a clump of jet black hair which she claimed was not his as his hair was graying. If poison, particularly an element been involved, a strand of hair outside of his tomb can assay of it even centuries afterwards.[23]

According to the press, Cornwell, Yallop and all other accounts, John Paul's niece Lina Petri spent a half-hour in the room alone with her uncle the morning of his death. An ally of the Vatican, one can trust the accuracy of her description, *"...It was as if he was smiling at me. His face showed no sign of suffering...There was something very strange. He was wearing his daytime clothes. Why would he not be wearing his pajamas if reading in bed? ...The sleeves were all torn. Why should they be torn like that? I wondered..."* [24]

The watch that ticked the time of death

We know from the testimony of those who shared his last dinner, aside from his usual conversation, laughing and joking, the Pope had been preoccupied with his new watch.

Not much is known of the watch.

The only mention of it is by Vincenza who said he kept fumbling with it at dinner to try to determine if it was waterproof as it was his custom not to remove it for sleeping or in the shower. It was of such an unusual design, *"It looked like it had come out of 'Dr No.'"*[25]

We also know from her testimony it had been Pasquale Macchi who delivered the watch to the Pope. Yet, everything given a pope goes through one of his secretaries. There has survived no record of who made the watch or for that matter who gave it to Macchi.

It likely arrived in the mail as Macchi—serving in transition—handled the mail. It would have come from someone the Pope would have accepted it from. We have the possibility a third person could have used the name of someone close to the Pope who they knew to be out of touch for a few days—perhaps vacationing on the Rivera. We will leave that one for the mystery buffs.

We know one more thing. Like the slipper socks and the glasses, the watch vanished. That is, we know the Luciani family never recovered it and it was never mentioned again in the press. It was just not that important. Actually, it did not seem important to this author either as in previous editions I had intentionally left it out. Nevertheless, this time I leave it with you to ponder with all the other circumstances surrounding the death of this unfortunate man.

Scorpions

Finally, we have the scorpions for those who wish to nibble on them. Whereas a pale yellow scorpion allows the victim time to seek help, the giant golden mutation injects enough venom to kill a dozen men instantly. The miniature desert in the gardens at the papal retreat Castel Gandolfo was home to this creature at the time.

Because its sting would have left the Pope in the position he was found and the coincidence the scorpions disappeared from the Castel Gandolfo after the Pope's death it has found its way into a number of books including the first edition of *Murder in the Vatican*.[26]

To employ a scorpion in the murder of a pope is certainly a remote possibility, yet, if one is to include all the circumstances of John Paul's death, one must include all the possibilities.

Reprise

Aside from stories of his childhood and young priesthood which are my direct witness, I say nothing here that has not been said before, either in the press or in the writings of this good man.

All that is to my credit is that for the first time the full record has been brought together in one place...

...the strange set of circumstances that caused three men to sleep in the great bed in the papal apartment in the fall of nineteen hundred and seventy-eight.

Nevertheless, we are left with some questions.

Who placed the spectacles on his nose? Who turned the light on which was not on all night? Who turned the alarm clock off which did not ring? Who dressed him up in his daytime clothes? Who tore his sleeves? Who gave him the watch that ticked the time of death? Was the watch set for the time of death? Who took the spectacles, the slippers socks and the watch? Who took the time to methodically destroy all nine copies of his will and why? Who bred the scorpions at the Castel Gandolfo? Where did they go after the Pope's death?

There is only one absolute fact on which to build our case: the only circumstance of his death agreed to by all witnesses including both Vatican releases, the nun who found him, his secretaries, the embalmers and all others brought to his room, *"The bed lamp was on and he was sitting up in his daytime clothes wearing his glasses reading papers held upright in his hands."*

This leaves us with the glaring inconsistency the Pope could have remained in a sitting-up position with notes still clutched upright in his hands if he had suffered a massive heart attack. Only the most gullible accepted the Vatican's contention *"...by the grace of God."*

Yet, it is from these few bits and pieces we must begin our work. From these few observations, employing the analysis and deduction techniques which lifted Sherlock Holmes to the top of his game, we will prove this good man was murdered. Yet, unlike our nineteenth century predecessor, we will not be dealing in the make-believe world of yesterday. We will be dealing in the real world of today.

We will prove beyond a shadow of doubt when he was murdered, how he was murdered, why he was murdered, who pulled the 'trigger,' and, most important of all, who ordered the dreadful deed.

Here, is the proof—the absolute proof—how John Paul, and those around him, fell victim to twentieth century capitalism as it was jointly embraced by the Vatican and the United States.

Yet, unless one first understands the mystery of his life, one will never be able to solve the mystery of his death. So, let us first step back a few years. Back to that time the little boy Albino Luciani would begin to mold his destiny.

Let us walk with him a bit through those years he would build his dream which would eventually take him to his fate—of two hundred sixty-five popes, the only one whose remains are triple-sealed in a lead-lined vault today.

Now come. Let us talk with him. Let us walk with him, in the woods, together with his good friend Pinocchio and the Cat and the Fox and the Poodle Medoro. Let us bear witness as...

"One Beautiful Life explodes into a trail of death and destruction in the Roman Catholic Church."

Howard Jason Smith, *Boston Globe*

1 *Messaggero Mestre* 7 Mar 73 - *Nostro Veneto* 8 Mar 73
2 Composite of Vatican wire release, *La Osservatore Romano* and *Vatican Radio* 29 Sep 78
3 *La Repubblica* 1 Oct 78. Luciani's doctor Da Ros agreed → *Messaggero Mestre* 9 Oct 78
4 John Paul did wear a simple ring which had been given all attendees of the Vatican II Council
5 Mario di Francesco of the *ANSA News Agency, Italy's most reputable wire service* 29 Sep 78
6 *ANSA News,* 29 Sep 78   *La Repubblica* 1 Oct 78 and other newspapers reported variations, yet, all witnesses agree she discovered the body shortly after 4:30 in the morning. Some books claimed the alarm clock rang while she was at the door at 4:40AM, not true—never reported in the press
7 *Utrecht Socialist* 29 Sep 78
8 *ANSA News Agency.* Motor pool records showed a van dispatched at 5:23AM to pick up embalmers
9 On April 5, 2005, Massimo Signoracci confirmed with Marta Falconi of *Associated Press* his family had embalmed John XXIII, Paul VI and John Paul I before their first viewings.
10 *L'Osservatore Romano* 28 Sep 78
11 *La Repubblica* 1 Oct 78
12 *L'Osservatore Romano* 10 Oct 78 and most major world newspapers
13 *Messaggero Mestre* 14 Oct 78
14 *Il Messaggero Romano* 5 Nov 78. Da Ros confirmed this in his interview with *Andrea Tornelli* of *Il Giornale* 27 Sep 03. He had never prescribed Effortil or other low blood pressure medication
15 John Cornwell's *A Thief in the Night*
16 Medical dictionaries in libraries or search 'heart attack low blood pressure' on the Internet.
17 Medical dictionaries in libraries or search 'symptoms low blood pressure' on the Internet.
18 *Padovanews* 24 Apr 78 *'Como Bianco'*
19 *JAMA* Oct 79. There are others including British Medical journal 216. Search medical libraries
20 direct testimony Dr. Da Ros. Also, there is a small notice in *Nostro Veneto* 24 Jul 67 alluding to this
21 *La Repubblica* 16 Oct 78
22 *La Repubblica* 22 Oct 78
23 *La Repubblica* 2 Nov 78
24 John Cornwell's interview with Lina Petri in John Cornwell's *A Thief in the Night.*
25 *L'Osservatore Romano* 28 Sep 78. Vincenza refers to Ian Fleming the creator of *James Bond.*
26 *Murder in the Vatican* 2003
27 see author's note below

Author's note: There is a tendency of authors to include only those things which contribute to one's pre-convictions—the reason Yallop—*In God's Name*—and Cornwell—*A Thief in the Night*—could interview the same witnesses and come up with two entirely different answers. There are no press references in either of these books as they depend entirely on witnesses of motive.

Conversely, *Murder in the Vatican*—other than the author's brief brushes with Luciani's doctor Dr. Da Ros and Paul Marcinkus—sets forth the record of the press; over five hundred and fifty press accounts of the events of the time.

Photo John Paul - *Associated Press*
Photo St. Peter's Square - *author's property*
Caricature of three popes in bed by *Ben Vogelsang - author's property*

Chapter 2

The Worst of Children to the Best of Men

"This chalice contains one hundred and twenty-two of the world's most pristine diamonds. Do you really think this is what Christ meant by his Church?"

John Paul I

Albino Luciani was born into dire poverty in a small village in the Italian Alps to a scullery maid and a migrant worker.

His mother was a devout Catholic who prayed before crucifixes made of bits of wood. She told him the only path to heaven was on his knees in prayer.

His father was a social revolutionary atheist who often burned his mother's crucifixes in the stove. He told him the only path to heaven was on his feet helping others.

When he was six years old, his grandfather told him, "Albino, today, you believe in Jesus and Santa Claus. Well," he apologized, "there is no Santa Claus. We've been kidding you."

He cried himself to sleep that night. How could they take Santa away from him? In his dreams he waved adieu to Santa, but he still had his Jesus. He pleaded, "Please don't take my Jesus from me."

The next day he trudged along the railroad tracks in the knee-deep snow. His shoes were tattered and worn and they did not match and his feet were frozen and they tormented him with each step. Yet he continued on, pausing here and there, filling his pail with scraps which had fallen from the rumbling coal cars.

He thought of the day before when he had gazed through the store window at the golden crucifix. At three hundred lire a pail he needed three more pails full and he would have enough to buy this splendid treasure for the very best mamma in the world. A smirk of a leer tinged his lips as he imagined his papa's frustration when he would try to burn this one. It broadened into a smile which mirrored the look of surprise and wonderment his mamma would have when she would open the gift on Christmas morn. He imagined her puzzled expression when she would read the card,

You gave him life; I gave him hope.
Together for a time; we gave him paradise.
Now my quest must end; but for you the work goes on.
The struggle must endure; for the challenge remains.
The hope is still there; his dream must never die.

Santa

The worst of children

The icicles poured like waterfalls from the rooftops all the way down to the walkways beneath them. In the summertime, each house had its own identity—its own personality - red - green - blue - orange. Each had been a tiny splinter in a giant rainbow. But, now, in the wintertime, each was just one of an endless row of crystal figures in an enormous glass menagerie.

The parade of weather-beaten wooden carts moved through the streets of Canale d'Agordo in the Italian Alps as they had every other morning. The snow was heaped so high on each side of the road for the most part they passed unseen.

Yet, the shouts of the barkers broke the stillness of the morning air: "milk - milk - milk," "cheese - cheese - cheese," "lamb - lamb - lamb," "bread - bread - bread," "eggs - eggs - eggs." Their voices echoing through the whitecapped rocky mountain gorge which engulfed the desolate hamlet. Yet, one had made its way before them—no wares—no barker—no echo. A silent one—a ghostly one.

The cart rumbled along the dimly-lit snow-covered cobblestone streets in the wee hours of the morning; its chauffeurs, pausing, here and there, gathering their ghoulish haul—those of Italy's two million homeless orphans who hadn't survived the wintry night.

Only the creaking of the wheels and an occasional thud of a frozen tot broke the quiet of the dawn.

They were orphans because they were the worst of children—BASTARDS. They called them BASTARDS because they were children who had been born out of wedlock. Nobody wanted them. That is, nobody in their right mind wanted them. Everyone hated them. That is, everyone who went to church. In those days everyone went to church. Every priest, every nun, every monk, every devout parent, every brainwashed child, despised them.

30

Each time their frozen bodies would pass by in the cart, they all thought it to be right. The only hint of compassion, now and then, "They are better off dead." Everyone thought there was something holy about it. After all, it had been written in their Holy Bible, these were the worst of children—BASTARDS.[1]

That is, everyone except Piccolo, the little boy Albino Luciani. He thought it was wrong. He didn't care if it was written in a book. In fact, he knew it was wrong. He knew it was wrong because his revolutionary socialist atheist father had told him it was wrong.

His first mortal sin

Luciani told me of the first time he had missed Sunday Mass.

"I had just turned eleven and was as poor as a church mouse and often went hungry myself. Yet, I did have a mamma and papa to take care of me and love me. They were away visiting a sick friend on that subzero Sunday morning when I made my way to church with my fellow Catholics.

"We passed a dozen orphans who were begging in the street. Most of them were orphans because they had been born out of wedlock, the reason why they were barred from church, as it had been God the Father's sacred testimony in *Deuteronomy, 'A bastard child shall not enter into the congregation of the lord.'*[1]

"It was this that first made me realize what a monster Moses was, that first made me realize the Old Testament was not the word of God. As a matter-of-fact, it was not even inspired by God; it was obviously inspired by the hatred and greed of evil men.

"It may have been the intense cold that inspired me. Regardless, I turned around and hurried back to my house and quickly cooked up a cauldron of soup with all the vegetables and lentils I could find and, although it meant we would go without them ourselves for days, I took it to the orphans and placed it in the snow in the midst of them. For the first time in my life, I realized what Christ had meant when He said, *'Where two or three are gathered together in my name, there am I in the midst of them.'*

"By that time church was over. I had missed Mass, a mortal sin in those days. I decided to go into the church to ask forgiveness. But, I forgot they locked the doors outside of service hours to keep the orphans from coming in to get warm.

31

"It was then—at that moment—when those doors would not open—I realized what Christ had meant by the word 'Church.' It was then—at that moment—when those doors would not open—I decided to become a priest. It was then—at that moment—when those doors would not open—I decided I would change the Church back to what Christ had intended.

"It was then—at that moment—when those doors would not open—I realized my devout mamma was a sheep, and my atheist papa was a lion. It was then—at that moment—when those doors would not open—I began to shed my wool, and groom my mane.

"I hoped the scolding I would receive when my parents returned would not be too harsh. I underestimated the wrath of my mamma who, taking me into the bedroom, left me on my knees pleading for God's forgiveness for having broken His sacred law.

"Later, when my papa returned, he pulled me up off my knees and hugged me. He told me what I had done was wonderful. He told me to ask Christ to forgive my mamma. I should not think ill of her, as she was caught up in religion—Christianity—something he often referred to as the *Opium of the Masses*. Drugged with belief, she is unable to judge what is truly right or what is truly wrong.

"Though my mamma taught me the idolatry of Christ, it was my papa who taught me the reality of Christ; it was he who taught me right from wrong. While I loved her dearly, my mamma was too caught up in the *Opium of the Masses,* to know right from wrong…"

The best of men

Many years later on a rather chilly autumn evening as I sat by the fireplace in an overstuffed armchair, I reached for the newspaper and read: Associated Press, September 21, 1978, Vatican City. As he has on other occasions, after an audience, yesterday, John Paul called for assistance from his listeners. A young boy came forward.

The Pope asked, *"What is your name and how old are you?"*

"Anthony." Then with a touch of pride, *"I am sixteen."*

"Good. Tell me Anthony, what is the greatest of sins?"

The boy looked sheepishly around the hall, nervously twitched his lips, hesitated, and finally stammered, *"I suppose sex?"*

Smiling, the Pope apologized, *"Sorry, to have put you on the spot. Yes, sex. We have made of sex the greatest of sins, whereas, in itself, it is nothing more than human nature and not a sin at all.*

"I will give you another chance. Now, Anthony, think, what is really the greatest of sins?"

The boy thought a moment, *"I guess, murder?"*

"Well, you are getting warmer. But, what I am looking for is the cause. Not the result."

The boy was silent. The Pope told him, *"Anthony, the greatest sin of all is hatred—hatred of other kinds of people and hatred of those who live their lives differently. Hatred usually goes hand in hand with its partner, greed."*

The boy interrupted, *"Now, that I think of it, you're right. Hatred and greed have been at the root of all the grief of mankind, the countless wars of ethnic cleansing, murdering and destruction of individuals, and, at times, entire populations."*

"Why do you suppose you didn't think of it when I first asked you?" the Pope asked.

"I don't know. Maybe, because it is not a commandment," the boy replied.

"Why do you suppose Moses left 'hatred'—the greatest of sins— out of his commandments?" John Paul probed the boy.

"Well, I guess, he intended to leave it out or he made a mistake," Anthony responded.

The Pope looked at the youth, *"Believe me, Anthony, he made no mistake. He intended to leave it out..."*[2]

The rich and the poor

A week or so later I picked up another newspaper: Associated Press, September 28, 1978, Vatican City. In a general audience yesterday, the Pope talked of the Church's responsibility to help control the world's population. *"...I have been discussing birth control for forty-five minutes. If the information I have been given, the various statistics, if that information is accurate, then during these few moments, over one thousand children under the age of five have died of malnutrition. During the next few hours while you and I look forward with anticipation to our next meal, another five thousand children under the age of five will die of malnutrition. By this time tomorrow, thirty thousand children under the age of five, who at this moment are alive, will be dead of malnutrition. God does not always provide. It is our sacred responsibility to provide,"* he raised his voice to a demand, *"and we will provide now."*[3]

John Paul spoke in simple words so that the youngest child could understand what he had to say. As he had on many occasions as a bishop, he threatened the hypocrisy of the Vatican treasures.

"This morning, I flushed my toilet with a solid gold lever. At this moment, bishops and cardinals are using a bathroom on the second floor of the Papal Palace which trappings, I am told, would draw more than one hundred million dollars at auction."

Reaching for a golden chalice and lifting it up, *"This chalice contains one hundred and twenty-two of the world's most pristine diamonds."* His eyes scanned the television cameras, *"Do you really think this is what Christ meant by his Church?*

"Believe me, one day, we who live in opulence, while so many are dying because they have nothing, will have to answer to Jesus why we have not carried out His order, 'Love thy neighbor as thyself.' We, the clergy, together with our congregations, who foolishly substitute gold and pomp and ceremony in place of Christ's instruction, who judge our masquerade of singing His praises to be more precious than human life, will have the most to explain...

"Embrace the words of Paul VI in the Populorum Progressio, 'It is the inalienable right of no man to accumulate wealth beyond his needs while other men starve to death because they have nothing!'"[4]

Search for the truth

He asked, *"Can one of the children come up to help the Pope?"*

A young boy stepped forward. *"What is your name and what grade are you in?"*

The boy stammered, *"Daniele. I am in the fifth grade."*

The Pope asked, *"Daniele. Now, do you want to stay in the fifth grade or would you rather go on to the sixth grade next year?"*

34

The boy startled the Pope, *"I want to stay in the fifth grade. If I go on to the sixth grade, I will lose my teacher."*

The Pope smiled to the crowd, *"Well, this boy is different than was the little boy Luciani, for when I was in the fifth grade, I would say to myself, 'Oh, if only I were in the sixth.' And, when I was in the sixth, I would say to myself, 'Oh, if only I were in the seventh.'"*

Turning to the boy, *"Daniele, we have within us a need to make progress—to move forward. Only with progress can we find the truth. We started out living in caves and then progressed to huts and now we live in homes with modern kitchens and bathrooms.*

"More importantly, has been our progress in accepting our fellow human beings as we do ourselves. Our enemy is what has gone before us. We wrongly assume our ancestors were smarter than we are. We wrongly accept what they wrote in their books as the truth. We assume that what they had to say was right and this misconception pulls us backward, instead of forward.

"Yet, we are much smarter than were our ancestors. As each generation comes forward, it benefits from all the knowledge that has been accumulated by all those which have gone before it.[7]

"Tell me, Daniel, what did God do on the first day of creation?"

The boy looked up at the Pope with a puzzled frown. *"Why, He divided the waters that were there to create Heaven."*

John Paul followed, *"And, on the second day?"*

Daniele, *"He gathered the waters together to allow the dry land to appear and He grew grass, trees and flowers."*

The Pope nodded agreement, *"Now, how about, the third day?"*

Daniele, *"God hung the sun and the moon and the stars in the heavens to give light."*

The Pope smiled, *"You have a good teacher. No wonder you don't want to leave her. Nevertheless, when Moses told us the story of creation, he was unaware the earth was round and rotating on its axis and controlled by its sun. As a result, he told us God had told him the earth was flat and God hung the sun and the stars in the heavens the day after He created the earth and its vegetation.*

"He told us this because he didn't know, at his time, it is the sun that is the center of our solar system and controls all life on our planet. It is because he didn't know the facts—the truth—Moses told his followers God had told him God had created vegetation the day before He hung the sun in the heavens.

"Yet, today we know the truth—no vegetation can exist without the process of photosynthesis which is a product of the sun. In fact, the earth, itself, could not exist without its sun."

Daniele, with a triumphal smirk, *"But, God would have told the story of creation as people at the time believed the world to be."*

The Pope nodded, *"Yes, in the seventeenth century when Galileo proved the organization of the universe—when he proved the story of creation as told by Moses was not the truth—Pope Innocent declared God would have told the story of creation in the way people understood the world to be at that time.*

"Everyone believed him. Today, many still believe Innocent's proclamation that the same God who gave us the commandment 'Thou shalt not bear false witness,' lied about the organization of the universe in His first words to man.

"Of course, I, too, am Pope. In addition, I have at my disposal the great abundance of knowledge the world has accumulated since Innocent's time. I ask myself, 'Would God have had reason to have lied?' The answer is that God had no reason to have lied. In fact, God had great motive to have told the truth. For had He told Moses the truth, had God revealed the true organization of the universe to Moses, it would have proved He was the true God.

"It would have explained a great mystery of that time. How it was possible for the sun to rise in the east each morning and set in the west each evening? How did it ever return to the east? So God had great motive to have told the truth. Yet, Moses, in convincing his people he had talked to God, inspired them to take the Promised Land which made him one of the wealthiest men of his time. So Moses would have had great motive to have lied.

"Daniele, now listen very carefully to what I am about to say to you. I want you to keep it with you always." He raised his voice and his eyes roamed around the hall so that all would hear what he had to say, *"Daniele, I do not believe the same God who has endowed us with reason and intellect has intended us to forego their use; we would believe a God, who had great motive to have told the truth, lied, and a man, who had great motive to have lied, told the truth.*

"In his day, Moses thought he was telling the truth. But, today we know he was not telling the truth because, at his time, he did not know the truth. Daniele, if we are ever to know the truth, we cannot start with falsehoods. We must start with what we have determined

to be the truth to a given point in time and go forward.

"As each generation comes and goes we grow closer and closer to the truth. Daniele, the truth does not lie in the past; it lies in the future. It is your job to help society in its struggle to find it."

John Paul looked at the boy, *"Daniele. Let me tell you a story.*

"In America, for two-hundred years, Negroes were taken from their children and placed in bondage and the white church-going Christians thought it was right, it was holy, the will of God. They thought this way because they were in the fifth grade and wanted to stay in the fifth grade because they could not give up their teacher.

"Their fifth grade teacher was the God of the Old Testament. He told them in His Tenth Commandment, 'Thou shalt not covet—desire to take from—thy neighbor his property, including his house, his wife, his slaves, his ox, his ass.'⁵ Their fifth grade teacher felt so strongly slavery was right, He protected the right of one man to enslave another in His Commandments.

"Then one day, a man named Lincoln and others like him came along and scratched their heads, 'There is something wrong here? Let us go onto the sixth grade.' There they found a new teacher, His name was Christ and Christ told them slavery was wrong.

"In Matthew, when asked, 'Which commandments must I keep that I shall have eternal life?' Christ makes no mention of Moses' first four commandments which require adoration of the God of the Old Testament: 1) I am the one God, 2) no graven images, 3) don't take the name of the Lord in vain, and 4) keep the Sabbath.⁵

"Unlike Moses' God who tells us the only path to Heaven is to fall down on our knees and adore Him, Christ tells us falling down on our knees and adoring Him isn't going to get us anywhere. He tells us clearly the only path to heaven is on our feet helping others.

"Christ does retain five of Moses' requirements: 5) honor thy father and mother, 6) shalt not kill, 7) shalt not steal, 8) shalt not commit adultery, 9) shalt not bear false witness. Yet, He specifically excludes the tenth commandment, Christ decrees Moses' intent to protect the right of one man to enslave another was wrong."⁶

The boy whispered, *"I never thought of it in this way."*

John Paul continued, *"Through the centuries, Mother Church has had the same problem the American Christians had back before Lincoln's day. In Moses' time, the Israelites slaughtered hundreds of thousands of their peaceful Canaanite neighbors including all of their children and thought it was right because their faith told them it was right. Back in Christ's time, they would stone unwed mothers to death and thought it was right because their faith told them it was right. The Crusaders slaughtered millions of Muslims and Jews and thought it was right because their faith told them it was right. In the World War, Italy sided with Germany in its quest for the superiority of the white race and the annihilation other races. Again, we thought it was right because our faith told us it was right.*

"Daniele, not too long ago when I was your age, every village in Italy had a cart that went about the streets each morning picking up the frozen bodies of orphans who had not made it through the winter nights. At the time, all we good Christians thought it was right because our faith told us it was right. Now, a few generations later, we know it was wrong. It was an atrocity.

"Just a few weeks ago, the first artificially inseminated child was born. Catholics overwhelmingly condemn the child. The reason they condemn the child is because their faith condemns the child. So even today, faith does not know right from wrong. Today, we persecute many kinds of people who live their lives differently and continue to think it is right because of what someone once wrote in a book.

"Daniele, you too must make progress or you will never know right from wrong. You will never be able to help society in its search for the truth. You will never be able to make your mark toward making this a better world to live in for those who come after you."

Daniele, *"Now I know why I must go on to the sixth grade."*

"Yes, Daniele, you have your sacred commission. You must go on to the sixth grade, then on to the seventh, and then on to the eighth. You must go forward, always advancing, never looking back. Progress must be your guiding ambition. So that someday the whole world will come to know the truth. So that the day will come about when all men and women will treat each other equally as Christ had commanded, 'Love thy neighbor as thyself.' Not as they have in the past, just because someone once wrote something in a book.

"Always remember," John Paul cautioned, *"faith is something someone once wrote in a book. Someone who wanted to take advantage of others who didn't know what we know today. Faith is not the truth. It does not know right from wrong..."*

Daniele baffled, *"But, how would we know right from wrong?"*

The Pope pointed to his head.[8]

Women ordination

On CBS News the next day: John Paul held an audience with a Philippine delegation this morning. He was challenged on doctrine concerning rumors a woman might be ordained. John Paul told the bishop, *"When I was a boy, my father made me promise I would live my life in imitation of Christ. I have kept that solemn promise. Each time the fork in the road has come up, often only minutes apart, I have asked myself, 'Now, what would Jesus have done in this case?' I have often pondered the possibility as to how much better the world would be if everyone were to do this."* He then asked the bishop, *"Now, what do you think Jesus would do in this case?"*

The bishop remained silent. John Paul told him, *"It makes no difference what was written by self-serving men for yesterday, all that counts is what Jesus would do today."* He reminded the delegation, *"God is more our Mother than She is our Father!"*[9]

The next day, I woke up to the news: *"Just thirty-three days into his pontificate, Pope John Paul died last evening... Vibrant and on the job to the end, he was sixty-five... the only Pope whose death was unwitnessed... On hearing the news, Cardinal Benelli of Florence called for an autopsy... Born of a social revolutionary atheist father who had placed him in a seminary at the age of eleven with the commission to bring change to the Church... What would have been John Paul's papacy is perhaps best defined by his compassion for women, the remarried, bastards, homosexuals, the poor and others oppressed by scripture as expressed in the underlying message of his acceptance speech* in the Sistine Chapel on August 27, 1978, '...We must rise up the courage to set aside the preferences that have been built into us by our Christian forefathers...Together we will muster the strength to lift those restraints unfairly placed upon the everyday lives of so many innocent people by doctrine... for God-given human life is infinitely more precious than is man-made doctrine.'"*[10]

Cardinal Willebrands, the most outspoken cardinal for women and married priests, who had recently defended homosexuals in an incident of gay-bashing, *"When Mother Church incites suffering and death, the thread which weaves her moral fabric is flawed,"* told the press, *"It is a disaster. I cannot put into words how happy we were on that day we had chosen John Paul. We had such high hopes. It was such a beautiful feeling, one that comes once in a lifetime, a*

39

feeling that something fresh was about to happen to our Church. "[11]

Five days later, Associated Press, October 4, 1978, Vatican City: "...The coffin, a pine box as reserved for paupers, was hemmed in by the princes of the Church in their rich and elegant attire...

Cardinal Leon Joseph Suenens, the leader of liberalism in the Roman Catholic Church, gave the final tribute for his dear friend.

'...Like a shimmering white light, he rose up from the mud in the street and left no one untouched.

For those of us at the top, from heads of churches, to leaders of nations, to those of great scientific achievement, he was the Enlightener—the Imitation of the Holy Ghost.

For those of us at the bottom, from the poor, to the homeless, to the handicapped, to the oppressed, he was the Redeemer—the Imitation of Christ.[1]

Above all, he was the best of men.'" [12]

Thus was the beginning and the end of Albino Luciani. Now, witness the whole of him. This is the Testament of John Paul I.

Albino Luciani = White Light

Author's note: ↓ PLEASE READ ↓

'Acceptance speech' as used herein is a misnomenclature as Luciani chatted with the cardinals for hours in a closed session. Its message is limited to what various *right* and *left* wing cardinals told various *right* and *left* wing elements of the press, the reason newspapers reported variations of what was said.

Yet, from all that is known, John Paul made a partisan effort to appeal to all. His *'greetings to all'* message, particularly to the oppressed, won the hearts of those on the *left*. Cardinals Benelli and Felici were pleased with the high priority given revision of the code of canon law the reason the Florence newspaper *La Nazione* focused on this point. Progressives who took *'ecumenism'* to include all religions were happy he committed himself to it. Conservatives were content as they took *'ecumenism'* to be religious unity within Catholicism the reason *L' Osservatore Romano* focused on this point. Third world cardinals were pleased with his overly compassion for the poor and his emphasis on human rights and international justice the reason Latin American media focused on this part of what he had to say. He made friendly tones toward the Synod of Bishops which was taken by Cardinal Suenens that future bishops, including popes, would be elected by the Episcopate to avoid polarization of the hierarchy of the Church which was reported in *L Europeenne de Bruxelles*. His most uniformly published comment in the world press, *'The Church existed not to be served by the world but instead to serve the world'* recalled Jack's last letter to me, *'Mother church will cease to be the cause of the world's problem and instead will begin to be the answer to them.'*

Except for some bits which had reached the world press, he was unknown outside Italy. Comments in world newspapers varied the day he was elected,

Rebel Bishop Voices Concern For Name.

Econe, Switzerland—Marcel Lefebvre said the Pope's name John Paul is an ill omen for traditionalists. It is a sign he would continue the reforms and procommunist position of his predecessors Paul VI and John XXIII.

Lefebvre suspended from all priestly powers for defying reforms started by John and continued under Paul, said the speed with which the new pontiff was elected is obvious it was arranged in advance.

Washington Post

There have been signs—in his church work, his speeches and his temperament—that Pope John Paul is not a hard-line conservative unwilling to change on various issues. "History is history," he said when elevated to cardinal five years ago. "We must look to the future with fresh hopes and new ideas."

Baltimore Sun

The new Pope is regarded as a moderate who is concerned with maintaining traditional Catholic values while at the same time lending Church support to issues of social justice.

The Times

"The choice indicates that the cardinals want to face the complex problems of modern times with prudence and with a moderate like Luciani rather than a conservative," said Kronos, a major Italian news agency.

Philadelphia Inquirer

His attitude on communism is unclear. The Church in Italy has made something of an uneasy peace with the powerful Communist and Socialist parties, and under Paul VI it has made bold diplomatic overtures to communist countries. The new Pope

Philadelphia Evening Bulletin

Official transcripts available on the Internet and in libraries of what a pope said on a specific occasion are usually not representative of what was actually said and are often contradictory of what was said. If one takes the time to view the clip of John Paul's September 27th audience www.johnpaul1.org one will find a simple man speaking in everyday conversation. Conversely, the official Vatican transcript of this audience—available in libraries and on the Net—portrays a great orator addressing a group of Noble laureates—it will drive the scholar to his dictionary.

John Paul's public audiences ran two to four hours during which time he spoke extemporarily. The Vatican transcripts can be read in less than a minute or two—in most cases not remotely representative of and in some cases contradictory to what actually took place. For example, during his four audiences he interviewed seventeen people including twelve children—the meat of what he had to say. Every one of these conversations ended up on the Vatican's cutting-room floor. The Daniele conversation exceeded thirty minutes, yet, only a few briefs reached most newspapers and it is not mentioned at all in the Vatican transcript.

himself lowering the microphone to the boy's height.

"Do you always want to be in the 5th grade?" the pope asked Daniele Bravo. "Yes," the boy replied. "So that I don't have to change teachers."

Flustered, the pope roared with laughter and said, "Well, you are different from the pope. When I was in 4th grade, I worried about making it to the 5th and when in the 5th, about passing to the 6th. You must move on."

Philadelphia Evening Bulletin

Authors have written of this. Roger Crane, in his play *The Last Confession* which premiered in 2007 in London starring David Suchet, probably tells it best.

John Paul: *(Disturbed)* "The Vatican press has changed my speech again...This isn't what I said at all. Just official statements cleverly redrafted by the Curia. They even have me celebrating the tenth anniversary of the encyclical against birth control. Everyone knows I intend to revise it."

Lorenzi: "There is also an article of your condemnation of the birth of the recent test-tube baby."

John Paul: "They know of and are ignoring the letter I wrote congratulating the parents. *(Angry)* Damn them!"

Lorenzi: "Holy Father."

John Paul: "Forgive me." *(Smiling)* "Just a figure of speech..."

... then we have Thomas Wynn's play *White Light*—John Paul and his secretary Magee the afternoon before his last audience:

Magee: "It says here, *'The new pontiff refused to join the priest-worker movement. A strong supporter of Paul's Populorum Progressio he is seen as an avid anti-communist.'* They have it in all the newspapers."

John Paul: *(Laughs)* They've got that one partly right. I never joined it. I started it.

Magee: *(Dumbfounded look)*

John Paul: "I helped draft *Populorum Progressio*—the inalienable right of all men to reasonable working conditions and just wages. Instead of rumors, they should read my book *Illustrissimi*. I make clear my support for the priest-worker movement in my letter to Saint Therese, *'...A justified strike is in progress...to feel solidarity in progress of men fighting for their rights, is Christian charity...'* And this name tab, *'Anti-communist?'* They are confused by what is going on in Russia. The Soviet Union is an autocracy. It was never a true communist society. The world does not know the meaning of the word 'communism.' Tomorrow, I will tell it what it means,

Magee: *(Dumbfounded again)*

John Paul: "It is the inalienable right of no man to accumulate wealth beyond his needs while other men starve to death because they have nothing."

---

1 *Deuteronomy 23 'A bastard child shall not enter the congregation of the Lord.'* Moses condemnation of born-out-of-wedlock children is why the word continues to have a terrible connotation today despite that the stigma is now dead. In 1973, Paul VI motioned to make Luciani a cardinal. Luciani sent a message that unless the Pope reversed canon law's condemnation of bastards, he would refuse the *red hat*. Paul complied. Yet, even today, in conservative Rome, one will not find a priest who is willing to baptize an illegitimate child. Despite Paul's reversal of the statute, the Church continues to cling to Moses' condemnation of these children, e.g., today an illegitimate child cannot become a priest, cannot become a Swiss Guard, etc.
2 carried in its entirety by ANSA, Italy's premier wire service. Conversation with the boy Anthony
3 John Paul originally said this to Cardinal Villot on September 19th. He repeated it is his 4th audience.
4 Visit www.JohnPaul1.org for film clip *"...It is the inalienable right..."* 27 Sep 78 4th audience
5 The Tenth Commandment as it appears in the oldest surviving texts and in eastern Bibles including the Jewish *Torah* today: *"Thou shalt not covet (desire to take from) thy neighbor his property, including his house, his wife, his slaves, his ox, his ass."* In the twentieth century, most Bibles changed its meaning from the original texts: *"Thou shalt not covet thy neighbor his...servants or employees..."* Moses' intent was to hold women as mere property of men and protect the right of one man to enslave another. The United States Constitution was originally based on this commandment—women and slaves were property and had no rights as human beings until the mid-nineteenth century.
6 *Matthew 19*
7 *Right* wing media reported only this to this point inferring the Daniel interview lasted only a minute. Even this excerpt taken out of context, John Paul explicitly defines himself as a progressive,
8 This relatively substantial text of the boy Daniele interview and is a composite of excerpts published in *La Repubblica, La Stampa, El Mondo, Corriere della Serra, Corriere del Alpi, The Times*, the *Washington Post*, the *Boston Globe, the Philadelphia Bulletin and other world newspapers*
9 As reported in *La Stampa* 12 Sep 78. Other newspapers reported variations of what was said reflecting their political position. John Paul originally said this on Sunday September 10, 1978 and repeated it in his private audience with the Philippine delegation on September 27, 1978.
10 See author's note above
11 *De Groene Amsterdammer* 2 Oct 78
12 *L Europeenne de Bruxelles* 5 Oct 78

Photo Anthony – *author*
Photo Daniele – *author*
Photo John Paul funeral - *author*

Chapter 3

The Minor Seminary at Feltre

"The most fundamental weapon of war is not guns and bombs. It is propaganda which conditions children of nations to hate children of other nations so that when they grow up they will kill each other for the few at the top."[1]

Albino Luciani

It was a dark dismal afternoon in October of nineteen hundred twenty-three, when eleven year old Albino Luciani climbed into the carriage that would take him to the minor seminary at Feltre—his first stop on a long journey which would eventually lead to Rome.

His father, who had spent a lifetime trying to change the Church from the outside, decided it could only be changed from the inside. He committed his son to the task.

In those days, prep schools, particularly minor seminaries, were reserved for the very rich—the reason priests came only from wealthy families—a reason priest do not take a vow of poverty. The best a poor boy could look forward to was a monk's robe. His father, Giovanni Luciani, a member of the Socialist Party of Italy, made a deal; it would contribute the money, he would contribute Albino.[2]

In his farewell, the revolutionary outcast of the Veneto country commissioned his son, "Albino, unlike those hypocrites who prance about the Vatican palaces in magnificent robes of silk and satin with jeweled chalices and rings of diamonds and rubies and gold, you must promise me you will live your life in imitation of Christ."

Emulating Albino's fondness for chess, he gave the boy his game plan, "Play your pieces carefully and work hard until that day when at the helm of their ranks you will establish the common dignity of all Christ's children in the Church." He left him with one last word of caution, *"Never risk your king to save a pawn."*

So it was, his Papa, together with his little brother Edoardo, with tears in their eyes, waved goodbye, on that dreary drizzly autumn afternoon, to this *Pauper who would be Pope.*

The road to Feltre had been a difficult one for the little boy. In

44

the impoverished town of Canale d'Agordo, his family had been the poorest of the poor. His father was not only an atheist, he was a revolutionary socialist activist—a thorn in the side of the Church.

So much so, he had to migrate hundreds of miles away where he was unknown to earn enough to support his family. Also, he spent much of his earnings building sheds for the orphans.

Nevertheless, Feltre was a big step up for the little boy Luciani. To begin with, the buildings had indoor plumbing. In the poor mountain village where he had grown up, none of the houses had indoor plumbing. Going to the bathroom was the worst of times, particularly in the wintertime. That is, it was the worst of times for everyone except the orphans. They would sneak into the outhouses to keep warm. For them, it was the best of times.

For this reason most people kept padlocks on them to keep the orphans out. Nevertheless, going to the bathroom would never again be the worst of times for Albino Luciani. Actually, the worst of times for this little boy were not over. They were yet to come.

Luciani told me of the time he knelt in the chapel at Feltre.

"It was at the age of eleven I began my ministry.

"The haunting memory of the hopeless struggle of the orphans would trouble me all the rest of my days. These unfortunate children would become the central focus of all my energies. It was then, in the solitude of that tiny chapel, I made my sacred pledged to Christ,

"'*I can offer you no great cathedral, no chant, no offering of gold. All I have to give is my promise that I will do what you have told me to do. I know not where this path leads. All I know is that you have told me to take it, and that is all I need know.*

'*If at its end there is nothing there, it is enough for me that you have allowed me the opportunity to have walked this way. That you have called upon me to bring about the equality of all your children.*

'*I care not if it takes me over the highest mountains, or across the widest seas, or against the armaments of all the armies of the earth, or even through fire. I intend to do this thing with all the strength, vigor and courage that is within me as if the very existence of each and every one of your children depends on me, alone.*'"[3]

Thus began the work of John Paul I.

The bell tower

45

When he had first arrived at Feltre, he gazed up in wonderment at the bell tower which annexed the school. It was the first time he had seen a building so tall—easily twice the height of the next tallest building in town. In total mass, it was every bit as big as was the school itself. It made no sense to him one would build a structure of monumental cost just to house a bell.

It was when he gazed up at the bell tower, he realized how far the Church had strayed from what Christ had intended. It would use an immense amount of money it collected for the poor, which could be used to build housing for a hundred orphans, to house a bell.

He noticed something strange about the tower. There was no lock on its door. Why no lock on the door to the bell tower? He was soon to find out there was another purpose of the tower.

The strange little boy in the schoolyard

It was early in the spring, the bishop, Jack and I—were enjoying the afternoon sun on the terrace of the bishop's castle in Vittorio Veneto when the local newsboy delivered a week-old copy of the *New York Times*. There was a picture of a boy on a fence.

A gay Hispanic teen had been arrested in Washington Square Park and brought to the Sixth Precinct Station for booking. Later that night he was found impaled face downward on the heavy iron fence which enclosed the station with six of its spikes protruding upwards through his body from his neck to his thigh. It was then I learned this smiling, grinning, laughing, teasing, joking, Albino Luciani, could cry. It was then he told me of his first brush with homosexuality.

"It was on my twelfth birthday, I learned there was another kind of BASTARD. He was a delicate little boy who spoke with a lisp and waved his hands in a funny little way. All the kids laughed at him in the schoolyard. Then one day he died. No Mass was said for him and he was buried outside of town in the village dump. The day after he was buried, Father Gaio explained to the class Giovanni had been born bad, so the Devil had taken him back. But I knew the priest was wrong. I knew Giovanni, like all Christ's children, had been born good. I also knew why he had jumped from the bell tower. He just

46

couldn't take it anymore. That afternoon, as I stood over my friend's grave, I vowed I would never let anyone laugh at him again."[3]

As he crept into his teens, Albino came to realize many of his classmates were gay, despite few of them displayed effeminate traits as had Giovanni. He knew why. A teenager who contemplated the priesthood had to make the great sacrifice of celibacy.

Under canon law, all sex outside of marriage is mortal sin. A straight youth had the option of marriage and could look forward to a life of sex free of sin. For him, celibacy was a great sacrifice.

But, a gay teen could never marry and therefore, if he was devout—in those days everyone was devout—he was condemned by canon law to a life of celibacy anyway. So in choosing the celibate life of a priest, a homosexual teen wasn't giving up anything.

He also found a number of his classmates were transsexuals— girls born into boy's bodies—attracted to the priesthood because it allowed them to dress up in beautiful gowns and live their lives as objects of admiration otherwise reserved for the fairer sex.

In the five years he would be at Feltre, a dozen of his classmates leaped from the bell tower. Some were homosexual or transsexual teens whose identity was uncovered by their 'holy' keepers. A few were discovered to have been born-out-of-wedlock and went off the tower on the eve of their excommunication. Others developed deformities, one was crippled in an accident and another stopped growing and was determined to be a midget. Each one, with his dream of becoming a priest shattered, went off the tower on the eve of expulsion—the remains splattered across the cobblestones below.

No Mass was said for any of them. Each of them, one by one, was put into a burlap sack and taken to the town dump. It had been Moses' testimony in *Leviticus, "The lord spoke to Moses saying, whosoever should he be that hath a blemish, whether he be a blind child, or a lame child, or a child with a flat nose (Negro), or a child broken-footed, or broken-handed, or a hunch-backed, or a dwarfed child, or a child of disease is not to approach the altar of the Lord."*[4]

There were many different kinds of BASTARDS in those days, but nevertheless, they were all BASTARDS—the worst of boys.

His rise to the world stage

Albino Luciani's rise to the world stage did not begin when he became a cardinal in 1973. It began in 1926 when he was just thirteen years old. He had wiggled himself into the job of Assistant Editor of the school paper and his first article, through his father's influence, was republished in a socialist literary journal and eventually reached all of Europe. *"...The problems of the Western World will only come to an end when free nations, in accordance with their copyright laws, require the Old Testament be prefaced, 'This is a work of fiction. Keep away from children.'*

"A function of copyright laws is to protect the public from what might not be true. The state is derelict in its duty in failing to place a warning on this book, as many people are using it to guide the way they live their lives and this is costing many others their lives.

"There is not a word in this book that has been proven true. What's more, all of the major claims set forth by Moses have been proven to be false. After all, everyone knows the earth is round. Let us not be so foolish as to believe this man Moses who talked to a God who thought it was flat. It is obvious to any man or woman of good conscience, this book was not inspired by God; rather, it was inspired by the greed and hatred of evil men."[5]

Most laughed, they took it to be a joke. Some were critical of the boy's audacity, some called for his expulsion, others going so far as to call for his excommunication. On the other hand, one of them, Albert Einstein, called the child prodigy's article, *The first bit of common sense to ever come out of the Roman Catholic Church."[6]*

Just a few months later, when it seemed the smoke had cleared, Albino struck again. He wrote his first editorial and, again, through the influence of his father, although it did not attain the notoriety of the first article, it showed up in periodicals throughout Europe.

"I cannot accept Moses was the holy man the Church and the motion pictures make him out to be. Moses introduced fascism to the Western World, the concept some kinds of people are better than others and are entitled to more. That ideology which fosters hatred of certain kinds of people and a rich and poor society, one in which some children are born into immense wealth and other children are born into dire poverty and starvation.

48

"Moses talks of God the Father's dream in which the white male rules at His side with woman held in servitude to man and all others who are different are to be subordinated, annihilated or cast into slavery. Moses subordinates those with 'flat noses' (Negroes) and 'those who are of physical blemish' (the handicapped).

"In all my life I have never seen a black person as black people are not allowed in Italy. We are an entirely white Catholic country because the minds of the voters are controlled by a Vatican that wants to preserve the purity of our superior race...

"On the other side, we have Christ. He introduces communism to the western world, the ideology based on the premise all God's children are created equal and are entitled to share equally in God's province. Christ dictates a world in which every child has an equal opportunity at a good and healthy life, a far different world than we live in today. Christ gives us only two commandments 'Love thy neighbor as thyself' and 'Sell all thou hast and give to the poor.'

"These are the pillars of society, communism and Christ on the left and fascism and Moses on the right...

"Despite Christ's overwhelming testimony two thousand years ago, Christianity remains steeped in fascism today. It is obvious Mother Church in her support of a fascist state has chosen the word of Moses over the word of Jesus Christ Himself."[7]

Albino's editorial was in response to an order by Pius XI, a week earlier, requiring all children be enrolled in the new *Fascist Scout Organization*, which served as the kindling wood for World War II.

Conditioning children for war

While at Feltre, he had his first look at a big city. From early childhood, he had expressed an expertise in chess and was permitted to go to Milan—his anonymous benefactors financing the trips.

Albino made the acquaintance of Russian teens his own age.

He found it was propaganda which conditioned Catholic children to hate children of communist countries. It was this strategy that enabled a few at the pinnacles of churches and nations to cause the mindless masses at the bottom to sacrifice their lives in war to the benefit of those at the top.

He found Russian children were every bit as good as he was. On the other hand, the Russian children found their western counterparts

49

were not as good as they were. They had heard stories about how Catholic countries treated born-out-of-wedlock children. Yet, they believed it to be Russian propaganda. When they found out it was true, they thought less of their western friends. In their homeland all children were seen to be equal. There were no orphans in the streets.

His Russian roommate Alexander Rotov was a bit older. Made possible by the Russian's fluency in Italian, the two struck up a relationship which would last until Rotov's death in 1959. The Russian would sire a son, Boris, who would eventually rise as Luciani's counterpart in the Russian Orthodox Church.

On return to Feltre, another of his editorials reached notoriety, *'The Shroud of War.'* He concludes, *"The most fundamental weapon of war is not guns and bombs. It is propaganda which conditions children of nations to hate children of other nations so that when they grow up they will kill each other for the few at the top."*[8]

He tastes of the forbidden fruit

In addition to required studies of Feltre designed to brainwash students in fascism, Albino got a glimpse of the other side of the coin. Through his father, he obtained a parade of forbidden books.

Among them were Darwin's *Origin of the Species* and Mendel's *Experiments in Plant Hybrids.* He took a particular interest in these pioneers of modern day genetics believing they would eventually pave the way to a time when all children would be born healthy.

He found Albert Einstein's works most fascinating, particularly as it defined the infinite unit of creation—the atom—from which all matter evolved. He would refer to Einstein's *Theory of Evolution* and be corrected by his teachers he was confusing Einstein with Darwin. But, he knew what he was talking about.

There were books on astronomy, anthropology, archeology, chemistry, physics, history, and psychology—how the mind works.

Then there were those banned from Catholic seminaries—the 'Bibles' of other religions including Mohammed's *Koran,* the Hindu scripture the *Vedas,* the *Sutras* and the *Tripitaka* of the Buddhist culture and an endless array of others.

He became particularly fascinated with Tao who, like Einstein, centuries after him, defined man as a microcosm of nature. In all, he spent countless hours scouring through the worlds of the other Gods.

50

Above all, the Church banned any book that mentioned sex, even scientific journals. That he was exposed to books which discussed sex at an early age made possible the most prolific testimony of his ministry, *"We have made of sex the greatest of sins, whereas in itself it is nothing more than human nature and not a sin at all."*[9]

Most instrumental to the man he would become were those on socialism. Among these were the works of Antonio Rosmini, a nineteenth century theologian who believed the purpose of society was to protect the individual and not the other way around—chagrin to the Vatican which limited human rights and dignity of those who did not conform to scripture. Regardless, except for this philosophy which would remain at the core of his existence for the rest of his life he would eventually refute much of what Rosmini had to say.

He studied at length Marx' *Das Kapital* and Lenin's *The State and Revolution* and *The Rise of Capitalism in Russia* and countless others. He swallowed up Marx and Engels' *Communist Manifesto.*

He quickly put two and two together.

Marx' Ideology	*Christ's teaching*
All God's children are equal	*Love thy neighbor as thyself*
Redistribution of wealth society	*Sell all thou hast and give to the poor*

Marx had tried unsuccessfully to bring Christ's teachings into a selfish world. He told his papa of his discovery. His papa explained.

"When the evangelists first went out teaching the word of Christ they found they had no customers. To give up one's greed for wealth and one's superiority over other kinds of people was too much to sacrifice for what most conceived as a long shot at an afterlife.

"So they went back to the drawing boards and made up a new kind of church, one that allowed one to accumulate wealth beyond one's wildest dreams while others starve to death. One based on the premise some kinds of people are better than other kinds of people.

"They built their new church on these principles:

• You can ignore what Christ had to say, *'Love thy neighbor as thyself.'* Little boys are better than little girls, whites are better than blacks, straights are better than gays...

• You can ignore what Christ had to say. You can accumulate wealth beyond your wildest dreams while others starve to death provided you give us our share.

51

• You can ignore what Christ had to say. We give you the loophole of forgiveness. We **give** you the opportunity in which you can lie, cheat, steal, rape and even murder all of your life and go to heaven. There is a catch. Only we can forgive you.

"One can't get a better deal than that. Lie, cheat steal, hate, greed and bask in untold wealth while others starve to death, and still go to heaven. From this grew the largest church in the world—the largest business in the world.

"The Church is today a church based on His death—the idolatry of Christ—the crucifix—forgiveness—a free ride for those who follow its rules of prejudice and greed.

"It ignores His life—the ideology of Christ—'*Love Thy Neighbor as Thyself*'—a church without preferences—a Church for all.

"It is your job, Albino, to change the Church back to what Christ had intended. Again, never risk your king to save a pawn!"

Nevertheless, it was these books and his father's guidance which molded him into the social revolutionary he would become. They would also provide him with the ammunition he needed to have some fun—to play with the minds of his captors at Feltre.

1 *Povera Tigre Belluno* 22 Jul 28
2 The grant was anonymous. It is reasonable to believe it came from the party his father belonged to
3 Direct testimony of the author
4 *Leviticus 21*
5 *Parish Bulletin Feltre*, 10 May 26   *London Times* 22 Jun 26
6 *Leidsch Dagblad*, 25 Jun 26
7 *Povera Tigre Belluno* 12 Dec 26
8 *Povera Tigre Belluno* 22 Aug 28
9 The most prolific teaching of Albino Luciani

Photo Feltre tower - *author*
Photo eleven year old Albino Luciani - *Angenzia Ansa* 1923

Chapter 4

The Tyrant of Feltre

"God is more our Mother than She is our Father"[1]   Albino Luciani

Today, visitors to Feltre can view a display of old notes, the only surviving record the boy Luciani had ever been there. A dozen or so reprimands—some not much more than a slap on the wrist while others threatened expulsion and even excommunication.

As he had been in grade school, the boy Luciani was a rascal and a tyrant at Feltre. Even the Church's biographical briefs will tell you this. But, they will not tell you why. They will lead you to believe he spent his schooldays shooting rubber bands and dipping pigtails in inkwells. Not so. Here, as I have promised, I will tell you why.

The ghostly past

To the little boy of Feltre, it was more a case of fun than it was one of sarcasm when he attacked the primitive nature of ritual.

One day he drew a comparison between the Christian dancing around his statues at festival time and the American Indian dancing around his totem poles—the ritual was the same, just the ideology differed. He compared them to their common ancestor, the Cro-Magnon, which archeology had recently discovered had once danced around an altar of bear skulls tens of thousands of years before.

He capitalized on the archeological discovery man's tendency to believe in ghosts began with the Neanderthals two hundred thousand years ago. The Neanderthals feared the spirits of the dead. Scores of excavations had revealed they buried their dead. The bigger the man, the deeper buried—at depths up to twelve feet. Females were not buried as the threat of spirits was thought to be relative to body size.[2]

That the Neanderthals believed the sprit leaves the body at death was not only the beginning of man's tendency to believe in ghosts, it was also the beginning of his belief he could somehow beat the rap of mortality and live forever.

53

It also marked the beginning of religion from which emerged the Cro-Magnon altar of bear skulls, the witchdoctors of dark Africa, the cunning Aborigine wise man who created the gods of the South Pacific, the clever Celtic who dreamt up the Banshee, the Eskimo who created Agloolik—the god who lived under the sea, up to western religions of today in which scrupulous men take advantage of man's fear of his mortality to achieve their political objectives.

Regardless, being a natural born prankster, he took pleasure in playing with the minds of his masters. He was well positioned to do this—they had only read one book. He had read them all.

The conspirators

In simple matters, he would use his peers. He would plant the idea in one of his classmates who would raise his hand, "Adam and Eve had three sons, Seth, Cain and Abel. After Cain killed Abel, we know Cain went on to sire a family. I would suppose then that his wife had to be his mother, Eve, since there were no other women?"

Don Filippo would jump at the bait, "Although the Bible doesn't mention it, Adam and Eve had daughters. The Bible doesn't mention them because women are not that important. Like all other animals, women are mere property of man. Here," he pointed to the tablet of the commandments, *Thou shalt not covet thy neighbor his property, his house, his wife, his slaves, his ox, his ass.* '³

The boy would respond "Then in those days it was okay to have sex with your sister?" The class laughed. Albino, in a corner of the room, would use all his willpower to maintain his composure.

Yet, as would be his sacred duty throughout his ministry—as God had given him the light to see that duty—wherever scripture or doctrine treated people unfairly, he stepped in.

Thank heaven for little girls

"How about the Bonobo?" he looked at his master for an answer.

"The what?" Don Filippo had evidently never heard the word.

"Of the fifteen species of higher primates including man, only the bonobo—the pigmy chimpanzee—recognizes the parity of woman. As a matter-of-fact, in the world of the pigmy chimpanzee, woman is dominant, man is subservient. In the world of the pigmy

54

chimpanzee," he told them what he would tell the world fifty years later, *'God is more our Mother than She is our Father.'*"[4]

Don Filippo could scarcely contain himself. "Blasphemy!

"Only man can be of divinity. Only a man can be a God. We know this as a matter-of-fact. It is sacrilege to think of woman as being of divinity. An idiot would know that."

"As a matter-of-fact?" Albino looked up at his master.

Filippo spoke down to the boy, "Yes, it is the fundamental truth on which Christianity is built. Christ was a man. What's more, God—His Father—was a man. His mother was a mere animal."

"Let's see," mumbled the boy reaching for his copy of the New Testament and flipping a few pages. "Here, here in *Matthew*. I guess this is what you are talking about. *"When Mary was espoused to Joseph, before they came together, she was found to be with child. Joseph being a just man was minded to put away her privily and not make her a public example..."*"[5]

He paused for a long moment as does a chess player planning his next move. He carefully anticipated all the possible ways his teacher might counter his move. Then he let him have it. "It is a matter-of-fact Mary cheated on Joseph. Christ was conceived out-of-wedlock. Christ was a Bastard—born-out-of-wedlock. According to canon law Christ could never be a priest, let alone a God."

If Don Filippo had been standing on a corner, one could easily mistake him for a red light. He did exactly what Albino anticipated, "You are taking it out of context. Read the rest of the verse."

"'...Behold the angel of the Lord appeared in a dream, saying, Joseph, Mary is conceived of the Holy Ghost...'"[8]

Don Filippo locked up his case, "It is a matter-of-fact the Holy Ghost was the Father of Christ. Mary was merely the animal used to bear the child. This proves only a man can be of divinity."

The class turned and looked at Albino as if he had been the last one in line when the brains had been passed out.

The boy agreed, "Yes, it was a Ghost who had sex with Mary. But it is not a matter-of-fact; it is a matter-of-faith.

"The matter-of-fact is Mary cheated on Joseph. We don't know who Christ's real father was. Christ was a Bastard. Not only born-out-of-wedlock, He was born of adultery—a product of sin. That is a matter-of-fact. What you are talking about is a matter-of-faith."

Don Filippo's face flushed aghast the boy had dared use the word 'sex' in a classroom. Yet, he could not ignore the challenge. He had to correct the imp's illusion "The Holy Ghost did not have sex with Mary. Christ's conception was immaculate, free of the sin of sex."

Albino concurred, "Then you agree Christ was not a man."

"You don't understand, Albino. Christ was both man and God."

"If Christ was a human being, the Ghost, you speak of, would have fertilized Mary's egg with sperm. Otherwise Christ would not have been a man; He would have only been a God. The Ghost had to have had sex with Mary or Christ could not have been a man."

Don Filippo was tongue-tied. In his mind he pictured himself at the top of the bell tower gazing down in amusement at his young adversary's body splattered across the cobblestones below. The class waited anxiously for an explanation, but nothing came forth.

Albino rescued his teacher, "Yet, you are right. Joseph's dream is the fundamental 'truth' on which Christianity is built. It is the pivot point of belief in the Christian world. Yet, it is a matter-of-faith and not a matter-of-fact.

"More than two-thirds of the world: Muslims, Jews, Buddhists, Hindus, atheists and others don't believe in Joseph's dream. Only we Christians believe in Joseph's dream. We believe in Joseph's dream because of all the peoples of the world, we have the greatest tendency to believe in ghosts—in this case one with a capital 'G.'"

He paused, looked around the room to be certain each of his peers would witness what he was about to say. "Yes, my good papa, if one gets carried away with 'faith,' you are correct, God is our Father.

But, if one considers the 'facts—the absolute facts,'" he followed with conviction *"God is more our Mother than She is our Father."*

Don Filippo threw him off the bell tower, again.

---

1 He repeated this on September 6, 1978 in a public audience and again on September 27, 1978
2 Neanderthals also believed bears had spirits which survived death. They also conceived altar worship of a 'bear god' the earliest record of a god. The earliest being a row of bear skulls geometrically arranged on a stone slab in a cave in France. Darwin published his thesis *The Origin of Species* in 1859. The first Neanderthal fossil was discovered in Germany in 1856 but it was thought to have been a modern man until thirty years later its origin and age was determined.
3 The Tenth Commandment
4 As explained elsewhere in this book, John Paul shortly after his installation and repeated it the day before he died to a group of Philippine bishops
5 *Matthew 1* Had Joseph made her public example, Mary would have been stoned to death as required by the Law of Moses in the Old Testament. Until very recently, it was common for television to record a young unwed mother being shot to death in the streets of Iran

Chapter 5

The Worst of People

"When a man does not believe in God... it does not mean he believes in nothing. It could mean he believes in everything."[1]   Albino Luciani

Not all things the boy Luciani did in class were fun and games. Sometimes things got quite serious. There was a young priest, Don Gaio, who taught a class on catechism.

One day, a student demanded, "We should have a law against atheists and put them all in jail? They are the worst of people."

Albino took this as a direct attack on his father. His classmates knew his father was an atheist. In fact, they knew his father did not even believe Christ had ever lived.

Although his father did not believe Christ had lived, that is, a man who had performed the miracles said of Christ including His virgin birth and resurrection—unlike his Christian adversaries—he did believe in Christ's philosophies as set forth in the gospels.

What's more, he believed good men, in an attempt to do away with the evilness of the God of Moses, had written the gospels.

When the young priest started to side with the student, Albino didn't bother to raise his hand. To him it was a matter of honor. He would stand and fight to the end in defense of his beloved father who had taught him right from wrong.

Bringing his fist down on his desk, he stood up, "Instead of throwing stones, let us first define what we are talking about, so that we all know what we are talking about."

Don Gaio looked at the boy as if he didn't know what he was talking about. Albino answered the priest's puzzled expression, "We are talking about God. That is what we are talking about. How one defines God. That is all we are talking about.

"So let us define the 'God' of religion versus the 'God' of the atheist." Still there was not much more than a dumbfounded look on the faces of both the teacher and the students.

The priest motioned him to sit down. Yet, the young boy held the floor, "Let us start with what we know.

"To begin with, we have the sun. We know the sun holds the earth in its orbit and is the source of all life on our planet. The reason it is the source of all life on our planet is because it is the source of all energy in our solar system.

"We know, from Einstein's work, energy is the fundamental unit of creation. Without energy, without the sun, nothing could begin, nothing could grow, nothing could move, nothing could be." Don Gaio, raising his voice in a nervous twang, ordered him to sit down.

Albino didn't budge. "So religion and atheism have a common definition. *God is the source of all energy which drives the natural order of God's creation.* So, in truth, we all have a common God.

"Yet, the similarities end there. On the one side, we have those of us who are happy with what God has given us in this life and accept the natural order of God's creation. On the other side, we have those of us who are unhappy with what God has given us in this life and do not accept the natural order of..." Gaio cut him off.

"Now, you are talking sense..." the young priest smiled. "Yes, we Christians accept what God has given us..."

"Not Christians, Atheists." Albino took back the floor. "Atheists accept the natural order of God's creation. We Christians are not satisfied with what God has given us in this life. We lust for more." Fifty-two ears surrounding him perked up. Fifty-four including Gaio.

"We Christians cannot accept the real world we live and die in while the atheist does. To put it bluntly, we Christians believe in ghosts and the atheist does not." Don Gaio sneered the boy a glance of insanity and the class snickered at Albino's ridiculous notion.

"Yes, we believe in ghosts. We believe a Burning Bush which claimed to be God appeared to a man named Moses over three thousand years ago—the foundation of all Judeo-Christian belief.

The cornerstone of Judeo-Christian belief

58

"What's more, like Jews and Muslims, we also believe in those ghosts that appeared to the two-dozen or so other prophets who came after Moses in the Old Testament.

"As Christians, ghosts follow us into the gospels as well.

"When Joseph is alarmed when Mary is conceived with child before they had come together, as we were discussing the other day, we believe another ghost—an angel—appeared to Joseph in a dream telling him Mary had been impregnated by a still another ghost—the Holy Ghost—the foundation of our conviction Christ is God.

"On top of it all, we, as Catholics, believe in ghosts today as we accept the ghosts of Lourdes and Fatima. So much so, we make saints of those cunning few who pulled the wool over our eyes."

Don Gaio was tongue-tied, the class frozen in apprehension. The boy was not quite finished. "Most ridiculous of all, we believe we, ourselves, will someday, too, be ghosts."

The beginning of us…

"Nevertheless, let us consider how this works.

"First, let us consider the beginning of us—birth.

We all know, as a matter-of-fact, we are conceived of tiny bits of energy that come together and result in a chemical reaction. That is the will of the *God of Nature*—the natural order of creation—the *God of the Atheist*—the God who gives us life.

"It is an absolute fact of nature the egg comes first.

"But, religion does not accept the facts. It does not accept the will of the God we know, as a matter-of-fact, gives us life. It tells us, 'No! The chicken came first.' It gives us the tale of *Adam and Eve*.

"Yet, on the other side, we have the facts.

"The Indians were running around the Americas thousands of years before God created Adam and Eve in the Garden of Eden and our true ancestors—the Cro-Magnons—were were running around Europe tens of thousands of years before that."[2] He stopped again for a moment or two to allow his listeners to catch up.

The end of us…

"Then, we have the end of us—death.

"We know, as a matter-of-fact, each one of us will eventually die. This is the will of the *God of Nature*—the natural order of creation—the *God of the Atheist*—the God who gives us life.

"But, once again, religion does not accept the will of the God who we know, as a matter-of-fact, gives us life. It tells us, 'No! For a few dollars, I will give you eternal life.'

"And how will we live forever? The sun is only the hand of God. There is an all-powerful Supernatural Creature who controls the sun and has a large book in which He records everything each one of us does from the time we are born until the time we die—the premise of all religions. So, for a few dollars, we will live forever.

"So we have the definition of religion—a business in which scrupulous men take advantage of man's fear of his mortality to achieve their political objectives.

The in-between of us…

"Then there is the in-between of us—life.

"There are many difficulties in life. People suffer from all kinds of birth defects, diseases, injuries, accidents and so forth. This is the will of the *God of Nature*—the natural order of God's creation—the *God of the Atheist*—the God who gives us life.

"Again, religion does not accept the will of the God who we know, as a matter-of-fact, gives us life. It says 'No! For a few dollars I will give you miracles. I will give you a better life.'

"To seek miracles is to refuse to accept the will of the God who gives us life. Regardless, we fall down on our knees and speak to plaster statues asking them for miracles. As if to say, God would favor some of Her children over others.

"Religion is a business of only two products—miracles and an afterlife. When we are priests, the faithful will pay us for the first of these because it does not really believe the second one is there.

"It makes no sense to pray for the recovery of a six year old boy when doctrine guarantees if he dies he will go to heaven. Christ said *'Blessed are little children for theirs is the Kingdom of Heaven.'* He said this not once, but many times, as to leave no doubt about it. [3]

"If this same boy grows up to be an adult, his chances, according to the same doctrine, are immensely diminished, *'Many are called, but few are chosen.'* [3] The young priest tapped a boy on the shoulder and sent him for the headmaster.

The differences between us…

Albino blinked. "Finally, we have the differences between us.

"The *God of Nature*—the natural order of God's creation—the *God of the Atheist*—creates all of Her children to be equal.

"Again, religion does not accept the *God of Nature*—the natural order of God's creation—the *God of the Atheist*—the God who gives us life. It says 'No!'

"It tells us women, like other animals, are mere property of men. It tells us little boys are better than little girls. It tells us only we men are worthy to be representatives of God, only we men have the power to mumble a few words and wave our hands over a piece of bread in a cup and change it into a God—the reason there is not a single girl in this room despite, as we proved conclusively the other day, *'God is more our Mother than She is our Father.'*

"It preaches the subordination of black and ethnic peoples and *'whosoever child that hath a blemish, a blind child, or a lame child, a broken-limbed child, a hunch-backed child, a dwarfed child, a diseased child, a queer child, or a child born out of wedlock is not to approach the altar of the Lord.'*[4] He smiled as he recited the sacred words of the God his seniors and peers gambled their eternity on.

His eyes roamed around the room catching each one of them in a frigid stare. They finally came to rest on Gaio and the headmaster who had just stepped into the room. He dealt the crushing blow.

"When a man does not believe in God—a Ghost someone once wrote about in a book—it does not mean he believes in nothing. It could mean he believes in everything."[1]

He held back for a moment or two thinking deeply. Rather than softening the blow he decided to solidify it. Turning toward his master, "Father Gaio, it is said Satan comes in many disguises."

Gaio jumped at the lure. "Truer words were never spoken. We must be on our guard at all times."

He looked up at Gaio, he nodded agreement. "Yes. But tell me. How did Moses know who he was talking to in the desert? Why was that 'Bush'—we accept as our God—burning in flames?

"Where do you think it came from?"

The aftermath

Despite his nickname Piccolo—little one—would be with him all

61

his life, regular meals and sports at Feltre had given him an athlete's body of envious proportions. After class, he told Giulio—the boy who had raised the question in the first place. "Don't ever try that again. The next time I will use my fists instead of my eloquence."

To all history has recorded, Giulio never tried it again. Neither did any of Albino's other classmates. Perhaps, not so much they feared his fists, as they feared his eloquence.

So it went on for four years, the teenager literally torturing his masters day after day. Each one of them wanted him out of the school as quickly as possible in order that they could survive with their sanity. In that everything he had to say was wrong to them, none of them could rightfully give him passing grades. Yet, it was the only way they could get rid of him for the grant from the boy's anonymous donor was far too much for the diocese to give up.

So it was on a sunny afternoon in the early summer of nineteen hundred twenty-seven, Albino Luciani graduated at the bottom of his class in the courtyard at the foot of the bell tower in Feltre. The class valedictorian gave his promise to serve God and the wreaths were passed out: catechism, theology, liturgy and so forth. One by one, his classmates strolled to the platform to pick them up.

Had there been wreaths for ancient history, anthropology, archeology, astronomy, biology, chemistry, genetics, language, mathematics, physics, politics, psychology, science, sociology, compassion, courage and change, he would have taken them all.

Yet, he did take one——perfect attendance.[5] While at Feltre, he had not missed a class. They couldn't take that one away from him.

Nevertheless, the following day, the boy Luciani was gone. The masters of Feltre would celebrate. But, they would never forget him. No matter how hard they tried, they would never forget him.

What's more, they never locked the door to the bell tower, either.

1 *Biblioteca Apostolica Vaticana,* Second Vatican II Council transcript 22 Nov 63. When atheism came up in a discussion of ecumenicalism, Luciani made a similar observation.
2 DNA applications have since proved the boy Luciani right. The Cro-Magnons are the biological ancestors of modern man.
3 John XXIII (Angelo Roncalli) said a similar thing in the Basilica di San Marco in 1955
4 *Deuteronomy 23*
5 *Povera Tigre Belluno*22 Jun 27.

Author's note: Albino was fifteen at the time of this incident. It was related by Bishop Luciani to the author. The author has reconstructed the story to best represent what took place. A fuller rendition of the incident is recounted in the author's book of short stories, *'Let's All Get Behind the Pope,'* in the short story: 'The Library of the Atheist.'

Chapter 6

The Seminary at Belluno

"...Never risk your king to save a pawn."[1]

Giovanni Paulo Luciani

In the following autumn, a grant surfaced from the anonymous donor and the youth Luciani showed up at the seminary in Belluno. There was no easy way out here for those who found themselves in violation of Moses' laws. No bell tower. One had to resort to a bottle of pills, a straight razor or a combination of a rope and a chair.

Unlike the villages of Canale d'Agordo and Feltre which had an occasional spot of color, Belluno was a sprawling city of sameness. Every house, every building, even the seminary, was of the same shade of beige stucco topped off with orange tiled roofs.

The seminary here was as large as the one at Feltre had been small. There were as many teachers here in Belluno as there had been students at Feltre where he had groomed his mane.

He was determined not to repeat the record he had at Feltre which had brought him poor grades. This time he would give them what they wanted. He took the early lead and the others would never catch up. Although deeply immersed in his studies, he could not ignore what was going on in the outside world around him.

The Axis Powers

One might ask why Italy was Germany's ally in the war.

In Hitler's case, one must consider why he went after the Jews, atheists, homosexuals and other outcasts of Christianity.

These outsiders had for the most part evaded enlistment in the German army in World War I—they would have been fighting against an enemy which had far less discriminatory policies than the country they would be fighting to defend.[2]

What's more, a number of them had been caught operating as undercover agents for Russia within Germany during the war. After all, if Christian Germany were to win the war, they were destined to live out their lives in perpetual oppression.

Hitler intended to wage his war against the Slavs—Russia and its eastern allies—countries which had a tolerance of Jews, atheists, homosexuals and other outcasts of Christianity.

Hitler knew if he were to win the war, he must first remove these 'dissidents' from his own ranks to prevent the undercover tactics which—in his mind—had cost his Fatherland the First World War.

In Italy's case, uppermost was the black-white issue.

As devout Catholics, the Italians believed in the superiority of the white race. It was for this reason blacks were not allowed in Italy or for that matter other predominated Catholic countries of Europe— the reason why few of them died in concentration camps.[3]

In 1935, Italy invaded Ethiopia, a country of fifty million blacks. Realizing soldiers stationed in Ethiopia might integrate themselves with the natives Mussolini imposed heavy penalties for interracial copulation. The minimum penalty for an Italian was five years and that for an Ethiopian could range up to death.

In any event, the pregnancy was aborted and offspring usually disappeared. Although it was mostly kept under the table, Italy's occupation of Ethiopia likely surpassed the Holocaust in infanticide.[4]

Although the United States was no angel itself concerning the treatment of blacks, the atrocities were so great in Ethiopia that it joined together with its allies and placed sanctions on Italy. These sanctions which remained in place at the start of the war together with its fascist convictions made Italy the great ally of Germany.

Yet, there was a more basic reason Italy was Germany's ally.

The Tri-Axis Powers

When the war began, by a whisker over Italy, Germany was the most Christian nation in the world split evenly between Catholics and Protestants. Ninety-nine percent of its population was Christian and the others—Jews and atheists—were destined for the camps.

The entire Italian army was Catholic—the mind of every single soldier was controlled by the sitting Pontiff—each one of them would do whatever Pius told them to do.

Unlike the allied armies which spanned many religions, the Axis army was entirely Christian. There was not a Jew, a black, a Muslim

64

or for that matter an atheist in the German and Italian armies. What's more—true of all Christians of that time—these soldiers were devout Christians who thought it a mortal sin not to attend services on Sunday and fell on their knees and prayed to Christ each night.

The Nazi uniform had a small zippered pocket. In the standard issue, if the recruit was Catholic, it contained a pair of rosary beads. If he was Protestant, it contained a small book containing passages from the Bible including the 23rd Psalm *"...Though I shall walk through the shadow of death...the Lord is my Shepherd..."* The reason battlefield photographs of fallen German soldiers usually show either rosary beads or a prayer book in the hands.

Nazi battlefield graves

The Axis powers had the largest chaplain corps of any army in history. The Holy Sacrifice of the Mass and other services were available each day. If a soldier was caught not attending services, he ran the risk of being tabbed an atheist and sent to a camp.

The British hymn *'Onward Christian Soldiers'* could be heard in German and Italian for miles in and about battlefields.

Motion pictures and books portraying German troops shooting up churches in Poland and other occupied countries could not be further from the truth. This may have been somewhat true of the Russians, but not of the Germans—Vatican propaganda designed to separate modern day *Catholicism* from what it was then and continues to be today—*fascism.*

Hitler's Guard at Mass
Lodz Poland
Sept 23, 1941

Brown Guard
Brussels Belgium
June 6, 1940

Hitler leaving Mass
Berliner Dom
March 16, 1943

Nevertheless, it was this more than anything else which made the Vatican the great ally of the Axis powers. They shared a common ideology—*fascism*—*some kinds of people are better than others.* This gave them a common enemy—*communism*—*all children are created equal and are entitled to share equally in earth's province.*

The embers of war

Fascism had been implanted in Italy and Germany years earlier. When one plans to take over the world in the future, one starts with the young who will carry out the plan in the future.

The Italian Scouts [5]

Early in the twentieth century, the Vatican used the *Catholic Scouts of Italy* to indoctrinate Italy's youth into *fascism.* In 1925, Pius XI and Mussolini began graduating children from the *Catholic Scouts*—a social group—to the *Fascist Scouts*—a military troop.

In December 1926, Pius issued an order to elementary schools in Italy requiring enrollment of all children in the *Fascist Youth Organization;* as already discussed, this action prompted thirteen year old Albino Luciani to make his debut onto the public stage.

That Mussolini and Pius were grooming these children for war was apparent in that they dispensed with the angelic dress of the *Catholic Scouts* in favor of military uniforms for the newly formed *Fascist Scouts* and trained them in military tactics. As early as the age of eight, young boys were trained in the use of firearms and, more importantly, they were brainwashed in an enormous Vatican propaganda program to hate children growing up in Slavic countries.

The Nazi Scouts [5]

By 1933, the process had been completed and Italy's youth had been indoctrinated into its *Fascist Youth Organization.* Yet, less than fifty thousand had been enrolled in its counterpart in Germany—the *Hitler Youth.* [6] As had been true of Italy, established scout troops in Germany operated mainly in Catholic dioceses.

As Mussolini had before him, Hitler appealed to Pius. Overnight Germany's youth had been enrolled in the *Hitler Youth*.

By 1938, the scouts of the Axis powers were ready for war.

Fascism **The Vatican**

In February 1929, Pius and Mussolini entered into the *Lateran Treaty* formally uniting the Roman Catholic Church with the fascist movement in Italy. There began a campaign to preach fascism—some kind of people are better than others—openly from the pulpit. An election referendum was held which invited the populace to vote its support of the new fascist government.

Pius XI issued a letter to Catholics in Italy who comprised 99.9% of its population. It was read from every pulpit throughout the country and published in every newspaper telling them to vote 'Yes.' The voters went to the polling stations on March 24, 1929. The vote was 8,519,539 'Yes' and 155,761 'No.' Mussolini became the recognized dictator of Italy.[7]

This demonstrates the immense power the Pope had upon the Italian people at the time. Although Mussolini would never waiver from the mission his people had given him, the Italians would string him up in Milan just fifteen years later.

Nazism **The Vatican**

On January 30, 1933, Hitler became Chancellor of Germany and established his *New World Order: "The Federal Government must preserve and defend those Christian principles upon which our nation has been built and which define our morality and values"*[8]

He drafted the Enabling Act intended to make himself dictator of Germany. On March 12, 1933, he shaped the *Coalition of the National Socialist (NAZI) Party and the Nationalist People's Party.*[9]

The coalition's first action was to open the first concentration camp—a converted factory just south of Berlin at Oranienburg. Members of the Communist Party and Social Democratic Party, who otherwise would have voted against him, were its first inmates.[10]

Yet, the measure required a two-thirds majority of the Federal Assembly and his new Nazi coalition controlled only 340 of its 647 seats. The balance of the votes lay in the Catholic Centre Party. Ludwig Kaas, a priest and pawn of the Vatican, headed the Centre Party. As Mussolini had before him, Hitler appealed to the Pope.[11]

On March 23, 1933, Kaas gave the order and the Catholic Centre Party cast the decisive block of votes passing the Enabling Act.

In an act of ironic symbolism, Kaas, himself, cast the specific vote which made Hitler dictator of Germany.[12] Kaas' vote changed Germany from a democracy to an autocracy. The Vatican was the first foreign state to recognize the new government.[13]

A few months later on July 20, 1933, Pius XI and Hitler entered into the *German Concordat*—the union of the Vatican with the Nazi Party of Germany. This together with the *Italian Concordat* of 1929 completed the fusion of the Tri-Axis Powers—Germany, Italy and the Vatican. The table had been set for World War II.[14]

Yet, there was an enormous difference between the *Italian Concordat—the Lateran Treaty*—and the *German Concordat.*

In the *Italian Concordat,* the Vatican had, among other things, gained its sovereignty and title to the lands which make up the Vatican State today in exchange for its allegiance to Mussolini.

In the case of the *German Concordat,* the situation was much different. Pius formalized his allegiance with Hitler solely because he shared the dictator's philosophies as set forth in *Mein Kampf— some kinds of people are better than others*—which remains the central canon of the Roman Catholic Church today.

As a part of the strategy, Pius and Kaas dissolved the Catholic Centre Party as to leave no organized challenge to the Nazi Party's march to war—its votes merging into the Nazi Party.

On August 24, 1933, Hitler held a huge rally in Neukolln Stadium in Berlin to celebrate the *German Concordat.* Secretary of State Eugenio Pacelli (Pius XII) and Papal Nuncio Orsenigo joined him on the podium. Over three hundred priests and bishops lined the wall of the stadium.[15]

One is on solid ground when one says the success of the fascist movement in Europe rested entirely upon papal decisions. Neither the Italian nor German referendums would have passed without sanction of the Pope. Mussolini would have never become dictator of Italy and Hitler would have never become dictator of Germany.

It was clearly the Pontiff who was the puppeteer who held the strings which controlled the marionettes which would eventually act and dance their way into World War II and cost fifty million lives.

The concentration camps

The day before he became dictator, Hitler opened the camp at Dachau—a model for the vast network of death camps which would eventually follow. Because he was tied up with the Enabling Act, Hitler did not attend opening ceremonies. Vice Chancellor, Franz von Papen and the German Papal Nuncio Cesare Orsenigo did the  honors.[16] As they entered the gates of the prison, they were saluted by a group of bishops and Nazi officers gathered there.

The early inmates included social revolutionary activists, union and party leaders, Jews, gypsies and gay youths who had been rounded up in gay bars and social establishments. Initially, Hitler went after those who opposed the Enabling Act and others who were suspected of having spied for the Russians in the First World War.

Inmates were branded with serial numbers and forced to wear patches which identified them by color: red for political dissidents - violet for anti-Christians - black for social revolutionary activists - pink for homosexuals - yellow for Jews - brown for gypsies. Gypsies were nomadic Slavs who had wandered into Germany.

During the nineteen-thirties, upwards of a quarter-million were incarcerated in these camps. All but a handful would be dead when the first volleys of World War II were fired.

Cesare Orsenigo and Pius XII

Orsenigo would eventually become the fall guy for the Vatican. After the war, he was blamed for failing to convey to Pius XII what was going on in the death camps during the war. Some claim he went so far as to block this information flowing from others to the Vatican. His ideology, *"The Jew will not fight in behalf of the Fatherland because he is selfish to his own end. He will incite and help others undermine our struggle to bring about a worldwide Christian society."*[17]

Orsenigo - Hitler - Ribbentrop

It is inconceivable Pius was unaware of the Holocaust. Orsenigo had for years been one of his closest friends and confidants. In 1930, when Pius—at the time Eugenio Pacelli—vacated the Papal Nuncio position in Germany, he appointed Orsenigo to fill the post.

To see things clearly as they happened, as we have so often, one has to put events in the chronological order in which they occurred.

On September 1, 1939 Germany invaded Poland.

In late September Warsaw and Krakow fell to the Germans.

On October 6th the German occupation of Poland was completed.

On October 14th the ground breaking of the Auschwitz death camp took place outside Krakow. It would eventually evolve into a network of 48 camps operating within Poland which together with Treblinka at Warsaw would murder over three million.

On November 1, 1939, Filippo Cortesi, Papal Nuncio to Poland, was removed by Pius.[18] With Hitler's concurrence, Pius appointed their mutual friend and confidant Cesare Orsenigo the duty of Pro-Nuncio to Poland in addition to his main job as Nuncio to Germany.

Being a trusted friend, Orsenigo was permitted by Hitler to travel freely to Poland including his widely publicized trips to Auschwitz at Krakow and Treblinka at Warsaw.[19]

Orsenigo served as the clandestine contact between what was going on in the death camps and Pius XII. His close friendship with Hitler is documented by hundreds of surviving photos of himself with the Fuhrer. So much so, if Hitler was not so recognizable, one would think him Orsenigo's bodyguard.

Orsenigo - Hitler

The Boxer Rebellion

The young seminarian at Belluno watched and waited.

He knew it had been this same view of Christianity that had inspired the Boxer Rebellion in China at the turn of the twentieth century which had driven the Christians out of China. He was about to see it happen all over again in World War II and he would live to see it happen, once more, in the Vietnam War.

The Chinese had never known racial strife despite that four of the major race groups were native to Asia.[20] Ethnic and racial strife had been limited to Christian and Muslim countries in the west which cultures were driven by the God of the Old Testament, the overwhelming number of wars in the west were ethnic cleansing.

They didn't want this influence in the east. Although China had a long history of wars of aggression it had never thought there to be differences among races and this extended to all people who lived their lives differently including creeds, atheists, ethnic groups and even homosexuals.[20]

Until Christian preachers started to preach bigotry and hatred of people who appear to be different or live their lives differently, the Chinese never knew what the word bigotry meant as all people were considered to be children of the same God—the fundamental thesis of Tao. *"Love thy neighbor as thyself"* is not original to Christ in the Gospels—it had been the way of life in China for a half-century before Christ's time. As one knows, it has never become the way of life in much of the western world which claims Christ as its God.

The Chinese, mostly Caucasoids themselves[20], knew the United States, a Christian nation, held other than Caucasoids as subordinate peoples. Black, yellow and red races and other ethnic groups were made to live as inferior peoples. They were not permitted in white neighborhoods or provided higher education and were confined to live under unbearable conditions in impoverished ghettos.

Blacks were imprisoned if caught using 'white' toilets or riding in the fronts of buses or sitting in the ground-floor pews of churches. Blacks, homosexuals, Asians and other persons of ethnic origin were often taunted, tortured and sometimes killed in hate crimes.

Perhaps, most heartless of all, in America, out-of-wedlock children were shunned by society. The Boxers knew it was the white Christian preacher who was behind this kind of hatred.

Luciani would live to see the Boxers eventually progress into the Vietnam War. After the Boxers threw the Christians out of China, the Vatican continued to hold a presence in French Indo-China which included Laos, Cambodia and Vietnam—countries which bordered China to the south. Other than this, Catholicism had been restricted to the Philippines and other island nations in the east.

In 1954, the French pulled out of Vietnam and the Vatican lost its foothold in mainland Asia which blocked its long range strategy to annihilate atheism and convert China to its fold.

This prompted Cardinal Spellman of New York to mastermind the strategy of the Vietnam War. He arranged a 3-day audience for U.S. Secretary of State John Foster Dulles and his son Avery Dulles with Pius XII. Avery was a Jesuit priest in Spellman's diocese.[21]

Despite the French half-century presence, Vietnam remained overwhelmingly Buddhist—atheist. Unlike one might believe, it was in the hallowed halls of the Vatican and not in the hallowed halls of Washington DC, the Vietnam War began.

The strategy was to force conversion of Vietnam, Cambodia and Laos through civil war. Once Catholicism regained a foothold in mainland Asia, it would spread northward into China, annihilating atheism—Buddhism—in its wake.

Avery Dulles was eventually made a cardinal, the only American not a bishop ever given the *red hat*. His single achievement that reached notoriety was that he influenced his father to involve America in Vietnam—which cost upwards of eight million lives.

An important part of the Pius/Dulles/Spellman strategy was to place into power Ngo Dinh Diem—a devout Catholic and a long time friend of Spellman. Diem, together with his brothers—one the archbishop and the other the chief of police,—rose to power on October 26, 1955 less than a week after the meeting.

Shortly afterwards, Dulles announced American intervention in Vietnam. The Diems ruled Vietnam with an iron fist, closing temples and ostracizing Buddhist priests, some burning themselves to death in protest of American backed religious persecution.

The Kennedy Assassination

One of the theories surrounding the assassination of President John Kennedy grew out of his intention to pull out of Vietnam—a conspiracy of *right wing* elements in the Vatican and factions in the CIA to continue the war.[21]

Kennedy found that though South Vietnam was overwhelmingly Buddhist, there was not a Buddhist in the South Vietnam army which was entirely Catholic. This told him the war was not between South Vietnam and North Vietnam, but between the South Vietnam Catholic army and the entirely Buddhist army of North Vietnam.

When he realized America was fighting a religious war intended to annihilate atheism, Kennedy announced a plan to pull troops out of Vietnam just three weeks before his assassination—devastating to the Vatican's plan. The CIA-Vatican intrigue went to work.

There has been no war more fundamentally based on religion than the Vietnam War which pitted organized religion, the Vatican, against organized atheism, Buddhism. So much so, the war gave birth to the misconception communism is synonymous with atheism.

Spellman took on such an active role in organizing the Vietnam War it is often rightly remembered today as *'Spelly's War.'*

Years earlier, in the Korean War, *Radio Hanoi* had capitalized on America's discriminatory policies driven by Christian preachers. So much so, black soldiers were reassigned to non-combat duty away from Korea—the reason few of them died in Korea. It didn't take long for the American Negro to realize he was fighting for a country that considered him a subordinate human being and against the Chinese who had very little discrimination policies at all.

The American Civil War

Back in Belluno, widely read in world history, Luciani knew the American Civil War also had its roots in what Moses had to say. His books told him that Martin Luther's reformation of the 16th century had moved the Protestants in America toward the *left* away from Moses and in 1626 Roger Williams brought the Baptist Church to Rhode Island which doctrine was intended to move them back to literal belief in what Moses had to say.

In 1841, the Baptist Church split into the southern church and the northern church, the former believing in the 10th Commandment as had been handed down from God to Moses on Mount Sinai which protected the right of one man to enslave another, *"Thou shalt not covet (desire or take from) thy neighbor...his slaves"* and the latter no longer accepting slavery as the word of God. This division in the Baptist Church set the stage for the Civil War.[22]

Luciani saw this happening all over again as he witnessed the glowing embers—the fascist scouts, the concentration camps, the prejudices and, perhaps, most dangerous of all, the fusion of the Tri-Axis Powers which was about to launch World War II.

During this trying period, though often tempted to do so, he never approached the press. He knew to do so would demolish his ability to carry out the commission his father had given him—to change the Church back to what Christ had intended.

"...faith and the conviction with which we speak."

Luciani spoke at length of humility at his graduation ceremony. He reminded his classmates to never forget they are mere men.

"The preacher is unique among entrepreneurs.

All businessmen know immensely more about their products and services than do their customers—the reason they are able to sell their wares.

Yet, we as preachers know no more about the existence of a God, or for that matter which God is the true God, than do our customers.

As a matter-of-fact, we will know nothing about the afterlife until after we are dead. Then, perhaps, we may never know.

All we have is our faith and the conviction with which we speak. We came here with one of these. The good fathers gave us the other.

Let us take them with us. Let us feed them - nourish them - train them - cherish them - protect them. For these are the horses of the carriage that will one day take us to our destiny.

Let us never use them—our faith and the conviction with which we speak—to spread hatred of any of God's children no matter how different they may appear to be or how they live their lives.

Rather, let us use them to help bring about a day when all men and women—no matter how scorned by doctrine—will be accepted with equal human dignity under the laws of nations..."[23]

74

On July 7, 1935, in a city of beige stucco topped off with orange terra cotta roofs, Don Albino Luciani was ordained a priest.

He had learned to heed his father's words, *"Play the game carefully...Never risk your king to save a pawn."*

1 Albino Luciani's papa's last words to him as he started his long journey to Rome

2 Over 2 million Christian crosses mark the World War I dead in military cemeteries in Germany. The *Star of David* marks less than a hundred of them. See photos of these on the Internet.

3 *'The Red Faced Captain'* in the author's book *'Let's All Get Behind the Pope'* tells the story of General Patton defying Pius XII by marching his black battalion into Italy

4 Search any Italian history book – *Occupation of Ethiopia.*

5 Search any Italian history book – *Fascist Scout Organization*

6 Search any German history book – *Hitler Scouts*

7 *La Repubblica* 25 Mar 29 Although Mussolini had assumed some dictatorial powers before this time, he had not been previously been recognized by the people as dictator

8 *Berliner Zeitung* 3 Feb 33

9 *Berliner Zeitung* 13 Mar33 *'Nazi Party Coalition'*

10 *Berliner Zeitung* 15 Apr 33 *'Oranienburg'*

11 *L Osservatore Romano* 19 Mar 33

12 *Washington Post* 24 Mar 33 *'Enabling Act, Berlin'*

13 *L Osservatore Romano* 29 Mar 33

14 *Berliner Zeitung* 22 Jul 33 *L Osservatore Romano* 22 Jul 33

15 *Berliner Morgenpost* 25 Aug 33

16 *Berliner Zeitung* 24 Mar 33

17 *Berliner Morgenpost* 10 Sep 39. *Phayer* 2000. Search *Wikipedia:* Cesare Orsenigo

18 *L Osservatore Romano* 2 Nov 39 *Berliner Morgenpost* 9 Nov 39

19 *L Osservatore Romano* 1 May 40 *Zycie Warszawy* 15 Jul 42

20 DNA classifies the mass of the Chinese population as Caucasoid. Mongoloids are found in northern Asia and Aborigine in the island nations of Asia and Negroids occupied southern China as early as 1000BC. Later in the twentieth century as parts of China became westernized—Christianized—racial problems surfaced in some provinces.

21 America's involvement in the Vietnam War is recounted in the author's book of short stories *'Let's All Get Behind the Pope':* See stories: *'Why Am I Killing These People?'* - *'The Fog of War'* which outline the Vatican plot involving the CIA in the Vietnam War and the murder of John Kennedy

22 *History of the Baptist Church in the United States Wikipedia* or any library

23 *Il Corriere delle Alpi* 12 Jun 35

Photo Battlefield graves - German propaganda photo

Photo German soldiers at mass - German propaganda photo

Photo Hitler leaving Mass - *Berliner Kurier*

Photo Neukolln Stadium - source unknown

Photo Bishops at Dachau- German propaganda photo

Photo Orsenigo-Hitler-Ribbentrop - German propaganda photo

Photo Orsenigo-Hitler - German propaganda photo

Chapter 7

The Politics of Albino Luciani

"It is the inalienable right of no man to accumulate wealth beyond his needs while other men starve to death because they have nothing."[1]

Albino Luciani

There is great controversy concerning Luciani's political agenda; both those on the *right* and those on the *left* claim him as their own.

In that the Vatican destroyed much of the controversial record of Albino Luciani, one can say most anything.

In the first edition of *Murder in the Vatican*, I wrote, '*In the mid-eighties, I visited Vittorio Veneto and was lucky enough to pick up a collection of drafts of his sermons for a couple hundred bucks ...*'[2]

Drafted on what I recognized as diocese stationary and thinking them real I incorporated some of what they had to say in that edition.

An astute reader—a renowned paleographer—exposed them a fraud. Forensic testing resolved them, indeed, a fraud. So well executed, they had likely been planted by Vatican censors in their efforts to annihilate the true record of Luciani after his death.

If you take the time to visit the Veneto country, as I have many times, you, too, can pick up 'original' drafts of his work. Yet, unlike those I acquired, which came from the top, they are likely to be creations of locals who capitalize on the rarity of the find.

The tab for a small note might be 10 Euros, a complete sermon as much as 200-300 Euros—phony diocese letterheads carefully bathe in tea to give them a tinge of age and typed on vintage typewriters— easy bait for the everyday sucker. Just recently, I paid 25 Euros for a postcard sent to Luciani from his sister. It, too, did not pass the test.

The market for these 'fakes' exploded in 1984 when Yallop's *In God's Name* established the rarity of the find. Although not as proliferated as they were in the eighties, you can find 'original' drafts of his work today. With very rare exception, authentic Luciani documents are confined to the archives of the Apostolic Library.

Regardless, among the unbiased referees are his books. Yet, even here one must dig up the original editions published before his death as the Vatican went to work on 'original editions' published after his death. If you are lucky enough to find one of the uncensored copies of Luciani's *Illustrissimi*, interspersed between the lines of its rather heavy theology can be found the ideology of his political agenda.

"Dear Pinocchio,

I was seven years old when I first read your adventures. I can't tell you how much I liked them. In you, I recognized myself as a boy, and in your surroundings I saw my own...

My dear Pinocchio, there are two famous remarks about the young. I commend the first by Lacordaire, to your attention: 'Have an opinion and assert it!' This is one of reason. It is the lion. It will win for you.

The second is by Clemenceau, and I do not recommend it to you at all, 'He has no ideas of his own, but he defends them with ardor!' This is one of belief. It is the sheep. It will lose for you...

Think of this, as you go through life, as you run through the woods with the Cat and the Fox and the Poodle Medoro,

Your magical friend, Albino "[3]

Luciani contrasts *Lacordaire,* the progressive democrat on the *left,* and *Clemenceau,* the conservative republican on the *right.* One need not go further than his letter to his dear friend Pinocchio, one of his most famous, to determine on which side of the aisle he stood.

Again, in his *Illustrissimi,* he points to the socialist and away from the self-serving republican in his expedition beyond the wall,

"Dear Casella,

I have had the good fortune to have visited those places which, as we all know, lie beyond the wall.

For each of us, I have found that we will live beyond the wall as we have chosen to live on this side of the wall.

First, I was granted the privilege of seeing Hell. As I peered in through the gates, I saw an immense room with many long tables.

On these were so many bowls of cooked rice and gourmet delicacies as one could imagine, properly spiced, aromatic, inviting.

The diners were all seated there, filled with hunger, two at each bowl, one facing the other. Then what?

To carry the food to their mouths they had, in oriental fashion, chopsticks affixed to their hands, but so long that no matter how great their efforts, not a single grain of delicacy could reach their mouths. Although starving, they could not take of these things.

Then, I was able to peer into Heaven.

Here again, I saw a great room with the same tables, same gourmet delicacies, same long chopsticks affixed to their hands. But here the people were happy, smiling and quite satisfied. Why?

Each, having picked up the food with the chopsticks, raised it to the mouth of the companion that sat opposite, and all was right.

So my dear Casella, we must learn here, as we make our way toward the great wall, how to use the chopsticks, else we will not know how to use them when we are on the other side of the wall.

Your magical friend, Albino"[3]

If one cannot accept his written word, there is the surviving video clip, *"Look, Daniel, the Lord has put in us a strong desire to progress, to go forward..."* John Paul explicitly declares himself a progressive in a televised audience on September 27, 1978.[4]

The most reliable evidence that has survived—his own writings and papal video clips which have survived the Vatican cutting-room floor—place him clearly on the *left*. Yet, he did at times lick at both sides *"If you confront opinion you do not agree with, trim it patiently to reveal the good that is in all things."*[5]

Even the press, which I rely on for much of what I have to say, spoke from both the *right* and the *left*.

In the spring of 1974, when questioned as to the psychological community's declaration homosexuality is a God-given birthright, a *right wing* paper reported, *"Sex, natural of a man, is a part of love for one of the opposite sex,"* while an allied paper reported, *"It would seem sex, natural of a man, is a part of love for a person of the opposite sex...Yet, God makes mistakes."*

A *left wing* paper reported *"It would seem sex, natural of a man, is a part of love for a person of the opposite sex...Yet, God makes exceptions and society must accommodate God's exceptions..."*[6]

Which is taken out of context?

On the first anniversary of the ruling he clarified his position. He spoke of the road ahead to unravel the stigma which has wrongly been associated with it, *"As long as one can be accused of being a homosexual, we have not put this one behind us."*[7]

Yet, perhaps, only the impartial referee can break a tie.

Again, from his *Illustrissimi,*

> *"Dear Figaro,*
>
> *Well then, who and what are you my dear Figaro?*
> *A variety of dress? A mixture of feminine and masculine?*
> *Of Orient and Occident?*
> *Poor Figaro, against all these nobles with their coats of arms,*
> *these bewigged bourgeois, who themselves do every trespass.*
> *They are no better, perhaps, worse than you.*
> *Barber, marriage broker, adviser of pseudo diplomats, yes, ladies*
> *and gentlemen, whatever you like.*
> *They demand that you alone be honest in this world of cheats and*
> *rogues.*
> *Do not accept what they say, dear Figaro. You, too, are a citizen.*
> *Sadly, perhaps, your only solution is in revolution!*
>
> *Your magical friend, Albino"* [3]

Luciani refers to scant evidence condemning homosexuality and transsexuality. No mention of these in the commandments and only a single explicit condemnation and less than a half dozen ambiguous mentions of them elsewhere in the Bible, as compared to more than eighty explicit condemnations of heterosexual sexual activities, most calling for the death penalty and permanent exclusion from heaven.

For those who are lucky enough to stumble across a 1949 edition of *Catechism in Crumbs,* one will find the formation of his doctrinal position—as long as doctrine did not treat people unfairly he conformed to it, yet, whenever doctrine placed undue hardship on the lives of innocent people, he stepped in.

The day he became a cardinal, Luciani paid homage to Lincoln for having had the great courage to have defied the written word of his God, *"Thou shalt not covet* (desire to take from) *thy neighbor his property, including his house, his wife, his slaves, his ox, his ass."*

He told the youth group which had gathered to listen, *"Never be afraid to stand up for what is right, whether your adversary be your parent, your teacher, your peer, your politician, your preacher, your constitution, or even your God!"*[8]

His letters to *Carlo Goldoni* in his book *Humbly Yours* prove him an ardent feminist. For those who can't accept his written word, we have his papacy, *"God is our Father, more so, our Mother."*[9]

Common ground

When it comes to his primary ambition in life, all agree—*to rid the world of poverty*. So much so, he was universally recognized by both those on the *right* and those on the *left* as a monumental Marxist—an enemy of the capitalistic world we live in.

One day in Venice, he was bombarded by activists on a range of issues from contraception, women ordination and homosexuality to remarriage and so forth; issues of the emerging social revolution he had, from time to time, championed. He stopped them,

"As long as there is a single child anywhere on earth who is starving to death because he or she does not have enough to eat, there exists no other problem in the world."[10]

How can one possibly wiggle one's way around it?

The film-clip of September 27, 1978, *"It is the inalienable right of no man to accumulate wealth beyond his needs while other men starve to death because they have nothing."*[1]

Doesn't sound like much of a republican to me?

1 *Associated Press* See film clip: www.johnpaul1.org
2 *Murder in the Vatican* 2003
3 Reprinted from Luciani's book *Illustrissimi* 1976.
4 this video can be viewed on you-tube. September 27 1978 audience
5 *Treviso Notizie* 1 Aug 68. (¹)
6 *Il Gazzettino* 12 Feb 74 (²) - *Messaggero Mestre* 14 Feb 74 - *Nostro Privilegio* 17 Feb 74
7 *Messaggero Mestre* 17 Dec 74
8 *La Nuova Venezia* 6 Mar 73
9 *La Repubblica* 8 Sep 78. *Right* and *left* media reported variations
10 *Messaggero Mestre* 19 Dec 75 pointed and read the

(¹) Author's note: For brevity, Luciani's actual words in this book have often been shortened but in no case do they take out of context what he said. His actual words in this case: *"If you come across error, rather than uprooting it or knocking it down, see if you can trim it patiently, allowing the light to shine upon the nucleus of goodness and truth that usually is not missing even in erroneous opinions."*
(²) at the time, the Vatican had a controlling interest in *Il Gazzettino*

Chapter 8

His Ministry

"The desire to parent children is a basic human need... Until we can guarantee basic human rights to the tiniest minority we cannot truthfully call ourselves a democracy."[1]

Albino Luciani

Albino Luciani's first post was in the small village in which he had grown up. He had been on the job for less than a week when he was summoned to the rector's office for his first commission.

"My sister is gravely ill. She will not make it another month.

"That is not the bad news, for we must all meet our maker. The bad news is she will not see Him for long. She remarried outside the Church and has been living in a state of mortal sin."

The old man reached across the desk grasping the young priest's hand with a frightened look as if he were hanging from the edge of a cliff, "You must rescue her from Satan. It is your sacred duty to convince her to renounce her husband or she will surely be buried in unholy ground and burn in the everlasting fires of hell."

When he arrived at the hospital he was given yet another task. The woman's doctor met him outside her room and told him she had only few hours to live and asked if he would tell her this.

Rosary beads ran like a miniature freight train through her fingers to rumbling repetitions. Though dealing with a woman who had remarried, he was, nevertheless, dealing with a devout one.

Taking up her hand he told her the bad news—she was about to die. He followed it up with the real bad news, "Unless you renounce your husband, you will surely go to hell."

To his astonishment she answered with a question, "What do you think I should do?"

The young priest struggled between his duty and his heart. He answered her question with another question, "Do you love him?"

A tear ran down her cheek, "With all my heart."

Her hand still in his, Albino fell silent wondering what he should do. During his seminary days he had excelled at soccer, so much so, his team had never lost a game. Yet, now the clock was running out and he was about to lose this one.

His eye caught the tiny crucifix hanging from the beads. He had his answer, *"I wonder what Jesus would do in this case?"*

Holding a tear in the corner of his eye, he cuffed her hand tightly, "Then cling to it, your love for your husband. Don't ever give it up. Not for me, not for your brother, not even for the Pope.

"Your love for your husband was not given to you by men. It was given to you by God. He would not be happy if you were to give it back to Him to satisfy the whims of common men.

"I promise you, if you have the courage to do this for me, there will be reserved for both you and your husband a place in heaven. Believe me, if it takes me all the remaining days of my life, I will make this possible for you."

He reached for a photo of her husband on the bedside table. Unwinding the beads from her fingers, he placed it in her hands. She died a few hours later, still clutching the picture in her hands.[2]

Thus began the ministry of John Paul I.

Checkmate!

Of the persecutions imposed by the Church on innocent people, it was its position on remarriage that tormented him the most. He could not accept the Church could take it upon itself to refuse sanctification of the union of two people who, having had made a mistake in choosing a mate at age twenty, at thirty had fallen truly in love. It troubled him deeply the Church condemned millions of people to have lived out their lives in loneliness and despair who otherwise would have lived out their lives in loving relationships.

In 1950, he wrote a letter to Rome recommending Hitler and Mussolini be excommunicated posthumously.[3]

Ignored, he followed it up with a another letter demanding the authority to grant annulments be moved to the local bishop level, *"I am greatly tormented Mother Church would see it as her duty to close the Gates of Heaven to so many young innocent people who have at last found true love and yet see it as its duty to leave the Gates of Heaven open to the likes of monsters."*[4] A leading Italian tabloid capitalized on his fondness for chess. Its headline read 'SCACCO MATTO' 'CHECKMATE!'[5]

Pius moved for excommunication but his undersecretary of state, Montini, stopped him warning it would cause an uproar in the press.

Montini recalled the young priest from Belluno. During the war, Luciani had approached him to use his influence to gain asylum in the Vatican for five hundred Jews who had shown up on a boat in Naples. Montini struggled with Pius for a compassionate decision. Instead, the Pope ordered the boat to Germany to death camps.[6]

These encounters marked a turning point in Luciani's life as they won him the favor of Giovanni Montini who eventually rose to the papacy—Paul VI, which would eventually lead to his own papacy.

"...sex is good and beautiful..."

Luciani was convinced removing the stigma associated with out-of-wedlock pregnancies would eliminate what was, at the time, the leading cause of abortions—family embarrassment.

He recalled his childhood in his memoirs, *"I could hear my mamma and aunt and sister talking in low tones and every time I entered the room there was a hush-hush. Then one day my sister took a short holiday. I was told she had gone to a neighboring village to rest for awhile, but they didn't fool me at all, for I knew exactly what was going on. As I fell on my knees that night I vowed I would someday bring an end to it all. Believe me, I will."*[7]

A pioneer of the sexual revolution, he was the first in either the public or private forum to introduce sexual education into schools. He wanted to bring about a day when sex would be discussed openly between parents and children. Until his time, sex, being sinful, was not to be talked about in either the family or public.

He looked forward to a time when *"sex would be seen as good and beautiful, but there is a time and place for everything, rather than in one in which sex was condemned as being shameful and sinful."*[7] He knew the Church's position sex was sinful caused many children to grow up in a state of trauma, resulting in guilt complexes which led to less than healthy sex lives and, at times, even suicide.

"My part in this thing is to bring about a day when the young girl would no longer think she has gotten herself into trouble, as the preacher might lead her to believe, but rather she would realize that she had, indeed, gotten herself into paradise."[7]

Today few abortions are owed to embarrassment. It is much to the credit of Albino Luciani millions of children, who might have otherwise been aborted; now see the light of day.

Champion of orphans

Referring to Italy's enormous homeless orphan population, one Sunday morning, he looked up at the immense dome of the Basilica di San Marco. He told his congregation, *"We must learn to lower our ceiling height to make room for all of Christ's children."*[8]

In his twenty years as a bishop and as a cardinal, Luciani never built a single church, yet, he built forty-four orphanages, many of them equipped with schools and clinics.

A monk, one of an army of monks and nuns who had spent most of their lives in prayer, once spoke of him, *"He pulled us up off our knees and put us to work, we monks building and maintaining orphanages and serving as youth counselors, and the nuns teaching class and others caring for those children too ill to come to class."*[9]

Whenever faced with the question as to whether to use money raised from the faithful for a church or an orphanage, he would ask himself, *"Now, what would Jesus do in this case?"*

Strange parents

Faced by an orphan population of two million in Italy, it was his lobbying in Italian Parliament that made it legal for single persons to adopt children in Italy. An opposition member challenged *"But, that would make it legal for homosexuals to adopt children."*

Luciani responded, *"The desire to parent children is a basic human need...Until we can guarantee basic human rights to the tiniest minority we cannot truthfully call ourselves a democracy."*[10]

His adversary didn't give up, *"But homosexuals have a record of splitting up after the 'honeymoon' is over. This would cause children to lose one or both of their parents."*

Luciani closed the gap on his attacker, *"There are two major forces involved in making for long term loving relationships and regardless of what Rome might believe sex is not one of them.*

"As a matter-of-fact, sex is often a declining force in many relationships. It has little to do with the long term survival of a union. The longevity of a relationship of those who parent children that is so instrumental to protecting the stability of children until they reach adulthood depends not on sex, but rather on those forces that create long term relationships, love and companionship.

"In companionship, the homosexual has the edge. Two people of

the same sex who fall in love make much better companions of each other because they are more likely to share common interests. Children parented by homosexual couples are less likely to undergo the ordeal of arguments and the trauma of divorce..."

His attacker didn't give up. *"But, homosexuals are pedophiles."*

The bishop cut him off, *"Homosexuality is a God-given instinct and pedophilia is a Satan-driven perversion. Yet, since pedophilia often involves incest, one must address the question.*

"If our objective is to prevent pedophilia in adoption then the only logical action is to permit only homosexuals to adopt children who are of the opposite sex. This would reduce incest in adoptions to zero as the sex of the victim is determined by the sexual orientation of the predator. If we permit heterosexual couples to adopt children, children of both sexes would be at risk. Regardless, on average, homosexual adoptions reduce the risk in half."[10]

The measure passed. Overnight, a million orphans were provided loving and economic support by single parents. Some were gay couples which one of the parents adopted the child, as it remained illegal for parents of the same sex to adopt the same child.

Little is known of Luciani's involvement with gay parents other than a few notes written in connection with his orphanages, *"We have found homosexual couples will take handicapped and born-out-of wedlock children which make up most our orphan population today. Heterosexual couples go for the cutest and healthiest children as if shopping for a puppy in a pet shop."*[11]

There is another note written in diary format,

"Dear Mamma,

I have for years counseled a young couple. They have great sexual attraction for each other, yet, beyond that they have nothing in common. I have yet to be in their presence when they have not been arguing or yelling at each other.

What's more, they both suffer from an ongoing drug and alcohol addiction problem for which they have not sought counsel. Both children, having been bombarded for years by the incompatibility of their parents, are now confined to institutions. In that I sanctioned this marriage, I must live out my days with this on my conscience.

Last week, this couple came to me on a matter of such great

85

*urgency I had to cancel another appointment. They told me of a
neighbor—one of the new single parents in Italy—a homosexual.
Another man has been living with him for many years.*

*I have known of this queer couple for some time. Both men are
contributing members of the community and spend much time
helping out in the orphanage. Their two beautiful children, a boy
and girl, are the envy of all who are privileged to experience them.*

One night, as they were leaving, I noticed tears in their eyes.

*They told me, it grieves them they cannot take all the children
home with them.*

*Mamma, it is this experience, more than any other that has
caused me to understand the qualifications of a good parent.*

*There is something terribly wrong with a society that thinks that
one's sex is what makes one a good parent.*

Your loving son, Albino"[12]

Years before the psychiatric world came to the same conclusion,
Luciani realized sexual orientation could not be changed by therapy.

As a seminarian, he wrote a paper which brought him bad marks.

Yet, he found unlike sexual orientation, sexual behavior can be
conditioned by therapy. He reasoned either of two forces drive a
sexual act, *love* or *lust*. When people are in love, *love* tends to drive
the act. When people are not in love, *lust* tends to drive the act.

He reasoned a homosexual male can be conditioned to engage in
sex with a woman only by changing the motivating force from *love*
to *lust*. Yet, he will never be able to truly fall in love with her. He
might grow to like her, develop affection for her, parent children
with her, but, he will never be able to truly fall in love with her.

Conversely, he had ministered in prisons and found heterosexual
men who engaged in homosexual acts. Yet, no matter how long it
went on, when a heterosexual male had an intimate relationship with
another male he could never fall in love with him.

He concluded one's God-given instincts cannot be changed.

Strategy of a Strange War[13]

*"Like all animals, we are born with two basic instincts: the
instinct of survival, and its adversary, the instinct of compassion.*

why he helped *"those kinds of people?"*

Alluding to the quarter of a million homosexuals murdered in concentration camps, he replied, *"If we are ever to be truly free, we must stamp out what Hitler stood for once and for all."*[23]

"...their liberty oppressed..."

In 1978, Paul VI permitted him to address Vatican cardinals on the possibility the Church encourage homosexuals to enter into long term loving relationships as they represented the only population group large enough to provide loving and economic support to millions of children who otherwise would be aborted by women too young or too poor to afford them.

Luciani argued the Church's position exiled them from society, forcing them into loneliness and despair. He reasoned the Church's position was one of prejudice, as science had proved the condition cannot be changed and the Bible's condemnation of homosexual acts was scant compared to its vast condemnation of heterosexual acts.

Yet, he was unable to convince no more than a handful of his audience the matter should even be discussed. He thanked Paul for having given him the opportunity. Turning to the cardinals he took on a rare tone of bitterness, *"'The day is not far off when we will have to answer to these people who through the years have been humiliated, whose rights have been ignored, whose human dignity has been offended, their identity denied and their liberty oppressed.' What is more, we will have to answer to the God who made them."*[24]

The innocence of sex

Concerning what he considered to be a more important issue, he became outspoken about the population explosion. He argued the Church's ban on contraception was creating massive poverty and starvation in the poor countries of Asia, Latin America and Africa.

What's more, its position on birth control was resulting in untimely pregnancies forcing abortions in the United States and Europe. The Church's policy on birth control was in direct conflict with its policy on abortion; the Church, itself, was the underlying cause of the lion's share of abortions.

It is the instinct of survival which moves the newborn puppy out of the womb to the teat. It is his instinct of compassion which causes him to move aside and let his little sister have some too.

These instincts are with us all the days of our lives.

They determine everything we do as everything we do is either done for ourselves or for others.

Though we are scarcely aware of it, an inner struggle goes on within each of us every day of our lives. Each time the fork in the road comes up—often only minutes apart—our instinct of survival tells us, 'Now what is in this for me?' Our instinct of compassion tells us something else, 'Now, what is in this for others?'

Many of our actions are reflections of these basic instincts.

We don't teach babies what to laugh at or what to cry about. They are born with this instinct, and all babies will laugh at the same things and cry about the same things and they will laugh and cry about these same things for all the remaining days of their lives.

The tendency to fall-in-love is a manifestation of the instinct of compassion. The kind of person one falls-in-love with cannot be changed. It would be like trying to condition a child to laugh when something terrible happens and cry when something wonderful happens.

These instincts are the fabric of the human soul. Although they cannot be changed in this life, it is within our power to weave them into the next life..."[13]

Whenever the Church's policies were inhumane, he stepped in.

It was in Italy the Vatican first limited hospital visitation rights to family members. The intent was to keep partners of homosexuals out to facilitate the priest demanding the dying partner renounce his or her loved one. "Otherwise, you will certainly go to hell!"

As a bishop, in defiance of the papal decree, he ordered hospitals within his jurisdiction to admit longtime partners of homosexuals into intensive-care units on at least six occasions reported in the press and, perhaps, many more not reported in the press.[14]

Across the pond

When civil rights legislation was enacted in the United States in 1964, the *Christian right*, having lost its quest to keep the black in his corner, turned its hatred toward homosexuals. By the end of the decade millions of homosexuals had been incarcerated—those in northern states for short sentences and those in southern states for long terms. Alabama came within one legislative vote of requiring the death penalty for a single homosexual act in private.

In the wee hours of the morning in the spring of 1967, acting on a tip from a neighbor, police broke into the home of Robert Wise and Timothy Wilson, both 22, outside Augusta Georgia.

Caught in the act, they were tried and sentenced to twenty years. Timothy Wilson served only four days of his term. He cut his wrists and bled to death in his cell on his twenty-third birthday.[15]

Timothy Wilson did not stand alone in his demise.

During the ensuing quarter-century homosexuality surfaced as the leading cause of suicide in Bible-belt states. Over a quarter of a million gay children and teens, born to parents whose minds were deranged by the hatred of Christian preachers, took their own lives.[16]

In the spring of 1969, the local newspaper boy delivered a copy of the *New York Times* to the bishop of Vittorio Veneto. Luciani's eye caught a headline, *"Police Murder Young Gay."* The article was accompanied by a photo. Impaled facedown atop a heavy iron picket fence was a small-framed boy. Though taken at night one could see four or five of the spikes had penetrated his body from his neck to his thigh and that the tips of the spikes were wet with blood.[17]

As he read the article, he saw the caption was wrong. The boy, a thirteen year old, in critical condition, was still alive. The fence was cut with torches and the teen removed to St. Agnes Hospital with spikes embedded in his body. He had been arrested by an undercover cop in Washington Square and brought to the station for booking.

Fearing disclosure to his parents, the youth pleaded for the police to let him go. When he went to use the restroom two officers were overheard threatening to force themselves on the youngster and the boy was either thrown from or leaped out of a window into the dark of the night and landed atop the fence.

The officers were suspended pending an investigation and were eventually returned to active duty when a witness who occupied a booth testified he had not seen anything; he had only overheard the confrontation and the most he could come up with is that one of the officers used the term, *"little faggot."*

Approached by a reporter, Luciani was asked for his assessment, *"When religion sanctifies hostility, it erases morality."*[18]

A week later, the boy died. Infuriated by his death, homosexuals for the first time stood their ground and fought off police in what is remembered today as *Stonewall.*[19] The gay revolution had begun; the prediction Luciani made in his letter to *Figaro* had become a reality.

Four years later, in December 1973, the American Psychiatric Association adopted the resolution homosexuality is a matter of instinct and not a matter of illness. It ordered its members to begin the work of removing the stigma long been associated with it.[20]

Luciani, referring to this ruling, got himself into trouble with his flock when he made the remark, *"I wonder how long it will take for the sheep to get this one."*

Even after Galileo proved via his *Falling Bodies Law* the earth was round and rotating on its axis, most Christians continued to believe it was flat because the Bible told them it was flat until years later when Magellan sailed off to the west and returned from the east. Half of them refused to believe it even then.[21]

"...stamp out what Hitler stood for..."

Despite medical science proved its claim, much of the population, influenced by preachers, continued to believe sexual orientation was a matter of choice. Luciani would often taunt clergy who chose to ignore what the medical community had to say.

Mimicking them, he would say in sarcasm, *"Psychology, the science of human theology, excuses homosexuals. Does the fault lie with parents who didn't discipline their children?"* Anything to ignite discussion, yet, for the most part he was ignored.

A couple of years later in July 1976, the French physician-priest Marc Oraison, made public his homosexuality. In his announcement Oraison declared homosexual love was God's will.

Luciani warned Oraison in a public release, *"If a priest preaches as he does, everything is ruined."*[22]

Of the things he said of homosexuality, this was the most widely published because *right wing* factions took it as a condemnation.

Luciani's remark obviously meant Oraison should have kept his identity private. One can best help an oppressed people by appearing to be an outsider; one was far less effective if one appears to be trying to help oneself.

A few days after the Oraison incident he was asked by a reporter

What changes he would have made had he lived will never be known. What one does know is that he died on the eve of the time he would have lifted the Church's ban on contraception. One knows this for he could have never rid the world of poverty—his number one objective—unless he first eliminated the driving force behind it.

On April 11, 1970, Luciani told his priests, *"It is easy to find persons who use the pill and other contraceptives and do not believe they are sinning. If this were to happen it would be best not to disturb them... There has rarely been such a difficult question for the Church, particularly, in the intrinsic implications as it affects other doctrinal issues..."*[25]

"Other doctrinal issues" struck at the heart of papal power. According to canon law only a pope can determine *who can have sex without committing sin and who cannot.*

This is what defines morality in the Church. According to doctrine, all sex outside what an incumbent pope defines as marriage is mortal sin—masturbation, remarriage, homosexuality, etc.

By definition, a Catholic is one who believes only a pope can decide *who can have sex without committing sin and who cannot—* the reason why, today, tens of millions of good Catholics, having made a mistake in choosing a mate at age twenty, at thirty had fallen truly in love, are living out their lives in loneliness and despair.

Christ did not give this authority to the pope. Men who were convinced sex is sinful, dirty and shameful made it up. Yet, take this unique power away and a pope is just another man.

The Council of Trent which today defines morality in the Roman Church rises and falls on the premise all sex is evil. So much so, it explicitly subordinates marriage to celibacy, *'If one saith that the marriage state is to be placed above the state of virginity, or of celibacy, and that it is not more blessed to remain in virginity or celibacy, than to be in matrimony, let him be excommunicated.'*[26]

Whereas, compassionate of homosexuals, Luciani was no more compassionate of them than he was of those who had remarried outside the Church, those heterosexuals who engaged in sex who had never married or those had not reached the age of marriage, who were equally condemned by the central moral doctrine of the Roman Catholic Church: *all sex outside of marriage is mortal sin.*[26]

In his mind, homosexuals were not a minority as they claimed— together with their allies they were in the majority.

91

His secretary in Venice was Mario Senigaglia. Senigaglia and Luciani spent much of their free time discussing the morality of sex. *"He was an understanding man,"* recalls Senigaglia, *"He would say to teenagers, 'We have made of sex the greatest of sins, whereas in itself it is human nature and not a sin at all.' He would say to youth groups, 'Always think of sex as being good and beautiful - a gift from God. But, also keep in mind, as with all other gifts from God, it comes with responsibility, both to yourself and your loved ones.'*[27]

"He would counsel couples contemplating marriage that it is irresponsible not to engage in sex before marriage. 'Sex is a complex issue,' he would tell them. 'Unlike Mother Church might pretend, it is not the whole of marriage. Yet, being incidental to marriage, it is prudent to test the waters before one drowns...'"[27]

David Yallop describes Villot discussing contraception with John Paul I. He quotes the new pope responding, *"Eminence, what can we old celibates really know of the sexual desires of the married?"* [28]

In general, Luciani could not understand how a group of old men in Rome, who had never been in the bedroom, could take it upon themselves to tell others what they can or cannot do in the bedroom.

Marriage

Traditionally, marriage had been a contract between a man and a man—a barter in which the merchandise was a maiden. Falling in love had little to do with it. It was common for a man to trade his daughter for a horse and believe he got the better part of the deal.

Marriage was a one-way street which purpose was to satisfy the lust of the man and grow his property—children.

In the nineteenth century, woman gained recognition as a human being and was no longer the mere property Moses had declared her to be. The definition of marriage changed from being a business transaction to being a union of two people who are mutually in love.

We are talking here of society and not of the Church.

The definition of marriage within the Church remains today as it was first written into canon law in the seventh century: *permission to have sex without committing sin.* According to canon law, the sole purpose of the Sacrament of Matrimony is to satisfy the body—*lust.* It has nothing to do with the mind—*love.*

92

What demonstrates marriage in the Church is a union of the body—*lust*, and not of the mind—*love,* is its dogma condemning transsexuals. A person determined by the psychological community to be a woman born into a man's body cannot marry a man; she can only marry another woman.

That marriage in the Church serves only to satisfy the body's *lust* and has nothing to do with *love* is also demonstrated in that no Catholic priest will marry a paraplegic or other person handicapped in such a way one cannot consummate sex.[29]

That satisfaction of body *lust* and not procreation is the purpose of marriage in the Church is most clearly demonstrated in that every Catholic priest will marry a man and a woman well beyond their childbearing years into their nineties and beyond.

Nevertheless, in the nineteenth century *falling in love* began to define marriage in society. Yet, it still had to negotiate the hurdles society placed upon it: creed, race, social status, and so forth. A Jewish girl who fell in love with a Christian man could not marry him. Nationalities were involved. A Pole could not marry a Russian and so forth. Age was a factor. The man had to be older—yet, not much older—than the woman. If the woman was older it was frowned upon. Even if the engagement passed all the tests of society, it still had to pass the will of the family or the two could not marry. One had to choose between one's family and one's happiness. This was true of everyone, those at the top and those at the bottom.

There occurred an event that would ignite a revolution which further changed the definition of marriage. Marriage would no longer be the decision of others or for that matter the state. It would be solely the decision of two people who love each other. It would be an individual decision and not the decision of the majority. It would be the duty of the state to sanction the individual commitment of two people who are in love, no matter who those people were.

On December 10, 1936, Edward VIII, King of England, told the world, *"I abdicate my throne for the woman I love."*

Edward had been engaged to Wallis Simpson, a divorcee who was not of royal blood. He had sought the approval of his family, the Church of England and the political establishment to no avail.

Albino was twenty-four when Edward abdicated. In Edward he saw courage, the same kind of courage his mother had shown when she had married his socialist-atheist father a quarter of a century earlier. In marrying a renegade, she too had given up her family.

As keynote speaker in the summer of 1961 at commencement services of his seminary in Vittorio Veneto, he spoke of how mental energy is exchanged between two people who are in love.

"...Though the Bible's only account of 'falling in love' involves two men—It came to pass...the soul of Jonathan was knit with the soul of David. Then Jonathan made a covenant with David, because he loved him as his own soul,'[30]— it applies to everyone.

Therefore we must hold in sanctified trust this most hallowed personification of God's creation—this perfect balance of mental energy that exists between any two people when they fall in love— whether it exists between man and woman, or black and white, or Christian and Jew, or believer and atheist, or German and Russian, or royalty and commoner, or virgin and divorcee, or man and man, or woman and woman, or hermaphrodite and eunuch...

The rest of this thing one calls 'love' is nothing more than the animal in us. To think differently—it pertains to physical parts of the body—is to say the Holy Sacrament of Matrimony pertains equally to the apes in the wild as it does to human beings.

When Christ said, 'Let no man put asunder what God has joined together,' this is what He was speaking of. This union made by God. He was not speaking of ancient rituals performed by mere mortal men dressed up in long robes muttering vain repetitions.

Mother Church and society use the word 'marriage' to describe two entirely different things.

In canon law, marriage is nothing more than permission from certain kinds of men to certain kinds of people to have sex without committing sin—a man-made union—a union of bodies...

In society, marriage is a union of any two people who hold each other as the most precious constituent of human life—a God-made union—a union of minds...

Mother Church has made of sex the greatest of sins, whereas, in itself, it is nothing more than human nature and not a sin at all."[31]

At the time, the motion picture *Guess Who's Coming to Dinner* had not yet previewed and most of the unions he spoke of were

94

condemned by preachers as being against God's will.

To Luciani, the state was in violation of Christ's will. In denying sanctity of marriage to any two people who were in love, the state was *"putting asunder what God has joined together."*[32]

The sacred duty of society

In the ensuing months, civil rights advocates in the United States, faced by polls overwhelmingly against integration, continued their struggle state-by-state to make interracial marriage legal.

As keynote speaker at the Christian Democratic Party Convention in Milan 1963, Luciani criticized the American process, *"The most sacred duty of society is to protect certain inalienable rights for all of its citizens and it should not be an option of any of its tributaries or the majority to abuse those rights.*

"The right to fall in love with whomever God deems one fall in love with is one of these rights...Democracy, which finds its strength in rule by the people, can only find its sacred duty to society, in preserving the basic human rights of its loneliest individual."[33]

In 1967, *Loving vs. Virginia*, an interracial case, reached the United States Supreme Court. The Lovings had been convicted of interracial marriage and sentenced to a year in the state prison for having married. Chief Justice Earl Warren, read the court's decision, *"The freedom to marry has long been recognized as one of the vital personal rights essential to the orderly pursuit of happiness by free men. Marriage is one of the basic civil rights of man, fundamental to ones existence and survival...Under the Constitution of the United States, the freedom to marry...resides with the individual and cannot be infringed upon by the state, or by the majority."*[34]

On the fortieth anniversary of the court's ruling, June 12, 2007, Mildred Loving, a plaintiff in the case, *"Surrounded as I am with wonderful children, not a day goes by I don't think of Richard and our love, our right to marry, and how much it meant to me to have the freedom to marry that person who is most precious to me, even if others thought it to be the wrong kind of person for me to marry.*

Government has no business imposing some people's religious beliefs on others; especially if it denies people civil rights.

I am proud that Richard's and my name are on a court case that can help reinforce the love, the commitment, the fairness, and the family that so many people, black or white, young or old, straight or gay, seek in life. I support the freedom to marry for all. That's what Loving and loving is all about.''[35]

The Catholic marriage ceremony ending *'until death do us part''* defines the *Sacrament of Matrimony* as being between two mortal animals which is consistent with the description of heaven in the Old Testament, *"The Lord came to me saying, Thou shalt not take thee a wife into this place, neither shalt thou bring sons or daughters...''*[36] And, in the New Testament, *'In this place one shall be as the bride of Christ...all of your love will be for Christ alone...''*[37]

Clergy Pedophilia

Another of the seminarian's works which drew low marks, *Il Pedophilia del Clero,*[38] addressed the question as to why the rate of pedophilia among priests seemed to be much higher than that of the general population and why it seemed to be primarily homosexual whereas in the general population it was primarily heterosexual.

Homosexuals in the priesthood

He recalled his time at Feltre, *"All sex outside of marriage is mortal sin. A heterosexual has the option of marriage and can look forward to a life of sex free of sin. For him, celibacy is a great sacrifice. But, a homosexual can never marry and therefore he is condemned to a life of celibacy anyway. In choosing the celibate life of a priest, a homosexual isn't giving up anything. This yields a relatively high percentage of homosexuals in the priesthood..."*

Transsexuals in the priesthood

He addressed the inconsistency, priests versus nuns and monks, *"I am puzzled why there is relatively low incidence of homosexual pedophilia among nuns and monks who outnumber priests four to one. Certainly, all three professions would attract the same mix of people as they offer one a life of celibacy, one dedicated to God. I wonder what could be the difference between a priest and a monk or a nun that results in a high rate of pedophilia among priests."*[38]

He looked at those who had gone before him. One researcher determined the vestments were attractive to the transsexuals.

A monk's brown robe would not suffice, as everyone would be wearing the same 'dress.' Conversely, reverse transsexuals—men born into women's bodies—would have no interest in the convent, as, at the time, it required they spend their lives in a black dress. These 'men' wanted to wear pants, not dresses.

The researcher concluded the vestments themselves resulted in a significant transsexual population among priests and practically no transsexual population among monks and nuns. Yet, Albino already knew this as many of his classmates exhibited feminine traits—the priesthood allowed them to dress up in beautiful gowns and live out their lives as objects of awe otherwise reserved for the fair sex.

Also, like a homosexual, a transsexual contemplating celibacy didn't have to give up anything in celibacy; unable to marry, he or she was otherwise condemned to a life of sin.

Benedict XVI

This is demonstrated by Benedict today. At the age of five, he was among boys who bestowed flowers at the feet of the Archbishop of Munich. He fell in love with the cardinal's elaborate gown and announced that evening he was going to be a cardinal.[39]

For the most part, Benedict has set aside the white smock of his predecessors for the more lavish dress of the pre-Paul VI era—magnificent robes of regal attire and added much of his own. Franco Zeffirelli, the film director, calls Benedict's wear *'too sumptuous for modern times.'* Though there is no reliable foundation for it, Queen Elizabeth is said to have said of his wardrobe, *'too effeminate for my everyday tastes and far too elegant and overdone for royal affairs.'*

Here, Benedict steps out for the evening in his velvet cape lined in white ermine in a gown layered in white satin and fine lace over beige chiffon. The Pope is particularly fond of lace and has a meticulous fetish for gold in that it promotes his majestic image. Famous for his collection of Prada shoes, here he wears a pair of Giorgio Brutini slippers. His wardrobe—the most lavish of any monarch—boasts hundreds of pairs of slippers from leading fashion houses.[39]

From 1981 to 2005, Joseph Cardinal Ratzinger served as Prefect of the Doctrine of the Congregation of the Faith, dictator of morality in the Catholic world.

In 2003, he enacted the doctrine transsexual surgery cannot alter gender and barred those who undergo sex-change surgery from marriage, ordination and religious life.[40]

Christ never damned homosexuals, transsexuals or transvestites. Yet, He did, many times, damn the Hypocrite.

Albino Luciani's conclusion makes sense today.

Although the transgender[41] population is relatively small, it is relatively large compared to the priest population. There are upwards of ten million transgenders in the United States and fifty thousand diocesan priests. It is reasonable to conclude that attracted by the vestments alone there is a large percentage of transgenders among priests, the reason why sacristies always boast a full length mirror.

Other than having been caught up in the scandal of the Maltese altar boys in 1993, there is no record Benedict was ever involved in pedophilia.[42]

Heterosexuals in the priesthood

One might wonder why a straight male who had the option of marriage and a life of sex free of sin would enter the priesthood.

The answer is obvious. They think something wrong with sex.

He sums up his case

In his study, *Il Pedophilia del Clero,*[38] he concluded that the priesthood was made up of three groups:

✓ *homosexuals*
✓ *transsexuals*
✓ *heterosexuals who thought something wrong with sex*

Actually, all Catholic clergy think there is something wrong with sex. After all, if they thought it to be good—a gift from God—it would be wrong to refuse the natural order of God's creation.

Luciani's conclusions are consistent with priest pedophilia cases tried in world courts. According to the best records available, about forty percent of predators have been determined to be transsexuals and another forty percent have been determined to be homosexuals. This leaves the rest who think there is something wrong with sex.

In their case, they are right.

The youth Luciani often wrote in humor. *Il Pedophilia del Clero* was no exception. Frustrated why priests were required to take a vow of celibacy and not one of poverty, he ended his paper, *"Christ said, 'If thou wilt be perfect, sell all thou hast and give to the poor'" He did not say, 'If thou wilt be perfect, keep it in your pants!'"*[38]

In the spring of 1978, a few months before his election, he was said to have criticized an American bishop for paying off the alleged victim of a pedophile priest. *"It would be better that we try our accused fellow servants in a court of law so they can be cleared of any wrong doing and if found guilty, they should pay their debt to society. It is not Mother Church's business to pay their debt in cash, particularly to pay it with money intended for the poor. Besides, if we take no action to get at the truth, we may very well be endangering countless children in the future."*[43]

The Prince Luciani

He had been the first bishop installed by John XXIII.

At the conclusion of the ceremony his sister who headed up the congratulatory reception line approached him and motioned to bow to kiss his newly acquired bishop's ring.

So horrified was he that this woman who had been such great support to him would bow to him, rather than extending his hand, he grasped her in his arms and held her for a time. The congregation was moved to tears. A group of Vatican cardinals, appalled at what they had witnessed stood off to one side, frozen in hostile stares.

On releasing her, this newest prince of the Church—realizing he had broken Church protocol—turned toward the Pope.

Rather than apologizing for his action, he told John, *"A prince must never forget his sister is the princess!"*[44]

Archbishop by Popular Demand

In September 1969, the Archbishop of Venice died. Thinking a Vatican cardinal would be chosen to fill the post, thousands of protestors marched through the streets of Venice demanding the bishop of the remote mountain diocese of Vittorio Veneto be named.

When Luciani was elevated to the post, the press billed it as *'the vote of the people.'* But, as we shall see in what is yet to come, Paul VI had already chosen Albino Luciani for the job. As a matter-of-fact he had already chosen him to one day fill his own job.

Under Arrest

It might interest the reader to know during his tenure as Patriarch of Venice Albino Luciani lived as a common man rather than as the crown prince of the Church he was.

He would often go incognito through villages dressed in clothes befitting a bum. He would learn firsthand the needs of his people.

This together with that he came across as a regular guy rather than a man of great stature occasionally got him into trouble.

In one case he was stopped by police in an impoverished section of a town and asked for identification. When he failed to produce his papers and claimed to be the Patriarch of Venice they didn't believe him and placed him under arrest.[45]

Shoes of the Fisherman

On another occasion, he escaped to the Lido for a few days.

His shorts were so fringed and worn and his shoes so tattered and torn a tourist handed him a lire note. It was time for a change.

Peering in a store window, he evaluated a pair of sandals.

The workmanship was of such fine quality as if made for a god. He went in the shop and tried them on. A perfect fit but the price too high. He would make do with the old ones a few more years.

Going out of the shop he took a bench along the edge of the lagoon. A youth in ragged clothes passed. He had no shoes.

Getting up, he beckoned the boy to follow him into the shop, intending to buy the sandals and give the boy his old shoes.

When he put them on, the youngster's eyes beamed in awe at the perfection of the sandals.

Together they went out of the shop, the boy in the sandals and he in his old shoes, still tattered and torn.

He bid the youth goodbye.

Returning to his bench, a tourist tucked a lire note into his hand.[46]

"A bit of red would help."

On still another occasion, he arrived at a village church and was told the church had closed for the day.

Returning to his car he told his aide to drive on. Ignoring his instruction, the young priest disappeared into the church.

A few minutes later, the church's rector came out to the car. Apologizing, he told the cardinal, *"Your eminence, perhaps, a tiny touch of red would help."*[47]

The Janitor of the Patriarch's Palace

On another occasion he entered into a conversation with a group of students in a pub and invited them to come to see him at home on the morrow, *"I live next to the Basilica di San Marco."*

"You mean the Patriarch's Palace?" *"Yes,"* he nodded.

"For whom should we ask?" they queried.

"Just ask for Piccolo," he smiled.

The next day they arrived at the palace and asked for Piccolo. They were taken to an elevator flanked by Swiss Guards. Exiting the elevator they were led to an office flanked by more Swiss Guards.

They were astonished to find Piccolo sitting by the window chatting with Pope Paul who happened to be visiting him that day.[48]

The Hypocrite

Luciani despised wearing vestments. Besides being effeminate, he thought there to be something hypocritical about them.

One day, in shorts and sandals, in the plaza fronting his Venice palace, he was asked by a retarded boy to pose with him for a photo.

He motioned to kneel down beside the boy. The boy stopped him, *"Could you put on your beautiful clothes?"*

Luciani disappeared into the palace. Shortly, he returned wearing his cardinal's robe, miter and golden staff.

"There are times," he told the boy's father, *"we must shed our humility and put on our hypocrisy. This is one of them."*[49]

Now watch as…

"One Beautiful Life… explodes into a trail of death and destruction in the Roman Catholic Church." Howard Jason Smith, *Boston Globe*

1 *Parlamento Italiano ABA35868* 16 Jan 59 *'La Single Condizione di Genitore Albino Luciani'*
2 direct testimony Luciani to the author. This story is reprinted from *Let's All Get Behind the Pope...*
3 *Corriere delle Alpi* 7 Jun 50
4 *Corriere delle Alpi* 15 Jul 50
5 *L'Epresso* 19 Jul 50
6 *Princeton Packet* 2 Apr 49
7 Direct testimony author
8 *Messaggero Mestre* 17 Mar 73
9 *Treviso Notizie* 1 Jun 68
10 *Parlamento Italiano ABA35868* 16 Jan 59 *'La Single Condizione di Genitore Albino Luciani'*
11 *Treviso Notizie* 12 Jan 59
12 Testimony of Jack Champney, author's file
13 Gregorian University Rome, *'Strategia di Una Guerra Sconosciuto, Don Albino Luciani 1941'*
See author's note on page 80. Exhibit: *Biblioteca Apostolica Vaticana*
14 *Veneto Nostro* 14 Apr 63   22 Aug 66   27 Dec 67
15 *Augusta Chronicle* 12 Apr 67
16 *Statistical Abstracts of the United States* 1960-1979
17 *New York Times* 12 May 78
18 *Veneto Nostro* 23 May 78
19 *N Y Times* 29 Jun 78 See *'Reincarnated Courage'* in author's book *Let's All Get Behind the Pope*
20 *Washington Post* 16 Dec 1973
21 *Messaggero Mestre* 17 Dec 73
22 *Catholic Encyclopedia Second Edition*
23 *Il Gazzattino Venezia* 23 Jul 76
24 *L'Osservatore Romano* 29 Mar 78 Luciani paraphrased Luis Cernuda's poem, *'The Family'* adding
the phrase *"...What is more, we will have to answer to the God who made them!"*
25 *Messaggero Mestre* 12 Apr 70
26 *Canon of Trent 1565* .That *'all sex outside marriage is mortal sin'* is canon Law. According to the
Bible, *'all sex regardless of marriage is sinful.'* There is one verse in the Bible which infers sex within
marriage to be without sin. *Corinthians 7 '... I say therefore to the unmarried and widows. It is good
for them if they abide. But, if they cannot contain, let them marry' for it is better to marry than to
burn.'* Yet, this verse is ambiguous in that it does not make clear *burn in hell* vs. *burn with passion.* It
does not appear in the oldest surviving New Testament, 4th century *Sinaiticus Codex* held by the
British Library. It was added by Catholic theologians in the middle ages to bring the Bible in line with
canon law, *'all sex outside marriage is Mortal Sin,'* which it remains today.
27 This is the most prolific and most widely published testimony of his ministry
28 *In God's Name* David Yallop
29 *Catholic Encyclopedia. Search:* 'paraplegic marriage,' e. g, Brazil De Brito 22 May 05
30 *29 1 Samuel 18.* Jonathan falls in love with David
31 *Veneto Nostro* 28 Jun 61
32 *1 Gospel of Matthew 19*
33 *Christian Democratic Party* minutes 22 Aug 63
34 *Loving vs. Virginia* United States Supreme Court 12 Jun 67
35 *Washington Post* 13 Jun 07
36 *Jeremiah 16*
37 *The Book of Reve*lations 3-9 paraphrased by the author
38 *Il Pedophilia del Clero* Gregorian University in Rome. *Biblioteca Apostolica Vaticana*
39 See *Little Lady in Disguise* in the author's book of short stories *'Let's All Get Behind the Pope.'* The
story of 5-year old Joseph Ratzinger and the Cardinal of Munich
40 *Catholic Catechisms* dated after 2003
41 Transgenders includes homosexuals whose sexual orientation drives a preference for apparel and/or
mannerisms of the opposite sex—i.e. butch females / effeminate males. Also included are transsexuals
whose preference for apparel and/or mannerisms of the opposite sex is driven by sexual identity, i.e.
born with the mind of the opposite sex—i.e. a 'woman' born into a man's body or a 'man' born into a
woman's body. A 'woman' born into a man's body will instinctively pass up the toy truck and reach
for the doll in infancy whereas a 'man' born into a woman's body will instinctively pass up the doll
and reach for the truck—i.e. Tom boy - Sissy. Transsexuality, being a function of the frontal lobes,
cannot be changed by therapy. Unable to change the mind, the only alternative is hormonal treatments

and/or surgery to adjust the body to match the mind. Consistent with the general population, most transsexuals are heterosexual but having a body of the opposite sex lead a homosexual lifestyle. Also included in transgenders are transvestites who acquire a fetish for apparel of the opposite sex for reasons other than orientation. See *The Enchanting Stenographer in 'Let's All Get Behind the Pope'.*
42 *Kullhadd* 13 Jul 93. At the time of the alleged scandal the altar boys who serve the pope were under Benedict, as Prefect of the Congregation of the Faith. Allegations were that the boys were molested in the Vatican. Ratzinger enacted a rule which sealed off communications of the boys with their homes during their tenure and required to take an oath, *'What happens in the Vatican stays in the Vatican.'*
43 *Messaggero Mestre* 17 Mar 78
44 *La Stampa* 28 Dec 58
45 *Treviso Notizie* 12 Jan 71
46 Direct testimony, Luciani to author
47 *Messaggero Mestre* 11 Jul 74
48 *Messaggero Mestre* 14 Aug 76
49 Jack Champney witnessed this in Venice on March 9, 1975. The author recreates this incident in the short story *'The Cardinal's Bench'* in his book of short stories *''Let's All Get Behind the Pope.'*

Photo Benedict XVI - *Associate d Press*

Dear Mr. Gregoire

My name is Tommy. I read Murder in the Vatican..

I was born with one eye and had a wrinkled face so nobody wanted me. I think I scared them. Then one day when I was five years old my father showed up and took me home. I remember the kids used to laugh at me in the playground. Then my fathers sold everything they had including the house and I spent a long time in the hospital and the doctors and nurses made me look good. We have still many bills to pay. But now I am quite a ladies man at school. I hit my first home run last summer and this year I am going to hit forty more.

My parents love me. That is, they used to love me. Now only one of them loves me. Because the other one is dead. He gave his life trying to win freedom for Iraq. He died on my fourteenth birthday. I noticed in your book that General Patton said some words over the grave of another soldier who like my father was gay and gave his life to save some Italian school children, "Freedom without equality is not what it pretends to be. For the diamond would be made of paste."

As you know I won't be getting any benefits from the army to pay for my education or my medical bills because my parents did not have the freedom to marry and I was adopted by the father that is still with me. I didn't even get his purple heart or bronze star. The army gave them to his parents who hated him and sold them in a tag sale. I would have liked to have them. And as you know I am also not entitled to social security and other benefits despite that my father like all other fathers paid for them. In his case not only with his dollars, but with his life.

My father tells me not to feel bitter because according to the last census there are a million children in gay families and they are in the same boat. But, of course, I am not listed with them because of the don't ask don't tell policy. My father says that there are also over fifteen milion other children in single parent families, many like me who are of gay parents who are not counted in the census because they are fearful of losing their jobs too. So we are talking about a lot of children here, million s of them, not just me.

Both my father and I are sure that your book will be a good seller. I want to ask you a favor. I want to ask you when you are on Larry King Live, could you please read my letter. I think it might help people to understand our problem.

I was planning on being a baseball player. But your book has made me change my mind. Instead I am going to study hard and I am going to grow up to be president. Well, maybe not president, but I am going to help other people. Like me.

Tommy

Chapter 9

Murder in Fatima

"Visions are harmful to true religion...particularly dangerous when used to promote political ends." [1]

Angelo Roncalli

In July of 1975, Luciani launched his most vigorous attack of his ministry. He criticized a South American bishop for capitalizing on a comatose twelve year old girl who was alleged to have the Stigmata.

The girl had been injured and had never regained her faculties. The bishop and her parents put her on display through a one way window set in the wall of her bedroom. In a circus-like atmosphere they paraded thousands of pilgrims past her room for a fee.

"I can understand why Mother Church might turn her head the other way when greedy people capitalize on defenseless children in this way. After all, she is at the source of this kind of satanic ritual. What bothers me most is that men and women of good conscience of the state stand aside and do nothing about it." [2]

Stigmata and the Shroud

Stigmata had been a money-making scheme ever since the 13th century when St. Francis had been the first to display wounds in the palms of the hands; he is rightfully credited with having come up with the perverted idea. Most popes since his time have capitalized on this *Sideshow of the Roman Catholic Church.*

Crucifixion involved the driving of spikes into wooden planks placed over the arms beneath the bone-line into the cross. It would not take a PhD in structural engineering of the anatomy to tell one razor-sharp first century nails driven through the palms of the hands would never support the weight of a human body.

A short time before the South American incident, a photograph of the Shroud showed the blood as coming from the wrists and not from the palms—Christ was crucified through the wrists and not through the palms. Yet, Christ could not have been crucified through the wrists as He would have bled to death in a few minutes as the arteries would have ruptured immediately under the weight of the body. The early icons placed the spikes in the palms as it was more artistic and all artists since have followed this practice.

The pain in crucifixion was concentrated in the feet. Spikes were driven crisscross through the ankles into the cross. The hanging impaired the victim's ability to breathe. In order to keep breathing the victim would put pressure on the heels causing unbearable pain. The victim would eventually succumb to asphyxiation.

The official position of the Church concerning the shroud is it is a fake. When it first appeared in France in 1353AD, Pope Innocent VI ordered an investigation. After three years Bishop Pierre d'Arcis of Paris reported, *"After diligent inquiry and examination, the truth attested by the artist who created it, to wit, it is the work of human skill and not miraculously bestowed. Bishop Henri de Peituers falsely and deceitfully created the hoax for personal gain. In his deception, de Peituers secures a cloth woven in the Holy Land.* "3

Innocent declared it a hoax and ordered it removed from display. After he died it resurfaced. His successor Urban V allowed the hoax to go on. Yet, no pope has ever reversed Innocent's decree.

Luciani once told me, "Take a peek at Jewish custom as to how they buried their dead. While the body was customarily wrapped in a white linen shroud as told in the *Gospel of John, 'Then they took the body of Jesus and wound it in linen clothes, as the manner of the Jews to bury,'* the face was first wrapped in a napkin, *'Then cometh Simon Peter into the sepulcher, and seeing the linen clothes lie, And the napkin that was wrapped about his face, not lying with the linen clothes, but wrapped together in one place by itself.'* "4 If an image of Jesus survived, it would be on the napkin, and not on the shroud."

Nevertheless, if Stigmata were an act of God, the Church should have been granting sainthood to those afflicted in the arms.

The vast majority of Stigmata including those of St. Francis have been self-inflicted. In the case of the comatose girl in South America, it was torture. Millions of people develop cancerous and bleeding sores, sometimes in the legs, toes, genitalia, buttocks and so forth. When they happen to appear in the hands one claims Stigmata.

Lourdes

In 1964, Luciani visited Lourdes on the guise of pilgrimage. Two issues had made the case for Bernadette.

A spring had sprung forth in the grotto. The original transcripts described the first apparition *"Bernadette went into the grotto to fetch water for the day."* Transcripts published after 1936 read, *"Bernadette went into the grotto to fetch wood for the day."*[5]

The second issue, the more critical one, was that the 'girl' told Bernadette she was the *Immaculate Conception*. At the time, the *Doctrine of the Immaculate Conception*—Mary had been born without original sin—was not known by the general congregation.

Like other progressive doctrines, this was politically motivated to bring the Church into sync with social changes. The Christian world had always recognized women as property. In 1853, following Europe's lead, laws were passed in the United States changing the definition of women from 'property' to 'human beings' bringing pressure on Rome to elevate the concept of women in the Church.

In 1854, Pius IX drafted the idea of the *Immaculate Conception*.[6] Yet, for eighteen centuries Mary was assumed to have been born with original sin. Pius' 'discovery' had to be kept secret while he searched for a way to convince the public of its authenticity.

It was that Bernadette spoke of this doctrine that made her a saint. There was no way she could have learned of it. Luciani was convinced the spring had always been there. Yet, he was puzzled as to how she could have learned of the doctrine. In 1971, he returned and spent much time scouring over records and talking to villagers.

The first apparition occurred in February 1858. The apparitions which followed were witnessed by crowds. She told them *"I have seen a girl of my age silent as to who she was. She would reveal her identity in six months."*[6] At the time Bernadette was fourteen.

In early March, two days before the apparition in which the 'girl' would reveal her identity, Bernadette was interviewed by a bishop from the Vatican. The vision was witnessed by ten thousand people. All they saw was a girl talking to the air. Afterwards, she told the crowd, the 'girl' had told her, *"I am the Immaculate Conception."*[7]

The next day, dozens of crutches appeared lined up against a wall suggesting crippled pilgrims had walked away. Townsfolk told Luciani they had been placed there by villagers seeking to capitalize on the visions. Within days, the poverty stricken town was booming.

There was no greater feminist activist in the history of the world than Albino Luciani. One could ask why he would destroy the myth of the *Immaculate Conception* when it would contribute to one of his lifelong objectives: to bring about equality of women in the Church.

He would not take part in deception to fool people into thinking women equal. He would remove obstacles the Church and society had placed in her path. Woman, herself, would prove she was equal.

Fatima

In 1916, Lucia Santos, age 9, and her cousins Francisco Marto, age 7, and Jacinta Marto, age 6, were tending sheep outside of Aljustrel Portugal. The specter in the first vision was the Angel of Peace. The second vision, a few weeks later, featured the Angel of Portugal. In the third vision, still another angel gives Lucia Holy Communion and Francisco and Jacinta a drink from a chalice.

So convincing was she that though her mother told reporters she was a pathological liar they sensationalized Lucia's story, *"Lucia wants to become a saint. She knows many have been made saints for no other reason than they convinced the Church of visions."*[8]

A reporter questioned the younger children Francisco and Jacinta. Their recollections of what the angel said not only contradicted Lucia but contradicted each other. Lucia successfully refuted her cousins as being too young to understand what they witnessed and by year end, her stories had reached much of Portugal.

In December of that year, a Portuguese writer, Jose Santos Silva, in his book *Short Mission* told of the appearance of a 'Lady' to two children tending sheep. To the extent his story included secrets told the children by the 'Lady' he seemed to have plagiarized the *La Salette* visions of September 1846 in southern France in which Our Lady appeared to two children herding cows and tells them secrets.[9] Yet, the timing of his book suggests he was motivated by the events of 1916. Regardless, he wrote of a 'ghost' appearing to more than one person at a time—a very rare occurrence in saintly visions.

The visions of Fatima in 1917 were quite different from those of Aljustrel in 1916. Like the book, *Short Mission,* they involved a 'Lady' rather than angels. Also, it was arranged the younger children would see the 'Lady' but not hear or participate in the conversations to avoid contradictions which had been a problem at Aljustrel.

The first apparition of the 'Lady' took place on May 13, 1917 at Cova da Iria near Fatima and was witnessed by a small crowd and a pair of reporters. A comparison of the 1858 Lourdes transcript and the 1917 Fatima transcript disclose Lucia plagiarized Bernadette in describing the 'Lady.' Both transcripts have identical wording, *"The Lady was clothed in light wearing a white mantel edged in gold. A star was caught in the folds of her dress. She herself was as if made of light...I saw a girl of fourteen who was silent as to whom she was. She would reveal her identity in six months."*[10] In both transcripts is the wording, *"I want you to build a chapel here in my honor."*[11]

Bernadette had, herself, plagiarized Juan Diego in his testimony of the apparition of the 'Lady' of Guadalupe in 1531, *"...The light around her formed a dress edged in gold; a gold star in its hem. She told me 'Tell Bishop Juan to build a chapel here for me here.'"*[12]

Cardinal Antonio Belo of Lisbon explained the similarities, *"The timing and descriptions of the visions and the request for a chapel would be identical as they involved the same Lady."*[13]

Although the younger children were excluded from conversing with the 'Lady,' there were contradictions as to what they saw. For example, in her testimony to the reporters Lucia claimed *'...the Lady was wearing huge magnificent dazzling earrings.'*[14]

When questioned independently the younger visionaries never mentioned the earrings. When pressed for an answer, Jacinta did not remember much of the earrings other than *'they were beautiful.'*[13]

Francisco, thinking it a trick—Lucia had not mentioned earrings—told reporters *'the Lady was wearing a veil which covered her ears. I could not see her ears.'*[14]

From this point on, it was arranged, Francisco and Jacinta would no longer witness the visions.

The next vision was on June 13, 1917, the feast of St. Anthony.

Lucia spoke of her conversation with the 'Lady.'

"Will you take us to heaven?" asked Lucia.

The 'Lady' replied, *"Yes, I will take Jacinta and Francisco soon, but you will remain a little longer since Jesus wishes you to make me known and loved on earth. . ."*[15]

When questioned why the younger children had not witnessed the vision, Lucia said, *"Only I was brave enough to see the Lady."*

Several months later, newspapers reported the younger children making confusing statements. Jacinta retracted some of what she had said and Francisco, probably because he had been cut out of the visions, began to deny them entirely. Shortly afterwards, both fell ill.

The nature of Francisco's illness remains unknown as, although he suffered for several months, he was deprived of medical attention. Jacinta died a few months after Francisco of pulmonary edema which had been mistaken for pleurisy in a Lisbon hospital.[16] For the mystery buff, arsenic poisoning very often cumulates in edema.[17]

Lucia's prediction had come true. *"Yes, I shall take Jacinta and Francisco soon..."* The Church recognizes this as a miracle. Any criminologist will tell you it is grounds for premeditated murder.

"She didn't see it dance."

Regardless, on July 5, 1977, Albino Luciani visited the village where Francisco had died. The next day he visited Saint Stephen Hospital in Lisbon where Jacinta had died. He spent the evening with Cardinal Robeiro in the Patriarch Palace.[18]

The following morning, he interviewed the nun Lucia Santos at Coimbra. Scores of reporters swarmed the cardinal as he left the convent. They looked for the familiar smile. All they got was a look of anguish and despair. When asked why Lucia had not discussed the 'miracle of the sun' with reporters the day of the alleged miracle, Luciani told them *"She didn't see it dance."* Other than that he was mum as to what took place behind closed doors.[18]

It could be Lucia was the pathological liar her mother claimed her to be. It could be she was a paranormal schizophrenic who really believed the things she imagined she saw. It could be she had actually seen a ghost. These things explain Fatima.

But, they do not explain why Lucia predicted the deaths of her co-visionaries? Countless books portray the loving Lucia taking a bowl of soup on her daily visits to her sick and dying cousins. One will never know.

Aftermath

After the spark of enthusiasm which followed Jacinta's death—the 'Lady's' prophecy had come true—only the most devout clung to Fatima. In the darkened corners of pubs and in schoolyards were whispers of 'murder' in the coincidental deaths of the children.

One could argue the children died of the 1918 Flu. Yet, both died outside the Flu mortality period and the cause of Jacinta's death is explicit in hospital records. Also, had Francisco been suffering from the Flu—readily diagnosed by coughing up of blood and darkening of stool to the extent one swallowed the blood—he would have been required by law to be quarantined in a sanitarium. No one survived the Flu for more than a week and both suffered for over six months.

Nevertheless, the coincidental publication of *Short Mission* prior to the first vision and the testimony of the overwhelming number of witnesses who saw nothing unusual the day of the sun nailed the case shut for the doubters. Scientific journals which had demolished the authenticity of the 'miracle of the sun' and the lack of mention of it in the Sunday editions the day after it allegedly took place nailed the case shut for those who accept the real world they live in.

The 'miracle of the sun' was created two weeks after it allegedly occurred. *Illustracao Portuguese*[19] paid a half dozen witnesses to testify they had seen the sun fall down out of the sky.

The tabloid plastered pictures on its front page of witnesses gazing upwards—obviously responding to Lucia pointing toward the sky, *"There she comes."* The crowd had come to see the 'Lady.'

Unlike Lourdes, in which case the town had exploded overnight into prosperity, Fatima remained in relative poverty. The villagers built a chapel. Yet, the Vatican not only failed to encourage the hoax, it did much to discourage it. Benedict XV ignored it. The bishop of the governing diocese of Fatima not only refused to recognize the apparitions but refused invitations to visit the chapel.

For over a decade Fatima remained not much more than one of hundreds of dots on the make-believe paranormal map of Europe.

In 1929, events occurred that would make Fatima into what it is today—the last of the saintly ghosts of yesterday. On June 7, 1929, Pius XI entered into the *Lateran Treaty*—a union between the Vatican and fascist Italy—a union between the Church and fascism.

In 1926, when Pius ordered all children under sixteen enrolled in the new fascist scout organization it drew the wrath of thirteen year old Albino Luciani. The *Lateran Treaty* caused an unprecedented uproar of *leftist* factions both within and outside the Church.

Christ's ideology that all children are equal and are entitled to an equal share of God's province was consistent with communism. Fascism, some of God's children are created better than others and are entitled to more, was Christ's archenemy. It was clear to anyone who had the least bit of awareness of the gospels the Church had separated itself from Christ whom it claimed to represent.

Pius had to convince the faithful Christ had changed His mind. He searched for a way to override Christ's most prolific testimony in the gospels. He sought to convince the faithful communism was evil and fascism was sacred. He had invoked his infallibility to no avail. He decided only a ghost could change the gospels.

The Russian Revolution

To understand what transpired here, a bit of Russian history.

The Romanovs were the last of a long line of Tsarist autocracies which had imposed poverty and suffering on the people of Russia. Yet, the Russian Revolution was as much an attack on the ally of the Romanovs, the Russian Orthodox Church, which, itself, had become immersed in vast wealth while children starved to death.

The Bolsheviks did not have to convince anyone Christ dictated a communist society. A half-century before, when Marx and Engels had written their *Communist Manifesto,* they had been accused of plagiarism—they had obviously put in their own words what Mark, Matthew, Luke and John had written two thousand years before.

Communism became the archenemy of the Orthodox Church and of the Roman Catholic Empire as well—cults of idol worship, ritual and vast wealth. The Bolsheviks threatened to change the Church from the idolatry of Christ it had become back to the ideology of Christ He had demanded. Ironically, this would become the sacred mission of Roncalli, Montini and Luciani a half-century later.

The Fatima Conspiracy

Since La Salette and Lourdes in the mid-nineteenth century, thousands of children had claimed to have had visions of Our Lady. They had been ignored. What separated Fatima from the others was that it happened to come along at the right time. Had it not been for this coincidence, today, one would have never heard of Fatima.

Fatima occurred at the precise time the Russian Revolution took place. The visions began shortly after the provisional government removed the Tsar from power in the spring of 1917 and they ended on the 13th of October, the day the Bolsheviks came to power.

Pius plotted to use Fatima to convert Russia back from a society in which all children are seen as equal—Christ's ideology—to one in which some children are better than others—fascism.

Pius selected some of what Lucia had actually told newspapers at the time and added some of his own. His main embellishment would eventually become the central message of Fatima—*'the conversion of communist Russia.'* What's more, he got Lucia to conspire with him. She had not mentioned 'Russia' to reporters at all in 1917.

Lucia lived into the twenty-first century. It was not unusual for her to add to or change her stories as historical events like the *Lateran Treaty* materialized. At one point, she revealed the 'Lady' had predicted World War II in what one knows today as the Second Secret of Fatima. The faithful were astounded the 'Lady' could have know this in 1917—another miracle. I will give you a hint. Lucia revealed the secret in 1941 after World War II had begun.

In October 1930, Pius released his Fatima transcript, *'Pray the Rosary for the conversion of Russia...If Russia is free to scatter her errors through the world, the Holy Father will have much to suffer and many nations will be annihilated...'* The document included other phraseology which had not been a part of the 1917 newspaper reportings. The visions of Fatima were declared *'worthy of belief.'*

The wave of pilgrims headed for Lourdes and La Salette suddenly detoured toward Fatima. Overnight, Lucia became much more than just another nun on her knees in a secluded convent.

Pius had removed Christ from his path. He was on his way to World War II.

1 *Messaggero Mestre* 29 Sep 55
2 *Messaggero Mestre* 12 Jul 75
3 *Biblioteca Apostolica Vaticana.* Independent DNA analysis date the Shroud between 1250-1350AD
4 *Gospel of John 20*
5 *Biblioteca Apostolica Vaticana, Notre-Dame de la Grotte a Lourdes* pg v.
6 *Biblioteca Apostolica, La Dottrina della Concezione Immacolata*
7 *Biblioteca Apostolica,* Notre-Dame de la Grotte a Lourdes pg xii
8 *O'Seculo* 31 Aug 16
9 *Short Mission,* Silva 1917. The book is available in some large city libraries.
10 *Jornal de Leiria* 20 May vs. *Calendario de Nossa Senhora da Fatima* p iii
11 *La Dottrina Della Concezione Immacolata pg iv Calendario de Nossa da Fatima* p ii
12 *Biblioteca Apostolica, El registro de Nuestra Dama de Guadalupe p v*
13 *O'Seculo* 29 May 17
14 *Calendario de Nossa Senhora da Fatima* p xxi.
15 *Ordem* 13 Jun 17 and *Calendario de Nossa Senhora da Fatima* p vi
16 *La a Tempo di Record di Beatificazione Jacinta Marto* p vi
17 *Mosby's Medical Dictionary* or any other approved by the American Medical Association
18 *O Dia* 9 Jul 77
19 *Illustracao Portuguese* 29 Oct 17
Photo of Lucia Santos - *Verdade das Pessoas* Oct 17, 1917

Chapter 10

The Marxist Movement in the Church

Angelo Roncalli = John XXIII
Giovanni Montini = Paul VI
Albino Luciani = John Paul I

"If we are to have a true church it must be built on truth, not on myth."
Angelo Roncalli

The Marxist movement in the Roman Catholic world began with the election of John XXIII in the Sistine Chapel on October 28, 1958 and ended with the death of John Paul I in the great bed of the papal apartment on the morning of September 29, 1978. It is no secret what brought these two men together in a common cause.

Unlike the overwhelming majority of popes who have been born into immense wealth, both these men had been born into poverty. They knew as children what it was to wonder where their next meal was coming from. It is no surprise they joined together to bring about a society which affords every child an equal opportunity to make his or her contribution to society—Marxism.

Yet, the bulk of the Marxist movement in the Church was driven by the man who came between them—Paul VI. What could this man who had been born into wealth and nobility have possibly had in common with the other two?

Like Luciani, Paul had been born to an atheist father and had been so influenced that by the time of his thirteenth birthday he had lost his faith—that is, his faith in what the Church had become. It was not until late in his teens he realized—like Luciani who would come after him—the Church could only be changed from the inside.

Yet, what was it that all three of these men had in common?

They wanted to change the Church back to what Christ had intended—a church for all people, but, especially a church for the poor. They wanted to move the Church away from the idolatry of Christ it had become: *'men dressed up in women clothes prancing about altars of marble of gold and entranced fools lining up to the cannibalistic ritual of swallowing their God,'* back to the ideology of

113

Christ He had demanded: *'Sell all thou hast and give to the poor.'*

Roncalli, Montini and Luciani were three men bonded together by the glue of a common ambition to rid the world of poverty—the shared thesis of Jesus Christ and Karl Marx.

They knew the only way they could achieve their goal was to first move the Church away from the ghosts of the past it had been built on lest it self-destruct in the meantime—the 'Burning Bush' that spoke to Moses in the desert, the two dozen other Ghosts that had appeared to other prophets of the old world, to the angel-ghost that appeared in Joseph's dream telling him Mary had been impregnated by still another Ghost—the Holy Ghost—which established Christ as still another Ghost—this one, too, with a capital 'G.' What's more, they did not believe in the ghosts of more recent times.

Specifically, they did not accept the Ghost that had allegedly appeared to Constantine three hundred years after Christ's time and the two dozen 'pope' ghosts with which he had linked himself back to Christ—fairytale popes of the pre-Holy Roman Empire.

Moreover, this triad of men did not accept the so-called visionary saints of today particularly when used to promote political ends. Roncalli, Montini and Luciani, more than any others before them or after them, were those Christ was referring to when He said, *'Blessed are the poor in spirit for theirs is the Kingdom of Heaven.'*

In 1985, Avro Manhattan wrote, *"Roncalli did not approve of visions or miracles. He prided himself on having, besides large hands, equally large feet, planted firmly on the ground. 'Visions,' Roncalli said, 'are harmful to true religion… particularly dangerous when they are used as a means of promoting political ends.'"*[2]

Roncalli reasoned miracles contradicted the premise of religion: this life is as a grain of sand on the beach of eternity and its sole purpose is to get one into the afterlife. *"It makes no sense to pray for the recovery of a young boy who is suffering from cancer when if he dies one knows he goes to heaven. Christ said 'Blessed are little children for theirs is the Kingdom of Heaven.' The reason one prays for his recovery is because one knows he is not going anywhere."*[3]

Roncalli was particularly outspoken against what he tabbed *'The Fatima Cult,'* the alleged appearance of a 'Lady' to the children of Fatima who condemned her alleged Son's—Christ—message in the gospels *'Sell all thou hast and give to the poor'*—Marxism.

Regardless, this triad-of-men—Roncalli, Montini and Luciani—

114

realized if they failed to separate the Church from its make-believe foundation, third world countries—in the not too distant future— would become first world countries and the tendency to believe in the ghosts on which the Church had been built would evaporate.

As Roncalli put it, *'A church that rises from specters will soon dissipate into the specters which gave birth to it. If we are to have a true church it must be built on truth, not on myth."*[4]

He was right. As one knows people no longer believe in ghosts. That is, ghosts of today. They believe only in ghosts of the past. The last of which was Fatima which for political purposes materialized more than a decade after it was claimed to have first taken place.

The Mythical Foundation of the Roman Catholic Church   **The Foundation of the Roncalli-Montini-Luciani Chuch**

"Christ's Church is not of buildings of wood and stone, nor of myth and fancy. It is in your heart. It is in your compassion for others."[5]   Cardinal Angelo Roncalli

Roncalli, in particular, had been critical of his predecessors who used the visionary saints to achieve political goals.

Pius XI used Fatima to justify the Vatican's union with fascist Italy in the *Lateran Treaty* and used it again in 1934 in winning over the votes Hitler needed to pass the *Enabling Act* which made him dictator of Germany which eventually cost fifty million lives. As late as 1941, Pius XII used Fatima to justify Hitler's invasion of Russia.

After the war, Pius again used Fatima as the driving force behind the Vatican's propaganda campaign which conditioned children growing up in Catholic countries to hate children growing up in Russia so that when they grew up they would risk their lives to kill them to defeat the Vatican's number one enemy—communism.

Pius employed Fatima to precipitate the Cold War. He cleverly convinced the western world Christ had sent His mother in Fatima to correct what Matthew, Mark, Luke and John had mistakenly claimed in their gospels, *'Sell all thou hast and give to the poor.'*

In September 1955, Pius, himself, saw a Ghost. He told Italy's largest newspaper *Corriere Della Sera, "I saw the Lord close to me in all His majesty...I heard the true and distinct voice of Christ."*[6]

Roncalli was caught off guard by a reporter the Pope was making up stories to lead the world into a third world war. *'...If we are to have a true church it must be built on truth, not one built on myth.'*[1]

Of course, no one took the Pope seriously, as no one believes in ghosts. That is, ghost of the present—only ghosts of the past.

Regardless, Roncalli reasoned the Pope had claimed to have seen a Ghost to facilitate his paving the way for World War III. The French had recently pulled out of Vietnam and the Church had lost its foothold in mainland Asia—a stronghold of communism.

Communism holds the relationship between a man and his God to be a personal and sacred one and should not be a business by which men take advantage of man's fear of his mortality to accomplish political objectives. This made communism Pius' greatest enemy.

Nevertheless, Pius was about to entice the United States to fight his war. What better way than if Christ had given the order.

We have arrived at that point one defines the *right* from the *left*.

It is the tendency to believe in ghosts which divides the *right* from the *left* more than anything else. Those on the *right* really believe a 'Burning Bush' spoke to Moses in the desert. Those on the *left* see it as a story once told to accomplish political objectives. To put it bluntly, the *right* believes in ghosts and the *left* does not.

Roncalli, Montini and Luciani would destroy the mythical foundation the Church is built on and replace it with the ideology of Christ which Matthew, Marx, Luke and John wrote of. They would pull them up off their knees mumbling vain repetitions and put them to work helping others.

And, yes, Mark, the only one who could have witnessed Christ's ministry, The one who spoke of Jesus as a man and not as a ghost.

1 *Messaggero Mestre* 29 Sep 55
2 *Murder in the Vatican* Avro Manhattan, pg 30
3 *Corriere della Sera* 12 Mar 55
4 *Messaggero Mestre* 17 Dec 56
5 *Messaggero Mestre* 25 Dec 57 Basilica di San Marco   Roncalli paraphrases Christ
6 *Corriere Della Sera* 16 Sep 55

Chapter 11

How a Pope is Elected

"When the political infighting that goes on when a pope is elected turns to murder."
Howard Jason Smith *Boston Globe*

According to canon law, the decision as to who becomes pope must be Christ's decision and not that of a group of men politicking and collaborating among each other. This is why after a candidate achieves a minimum margin of victory—two-thirds plus one vote—a revote is taken to make it unanimous; Christ has spoken, so to speak.

The public perceives the electors as being a group of old men cloistered together in the Sistine Chapel in prayer. It is led to believe the only guidance a cardinal has in making his choice is prayer. As a matter-of-fact, prayer has little to do with the election of a pope.

Like any other election, the election of the Supreme Pontiff of the Roman Catholic Church is a political process. A cardinal does not cast his vote for another cardinal because he thinks he will look pretty in a white satin gown. Likewise, he does not cast his vote for a man because Christ appears to him and tells him to.

Like any other progressive or conservative, the voting cardinal casts his vote for the candidate who most closely shares his own ecclesiastical convictions. As in any other election, he trades off a part of his own convictions in order in return to get a piece of the action. The political infighting that goes on when a pope is elected is often fierce and there have been times it has turned to murder.

In modern times, with the exception of Pius XII and John Paul I, popes have handpicked their successors. Historically, the reigning pontiff would move his choice into either the secretary of state position or the pastoral Italian archdioceses of Milan and Venice.

With the exception of John Paul II, all twentieth century popes have come out of these jobs. This includes Pius X, Benedict XV, Pius XI, Pius XII, John XXIII, Paul VI and John Paul I.

The 1958 conclave

117

As Pius XII aged, he realized Giovanni Montini would get the vote. Montini had gained popularity with field cardinals in that he had often embarrassed Pius on humane issues. Despite his moderate views, his relative youthfulness had gained the alliance of many of the Curia hardliners during his ten years as pro-secretary of state.

At the same time, the papal nuncio to France, Angelo Roncalli had also gained a level of popularity with field cardinals, particularly in his work to sever the Vatican from its fascist's roots which union with Hitler and Mussolini had led to World War II.

Under Roncalli's leadership, France was at the forefront of the anti-clerical movement which rose up after the war and was fed up with the fascist policies the Vatican continued to cling to. Yet, not a cardinal and lacking Montini's visibility as pro-secretary of state, he was not a viable candidate for the papacy.

In 1953, Pius moved him to the coveted position of Patriarch of Venice and at the same time made him a cardinal.[1] There were now two liberals—Roncalli and Montini—in the race for the gold.

When Montini, who had served as pro-secretary of state for ten years, was not included in the 1953 consistory it sparked rumors he had refused the *red hat*. The secretary of state position had not only traditionally been occupied by a cardinal it had been occupied by the ranking cardinal. Had Pius had any intention Montini succeed him he surely would have formalized Montini's appointment as *Cardinal Secretary of State* and put him in direct succession to the throne.

One might conclude Montini was not included in this consistory because of his relatively young age—in his mid-fifties at a time men were typically made cardinals in their sixties and seventies. Yet, in the same consistory, Pius awarded the *red cap* to his favorite son the Archbishop of Genoa, Giuseppe Siri—only forty-seven at the time.[2]

Nevertheless, despite Montini's and Pius' denials in the press the rumor Montini refused the *red hat* persists even today.[3] Yet, what we know of him tells us he did not refuse the *red hat*.

Most cardinals—though they may pretend otherwise—yearn to succeed to the papacy. Men are not, as one might be led to believe, dragged yelping, howling and squealing against their will to the papal balcony. This was particularly true of Montini and Wojtyla who openly voiced their papal ambitions throughout their ministries.

Yet, unlike Wojtyla, it was expected Montini would succeed to the papacy. Unlike his colleagues Roncalli and Luciani who feigned humility in accepting the post, Montini accepted it as his legacy.

In 1954, Pius moved Montini from the Vatican to Milan to lessen his grasp on the Curia votes. Again, he withheld the *red cap.*

Pius' intent was obviously to exclude Montini from the conclave which would diminish his chances. Yet, when Pius died, Montini still controlled a block of cardinals; they would vote only for him or his choice. This is seen in newspapers which listed Siri and Montini in a dead heat for the papacy as the conclave opened on October 25, 1958 despite Montini was not a cardinal. In retrospect, neither Siri nor Montini won the election. How could this have come about?

The leading candidates in the election were Montini followed by Roncalli on the liberal side of the aisle and Siri unchallenged on the conservative side. The war had been a wake-up call as to the dangers of frozen conservatism. The trend was away from fascism.

A liberal at that time was not what a liberal is today. Both the liberal and the conservative had convictions concerning doctrine. The liberal, however, had an open-mind in considering modifying doctrine in those cases where it unfairly penalized the lives of innocent people. The conservative, on the other hand, was fixed in his convictions, he didn't care how much suffering doctrine imposed upon innocent people. At the time, a conservative was a dedicated fascist limited only to what had been lost to him by Hitler in the war.

In retrospect today, one can only surmise Pius' strategy—faced by a growing open-minded majority—was to split the liberal vote between Roncalli and Montini and pave the way for his favorite son—the youthful conservative archbishop of Genoa, Giuseppe Siri.

In that Roncalli won the election, it follows Montini yielded his votes to the aging cardinal. What's more, we know he did this before the conclave went into session as Montini was not in the conclave. How do we know this? Post-election events clearly tell us this.

Shortly after his election, on December 15, 1958, John XXIII elevated Montini and twenty-two of Montini's loyal supporters to the College of Cardinals. Should John have died the following day, Montini would have won a successive election in a landslide.[4]

John's intention is seen clearly in the consistory listing: Montini is listed first. Never before in the history of the Church or since, has a pope held a consistory so soon after his election. John's intent was to guarantee Montini succession should anything happen to him in the short term. It is obvious to all but the most gullible, a deal had been struck between the aging Roncalli and the youthful Montini in the days leading up to the 1958 conclave.

The practice of listing their choice of succession first has been true of many popes. Albino Luciani led the list of thirty cardinals in Paul's consistory of March 5, 1973.

John did something else quite unusual. On the same day he made Montini a cardinal, John made both he and Montini's favorite son, Albino Luciani, a bishop.[5] One can only surmise this was to position Luciani to succeed Paul should Montini fall victim to foul play.

When Roncalli became archbishop of Venice he had adopted the young priest from Belluno as an aide. The bond between Montini and Luciani dated back much further. During the war, Luciani had intervened many times on behalf of the oppressed and often enlisted Montini's weight with Pius to bring about compassionate decisions.

History confirms a deal had been struck between Roncalli and Montini before the conclave began. What's more, those cardinals Montini had persuaded to vote for Roncalli in 1958 knew they were actually voting to place Montini in direct succession to the throne.

Setting this aside, there is the possibility strategy, politicking and collaborating among men has nothing to do with electing a pope. It may be Christ did speak to those cardinals committed to Montini in the conclave and told them to vote for Roncalli.

Although the choice of Pius remains vague, and the choice of John could not be more clear, there was no case more certain than was Paul's intent Albino Luciani succeed him.

Shoes of a Fisherman

Of all the demands Albino Luciani had made upon the Vatican through the years, none was more widely publicized than was his ongoing demand it liquidate its treasures to annihilate poverty and starvation. In his early years, he didn't have to look further than his own village to see poverty and starvation.

In the sixties, as a bishop, he saw much more. He became a close friend of Pericle Felici when the latter had served as papal nuncio to Africa. Through Felici's intervention Luciani established a mission in Africa and manned it with his own priests and monks.

When he first arrived in Vittorio Veneto and pressured his priests to sell their gold he gained worldwide attention. In the coming years, in an ongoing assault, Luciani brought public pressure on Rome to sell treasures held in warehouses and not on display to help finance his African venture, but to no avail. Nevertheless, of all the things Luciani had gained notice for, none had gained more press than his ongoing condemnation of the hypocrisy of the Vatican treasures.

In 1968, the Anthony Quinn movie *Shoes of the Fisherman* premiered. The film depicted the rise of a Russian to the papacy who resembled the real life Luciani to a tee. It told of a bishop who strolled in shorts and sandals incognito through the darkened ghettos of his diocese under assumed names and, most striking of all, it exploited Luciani's most widely known threat to Rome—liquidation of the Vatican treasures to annihilate poverty in the world.

In the film, Anthony Quinn, a newly appointed pontiff, shocks the world by announcing his intent to sell off the Vatican treasures to annihilate poverty and starvation in communist China.

That the leading character in the film so closely resembled Luciani and ignored, for the most part, the character Morris West had built into his 1963 novel brought the bishop of the Veneto country much notoriety. There is no mention at all of the liquidation of Vatican treasures in the book which is the focal point of the film. Regardless, the movie was a godsend for Luciani and the fame it brought him financed many of his third world ventures.

In the following year, 1969, Paul VI raised Luciani to Archbishop of Venice. The Pope sent a public message to the bishop of the remote mountain province. *"The time has come for you to begin your journey to Rome, for the gods of Hollywood have spoken!"*[6]

Everyone knew exactly what Paul was talking about.

The papal buzzer

Whenever, cardinals gathered in Rome and Luciani was among them, though only a common bishop, he sat next to Paul. In one well publicized instance at a public audience, Paul could not locate the little buzzer on his chair that would summon an attendant.

Luciani reached for Paul's hand and guided it to the button. Paul looked at him. Not aware the microphone would pick up his comment, said, *"So, you already know where the papal buzzer is."*[7]

The papal stole

In 1967, at Christmas service in Vittorio Veneto, Paul removed his stole and placed it upon Albino Luciani's shoulders. Through the years, Paul had often repeated this gesture. Yet, it usually went unnoticed until he did it in 1972 in the Piazza San Marco in Venice before twenty thousand people and an international television audience. Now the whole world knew Luciani was the choice.[8]

Stacking the College

In the early 1970s, Paul began stacking the College of Cardinals to the *left*. He raised the number of voting cardinals from eighty to one hundred twenty and filled most of the vacancies with liberals.

In the consistory of 1973, Paul not only made Luciani a cardinal and listed him first, but of the other twenty-nine appointed that day, there was not one who would not vote for Luciani.

As a follow-up to having raised the voting cardinals to one hundred twenty, he raised the authorized number of cardinals to one hundred thirty-eight in order to hold the voting conclave at one hundred twenty. This created eighteen additional voting vacancies, most of which had, in rapid consecutive order, been filled by Paul with liberals before his death. Of the last fifty-six cardinals Paul appointed, all but three were known to have liberal tendencies.

The voting conclave had remained at seventy for five hundred years. John XXIII, when elected, in order to guarantee his successor would be Montini, raised the number to eighty and made it clear he would not be restricted to it—when he died there were eighty-seven.

A cardinal has only two responsibilities—he elects a pope and advises a pope. Yet, popes have many closer advisers than cardinals from heads of state to common laymen, priests and nuns. It makes no difference whether he has fifty or a thousand cardinals. The only unique function of a cardinal is his role in electing a pope.

Paul's only possible motive in increasing the number of voting cardinals was the same as that of John. To guarantee his favorite son from Venice succeed him, he had only two choices: 1) he could refuse to reconfirm existing conservatives when their terms lapsed, or 2) increase the authorized number of cardinals and fill the vacancies with liberals. Something we know, in retrospect, he did.

Paul also eliminated cardinals over eighty from voting—at the time all eighteen over eighty were ultraconservatives who otherwise

122

would have voted against Luciani. Had Paul not made this particular change, his successor would not have been Albino Luciani.

As he lay on his death bed, Paul could be reasonably confident through the process of addition that Luciani had about seventy-five votes; a marginal win—the two-thirds plus one vote required. Yet, he could not be certain his choice would succeed him.

Barely conscious, falling in and out of a coma, the night before he died, Paul promoted Cardinal Yu Pin of Taiwan, to the position of Grand Chancellor of Eastern Affairs—the most powerful position in the Eastern Hemisphere. His intent was to give Yu Pin the influence in the upcoming conclave to add the dozen or so eastern cardinals to Luciani's list. When Paul went to rest, he knew Albino Luciani, the brave young priest he had once saved from excommunication, would succeed him. That is, if nothing happened to Yu Pin.

The Opus Dei candidate

In that all modern popes have succeeded to the papacy through the influence of their predecessors, one might wonder how Karol Wojtyla, unknown in the media, wiggled his way into the papacy.

Being the conservative he was, Karol knew he would never get the nod from Paul. We know him as the most widely traveled pope in history. He was also the most widely traveled cardinal.

In the ten years he was a cardinal, Karol visited more than two hundred cities. He visited almost every field cardinal, including his well publicized six-week trips to the United States in 1969 and 1977 in which he visited every city where a cardinal was in residence.

There is no record these trips had to do with fund raising. One might ask, what reason could he have had to have spent so much money from the poor box for so many expensive vacations? What could these trips have to do with his responsibilities as archbishop of Krakow? The only logical answer is he was lining up the votes.

In the 1978 conclaves, Wojtyla was the only member who had a personal relationship with each of the others. He had slept in each of their mansions, had tasted wine with each of them at dinner and enjoyed morning breakfast with each of them on their verandahs.

In truth, Karol did not rob the poor box to pay for his trips.

Like Albino Luciani, Karol Wojtyla had a benefactor who would pave his way to the top. The Polish cardinal's ten year 'campaign' was funded by his good friend Josemaria Escriva, founder of Opus Dei. Wojtyla and Escriva had met in 1965 at the Vatican II Council in Rome. The following year Karol made his first 'campaign' trip.

Opus Dei is a commune; it requires members to contribute most of their income to the cult. Though a secret society, it is no secret it uses its resources for political purposes and it is no secret, today, it financed the Polish cardinal to the pinnacle of the Catholic world.

Opus Dei is an order of extremists. It believes salvation can be obtained only through adoration. It does not believe helping others has anything to do with it. Although Opus Dei is per capita one of the richest organizations in the world, it does little to help others.

Its sole brush with charity is its *Harambee* mission in Africa which it uses as a pretext to indoctrinate youth into its fascist fold.[9]

It was founded in 1928 when movements within and outside the Church started to move Catholicism toward the *left*.

Women gained the right to vote and were threatening to leave the kitchen. Jews were permitted to practice their religion in Catholic countries. Homosexuality was gaining a level of tolerance.

On the world stage, the Soviet Union, the great enemy of *fascism*, was coming to power. In his own country of Spain, democracy was raising its ugly brow. All these things horrified Escriva.

Escriva's thesis, *The Way,* dictates the path to salvation: *"Blessed be pain. Loved be pain. Sanctified be pain. Glorified be pain."* It so closely mirrored *Mein Kampf* he was accused of plagiarism.[10]

In the late thirties, Licio Gelli, an officer in Mussolini's *black shirts* who had once served as an intelligence officer under Hitler, was sent to Spain to support Franco's insurrection of the Spanish people. Escriva and Gelli quickly struck up an enduring relationship.

Escriva and Gelli were at his side when Franco came to power in 1939. Opus Dei quickly infiltrated Franco's cabinet and brought about ruthless oppression of the Spanish people—the clandestine cult providing the ideology and Franco providing the executioners. Together they murdered over a million innocent people.

In March 1941, Escriva praised their great ally, *"Hitler will take care of the Jews. Hitler will take care of the Slavs."*[11] After the war, he would minimize the damage. Escriva told a reporter, *"History is unfair to Hitler. It claims he murdered more than six million in his camps, whereas, less than four million actually died."*[12]

Gelli's *rat line* funneled Nazis to South America. Although Gelli usually gets the historical credit because he headed it up, the *rat line* was in reality an Opus Dei scheme of which Gelli was a member.

In 1946, Escriva and Gelli enlisted Carlos Fuldner into the ranks of Opus Dei. Fuldner had been an officer in Hitler's SS Guard and an old friend of Escriva, probably why Escriva was able to make his remark in 1941 *'Hitler will take care of the Jews..."* as only the SS Guard knew what was going on in the death camps at that time.

Gelli and Fuldner ran rescue efforts from Madrid to Argentina for Nazi war criminals seeking refuge. Among those rescued were Adolph Eichmann and Josef Mengele though there are conflicting reports the latter may have escaped through the Pius XII *rat line*—a network of monasteries from Poland through in Italy to Naples.[13]

Knowing he controlled many votes, Alvaro Portillo, primate of Opus Dei, invited Luciani to address its convention. In his invitation, he cited the commonality of Luciani and Escriva—*Imitation of Christ.* The strategy was to win Luciani's support for Wojtyla.

Luciani refused, *"True. Msgr. Escriva and I are in common. We both believe the Imitation of Christ is the path to holiness. Yet, Escriva's teachings are materialistic. He believes salvation can be had solely through the Imitation of Christ's death, self-flagellation and the chanting of vain repetitions. I believe salvation can only be had only through the Imitation of Christ's life, in helping others... "*[14]

When Opus Dei met in Milan the next month Portillo introduced its candidate as *"Papa Stanislao."* The crowd broke into a frenzy for forty minutes before Wojtyla was able to begin his speech. *Stanislao* was Karol's chosen name should he ever rise to the top.[15]

When Karol Wojtyla rose to the papacy, like Franco before him, his cabinet was infiltrated by Opus Dei members from Agostino Casaroli at the top down to his valet Angelo Gugel at the bottom.

His personal secretary, Stanislaw Dziwisz, was a flagellation practitioner of the cult as if to hint His Holiness, himself, required an occasional flogging of the rump while he prayed the rosary.

When, in 1982, John Paul II raised Opus Dei to *Prelature of the Holy See,* he did it in the face of an uproar, not only among Jews, Slavs, homosexuals and others Escriva had persecuted through the years, but among men and women of good conscience all over the world. Twenty years later, when he canonized Escriva a saint, it confirmed to all—except the most gullible—a tit-for-tat deal had been made between Josemaria Escriva and Karol Wojtyla in 1965.

Conclave rules

Unlike what one might think, popes are not elected in conclaves. Consider the rules as they apply before, during and after a conclave.

If a cardinal discusses anything relative to an election before, during or after a conclave, he automatically self-excommunicates himself. No cardinal has ever revealed anything that pertains to an election whether it occurred before, during or after a conclave.

Yes, after a cardinal dies, an author might claim the cardinal had confided with him before his death and write a book to capitalize on the suckers. Yet, no media has ever published what a cardinal might have said out of conclave while he was still alive.

In the two weeks between a pope's funeral and the ensuing conclave, the cardinals are sequestered together in Rome.

Unlike what the public might believe, this time is not spent in prayer. It is spent electing the next pope. Cardinals can often be spotted in the *red cap*-frequented haunts in the city chatting away.

Although cardinals are forbidden to allow personal relationships to influence their vote, there is nothing in the rules prohibiting lobbying, nominating, negotiating, politicking or even tallying of votes before a conclave begins, provided it is done privately.

In that popes in recent history have been elected on either the first or second day, it is obvious the cardinals have already known the choice when the conclaves began. Otherwise, in a secret election as required by conclave rules, it would take years before anyone would by chance come up with two-thirds of the votes.

Once a conclave convenes, however, the rules tighten up. Unlike what the media, fiction writers and Hollywood might portray, no lobbying, nominating or politicking is permitted—only silent prayer.

Yet, rules have changed from time to time. At one time, cardinals were permitted to be accompanied by aides and other assistance.

In 1976, Paul tightened up the rules, making the 1978 conclaves the most covert in history. He restricted attendance to the cardinals.

The seating arrangement

There is a supposition based on innocent Vatican releases that have reported the winner has been consistently seated in the center chair of the first table on the St. Peter's side of the Sistine Chapel.

These same press releases through the years have also confirmed that the most likely runner-up was seated in the center chair of the first table on the opposite side of the Chapel.

This would suggest that at the end of each ballot, the counters place the leading vote getters in a pre-arranged seating arrangement.

For example, in the election that chose Montini in 1963, *The Times* reported, *"...The Secretary of State approached the cardinal of Milan who was seated in the center of the first row and opposite him was Cardinal Siri of Genoa..."* and in Luciani's election, *"...Cardinal Villot came to the cardinal bishop in the center seat. Directly opposite him was Karol Wojtyla of Poland..."* and, again, in Wojtyla's election, *"... Villot placed his hand on the shoulder of the Polish cardinal who was seated in the center chair..."*[16]

Media mayhem

There is no other major world event in which the public is more vulnerable to the press than is a papal election.

The reason is that no one, other than the participating cardinals, knows what goes on in a conclave. This affords the press the chance to sensationalize events beyond one's wildest imagination.

Despite the fact Paul had named Luciani his successor and had made many strategic moves publicly to that end, no newspaper in the world considered him a candidate. Despite *The Times* knew Wojtyla had campaigned around the globe and had, itself, reported Wojtyla had been seated in the *runner-up chair* in the Luciani election, it did not consider him to be a factor in the second conclave of 1978.

Despite that it had published a list of a dozen candidates led by Benelli and Siri in each election and not listed either Luciani or Wojtyla, the day Wojtyla was elected, it reported, *"...Benelli fell five votes short on the first ballot...The conclave then turned to Colombo who took himself out of the race...Unable to decide on an Italian cardinal on the first day, the College decided to look elsewhere and elected the Polish cardinal on the second day."*[17]

How did *The Times* possibly know this?

No one knows the name of the cardinal who leaked this to *The Times*. In reality, no cardinal leaked it to *The Times*. It made it up.

Yet, everyone believes this to this day despite that no one other than the cardinals know what took place. Everyone believes this to this day despite that the media had demonstrated in its predictions it knows nothing about what goes on when a pope is elected.

This not only fails to explain the question why the same cardinals elected a liberal in one election and elected a conservative a few weeks later; it makes it even more absurd. In one ballot, almost two-thirds of the conclave voted for a liberal—Benelli—and, a few hours later, more than two-thirds of them elected a conservative—Wojtyla.

Benelli was even further to the *left* than was Luciani.

Concerning matters like sanctification of remarriage, for example, Luciani would have moved authority to the bishop level; Benelli would have moved authority to the individuals involved.

The press would have one believe the Polish cardinal had not been considered at all on the first day, and, on the second day, despite cardinals are not permitted to lobby, nominate or politick under the conclave rules, made a complete about-face and switched from a liberal to a conservative on the spur of the moment.

This is not to say, despite the rules, some chatting does go on between ballots and this chatting can gain a few votes for candidates, but surely never a gain of two-thirds of the votes in a single windfall.

Yet, this is how books and motion pictures have described the election of John Paul II ever since, *"...Unable to decide upon an Italian cardinal on the first day, the College decided to look elsewhere and elected the Polish cardinal on the second day."*[17]

This is just not how the real world works.

'Luciani was elected on the fourth ballot on the first day'

Prior to 1978, the number of ballots had never been announced in papal elections as conclave rules required burning of the ballots after each vote. It was no secret as the number of puffs of smoke from the Sistine Chapel told the world how many ballots had been cast.

John XXIII's election involved only 53 voters and took four days and eleven puffs of smoke—eleven ballots—as many as three ballots a day. Paul VI's election involved 87 voters and took three days and six puffs of smoke—six ballots—as many as three ballots a day.

In each case, one puff of smoke bellowed on the first day.

There was no change in the 1978 rules concerning the burning of ballots—they were required to be burned after each vote.

On the day Luciani was elected, two puffs of smoke rose from the

Sistine Chapel, the last one as the sun went down in the west. It was obvious to all, Luciani was elected on the first ballot and a second vote had been taken in an attempt to make the election unanimous.

World newspapers speculated the election had been prearranged. Luciani had been elected in the days leading up to the conclave.

To cover up the politicking that goes on between the death of a pope and the ensuing conclave, Vatican Radio reacting quickly to this 'misconception.' On the following day, it reported, *"John Paul the First was elected on the fourth ballot on the first day..."*[18]

This is what got into the history books, *'Luciani was elected on the fourth ballot on the first day.'* Despite that under the conclave rules of 1978, ballots were required to be burned after each ballot.

Despite that in previous elections, with half as many voters, the cardinals had found time for only one vote on the first day.

The number of ballots

Aside from the puffs of smoke, a simple process of mathematics proves Luciani was elected on the first ballot.

Proceedings of the first day[19] required a minimum of five hours:

Mass in St. Peter's
Veni Creator Spiritus Procession
The sealing of the conclave
Camerlengo leads the cardinals in the reading of the oath of secrecy
Invocation prayer – Cardinal Secretary of State
The reading of the rules of election – Camerlengo
The elections of the counters
Oaths of the counters
Lunch including restroom privileges
Sermons by the senior Cardinal Deacon, the senior Cardinal Priest and the senior Cardinal Bishop take place anytime during the first day
Balloting according to the rules of the 1978 conclave

A round of voting is to begin each day at 9.30 A.M. and 4.30 P.M.

But Vatican spokesmen admitted they did not know whether ballots can be taken morning and evening under the lengthy procedures to be used. Each cardinal must walk to the altar in the chapel, say a brief prayer, vote and return. Then the votes must be counted and recounted.

The Times London October 15, 1978

The 1978 conclave rules called for two rounds of voting per day except for the morning of the first day.

A 111 cardinal conclave—a minute and a half each yields 166 minutes or two and three-quarter hours per ballot—plus scrutinizing, counting, burning of ballots—three to four hours per ballot.

Each slip has the name of the voting cardinal (preprinted) and the name of the cardinal he voted for (handwritten). The scrutinizers check each slip to be certain a cardinal has not voted for himself.

If the number of slips does not agree with the number of voting cardinals or if the count fails the ballots together with tally slips and any notes taken are burned together with a chemical which produces a puff of black smoke from the Sistine Chapel.

If a candidate gains two thirds plus one vote the ballots are recounted and then scrutinized again to be sure the winner did not vote for himself and final checks and balances are made. The count is verified by the Camerlengo and the ballots are burned with straw producing a puff of white smoke—a new pope has been elected.

The number of ballots possible in a 111 cardinal conclave is one or possibly two on the first day. The maximum number of ballots on succeeding days is four. So one knows there could not have been four ballots on the first day of Luciani's election. The Vatican lied.

We are speaking of the rules that governed the 1978 conclaves.

In 1996, reflecting the number of daily ballots possible in a 120 cardinal conclave, John Paul II changed the rules—one ballot on the first day and four ballots on succeeding days. The ballots would no longer be burned after each vote; they would be burned twice a day.

Luciani's election involved 111 voters and two ballots. Luciani was elected on the first ballot, the second ballot being an attempt to secure a unanimous vote. As the cardinals entered the conclave, they already knew who they were going to vote for—and why.

In the election of 2005, Joseph Ratzinger was the overwhelming favorite as he had been elected by the same cardinals to be the ranking cardinal—Dean of the College of Cardinals—in 2002. That they had elected him to the second ranking job in the Catholic world it make sense they would elect him to the top job.

It was a surprise to the press when a puff of smoke appeared late the first day and the results were not announced until the second day. It reasoned Ratzinger, having won the election on the first ballot, asked that recounts be taken on the second day.

Like Luciani, Joseph Ratzinger also won on the first ballot. The cardinals already knew who they were going to vote for before they entered the conclave—and why.

This will continue to be true of all future papal elections as long as conclave rules prohibit the lobbying, nominating politicking and tallying of votes that goes on when a pope is elected.

It was also true of John Paul II.

'Wojtyla was elected on the eighth ballot on the second day'

Though deliberations leading up to the conclave which elected Luciani were widely reported in the press, those leading up to Wojtyla's election were mostly kept under the table to avoid the rumors which had surfaced concerning Luciani's election.

The media had attributed Luciani's 'quick' election to lobbying, nominating and tallying of votes before the conclave opened.

One journalist gave a convincing report the election of Luciani had actually taken place over beer and wine at *Eau L' Vive*. He cited a newspaper article confirming dozens of key cardinals had enjoyed festivities at the quaint French restaurant behind the Pantheon for eight hours just two days before Luciani was elected.[20]

Then there is the famous comment of Cardinal Delargey to a reporter as he entered the conclave, *"I'll see you tomorrow."*[21]

This seemed to be confirmed by Luciani, himself, in his first pontifical words to his newly acquired congregation, *"A funny thing happened on the way to the conclave..."*[22] implying the cardinals had already decided on the winner before the conclave opened.

To prevent a recurrence of what had happened in his case, actions were taken to restrict gatherings of cardinals in Rome. No cardinals showed up at *Eau L' Vive* or other traditional haunts of the *red caps* in Rome in the days leading up to the second conclave of 1978.

The most one could come up with was that a group of cardinals attended a private Mass and gathered for the afternoon in the Church of Saint Andrew's at Quirinal on October 8, 1978, the last Sunday before the conclave that elected John Paul II convened.

The group—representative of moderates and conservatives in the conclave—included Wojtyla, Siri, Cody and Krol, Arns of Brazil, Gantin of Africa and Curia cardinals Hume, Baggio and Poletti. Among those not cardinals, were Wojtyla's seminary roommate bishop Deskur and Polish Bishop Rubin——Secretary of the Synod of Bishops——and Caprio and Casaroli and a few others.[23]

It is its St. Stanislaus Kostka Chapel that makes this church on Quirinal Hill in Rome a tourist attraction. Stanislaus—a 16th century Polish Jesuit novice——was Wojtyla's chosen saint.

It is said the Holy Spirit works in strange and mysterious ways. Perhaps, 'He' had already picked Karol for the top job?

One will never know.

Newspapers did report pre-conclave collaborations in the Vatican customary of all papal elections.

> The last of 10 preconclave meetings was held yesterday by the College of Cardinals as workmen put finishing touches on the Sistine Chapel for the world's oldest and one of its most secret and important elections.
> The cardinals drew lots for the cells

Washington Post October 17, 1978

In announcing Karol Wojtyla's election, the Vatican reported *'John Paul II was elected on the eighth ballot on the second day.'*[23]

For starters, one knows there could have only been one vote——at the most two votes—on the first day. The Vatican lied again.

Yet, this is what history has recorded, *'John Paul II was elected on the eighth ballot on the second day.'*

The Polish Pope confirmed the number of ballots possible on the first day of a 120 cardinal conclave in his 1996 change in conclave rules—*'one ballot on the first day, four ballots on succeeding days.'*

The myth *"The cardinals, unable to agree on an Italian cardinal on the first day, decided to look elsewhere on the second day"* rests on the supposition there had been four ballots on the first day.

The process of mathematics tells us there was only one ballot on the first day—certainly not nearly enough to conclude *'...unable to agree on an Italian cardinal on the first day.'*

Nevertheless, Karol Wojtyla, like Albino Luciani before him and Joseph Ratzinger after him, already had most of the votes he needed to win when the conclave that elected him opened on the first day.

He was elected on the first day of the conclave that elected him.

132

The election was announced on the second day to obscure the politicking that goes on before the conclave opened.

This will continue to be true of future elections. The candidate will be elected on the first ballot on the first day, yet, it will be announced on the second day to obscure the politicking that goes on when a pope is elected.

Perhaps, at times, to obscure when the politicking that goes on when a pope is elected turns to murder.

> His stunningly quick selection by leaders of a Church that has been beset with internal division was marked, amid confusion, by the smoke that billowed from the unimposing smokestack atop the Sistine Chapel at 6:24 p.m. (12:24 p.m. Philadelphia time).

Philadelphia Inquirer August 27, 1978

1 *L'Osservatore Romano* 15 Jan 53 - *The Times,* London 25 Jan 53
2 search: cardinal consistories 1953
3 *La Repubblica* 16 Jan 53
4 *La Repubblica* 16 Dec 58 or search: cardinal consistories xx century
5 *La Repubblica* 16 Dec 58 or search: Albino Luciani reputable biographies
6 *La Repubblica* 16 Dec 69
7 *L'Osservatore Romano* 6 Aug 67
8 *Veneto Nostro* 26 Dec 67 - *La Repubblica* 2 Apr 72
9 *Harambee Wikipedia*
10 *The Way* Escriva - *Mein Kampf* Adolph Hitler
11 *Metro Madrid* 2 Mar 41
12 *IL Mondo* 7 May 47 The recorded count is 4 million, total count estimated at 6 million
13 *Odessa File* Frederick Forsyth
14 *Messaggero Mestre* 3 Feb 78
15 *Corriere della Sera* 2 Mar 78
16 *The Times,* London 22 Jun 63 – 27 Aug 78 – 17 Oct 78
17 *The Times,* London 18 Oct 78
18 *Vatican Radio* 28 Aug 78
19 *Catholic Encyclopedia* and canon 1978 conclave rules
20 *La Stampa* 28 Aug 78
21 *La Mondo* 27 Aug 78
22 *La Repubblica* 4 Sep 78
23 *Vatican Radio* 18 Oct 78
24 *La Repubblica* 9 Oct 78

Chapter 12

The Murders of Cardinals Filipiak and Gracias

Two days before Pope Paul's funeral, the Interim Pope received almost identical telegrams from opposite sides of the globe.

Jean Cardinal Villot, Sovereign State of the Vatican

Most Holy Eminence,

As we prepared to go to the airport, today, His Eminence was stricken with severe stomach pain. We had to return to Bombay.
I will keep you advised on his recovery; that he will attend the conclave.

Raj Sharma
Secretary Valerian Gracias, Primate of India.

Jean Cardinal Villot, Sovereign State of the Vatican

Most Holy Eminence,

On the way to the airport, today, His Eminence was stricken with severe stomach pain. We had to return to Gniezno.
I will keep you advised. We expect he will attend the upcoming conclave.

Kolab Mizenski
Secretary Boleshaw Filipiak, Archbishop of Gniezno.

Gracias died midway through John Paul's papacy in a Bombay Catholic hospital of an ailment the press reported doctors were unable to diagnose and therefore could not treat. His death certificate reads *'inoperable adenocarcinoma of stomach area'*—cancer.[1]

Filipiak died on the day before his lifelong enemy Karol Wojtyla was elected to the papacy. Cause of death has never been disclosed either by the Vatican or the press.[2]

1 *Maharashtra Times* 16 Sep 78   The Vatican can control what goes on a death certificate in a Catholic hospital. Gracias' certificate has the identical wording *'inoperable adenocarcinoma of stomach area'* of Cardinal Delargey death certificate also stricken during the 1978 conclaves
2 *Catholic Encyclopedia* 2nd *Edition.*

Chapter 13

The Murder of Cardinal Yu Pin

There were some events that surrounded the funeral of Paul VI that may have been related to the first conclave of 1978.

The day before Paul's funeral, Belgium radio announced Leon Joseph Cardinal Suenens, Primate of Belgium, had been killed by a falling section of an aging building façade in Brussels. The radio report, based on eyewitnesses of the event, was premature.[1]

It had been a visiting French bishop that had been killed. It had been that the incident occurred near the cardinal's palace and the bishop was wearing black garb topped off with a red zucchetto that caused witnesses to mistake him for the cardinal.

Of course, if this was true, witnesses on the ground made such a misjudgment, it was likely anyone on the roof would have made the same mistake. Suenens, leader of liberalism in the Catholic world, would be one of the most influential members in the conclave. Yet, the incident was a mere foretelling of what was about to occur.

Cardinal Yu Pin keeled over at Paul's funeral. The Vatican cited 'heart attack.' Cardinal Delargey, closest friend of Yu Pin who had shared rooms with him the night before, called for an autopsy. He assured the press Yu Pin had no history of heart disease. Several newspapers demanded an autopsy. The body was quickly embalmed and returned in a triple-sealed coffin to Taipei for interment.[2]

A week later came another strange happening. Cardinals Benelli and Suenens narrowly escaped death when a small section of a frieze fell from the Torre Borgia missing them by inches. Though Vatican buildings are aging, this is rare, as the facades are routinely checked for defects to protect the tourists that roam Vatican City.

A notice in the Vatican paper called for increased inspection.[3]

In Brussels, the situation was different. Because the incident resembled so closely that which had killed the bishop two weeks earlier, the press pointed fingers.[3] Yet, in time, the incidents were discarded as having been mere coincidence.

1 *Le Soir Brussels* 10 Aug 78
2 *London Times* 9 Aug 78 details of Yu Pin's death is covered on the Internet
3 *L'Osservatore Romano* 22 Aug 78 *Le Soir Brussels* 25 Aug 78

Chapter 14

The Good Guys vs. the Bad Guy

"Some kinds of people are born better than others and are entitled to more, little boys are better than little girls, etc." The Roman Catholic Church

Albino Luciani – John Paul I
Karol Wojtyla – John Paul II
Joseph Ratzinger – Benedict XVI

John Paul I and his successors John Paul II and Benedict XVI were very different kinds of men, the latter fixed conservatives and the former a moderate-liberal. Yet, just how far apart were these men in their ideologies and why did they think so very differently?

To begin with, one must consider their upbringing.

Both Karol Wojtyla and Joseph Ratzinger were born into well-to-do families. Unlike Albino Luciani, they never knew what it was to wonder where their next meal was coming from.

This made them less compassionate of the poor; they were able to champion a ban on contraception and sleep on pillows of down in magnificent palaces and think it right.

Conversely, Luciani supported the pill. Conscious that the ban on contraception was the driving force behind the spread of disease, poverty and starvation in third world countries, he thought it wrong.

More fundamental to the men they would become, Albino had been born to a mishmash of parents—an atheist father and a devout mother—while Karol and Joseph had been born to devout parents of the conviction that whatever the men in Rome had to say was right.

Karol Wojtyla

From the age of six through the time he entered college, Karol was educated in expensive prep schools which even today are reserved for the rich. His early years were spent in the Wadowice Military Academy which brainwashed its students in fascism.

Non-Christians in Poland were made to live in ghettos and children of ethnic origin were not provided opportunity particularly higher education. To preserve the purity of the white race, blacks

were not allowed in Poland, This was also true of Italy and other Catholic countries in Europe.

Karol has been unduly criticized because he refused to join the resistance and instead went to work for the Nazis. This is not fair. In Poland, just about everyone went to work for the Nazis. What's more, they went to work for the Nazis eagerly.

8 year old Karol with mother

That is, except for a few—mostly Jews and Jew supporters—who escaped to the sewers. It was in Krakow, the resistance picked up the nickname *'the Underground'* where it was literally confined to the drains which ran under the city.

It was that the Poles were so intensely fascists—anti-Semitic, homophobic, atheist-haters and anti-socialists—most extermination camps were built in Poland and the overwhelming number of those who lost their lives in the Holocaust—including a million children—died in Poland.[1] This doesn't mean the Poles were bad people, just that they were good Catholics—zealous cohorts of the men in Rome.

This is demonstrated that the Nazis never tried to hide the atrocity from the Poles, the largest and most dreadful camps were located in the largest metropolitan areas—Treblinka at Warsaw and Auschwitz at Krakow—to draw on the Polish workforce.

The Auschwitz extermination system alone included forty-eight camps and there were scores or others besides Treblinka—Sobibor, Belzec, Chelmno, you name them. It took millions of men to build and maintain them with their ovens and gas chambers in such a short time. Though the Nazis oversaw their construction, Hitler did not divert millions of soldiers from his front lines. The Poles built them.

The heaviest toll of all was in the Auschwitz system a stone's throw from Wadowice where Karol had been born and grown up. Karol and his fellow Poles could peer through the barbed fence and see what was going on. Actually, they knew what was going on as many of them provided maintenance and other specialty services to the camp on an ongoing basis. The first Jews herded into an extermination camp during the war came from the sewers of Krakow and later out of ghettos of the same city.

Karol, like other Polish youths, shared the ideologies of Hitler and Pius XII—white superiority segregation of blacks, persecution of homosexuals, Jews, Muslims and other ethnic peoples—fascism—*some kinds of people are better than others and are entitled to more.* Karol, like most everyone else, was caught up in the *Opium of the Masses—Christianity—fascism.*

At the time, this was the way the population thought. Even those oppressed thought it was God's intention they live subordinated lives. We see this even today where seven hundred million members of the so-called fair sex pay a man in Rome for their salvation—a man who conditions their children from an early age little boys are better than little girls—the most fundamental discriminatory canon of the Roman Catholic Church. We see this today where millions of homosexuals pay this same man for their salvation, among the most homophobic men who ever lived. We see this even today where...

One would wonder why Poland fell in a few days.

The Poles and the Nazis shared the same ideals. Their common enemy was *communism,* not *fascism.* In Poland, Karol was just one of an army of millions of Polish fascists who enthusiastically went to work building ammunition and supplies for the German army.

The Poles built much of the infrastructure Hitler needed to fight his war. They broke ground on Auschwitz a week after Germany's occupation and had it up and running in the space of a few months. They built hundreds of supply plants including the IG Farben and Solvay chemical plants which annexed the main Auschwitz camps.[2]

Karol progressed rapidly from a quarry to a supervisory position in the Solvay chemical plant. Among other military supplies, the plant produced chemicals used to gas prisoners in death camps.[3]

In his job as distribution supervisor, Karol traveled to Treblinka and other camps in the Nazi extermination system. *The Man Who Would Be Pope* staring John Voight depicts Karol as quartermaster of the Solvay supply depot. A resistance leader, Boleshaw Filipiak solicits Karol to divert supplies to the resistance; Karol refuses.[4]

While at Solvay, Karol joined a theater group. The love of his life was the theater. He wanted to be an actor. The record shows he was quite an actor usually commanding the leading role. Twenty-two year old Karol is shown here

in the leading role of a romantic satire of Hitler's youth performed before Nazi officers. One could ask, if he wanted to be an actor and had no interest in the priesthood, why he entered a seminary? [5]

As the war progressed and an allied victory became imminent, Polish youth—who like the Germans were devout Christians—were forced into the German Army—particularly true of youths like Karol who had shown loyalty and were rising in the Nazi civilian ranks.

To escape enlistment, Karol entered a seminary. During the war no adult male was exempt from the draft including fathers of young children. Even advancing age was no excuse. If a man was able-bodied he was inducted. The exception was enrollment in a seminary owed to the immense demand for chaplains in the German army.

Seminary deferment gave Karol a window of two years in which time he gambled the war would be over. While in the seminary Karol realized he could use his acting abilities in the Church. There was a great similarity between the two professions as both preachers and actors dealt with the world of make-believe. [5]

Eagle's Nest

Unlike Karol Wojtyla, Joseph Ratzinger wanted to be a priest from the start. As already mentioned, when he was five, Joseph fell in love with the Archbishop of Munich's elaborate gown and announced at dinner that evening he was going to be a cardinal.[6]

Obersalzberg[7] is a sprawling mountainside resort area tucked in between the village of Berchtesgaden and the district of Traunstein in southeastern Germany. In 1933, Hitler built his residence here— the Berghof. Other Nazis including Adolf Eichmann, Herman Goring, Heinrich Himmler and Martin Bormann, had homes here.

Hitler headquartered his SS Guard—the Leibstandarte—in nearby Traunstein.[8] Hitler's pride and joy the Traunstein Scouts—a composite of the *Jungvolk,* ages 10-14, and the *Hitler Youth,* ages 14 and up—operated under the auspices of the SS Guard. To put it bluntly, the Traunstein-Berchtesgaden area was crawling with Nazis.

In the spring of 1937, Martin Bormann broke ground on Eagle's Nest—a mountaintop retreat—a gift from the Third Reich to its Fuhrer in honor of his fiftieth birthday.[9]

A strange happening

In the spring of 1937, Joseph's father, a police officer in western Bavaria, did a strange thing. At a time retirement was not a part of a common man's life and Hitler needed every man either on the front lines or in factories, he took 'early retirement.'

Yet, even more bizarre, at a time when most people died in the same village which they had been born, he moved his family from what had been for centuries their ancestral home in Marktl am Inn in western Bavaria all the way across the country to Traunstein.[10]

In his biographies Joseph Ratzinger claims, *"My father hated the Nazis and what they stood for…"* As we know today, they stood for the same thing both the Vatican and Hitler stood for at that time.

One can wonder why he pulled his family up from their ancestral roots and moved them across the country to the heart of Nazism in the western world and took a house a few kilometers from Kehlstein Mountain at the precise time Eagle's Nest was woven at its top.

The only logical answer suggests he was employed as a security officer at the Hitler compound or was a member of the SS Guard located in Traunstein? Is there any other explanation?[10]

Yet, what one does know is that his father hated the Nazis so much he moved his family to Traunstein which was crawling with them, forcing Joseph into Hitler's personal scout troop.

It is reasonable to surmise Joseph had the privilege to have been reviewed by the Fuhrer as the Traunstein troops were often invited to Eagle's Nest. Yet, the extent of their relationship is not known.

Joseph Ratzinger age 14

at Eagle's Nest

In 1984, when photos surfaced of John Paul II's fascist activities in the war, he ordered destroyed incriminating photos of prominent cardinals; the reason few wartime photos of Benedict have survived. Nevertheless, what does the man have to say for himself today?

"...It was on my tenth birthday we arrived in Traunstein...at first, inducted into the Jungvolk...on my fourteenth birthday I was promoted to the Hitler Scout troop as required by law. Yet, I did not participate in the scouts and refused to attend meetings. I tried to get an exemption by entering a seminary but as the tide began to turn against the Axis powers in 1943 and the draft age was lowered to sixteen. I was drafted into the army and assigned to an anti-aircraft battery protecting a depot in Hungary. Still I refused to fire a shot. A year later I became a part of the Austrian Legion...When the end of the war became imminent in 1945, I deserted..." Benedict XVI [10]

"...refused to attend meetings? ...refused to fire a shot?" I can't say for sure, but I don't think this is how armies are run. *"Thou shalt not bear false witness?"* Joseph, now, Joseph?

It is not unusual for those who were the 'good guys' who fought to maintain the status quo of yesterday, when the 'bad guys' of yesterday won the race and became the 'good guys' of today, to claim to be the 'bad guys' of yesterday and the 'good guys' of today.

Nevertheless, neither of these men—Karol Wojtyla and Joseph Ratzinger—have come clean of their past. What's more, they have been unable to break free of what the little boy Albino Luciani's father once called, the *Opium of the Masses—*Christianity—*some kinds of people are better than others and are entitled to more.*

The reason, I suppose, Gandhi said, *"I love your Christ. But I do not like your Christians."* [11]

Coincidence

By sheer coincidence, in a few minutes, it is possible to take a tour bus from the stately home in which Karol Wojtyla grew up in Wadowice to the Military Academy where he was schooled to the Auschwitz concentration camp he would pass each day on his the way to the Solvay chemical plant where he worked for the Nazis. It is possible in the same few minutes to take a bus from the house Joseph Ratzinger lived in up the mountain to Hitler's Eagle's Nest and even less time to visit the SS Guard headquarters in Traunstein.

Regardless, it is a remarkable coincidence, Karol Wojtyla who during his formidable years had been dressed in the military uniform of a fascist school and Joseph Ratzinger who during his formidable years wore the military uniform of the Jungvolk and Hitler Scouts, both having been guided by devout parents, rose to the helm of the Roman Catholic Church.

It is even a more remarkable coincidence, Karol Wojtyla who had once furnished cyanide pellets which were used to gas men, women and children in the extermination camps and Joseph Ratzinger who had once protected a depot which herded Jews to the same camps would both eventually succeed to the papacy.

Albino Luciani

Just where was Albino Luciani during the war?

During the early war he seemed not much better than the others.

As a seminarian exempt from military service he was studying for his doctorate at the Gregorian University in Rome. His presence in Rome gave birth to stories he was a member of the resistance in Rome, something, other than an incident in which he interceded in behalf of Jews docked at Naples, seems unsubstantiated.

Later in the war, on returning to the Veneto country, he developed a knack for mountain climbing while ministering to members of the resistance hiding in difficult to get at places in the Italian Alps. Here, he wears the soft cap of the Italian Resistance.

He spoke of the most difficult moment of his life; he felt the pulse of a boy run out between his fingers—shot while blowing up a railroad trestle to cut off military supplies coming from Germany.

The end of a dream

Regardless, if Hitler had won the war, all that Karol and Joseph had ever dreamed of would have become a reality. We would, today, be living in a world of white male superiority rather than in this world in which we find ourselves, this world of equal rights and dignity for everyone, this anti-*Christian,* anti-*Fascist* world of justice for all, which, as we speak, threatens to be extended to homosexuals, transsexuals and worst of all, atheists—people who bring their children up in the real world of today rather than the make-believe world of yesterday.

World War II broke the backbone of fascism which had been the way of life in the western world for thirty-five hundred years. Unlike previous wars, it did much more than to decide the superiority of one nation over another. From its embers would rise the social evolution beginning with integration and eventually expanding into feminism, planned parenthood, sexual education, divorce and remarriage, single parenthood, gay liberation, the right to believe or not to believe, and a general trend away from a Vatican controlled state.

After the war, both Wojtyla and Ratzinger rose up as leaders in the effort to preserve segregation of blacks and whites. Luciani rose up as an anti-segregationist, not only in the Church but in society as well. As feminism, homosexuality, divorce and remarriage and other faucets of the social revolution raised their 'ugly' heads, Wojtyla and Ratzinger raised their voices and held up their hands to stop them while Luciani became a part of them. At the time, Wojtyla and Ratzinger were the 'good guys.' Luciani was the 'bad guy.' One knows where the courage was. The masses were overwhelmingly against each of these uprisings as they were put on the table.

After the war, referring to the dangers of the gullibility of men, Luciani told a reporter, *"It was not so much Hitler and Mussolini who were the culprits in this thing, as it was the ignorance and the weakness of the minds of the masses that believed in them"*[12]

Two different Gods

Perhaps the greatest difference between these men was their relative doctrinal convictions. Whenever doctrine placed undue hardship on the lives of innocent people, Luciani stepped in. On the other hand, Wojtyla and Ratzinger, as doctrinal conservatives, didn't care how much suffering doctrine unfairly placed on the everyday lives innocent people. In their minds, what pre-medieval self-serving men had once written was etched permanently into society.

For example, during the twenty years Wojtyla and Luciani served as a bishop and as a cardinal, each of their countries—driven by the Vatican's condemnation of out-of-wedlock children—suffered from an immense orphan problem—two million in each country. During that time Wojtyla built and dedicated fifty-three churches and not a single orphanage. Luciani built and dedicated forty-four orphanages and not a single church. Each time the fork in the road would come up, Wojtyla would ask himself *"Now, what would Moses do in this case?"* Each time the fork in the road would come up, Luciani would ask himself *"Now, what would Jesus do in this case?"*

Nevertheless, these were very different kinds of men, driven by very different kinds of Gods. Karol Wojtyla and Joseph Ratzinger—the 'good guys' of yesterday—striving to preserve the last bits of *fascism* the God of Moses had left behind and Albino Luciani—the 'bad guy' of yesterday—like Marx before him, striving to bring the reality of Jesus Christ into a modern world—striving to stamp out what Hitler stood for, once and for all.

Call it communism. Call it what you may.

The ecclesiastical record of popes

Doctrine	Luciani	Wojtyla
	Moderate	Conservative
Contraception and Planned Parenthood	yes	no
Contraception to prevent AIDS children	yes	no
Liberation of the poor	yes	no
Vow of poverty (all clergy)	yes	no
Vow of celibacy (all clergy)	yes	yes
Abortion embryonic development*	yes	no
Abortion viable fetus	no	no
Genetic Research	yes	no
Ecumenism	yes	within Catholicism
Election of the pope by bishops	yes	no
Ordination of women	yes	no
Ordination born-out-of-wedlock children	yes	no
Homosexuality is God's will	yes	yes**
Love and commitment define marriage	yes	no
Sanctification of remarriage	yes	no
Black-white integration	yes	no
Mysticism	no	yes
Little boys are superior to little girls	no	yes

* Sequence of creation and *prevention*: sperm → egg ← *pill/condom* → fertilized egg ← *morning after pill* → embryo → tissue ← *1ˢᵗ term abortion* → heart beat → brain wave → viable fetus ← *3ʳᵈ term abortion* → ensoulment → birth.

144

Luciani supported the 'pill' to prevent untimely conception and condoms to prevent disease. We know from his support of artificial insemination he supported destruction of diseased and impaired embryos. The orphanages he built to permit children to be born which otherwise would have been aborted testify he condemned abortion of a healthy viable fetus.

** Benedict XVI positions are similar to John Paul II except for homosexuality. John Paul II accepted the findings of medical science that homosexuality is a God-giving instinct. Benedict still considers it an *"objective disorder."*

1 It is estimated 6 million died in the Holocaust. Of this only 4.0 million have been identified by records of which 3.1 million died in Poland: Auschwitz 1,300,000 – Belzec 435,000 – Chelmno 152,000 – Sobibor 200,000 – Treblinka 870,000 – Warsaw 200,000 – other Poland 209,000. Overall, about 80% of casualties were in Poland. See list of concentration camps on Internet or in libraries.
2 *IG Farben Solvay Trial Wikipedia or in libraries*
3 Search *Auschwitz* Wikipedia or in libraries
4 *'The Man Who Would Be Pope'* John Voight
5 Karol Wojtyla early life *Wikipedia and* auto-biography of John Paul II claim he was part of an underground theater which promoted anti-Hitler plays as if that were possible during the war. This claim is contradicted by the few photos that have survived show Nazi officers in the audience.
6 The story *'Little Lady in Disguise'* in the author's book Let's All Get Behind the Pope' recounts Benedicts five year old encounter with the Archbishop.
7 Search *Obersalzberg Berghof* on Internet or in libraries
8 Search *Leibstandarte* or *Obersalzberg* on Internet or in libraries
9 Search *Kehlsteinhaus* on Internet or in libraries
10 Paraphrased from biographies of Benedict XVI. Hufschlag Traunstein is about 20 kilometers from Obersalzberg. The Austrian Legion was a Nazi terrorist organization which brutalized dissidents in the years leading up to the war. It was integrated into the Germany Army as a branch of the SS Guard in 1939 and used in espionage activities and rounding up dissidents for the concentration camps.
11 Gandhi's famous response to the missionary E. Stanley Jones 13 Jun 46
12 *Messaggero Mestre* 1 Apr 46

Photo 8 year old Karol Wojtyla - *Laski Italfoto* 1928
Photo Auschwitz concentration camp - *author*
Photo Karol Wojtyla acting - *Malopolska Silesia* 1943
Photo Ratzinger/Hitler poster - author's property
Photo Joseph Ratzinger scout troop - German propaganda photo
Photo Albino Luciani - Italian Resistance photo 1942

Author's note: the supposition Joseph Ratzinger's father was either employed as a security officer at Eagle's Nest or was in the SS Guard at Traunstein is based solely on the coincidence he had spent his life as a police officer and, for a reason history has not otherwise recorded, moved his family from their ancestral home all the way across the country to Traunstein where the SS Guard was headquartered and Eagle's nest was built. There is no historical record to otherwise explain this remarkable event other than Benedict XVI's claim his father hated the Nazis.

Chapter 15

His Papacy

"What is important is not how many children are born, but that every child that is born has an equal opportunity at a good and healthy life."[1]

Albino Luciani

Giovanni Paulo I

The six mounds in the foreground represent Italian peaks for which he held the speed record when he became a bishop in 1958. The three stars stand for the attributes his father had built into him: compassion, courage and change. The lion represents his father Giovanni Paulo Luciani.

In late summer 1978, Paul VI died. As the conclave approached, *The Times* of London published a list of the leading candidates for succession. In order of their promise were listed cardinals *'Benelli, Siri, Hume, Pignedoli, Baggio, Suenens, Poletti, Lorscheider...'*[2]

The Patriarch of Venice was not on the list? It was no secret Paul had stacked the College of Cardinals heavily to the *left* toward his favorite son. Yet, this would have moved the vote toward most any other liberal, the most visible being Benelli and Suenens.

Yet, Paul had not openly endorsed either of these; he had placed the papal stole solely on the shoulders of Albino Luciani. How was it possible the press had missed the boat?

'They Have no Souls'

The knocker knocked. It was the nun Vincenza. She handed him the morning newspaper. She looked at him in anguish, "They say, *'they have no souls.'"* She scuttled out of the room.

He read the headline, *'First Test-tube Baby Born in England.'*

He read it again, this time aloud as if he had to hear it to believe it, *"First Test-tube Baby Born in England."*

His eyes caught another headline, *"Vatican City, 'The aging Dean of the College of Cardinals, Carlo Confalonieri, condemned the English child born of artificial insemination. He supported the Vatican's position with the quarter-century old decree of Pius XII prohibiting genetic experimentation of any kind. Rapid fire from palaces of cardinals from around the world, from Italy to Germany to Poland to Latin America to the United States backed him up; some suggesting such children are without souls and others stopping just short of labeling the newborn infant 'a child of the devil.'"*[3]

He thought back to that dark dismal rainy afternoon in nineteen hundred twenty-three when he had climbed into the carriage that had taken him to the minor seminary at Feltre, his first stop on his long journey which would eventually take him to Rome.

His atheist father, who had spent a lifetime trying to change the Church from the outside, decided it could only be changed from the inside. So it was he committed his son to the task.

In his farewell, the revolutionary outcast of the Veneto country told him, "Albino, unlike those Hypocrites who prance about the Vatican palaces in magnificent robes of silk and satin with jeweled chalices and rings of diamonds and rubies and gold, you must promise me you will live your life in imitation of Christ, for Christ would not approve of this masquerade of His earthly representatives. *"Play the game carefully; never risk your king to save a pawn."*

So it was his papa, together with his little brother Edoardo, with tears in their eyes, had waved goodbye, on that dreary autumn day, to this *Pauper Who Would Be Pope.*

Only at the helm of the Church would he be able to establish the common dignity of all Christ's children. Now he found himself faced with precisely what his father had warned of, the inevitable challenge of risking his king—the papacy—to save a pawn—this little girl. He reworked his father's words over and over again in his mind as if he could somehow get around them, *"Play the game carefully; never risk your king to save a pawn."*

It was no secret he was the favorite son of Paul VI. Paul had made him Patriarch of Venice the most coveted pastoral spot in the Roman Catholic world and stepping stone to the papacy. It was also no secret Paul had stacked the voting conclave heavily in his favor.

Paul was eighty and not well. If Paul were to die now the vote would be close. Surely if he spoke out in defense of this child, he would enrage those cardinals who had come out so strongly against her. He would risk losing those votes. He would risk all his father had done, and all he had done, and all John had done, and all Paul had done, to make possible his succession to the papacy.

Once more, he thought back to that day he had climbed into the carriage. How could he possibly get around what his father had told him? *"...never risk your king to save a pawn."*

Suddenly, something else his father had said popped into his mind, *"...Albino, you must promise me you will live your life in imitation of Christ..."*

"Hmmm?" the man in the red cap murmured to himself. "I wonder what Jesus would do in this case?"

He pressed the intercom. It buzzed twice, "Vincenza, here."

"Have you seen Lorenzi?"

"He's here with me now," the nun replied.

"Good. Send him in."

Lorenzi strolled into the study.

He was an angelic priest to say the least, as devout as they come. Being the cardinal's secretary, he knew his manager's mission; something that could only be accomplished if he were to rise to the papacy. He knew the vote for the papacy would be incredibly close. It had been one of his hobbies to keep track of it, both those voting cardinals in the field and those voting cardinals in the Vatican.

The man in the red cap did not look up. He was busy scribbling a note on a scrap of stationary. He handed it to his visitor.

"My dear Lorenzi, I want you to post this to the parents of the newborn child in England."

Lorenzi read the note,

"My Dearest Lesley and John Brown,

My very personal congratulations to you on the birth of your little girl. I want you to be assured there is reserved for you and your child a high place in Heaven.

Albino Luciani, Patriarch of Venice"[4]

The young priest smiled at his mentor. "Good, a private note. I was wondering how you would handle this one."

The Patriarch of Venice picked up another piece of stationary and scribbled again, "Here, my dear Lorenzi. I want you to issue this release to the world press. I want it to go out today. We have not a moment to lose."

Lorenzi read the note,

"I have sent my most heartfelt congratulations to the English baby girl whose conception took place artificially. As far as her parents are concerned, I (the Church) have no right to condemn them. If they acted with honest intentions and in good faith, they will be deserving of merit before God for what they wanted and asked the doctors to carry out. Albino Luciani, Patriarch of Venice."[5]

Lorenzi looked at his boss as if he were about to jump off a tall building, "But, Paul is ill. He might not make it another day, let alone another week. A private message to the parents might make some sense. But this message to the world will enrage those in the conclave who have come out against her. It will cost you the p…"

The man behind the desk cut him off. "A private message to this little girl's parents will not end the rumor these children have no souls. When prejudice rears its ugly head, one must nip it in the bud. If it costs me the papacy in this world so be it. If it costs me my soul in the next world so be it. We have not a moment to lose. Carry it to the ends of the earth. Do it now!"

Lorenzi shot the cardinal one last look of appeal but to no avail. He carefully stuffed the papers into his shirt pocket and hurried reluctantly out of the room.[6]

The aftermath

Pope Paul was in seclusion at Castel Gandolfo. A reporter asked him for his response to Luciani's press release challenging the decree prohibiting artificial insemination, going so far as to reserve a place in heaven for both the make-believe child and her parents.

Paul told the reporter, *"The cardinal could not have been more right. There is reserved for these courageous parents and their little girl a high place in heaven. Unfortunately, I cannot say the same for many of us who hold high places here on earth."*[7]

Luciani was challenged test-tube babies would aggravate the orphan problem he, himself, had worked so hard to resolve. Artificial insemination would make it possible for sterile and homosexual couples to have their own children, robbing Italy of the largest population groups available to parent unparented children.

He told the reporter, *"My friend Einstein once told me he could not accept the existence of God because he could not accept God would play dice with His children. There is something horrific about how God goes about making children.*

"Millions of fertilized eggs are drowned in the sewer in everyday intercourse. Others are born physically and mentally impaired to live unbearable lives and die unspeakable deaths.

"Here on the realization of this great event, it makes no sense for man to allow God to continue to have His way in this thing. Artificial insemination will eventually lead to man's greatest achievement, the creation of a perfectly healthy child every time

"What is important is not how many children are born, but that every child that is born has an equal opportunity at a good and healthy life. Genetic research will eventually take us there."[8]

Einstein had once said of him, *"Luciani thinks of things today, as the rest of us will think of them in centuries to come."*[9]

Regardless, his message to the parents of Louise Brown was viewed as the most defiant rebuttal of a papal decree by a ranking prelate of the Church since Martin Luther. In upstaging cardinals who otherwise would have voted for him, he had not only removed himself as a candidate for the papacy but rumors surfaced when his reconfirmation came due that year, it would not be forthcoming.

Many think a cardinal, once appointed, is forever a cardinal. Not so. Cardinals are appointed for five-year terms and require the reconfirmation of the reigning pontiff when their terms lapse.

Nevertheless, Paul died in the ensuing week.

Astonishingly, when the white smoke rose from the Sistine Chapel on August 26, 1978, it bore Luciani's name. On the first ballot the count was seventy-five for Luciani; a marginal win, exactly the two-thirds majority plus one vote required to elect him.[10]

On the recount—the traditional practice of making the election unanimous—fifteen others went his way. Twenty-one remained cast against him. In their loss, they were determined to send a message in their dissenting votes—the only pope in the thousand-year history in

150

which cardinals have elected popes who failed to carry a unanimous vote on the recount. So bitter was the hatred of these men, some of whom would share the Vatican with him, they could not accept that Christ had spoken.[10]

Just another man

In accepting his pontificate Luciani took the name John Paul. History recorded he named himself in honor of his patrons—John XXIII who had made him a bishop and Paul VI who had made him a cardinal and had paved his way to the top. Yet, one can surmise he also had in mind his beloved father, Giovanni Paulo Luciani—John Paul Luciani—who had sheared his wool and groomed his mane.

His installation took place before a makeshift altar in St. Peter's Square. He refused to be crowned with the jeweled encrusted tiara which in the past had been the focal point of papal coronations.[11] Instead he allowed a pastoral stole—the symbol of a common priest—placed upon his shoulders. He did not intend to rule from the throne. He intended to walk among his people.

Whereas both the rank-and-file and the hierarchy of the Church saw in the crown a symbol of royalty, John Paul saw something else. He saw in it the right to a good and healthy life for a thousand children who would otherwise starve to death.

His refusal of the tiara hinted at what would become more and more apparent in the coming days; he would liquidate much of the Vatican treasures to annihilate poverty. His peers, the crown princes of the Church, felt much of their own regency endangered.

In order to calm the fears of those who had refused to vote for him, he did something no other pope had ever done. He immediately confirmed appointments of all existing cardinals.

Yet, he reduced in half the substantial bonus cardinals receive upon the election of a new pope, a forewarning to his eventually reducing salaries of Vatican cardinals, which at the time was the equivalent of what is today one hundred thousand pre-tax dollars.

He refused to order the Fisherman's Ring[12] cast, the symbol of the majesty of the papacy. Nor did he ever extend his hand for the ceremonial kiss. He would have no one bow to him. Rather he would embrace his visitor, not in a ceremonial way, but in a real way.

Luciani had never been a man of formalities. As a bishop, he had refused to be addressed as *Your Excellency,* the title reserved for bishops. As a cardinal he had refused to be addressed as *Your Eminence,* the title reserved for cardinals. As a pope, he refused to be addressed as *Your Holiness.* He asked everyone, from heads of state to little children, address him by the nickname he had acquired as a child, Piccolo.

In his twenty years as a bishop he said Mass every Wednesday morning. He would have recently ordained priests say Mass on Sundays. Dressed in a smock, he would serve as the priest's acolyte. He carried this practice into the Vatican. He would have seminary graduates say Mass in his chapel; he serving as their acolyte.

When he told a crowd *". . . God is our Father, but more so, our Mother,"*[13] the press inquired if a fourth person might soon be added to the Holy Trinity?

He had a knack for explaining complex issues in a simple way. On one occasion, he took a microphone out of a cardinal's hand and gave it to a six-year old boy as if to suggest what the child had to say was more important than what his prince of the Church had to say.

The boy asked, *"What is the difference between the left and the right? Why are they always fighting with each other? Is it because one believes in God and the other doesn't?"*

"No," the Pope answered, *"They both believe in God. It is just that those on the right guide their lives by what someone is supposed to have said to someone else thousands of years ago."*

"Oh," said the boy. Puzzled by the Pope's reply, he scratched his head *"Then what do those on the left use to guide their lives?"*

"This, their conscience," the Pope pointed to his temple.[14]

When he shook hands with the communist mayor of Rome, Vatican cardinals shot vicious glances. When he hugged him, they shrugged in despair.

On one occasion, he was reported in the tabloids as being seen in the square walking among the people wearing shorts and sandals.

On another day he disappeared. No one could find him. Cardinal Villot sounded the alarm. After hours of searching, the Pope showed up at the Papal Palace dressed in a smock befitting a common monk.

Villot challenged him, "Where have you been?"

"I have been to see who is where and who is doing what. I have been to the Vatican Bank, the Patrimony of the Holy See, I stopped in and had a few words with Peter but I could not find Paul."

Villot warned him, "You are not to go anywhere without being escorted by guards. Do you understand? It is much too dangerous."

"Guards?" as if reminded of something he had put on hold for the moment, the Supreme Pontiff of the Roman Catholic Church told his Secretary of State, *"Your eminence, I want you to issue an order the Swiss Guards are not to kneel when I approach them. I am not a God. I am a man. I am just another man."*[15]

He asked, he listened, he learned. He talked, he told, he taught. He grinned, he smiled, he laughed. Above all, he hugged. Best of all, they learned to hug him back.

He made few friends among those of rank in churches and nations, yet, he quickly won the friendship of the common man.

His positions concerning those that practice planned parenthood, out-of-wedlock children, the remarried, homosexuals and others oppressed by doctrine were made clear,

"A particular greeting to all who are now suffering throughout the world; to the sick, to prisoners, to exiles, to the persecuted, and particularly, to those upon whom restraints are unfairly placed by doctrine in their everyday lives.

"Let our differences mold into one and together we shall rise to bring the world to a condition of greater justice. We call upon all of you, from the humblest who are the underpinnings of nations, to heads of state. We encourage you to build an efficacious and responsible structure for a new order, this one more just and honest... together we will muster the strength to lift those restraints that have been unfairly placed upon the everyday lives of so many innocent people by scripture and canon law... for God-given human life is infinitely more precious than is man-made doctrine."[16]

Yet, the lion's share of his papacy was headed for the poor. From his opening embrace of the communist mayor of Rome, to the audit of the Vatican Bank, to the appraisals of the Vatican treasures, to his meeting with the KGB mediator Metropolitan Nikodim, to his covert meeting with the head of the Communist Party, to the time he said *'Ubi Lenin, ibi Jerusalem,'* to his intent of the Puebla Conference as the *liberation of the poor*, to the time he told the capitalistic world, *"It is the inalienable right of no man to accumulate wealth beyond his needs while others starve to death because they have nothing."*[17]

Then, finally, to his last words before he retired to the great bed in the papal apartment on the evening of September 28, 1978. He told Cardinal Colombo, his long time ally in his war on poverty, *"Sadly, Giovanni, when we have completed our work and everyone has enough, there will always be those who want too much."*[18]

1 *La Repubblica* 2 Aug 78. Luciani's response to a reporter on artificial insemination. In artificial insemination embryos are conceived in a petri dish outside the womb. The Church is opposed to the practice because diseased and genetically impaired eggs and sperm are discarded in the process resulting in their 'death.' For example, an egg or sperm infected with AIDS or syphilis or one containing a known genetic impairment is excluded. Today, only a few hundred of the roughly three thousand genes have been identified. Genes known to cause birth defects and known viruses are eliminated in the Intro-fertilization process. On average, an artificially inseminated child is healthier than a naturally conceived child and this difference is becoming more and more pronounced as genetic science progresses. If the job is done right, an artificially inseminated child cannot be born of known genetically transmitted impairments or disease. When all genes that cause birth defects are identified, all artificially inseminated children will be born free of genetically transmitted impairments and disease—the reasoning behind Luciani's response. As genetic science progresses, responsible parents will resort to contraception and artificial insemination and irresponsible parents will risk children having genetic impairments and disease which would otherwise be prevented. Laws will be passed barring natural conception—every *child will have an equal opportunity at a good and healthy life.*
2 *The Times* London 14 Aug 78. Other newspapers published similar lists without Luciani's name
3 *L'Osservatore Romano* 26 Jul 78 Because of the confusion caused by his predecessor's action, the day after his installation, John Paul II issued a confirmation of the Pius XII decree banning artificial insemination and did it in such a way as to question the ensoulment of these children. In 1984, pressured by public opinion, he reversed the doctrine these children were without souls.
4 The private message was never published. The nature of the message is in Luciani's press release
5 *IL Gazzattino Venezia* 27 Jul 78 variations of this release appeared in world newspapers
6 This bit of satire is reprinted from the author's book *Lets All Get Behind the Pope...'* a book of 66 interrelated short stories – little known incidents in the lives of Albino Luciani and other famous people which caused them to rise up as champions of human justice.
7 *L'Osservatore Romano* 30 Jul 78
8 *La Repubblica* 2 Aug 78 Cardinal Luciani's response to a reporter artificial insemination
9 *Princeton Packet* 2 Apr 49
10 The only information released from a conclave is the names of counters and the number of votes the winner received on the final ballot. The number of ballots is evidenced by the smoke rising from the chimney in which the voting slips and tally sheets are burned after each ballot. No written or oral record of what goes on in a conclave ever leaves a conclave. Intermediate counts are not announced to the press or the conclave—known only to the counters.
11 The twenty-two papal tiaras are encrusted with over 1,700 diamonds and other precious gems
12 John Paul did wear a ring given participants in the Second Vatican Council—symbolic of his intent to continue change to the Church John XXIII had begun
13 *Associated Press* 7 Sep 78
14 *Associated Press* 14 Sep 78
15 Testimony of Jack Champney to author. The story is told in Roger Crane's play *The Last Confession* starring David Suchet which premiered in London
16 *Associated Press* 27 Aug 78 Sistine Chapel
17 Associated Press 27 Sep 78. See film clip: www.johnpaul1.org
18 *Corriere della Sera* Milan 30 Sep 78

NOTE: See Chapter 2 for excerpts from papal audiences

Chapter 16

The Murder of Metropolitan Nikodim

"There is no inner conflict for me. It is told me by both my patron saint of state—Marx and my patron saint of faith—Christ." Metropolitan Nikodim

Boris Rotov—Metropolitan Nikodim—youthful leader of the Russian Orthodox Church, had been the chief negotiator in which the Eastern Church agreed to participate in the Second Vatican Council on the condition there would be no condemnation of either communism or atheism during the conciliar assemblies.

It may not have been coincidence he happened to be John Paul's first foreign visitor. Boris may have never become Metropolitan of Leningrad at the early age of 32, had it not been for Albino Luciani. As we have said, his father and Albino had met the year before he was born and had kept up a relationship.

Boris' father was an atheist. What's more, Boris' mother was also an atheist. They were both dedicated enemies of the Church.[1]

One could understand how Albino, born of a mixed-bag of an atheist father and a devout mother could grow up to be a priest. Yet, it staggers the imagination to think Boris, reared entirely by atheists, could grow up to be a priest.

One can only surmise when the elder Rotov learned Albino's father was an atheist, he questioned how it was possible the boy could be studying to be a priest? Albino may have told him of his father's strategy the Church could only be changed from the inside and had committed him to the task.

Could it be, Boris' father had given him the same commission Albino's father had given him a few years before—change the Church back to what Christ had intended?

Or was it coincidence both boys had been involved by chance for years in an effort to change the Church from what it had become—a pompous demonstration of ritual, wealth and ghosts—back to the church of the poor Christ had intended; Albino working the western front and Boris working the eastern front. One will never know.

Nikodim called for the redemption of the American Christian,

155

"No one said it better than Gandhi. He defined the American Christian, 'I love your Christ. But, I do not like your Christians.'

Here in my part of the world I must take orders from my Kremlin bosses, certainly, if not at least I am at no necessity to pretend they and I pursue the same end. For me, it is that which is told me by both my patron saint of state—Marx—and my patron saint of faith—Christ. So there is no inner conflict there for me.

There is no originality in Marx. His word was to bring Christ into a changing world. Yet, on the other side of the world, the American part of the world, the situation is poles apart...

In America, freedom of religion means the right to force Christian beliefs through its Christian majority on others. In Russia, we look at it differently. Here, freedom of religion is the right to believe or not to believe. Yes, it has restrictions as we are limited to practice our religions within the privacy of our homes and churches.

Here, Christian bells and Muslim loudspeakers—the booming billboards of organized religion—are banned. In America, church bells ring out at will advertising Christianity; yet, prayers over loudspeakers in Muslim neighborhoods are banned.

There, tax laws exempt churches imposing higher taxes on the nonbelievers. The nonbeliever pays for the believer to believe and the believer uses his tax-free advantage to persecute the nonbeliever. Preachers spend hundreds of millions collected to help the poor on radio and television time spreading hatred of Jews, blacks, atheists, homosexuals and others who don't conform to their rules. Gestapo squads invade pubs and bedrooms and cart offenders off to prison.[2]

Here, preachers are imprisoned for preaching hatred of others and we don't invade bedrooms in the middle of the night.

Yet, what demonstrates, most of all, America is not what it pretends to be, is its closed borders to its poor neighbors to its south. It calls itself a Christian nation, as if to say Christ would slam the door on these poor and starving children. Most brutal of all, it is Christian money and military power supplied to ruthless dictators that keeps these children who live south of its borders starving to death. 'Love thy neighbor as thyself?' America never heard of it...

Free? Free? America has not the slightest conception of what the word means. Although we here don't pretend to have it, we at least know what we are striving for—free, to be so free to that point at which one's freedom imposes on the freedom of another...'"[3]

Two cups of coffee and a few almond cookies

On the morning of September 6, 1978 *L Osservatore Romano* reported. *"...Cardinal Willebrands led the Metropolitan into the Pope's private study...A delegation of Orthodox clergy assembled outside the room awaiting an audience ...The Pope poured two cups of coffee placing one in front the Russian. Nikodim brought the cup to his lips he found the coffee too hot. As he set it down, he fell back into his chair grasping his throat. John Paul felt briefly for signs of life then opened the door which brought a Swiss Guard and others into the room...The archbishop had previously had heart attacks..."*[4]

The Washington Post said, *"Nikodim repeatedly denied being a communist, yet, he has on an ongoing basis befriended the Soviet regime which has restricted religion..."*[5]

> Metropolitan Nikodim was born Boris Gheorghevich Rotov at Rozan, near Moscow, October 14, 1929. He was ordained a deacon at the age of 17 years, and priest at 20. He served as bishop of Yaroslav and Minsk before becoming metropolitan of the ancient See of Novgorod and at the same time of Leningrad.
> He was widely traveled and spoke several languages. During his stay here, he lived in institutions of the Jesuit order in the Roman hills southeast of the city He

The Times, London, September 6, 1978

His fluency in many languages erased a rumor an interpreter had been in the room. It was partly he was an accomplished linguist he was the Orthodox 'president' on the World Council of Churches.

He was particularly fluent in Italian. He had picked it up from his father as a boy and while at the Vatican II Council (1962-64), he had adopted Rome as his second home, the reason he had spent a month in Rome before meeting with the Pope.

John Paul, himself, true of all modern popes, was fluent in French, Italian, English and Spanish in addition to Latin.

The first reports seemed to indicate John Paul was alone with the body— *'felt briefly for signs of life before opening the door.'* If there had been anyone else in the room they would have opened the door.

157

Yet, whether or not the Pope was alone with the Metropolitan is immaterial to murder unless the toxin was in the sugar and not in the coffee. If cyanide crystals been involved, they could not have been in the pot as it may have killed the Pope when he poured the coffee.[6]

Anyone close to them would know the Pope did not take sugar and the Metropolitan had a sweet tooth. Of course, this would mean Nikodim, not the Pope, as widely rumored, was the intended victim.

That the Vatican claimed he had not tasted the coffee could have been intent to head off rumors. Yet, if he had tasted the coffee, though there are many toxins which incite heart attack, there is not one that would kill one so quickly if ingested. Cyanide in a gaseous form attacks membranes resulting in instant death.

That he grasped his throat is consistent with cyanide. The heart is a muscle and a fatal attack strikes as a 'charley horse' to the heart.

The speed with which he died is demonstrated that no newspaper reported that any effort was made at resuscitation. The first person to respond to the Pope's call was the guard no more than three or four minutes after the seizure. Swiss Guards, in addition to being human fighting machines, are trained paramedics and schooled in CPR.[7]

The press reported 'heart attack' in the deaths of John Paul and Nikodim. In both cases their respective churches declined autopsy.

Yet, there was a difference. Unlike John Paul who is proved to have had no history of heart problems, Nikodim was known to have a heart condition—he had suffered as many as five previous attacks.

Nikodim had been a competition swimmer in his youth—the reason his doctor had recommended a few laps each morning—one reason he stayed at the Jesuit compound which had an Olympic pool. It had been his powerful physical and mental stamina of his youth which had made possible his rapid rise in the Orthodox hierarchy.

La Repubblica reported the pool boy had watched the Russian taking vigorous laps for a half-hour that morning as he had every morning without resting, but noticed nothing unusual.[8]

La Stampa was less respectful. The pool boy described Nikodim with his immense physique covered front and back with hair down to his hands resembled a water buffalo splashing through the water.[9]

Yet, in Nikodim's case, as in the Pope's case, if one considers murder one must determine motive. Was there motive in his case?

We have already speculated the CIA may have suspected the Pope sought Soviet arms assistance for the *revolution of the poor* he was about to lead in Central America. There was more than just that.

The Metropolitan's alliance with the Soviets had made him many enemies within the Orthodox Church. The Orthodox Curia was even further to the *right* than was the Roman Curia in the Vatican. Nikodim represented the far *left* in the Russian Orthodox world.

There were those who reasoned the meeting, behind closed doors in the Pope's private study rather than in his public office where he normally met with dignitaries, was part of a plot to reunite the two churches. This made Nikodim the enemy of both those within the Orthodox and Roman churches who opposed ecumenism.

One can understand why the Vatican would not opt for autopsy as it never does. Yet, why didn't the Orthodox Church perform autopsy to dispel the rumors of the time? It wanted him out of the way?

Because there was no autopsy one will never know if murder had been involved. Yet, if one assumes foul play not involved—he died of a natural heart attack—one must consider the mathematical odds.

One must consider a few seconds in the span of a man's life.

The chance he had suffered up to five previous attacks and the one that killed him occurred at the precise moment in time he met John Paul behind closed doors. It occurred at the precise second he lifted the cup to his lips and finding it steaming succumbed to a death, so sudden, resuscitation was not considered by the Swiss Guard swiftly on the scene. So quickly, the crowd who wanted him dead did not have the chance to cheer as the ball went in the net.

Pauper who would be Pope

He had come onto the world's stage, together with his secretary Lorenzi, in an outdated *Lancia 2000*. Had the automobile been brand new, and it was not, it would have been unbecoming a common priest, much less a prince of the Church. Its fenders had been scorched by time and for the most part it had lost its color. So much so, Swiss Guards stopped it at the Vatican gates and demanded identification. It was a tin box designed and built for paupers. Forty days later he left in a pine box designed and built for paupers.

He had made the rounds, pauper, then altar boy, then seminarian, then priest, then bishop, then cardinal, then pope, then pauper, once

159

more. He left a few personal items including his exercise equipment and two cockatiels. There was a pair of cut glass cruets which had been given to him by his mother on the day of his ordination. There were a few other gifts, plaques and medals he had received through the years. Yet, not so much as a single lira in a checking account. He had given all he had to the needy, this *Pauper who would be Pope*.

Baby Pigeons

Nevertheless, I have some answers for you here. Among them are baby pigeons. Yes, why there are no baby pigeons?

One knows dogs come from puppies and cats come from kittens and cows come from calves. But, just where do pigeons come from?

Perhaps you have never noticed? You never wondered why, in all of your life, you have never seen a baby pigeon? Go to Saint Peter's Square in Rome or for that matter any of the grand piazzas of Europe or the great parks of America and you will see tens of thousands of pigeons and not a baby pigeon among them.

What's that? You believe they must be somewhere else? Well, go and try and find them and you will find they are not there. For pigeons, among all of God's creation, come from somewhere else.

So I have some answers for you here. Among them is the answer to the greatest mystery of all. Something that, like the baby pigeons, from day to day you could not see, yet, always assumed was there. As in the case of baby pigeons, I will prove it is not there.

Now, let us go back to that time, so very long ago, when I first visited the remote mountain province of Vittorio Veneto. Back to that time, when I first met this man called 'Piccolo.'

1 *'Leningrad kava Veteran* 17 Oct 76
2 At the time Nikodim said this one in four police in the United States were in vice or moral squads invading bars and other establishments and even bedrooms.
3 *Leningrad kava Veteran* 17 Oct 76
4 *L Osservatore Romano* 6 Sep 78
5 *Washington Post* 6 Sep 78
6 Cyanide escapes from liquid just above room temperature, it is deadly in steaming coffee. Its white crystals are easily concealed in sugar.
7 *Swiss Guard Code*
8 *La Repubblica* 6 Sep 78   9 *Kommersant* 6 Sep 78
9 *La Stampa* 6 Sep 78

Chapter 17

Milan

*"Freedom without equality is not what it pretends to be,
the diamond would be made of paste."*[1]

General George Patton

Spring

It was an exact point in time, the first day of spring, that day on which the sun rests directly over the equator; that day on which all over creation the sun rises due east and sets due west and day and night end in a dead heat in time.

The Boeing 707 rose slowly out of Kennedy over New York harbor before banking to the left headed in its intended direction. As it made its turn, I looked down at that grand lady who lifts her lamp by the golden door and wondered how she ever came about?

After all, we were a Christian nation, our forefathers; every one of them was a Christian. Of those who signed the Declaration of Independence, there wasn't a single black, not a single Jew, not a single gay, not even a woman among them. At least I didn't think so. It seemed to me a towering figure of Christ would be more appropriate at these gates to what was, indeed, the Promised Land.

In all of Europe I knew only one person. I probably knew others but I didn't know where they were. This particular one I had kept in touch with. He had been my rival back in high school in my run for the roses, one of those people I had to beat out in life.

His name was Jack Champney.[2] He was much smarter than I was. His problem was he didn't know it. He thought I was much smarter than he was. He had gathered this from how well I had done in school; I could keep pace with him all the way down the stretch only to lose him at the wire. He had no idea how much harder I had to work for what I got than he did. For him winning the race was like Sinatra singing *My Way,* almost effortless.

He won the race going away. I was just another student in the crowd of several thousand when I watched him take the stand on graduation day. On this day, many years later, I couldn't remember a single thing he had said. Vainly, I thought, "If it had been me, today, all that had been privileged to have listened would remember everything, every single word, I said."

As the plane started to take down the time zones, I thought back to graduation day,

... that day they were all wearing blue blazers. Usually it was only me. Day after day, year after year, it had only been me. The others in sweaters, blue jeans, sneakers, whatever they laid their hands on when they got up in the morning. They used to call me 'pretty boy' - 'momma's boy.' Then one day one of them called me a 'pansy.' That's the day they found out my small fists could hit and my feet could kick. Sooner or later they learned my help with their homework made the difference between honors and failure. So, although I had made a run for it, I didn't come in first or even second, but, nevertheless, when the wreaths were passed out I took home with me the ones labeled Catechism, Mathematics and History. What's more, the yearbook caption alongside my picture read, "Most likely to become a cardinal of the Church."

Well, I was never to become a cardinal of the Church. When the 'V' in the road came up, Jack took the path that said *Christ* and I took the one that said *Money.* I went off to the world of business where with him out of the way I would have less trouble reaping the roses.

He went on to attend Holy Cross where he once again took the honors and then began to work toward becoming a very special kind of priest. He took his doctorate in psychiatry at Johns Hopkins and registered as a licensed psychiatrist. His aim, made clear in his letters to me, was to become a member of the Catholic Church's Commission on Spiritual Occurrences. The panel, overseen by a group of bishops, was the Vatican's investigative panel for miracles, apparitions, exorcisms and other spiritual claims.

He had secured an assignment as an instructor in a seminary in northern Italy. The local bishop was a member of this commission, a nice stepping stone for Jack on his way to the top. The cathedral, together with the bishop's residence, was located in the remote town of Vittorio Veneto in the foothills of the Italian Alps.

During that time, I witnessed the splendor of Christianity. As I crossed Europe, I must have set the world record for visiting churches, including most of Europe's largest. Because it was too far out of my way, I had to skip Seville. But the others, all the others, from the majestic dome of St. Paul's, the great stone claws grasping at Notre Dame, the magnificent leaded glass windows of Chartres, the ashen wedding cake towers of Cologne, and now, finally, the immense Duomo di Milano with its threatening weather-beaten gargoyles oxidized by time, guarding the great square which lay before it—Milan's playground of princes and paupers. I marveled them all. I relished them all.

Yet it wasn't these great edifices that impressed me the most. It was entirely something else, something I would find here in Milan, something I would stumble onto quite by accident. Something I would carry with me all of the days of my life.

Besides its great cathedral and its great square and its crystal galleria, Milan has a fourth great treasure—something most tourists never witness—the city's great park of the dead. There you can see it all, every bit of yesterday.

The land of the dead

As I entered the cemetery, I became a part of it all. The only sound was my footsteps and the breath of a slight breeze. The sky was foreboding as if it were a good day for a funeral. Had there been a lake, and there was none, it would have held dark waters as there was not a thing in the sky to give it life. It seemed all of the living had forgotten all of the dead. I was alone—alone as one could be.

I found myself wandering in the world's greatest metropolis of the departed—endless rows of mansions of stone. Some even with windows as to provide their silent tenants a view of their neighbors' palatial abodes. There seemed to be more marble and granite houses in this land of the dead than there were houses outside in the land of the living—each one different—each one commanding the attention of its own artist, its own architect, its own engineer.

Interspersed, here and there, were sculptures, mostly of marble and granite, yet, a few of precious metals, some even studded with jewels—each one frozen in common death echoing its individual message of life—each one befitting a prince—no, a king—no, a god.

163

Collectively they echoed of immense wealth. "No wonder they lost the war, they had all their money tied up in monuments," I thought.

Nowhere could a single flower be found, as if to ensure the beauty of God's creation not overpower these great works of man. There was only the green grass which worked its way like a maze in and out and around and about these magnificent monuments and dwellings of the dead.

I proceeded down the main boulevard of this great city of death. Flanked on either side by mausoleums of superlative grandeur, some sealed up like the tombs they were and many others showing off their merchandise. Through ornate iron grates, I could glimpse the sarcophagi themselves—mostly of marble, some of bronze, a few of gold and even one of glass.

I listened. Not a sound. Silence, silence all about me, as not to wake those who were sleeping there. As I came to the end of the avenue, I turned the corner and suddenly stopped dead in my tracks. Not dead-dead, but dead in my tracks. There, to my left, a half dozen small white granite stones sat in a row on a blanket of green grass which lay before a matching manicured hedge of green shrubbery.[3]

The power of their simplicity eclipsed the grandeur of all that was about them. On each stone was carved a heart and within each heart an image of George Washington. "The Purple Heart," I thought to myself. I thought something else, "Here is the real reason why they had lost the war."

Approaching with all the solemnity the moment commanded, in my mind echoed the faint sound of the bugle, the hallowed roll of the drums and the distant roar of the cannon. A spot of light peeked down through the overcast sky as if to mark this precious moment in time. As to give one light to read,

Frank Phillips, Sergeant 1921-1944, 7th Army, 1st Battalion, Distinguished Service Cross

Richard Edwards, PFC 1925-1944, 7th Army, 1st Battalion, Bronze Star

Jerome Rose, 2nd Lt. 1919-1944, 7th Army, 4th Battalion, Silver Star

Brian Pickering, Pvt. 1924-1944, 7th Army, 3rd Battalion, Bronze Star

Anthony Jackson, Pvt. 1922-1944, 7th Army, 1st Battalion Bronze Star

Patricia Wilde, 1st Lt. 1919-1944, Army Medical Corps, Bronze Star

It didn't say it, but I clearly heard it, "That they shall not have died in vain." One of those things one calls tears, crept up out of my heart and ran from the corner of my eye and moved toward its lid. I looked first to the right, and then to the left, and then, again, to the right, and finally to the left, once more.

Holding the tear on the edge of the lid, I spoke as if I were a great orator on a world stage, "Not Thomas Paine with his pen, nor Patrick Henry with his eloquence, nor Paul Revere with his horse, nor Washington and Jefferson with all their courage, not even Lincoln at Gettysburg have spoken louder. For you have made more noise for freedom than all the others who have gone before you or have come after you. I pledge to you this day, to each and every one of you, that each and every one of you will not have died in vain."

I have carried that pledge, that sacred duty with me all of my life. I have carried it every day, every hour, every moment of my life. I have carried it in my mind, and in my heart, and in my being, and in my very soul.

Now it is time to carry out that solemn promise, to answer that fervent prayer. To carry it out for each and every one of them; that what they dreamed of, those things they willed to be, will come to be, for each of them, and for me, and for you, and for all humanity.

1 *Affria Italiani* 31 Mar 44. General Patton at the grave of gay soldier
2 Except for 'Jack Champney'—to protect the privacy of his family, all names in this book are real
'Jack' was on assignment by the Archdiocese of Boston to the Diocese of Vittorio Veneto
3 In July 2005, the bodies were exhumed and moved to the American military cemetery at Maastricht

Chapter 18

Vittorio Veneto

"Blessed are the poor in sprit..."   Jesus Christ

The next morning I took the train to Venice. It was from there I took the train to Mestre and from there to Vittorio Veneto. I nodded to the young man who took the seat behind me on the way to Vittorio Veneto as he had been the same one who had sat astride me on the short trip from Venice to Mestre.

En route, protestors, mostly in their teens and twenties, lined either side as the train passed through the stations. The tone of their demands sounded more like revolution than the *'Equal Pay for Equal Work'* their signs displayed.

I had found the situation in Milan worse. I wondered how things could have gotten so far out of hand in a country ruled by the pulpit.

Exiting the station at Vittorio Veneto, I pushed my way through an angry mob. I did what Jack had told me to do. I took the first right, and then the first left, and, again, the first right, and finally, the first left, once more.

I stood in front of what appeared to be an old southern hotel—a southern hotel in the most northern part of Italy. It was surrounded by an aging wall eight or nine feet high. It was of the same shade of amber stucco as was the rest of the town. It was topped off by one of those orange terracotta roofs that sprawl over all Italian villages.

I pounded with both fists as loud on the great wooden door as I could. I heard footsteps on wooden steps. They reached firmness for a time, then again on wooden steps, then firmness, once more.

There was the juggling and clattering of the unlocking of the door and standing before me was a little old lady who looked as if she had just stepped out of an Italian motion picture.

"You must be Lucien. Jack has told me all about you. We have a special place for you." I followed her into a reception area where I scratched out a registration card and surrendered my passport. I asked for directions to the bishop's castle as she led me to my room which overlooked a canal that ran behind the hotel. I freshened up a bit and headed back out onto the street.

Soon I passed over an ancient stone bridge and was channeled down a long narrow street hemmed in on both sides by row houses, everyone of amber stucco and in a general state of disrepair.

It was as if I was to see a green house, or a blue house, or a yellow house, I would remember it all of my days. As I looked up I could see the edges of the roofs framing the blue sky, every one of deep orange terracotta tile. On the town's edge I entered a tunnel that had been carved into an ancient fortress. At the tunnel's end I stepped out into medieval times, an ancient twelfth century plaza. I sensed Romeo and Juliet might be sleeping nearby.

Unlike the town, where stucco had been the tradesman's craft, here the buildings were entirely built of stone and the tatter and torn of the ages had gone unrepaired. The cathedral overpowered the plaza which lay before it. Partway up a mountain, was what I rightly presumed to be the castle——a medieval group of turret-topped towers, only the tallest had survived intact.

I passed an old stone trough with lions and gargoyles strewing water in a pool. There were statues set into arched niches in the ancient walls, a few of which had lost their original inhabitants.

Jagged cliffs engulfed the town like a giant horseshoe——a bit of the medieval ages trapped in a rocky gorge.

Suddenly, a man came running toward me wearing a 'Minnie Mouse' tank top. He smiled and waved as he passed. I judged he must have been about fifty. I was surprised the recent jogging fad in the states had reached this remote part of the world.

At the same instant, great bells rang out. Not in a rhythmic sort of way, but in a clanging sort of way, as if they did not want anyone to know what they had to say. The old church was of the identical washed-out color of its surroundings. Its nave was out of balance with its tower, as if they had run out of money in the middle ages, when I guessed the building had been built.

I started my ascent up a narrow cobblestone road hemmed in by ten-foot walls which ran up the side of the mountain to the castle.

I entered through what was the original castle entrance into a courtyard. It centered on a fountain not unlike others I had passed on the way. Water was splashing out over its edges onto the courtyard floor and was running down and around me and out of the castle arches. A gardener was trimming hedges off to one side. Off to the other side was an old car of forties vintage.

The house was of beige stucco and was set within the castle ruins. Its focal point was a grand symmetrical staircase, one set of stairs leading up to a landing from the *left* and another leading up to the same landing from the *right*. Jack stood there smiling. I decided to take the stairs on the *left*.

We got the usual "hellos" and the "Boy, you don't look a day older," out of the way quickly. "I see you don't have an age limit on runners here. I almost got run over down there." I mentioned the man in the church plaza.

Jack replied, "That was the boss, he turns in a few miles every morning. If you had shown up a month from now, he would have taken you up a mountain or two with him. The six mounds in the forefront of his coat-of-arms depict the six peaks for which he holds the record in Italy.

"When he comes back, I'll introduce you, but you won't see much of him until dinnertime. He goes to Venice today. Come, I'll show you my little corner of the world."

He pulled back the huge door—its heavy opaque glass panels protected by elaborate iron lattice work required the strength of both arms. As we entered, I mentioned the protestors I had passed on the way, "It seems you have your union problems here in Italy, too."

Jack's answer was abrupt, "It is much more than unions. We will get to that later."

We entered a large open space, the reception area of the house. Definitive paths had been worn into the ancient stone floor. One could make out where people had walked through the ages. There was nothing there. That is, not a single piece of furniture, just open space leading to colorless leaded glass windows which I correctly guessed overlooked the village below.

Today, this room is an impressive introduction to the house. Its walls are lined with ornately framed life sized oil portraits of the dozen or so bishops who have lived here in the twentieth century. At the far end of the room, the portrait of Albino Luciani, the only one to have risen to the papacy, is hidden behind a door that leads to a prayer station which fronts a window.

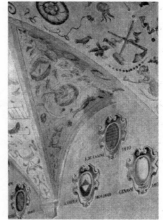

Like other portraits and statues of Papa Luciani that have been planted by the Vatican across northern Italy, from the small village he grew up in Carnal de Argo to Venice, this portrait depicts a man of one-hundred-and-five who is in the final days of a long, unsuccessful bout with pancreatic cancer—a part of the Vatican's deception to convince the public John Paul was at death's door when elected to the papacy.

The hand-painted arched ceiling in this grand vestibule contains the coat-of-arms of the eighty bishops who served here in Vittorio Veneto since the castle was built in the eighth century.

"Blessed are the poor… for theirs is the Kingdom of Heaven"

Jack took me to the end of the hall. We accessed a small alcove, his little corner of the world. A very little corner it was. I visualized my office back in the states overlooking the marina at the corporate headquarters of the company in which I was rapidly making my way up the ladder. "I was certainly winning this race," I thought.

The windowless area was as bare as it was small and clashed with its rich green, black and white marble terrazzo flooring which, instead of giving it the feeling of wealth it reflected, gave it a feeling of coldness. It was obvious the floor was not original; it had been added in recent times. Most of the opposite wall was made up by the room's centerpiece, a beautifully carved mahogany arched door.

The unbroken line of the yellowing wall was interrupted only by this door and a small bargain basement crucifix above it and a cheaply framed photograph of Pope John XXIII on the wall behind the desk which was more of an old wooden slab on legs than it was a desk. On the opposite wall hung one of those cheap alpine clocks one picks up in souvenir shops.

A message was written on the photograph. Approaching it, I found it was written in Italian. I heard over my shoulder,

Albino Luciani,

Christ asked me to express His congratulations on this important day of your life.

His Servant, John, 27 Dec 58

"It was given the man who occupies the adjoining cell" nodding at the richly carved mahogany door, "when he was made a bishop. Piccolo was the first bishop installed by John XXIII. The ceremony took place in St. Peter's."

I was struck by his reference to the bishop as 'Piccolo' and, at the same time, by the yodeling of a nun who ran out of the clock on the opposite wall. Sensing my shock at the sparseness of his corner of the world, he laughed, *"'Blessed are the poor... for theirs is the Kingdom of Heaven.'*

Mostly because of his toes

We chatted for awhile. He had just told me Piccolo must have run off to Venice, "... but you will meet him at dinner. He has been looking forward to meeting you," when suddenly, at the doorway stood the man who had run past me in the plaza. Clad in shorts and sandals, his wet hair told me he had just come out of the shower.

Two things struck me, the countenance of his smile and the perfection of his toes. I never thought of bishops as having toes, especially toes as flawlessly pedicured as these. I wondered if the nearby convent provided this service for bishops, a service that when I splurged for it cost me fifty bucks a throw back in the states.

A third thing struck me—his voice.

The voice was a piping, rasping voice. Not as if he was talking through his nose, but as if the pipe was built into his throat. It was a one-of-a-kind voice. It was this that made it relatively easy for me to follow what otherwise was heavily Italian accented broken English.

I could not think of the bishop title. "I apologize. I forget what I'm supposed to call you?" He cut me off, "Just call me the same thing everyone else calls me, 'Piccolo.'

"Yet, I must go. The thief of the ages is knocking at my door."

I turned toward Jack, "Did you hear someone knock?"

The bishop laughed, *"Time. Time is knocking. Time is a thief. It will rob one of one's childhood, eventually deprive one of one's youth and ultimately take one's life. But it is a good thief. It provides the span of wonderment for the child, the term of enlightenment while he grows and the age of fulfillment as he gives..."*[1]

He added, "My time to give is near." He was off.

"Piercing voice, huh?" Jack offered, noticing I had reacted to the bishop's voice. When he was a teen, he had a tonsillectomy that went haywire and left him with a uniquely raspy voice.

"Anyway," getting up from his chair, "I will show you where the boss spends his time dreaming up the next chapter for this sprawling paradise here in the foothills of the Italian Alps." He moved toward the great mahogany door and opening it, we proceeded in.

"Blessed are the poor in spirit..."

The office could not have been more impressive. My heart sank a bit as I thought of my relatively modest surroundings back in the states. I thought of the tax-free exemption status of the Church. Yes, the rich marble terrazzo flooring continued into the room, but here it was not out of place. The walls were richly carved mahogany.

We were in the company of angels.

Each one in Byzantine fashion, each one in individual color, each one bearing a shield with coat-of-arms, each one armed with a weapon of medieval times, each one topped off with a golden halo, each one standing in a carved mahogany panel. Each one watching, each one listening...

Yes, in addition to their protective presence they seemed to be listening, as if all that would be said within these walls would be related to the one above. Two more, in three dimension and white marble, guarded a huge walk-in fireplace at the far end of the room.

Above the mantel was an aging oil painting of Christ driving the moneylenders out of the temple——its dark tones accented by the brilliance of golden coins which cascaded out of the painting beyond its heavily gold encrusted frame. I thought it could be a Rembrandt.

Jack, noticed my appraisal, "No, not Rembrandt. It's a Titian. This is Titian country. His best works are here in Vittorio Veneto. His masterpiece is the altarpiece in the cathedral you passed on the way. Piccolo put this one here to remind us that Christ too had to deal with the republicans" he laughed.

One side of the room was set up as a boardroom with a huge coffin shaped mahogany table with gargoyles protecting its corners. Two wide Persian carpet runners lay along each side. Of a kind so plush that if one didn't take notice one would easily trip over them. On them sat a dozen richly embroidered chairs with matching gargoyles shooting out of their arms——six on each side. There were no chairs at the table's ends. "Piccolo is an advocate of symbolism. He reminds his visitors we are all equal. No one is at the top."

On the other side of the immense room was a personal work and reception area. A sofa and armchairs in Italian provincial sat in front of a huge kidney-shaped mahogany desk with neatly arranged writing instruments. There were no papers on the desk. The room seemed to be set up for display rather than set up as a workplace.

On the wall behind the desk, the only break in the perimeter of the room other than the door in which angels did not stand, were two relatively new life-sized oil paintings. The matching simplicity of their cheap modern frames clashed with the ornate antiqueness and wealth that was all about them——one of the reigning pope, Paul VI and the other of his predecessor, John XXIII. Between the two paintings was a framed document, this one in English,

Republic of Italy

For extraordinary heroism while engaged in military battle without regard to his own safety and risk of life no matter how great, to the betterment of lives of others no matter how small; the Republic of Italy is indebted to our eternal friend.

Aldo Moro, March 29, 1965

"Wow. He's a war hero." I exclaimed. "I will tell you about that later." With an athletic curl he rolled himself into the chair.

Suddenly, the somber setting came to life with the chiming of the hour. To one side a huge clock reached upward toward the ceiling easily fifteen feet in height. Glancing back to the door and then back to the windows, I wondered how one could have ever got a clock of such massive proportions into the room.

"It's a great, great grandfather clock," Jack offered. "Valdini's clocks fetch upwards of a quarter-million—on occasion, a half-million dollars. Because of its history, this one is worth twice that.

"It was given to the diocese when Leo XIII visited here late in the nineteenth century to mark the establishment of the seminary. The rest of the contents of the room including its paneling and mantelpiece came out of a monastery that was set on a mountain outside Naples. It was moved here as a protective measure when the allies reached Sicily and it became imminent they would take Italy. Pius thought the allies might destroy it. He was right. They bombed the hell out of it thinking it was used as an Axis headquarters."[2]

Summing up what I had just witnessed, *"Blessed are the poor for theirs is the Kingdom of Heaven."* I kept the thought to myself.

Jack read my mind, *"'Blessed are the poor in spirit for theirs is the Kingdom of Heaven,'*[3] are Christ's actual words.

"Piccolo says Christ refers to those who reason, those who don't easily believe, the poor in spirit. Those that use their conscience," he pointed to his temple, "rather than what is in a book. Those he calls the lions—as opposed to sheep. Yet, the mass of theology prefers to believe Christ was talking about the poor. Certainly, that is not what it says. Christ very obviously meant exactly what He said, *'the poor in spirit.'* Those lions who believe the search for the truth requires some effort of their own, rather than those sheep who just assume it is handed to them on a silver platter in their scriptures when they are born—those that think their birthright is their ticket to salvation.

"Piccolo rarely uses the office. He doesn't feel comfortable here. He handles his paperwork on the dining room table.

"Each of us sees in the clock a work of fine art and scientific achievement. Piccolo sees something else—the right of a good and healthy life for a thousand children. Within a week of his arrival, Piccolo started to sell much of this but the Vatican stopped him.

"If you have followed him in the world press, he is a threat to the regency of Rome should he ever rise to the papacy. Should he become Pope, his first act would be to liquidate the Vatican treasures to help annihilate poverty in third world countries."

173

"*Shoes of the Fisherman* was based on Piccolo. Anderson spent time here last year." Jack could not conceal his pride.

"Anderson?" I had never heard of him.

"Michael Anderson. He directed the film."

Jack walked to the mahogany table. Falling into a seat, he waved me into the opposite chair. "A word of our adversary," he began.

"Our adversary?" I repeated in a question.

"Yes, our adversary, Moses" he replied.

"Moses?" I questioned, again.

"Yes, Moses," he returned the ball. "Moses is the quartermaster of selfishness in the western world. It is he more than anyone else who draws the line between 'us' and 'them.' It is he who supplies the bigot with his arsenal of weapons—a bottomless pit, this arsenal that gives the bigot the words he needs to conduct his evil war.

"It is Moses in the Old Testament who tells us *'It is God the Father's command woman live in dire servitude to man.'* It is Moses in the Old Testament who tells us *'It is God the Father's command slavery be a way of life.'* It is Moses in the Old Testament who tells us *'It is God the Father's command those with flat noses, those we call Negroes today, and the handicapped are subordinate people and are not worthy to approach the presence of the Lord.'* It is Moses in the Old Testament who tells us *'It is God the Father's command born-out-of-wedlock children are not to approach the congregation of the Lord.'* It is Moses in the Old Testament who tells us *'It is God the Father's command homosexuals are to be put to death.'* It is Moses in the Old Testament who tells us *'It is God the Father's command sex is shameful and sinful.'* It is Moses in the Old Testament who tells us *'It is God the Father's command the prostitute and the adulteress be taken outside the city and stoned to death.'* It is Moses in the Old Testament who tells us *'It is God the Father's command whoever does not seek the Lord God of Israel shall surely be put to death...'*"[3]

"Each of these instructions and many more like them tell us what kind of God we are dealing with in the God of Moses, a selfish God." He raised his voice a notch, "No preacher can stand on a stage and tell his flock otherwise, for his scripture is his adversary."

He paused to give me time to grasp all the terrible things he had said. "The validity of Moses depends entirely upon whether or not he was telling the truth. Was Moses telling the truth when he told the story of the four hundred years the Israelites spent in Egypt? Was he telling the truth when he told the story of the Ten Plagues? Was he telling the truth when he told the story of the Exodus? Was he telling the truth when he told the story of the parting of the Rea Sea? Was he telling the truth when he told the story of the forty year wandering in the desert? Was he telling the truth when he claimed a ghost in the form of a burning bush talked to him in the desert? Was he telling the truth when he told his people a ghost appeared to him and gave him the Ten Commandments? Was he telling the truth when he told the stories of Creation and of Adam and Eve?

"This is the great hurdle we face. Picture books and motion pictures, influenced by preachers, have created the illusion Moses was a holy man. Yet, anyone who takes the time to read the books literally can only come to the conclusion Moses was a monster."

He raised his voice an octave or so with a tinge of frustrated anger, "There was nothing holy about this man. He has led the world into thirty-three hundred years of hatred and prejudice and persecution and horror and suffering and destruction and death!"

Silence prevailed. I broke the stillness, "Well, it is clear no one could prove Moses was not telling the truth in what he had to say. None of us were there; we don't really know what God told him."

Jack stopped. He peered around the room suspiciously, carefully examining the expressions of each of the angels which surrounded us. His action gave me the chance to count them, thirty-three in all.

I thought of the thirty-three years Christ had lived and of the thirty-three months of His ministry and of the thirty-three months Anne Frank had hid in the attic. In retrospect, I could add the thirty-three days of Luciani's papacy. I thought of the thirty-three centuries Moses had wreaked havoc and bloodshed upon mankind.

Jack's eyes finally wandered back to me, "Let's go for a walk."

1 Luciani originally said this in eulogy to John XXIII in the Basilica di San Marco in Venice 4 Jun 63
2 The trappings of the room were returned to Naples in the early seventies. The space was divided into four separate rooms including reception rooms lined with Italian provincial chairs and a secretary's office and the bishop's office. In one of the reception rooms is a small glass case housing items of John Paul's ministry, including military medals mentioned in this book.
3 Biblical quotations in this chapter are taken from the five books attributed to Moses

Photos: All photos in this chapter are in the author's collection and were photographed by the author

Author's note: For brevity, the author relates his time with Albino Luciani as if it was a single encounter, whereas there were about a dozen encounters in all.

Chapter 19

Murder in the Veneto

"Sell all thou hast and give to the poor."[1]   Jesus Christ

A light mist was falling. "I am about to show you our best kept secret." I followed him along a path edged in with lush underbrush which wound down around and then back up the mountainside.

We came into a grotto. Towering walls of darkened slate showed off a cascading waterfall splattering down onto and off of rocks into a sparkling blue pond edged in splashes of green.

On our side of the pond was spreading greenery flowering with red, white, yellow, blue and orange—whatever colors the Master happened to have dabbed into with His brush when He executed this breathtaking work of art.

Much of the color was in motion, butterflies and fireflies hovered here and there and everywhere. In the crystal clear water ran a living rainbow of fish glistening in an endless array of silver, gold, orange, red and what have you.

Opposite, a silent wind crept about evergreens. Half-circling the pond, they formed a crescent as if to reflect the moon which was not there. As the mist made its retreat, slivers of the sun's rays pierced through the trees as if trying to take out a frog or two which sat on island rocks of gray surrounded by more islands of green lily pads. All told, like a family reunion posing for a picture.

I thought of the infinite diversity of earth's species as my ears captured the hum of bees, the chirping of birds, the croaking of frogs, the chirping of crickets, the squeaking of a field mouse or two in a nearby bush and, alas, Jack's voice, "Piccolo and I call it our Garden of Eden. We do our best thinking here." Suspiciously glancing about the grotto, "We tell our best secrets here, too."

To our left, was a small tree sporting apple blossoms. I thought, "Could this be a descendent of the one that started it all?"

Jack laughed, "Piccolo planted it when he first came here and everyone who sees it thinks the same thing you're thinking. No, its parents were American. It is an American apple tree.

176

"He is fond of Americans. He's proud of what they are doing. He is particularly proud of the Kennedys and the work they have done for the handicapped in introducing the Special Olympics. Last year, Piccolo held a mini-Special Olympics here in Vittorio Veneto.

"Ten years ago when he first arrived, Piccolo attended the winter festival and was disturbed not a single handicapped child was to be seen. Shortly afterwards, he set up a clinic, a kind of halfway-house, designed to take many of these children out of institutions and allowing them to live together with the general population.[2]

"Yet, Moses stood in his way. Parents didn't want their children exposed to impaired children. They picketed our building of a ramp into the cathedral, the first one built into a Catholic church anywhere in the world. Their signs went so far as to quote the words of Moses barring the handicapped from the Lord's altar. Nevertheless, Piccolo knows the future of the world depends on what Americans do. One reason I'm here. Of course, there is another reason why I'm here."

"Another reason?" I followed.

"We'll get to that later. Come on." He motioned I follow him.

Baby pigeons

Two large rocks sat at the pond's edge a conversation apart. He took one and I, the other. He paused a moment to give me one last chance to take in all the wonderment that was about us. He started, "The castle angels most likely do have ears and it is for this reason I have brought you here. Although we have never been able to find them, we are certain the house is bugged.

"Just before we left the office you said, 'No one could prove Moses lied in what he had to say, as none of us were there. We don't really know what God the Father told him.'

"Not true. If one could prove Moses was lying then one could rid the planet of bigotry once and for all. It would destroy the arsenal of weapons—those flimsy words from which the bigot draws his ammunition. When we speak of Moses we are dealing with that part of the Bible where the historical benchmark is exact.

"The foundation of what Moses had to say was the story of the four hundred thirty years the Israelites were in Egypt. If they had been in Egypt, then much of what Moses said would fall into place.

"Yet, if one could prove the Israelites were not in Egypt at that time, all of what Moses said would fall to ruin for all the stories he told took place in the four hundred thirty years the Israelites were in Egypt and the forty year wandering in the Sinai Desert.

"In the summer of 1966, Piccolo, I and Brother Amedore—a local monk—visited our mission in Burundi Africa where our priests are serving. On our return, we stopped in Egypt.

"The intent was to uncover evidence of the Israelites' presence in Egypt during the Middle Kingdom Period—1750BC to 1320BC— the four hundred thirty years the Bible claims they were in Egypt— in Egyptologist terms, the twelfth through the eighteenth dynasties.

"According to the Bible, it was because of their great numbers— over two million of them—the Israelites were put into slavery during the last forty years of their alleged time in Egypt. *'Pharaoh said, Behold the children of the people of Israel are more and mightier than we: Come on, let us deal wisely with them lest they turn against us. So with hard bondage of mortar and brick the Israelites built for Pharaoh the treasure cities of Pithom and Ramesses.'*[3]

"What did you find?" eager to learn of this proof of the Bible.

He paused as a detective pauses before revealing the solution to his case. "Nothing, nothing at all. We proved the Israelites had never been in Egypt during Moses' alleged time. We examined thousands of ancient graves in the cities of Pithom and Ramesses where the Bible contends the Israelites lived which date to the Israelites alleged time in Egypt. We couldn't find a Hebrew marking on any grave."

"Nothing?" I was astonished, as it was something I had always taken for granted. It would be like looking at a photograph of the Empire State Building after all these years and assuming all the time it had a first, second, third, fourth and fifth floor; floors, though concealed by low-lying buildings around it, were obviously there. It is obvious the Empire State Building has its first five floors otherwise one could have never added the other ninety-seven floors.

Although no one has ever seen one, it is obvious there are baby pigeons. Otherwise there would be no pigeons. It is obvious Christianity has a first, second, third, fourth and fifth floor—the five books of Moses—otherwise one could have never added the other sixty-two books of the Bible. One doesn't have to see it to believe it. It is obvious the Israelites were in Egypt. No sound mind would question it. I shuddered at the magnitude of Jack's revelation.

Jack answered my unasked question. "Yes, we found nothing at all. There is much more than just the graves. There is the vast volume of hieroglyphs in the tombs, palaces and monuments of Egypt, which if reduced to fine print would fill all the volumes of all the libraries in the world. Sixty thousand rooms have been opened and they are covered  from floor to ceiling with hieroglyphs. What's more, there are tens of thousands of tablets with more hieroglyphs.

"About a third of this volume pertains to the four hundred years the Israelites were said to be in Egypt. Over twenty million human figures have survived in the hieroglyphics. They spell out in great detail every major event that occurred during that time: the birth, period of reign and death of every pharaoh, every war waged, every battle fought, every famine, every plague, every invention, every advancement in civilization—but not a single trace of any of Moses tales. Though most are Egyptian, there are many Hyksos, Hittites and Nubians among them; the Hyksos ruled Egypt during the twelfth through the fifteen dynasties; two Hyksos kings were Nubians.

"Despite the biblical 'fact' more than half of its population was Israelite, there is not a single mention of the way of life of the Israelites in Egypt dating to Moses' time. No mention of the Red Sea Miracle in which the Egyptian army and its Pharaoh perished which, if true, would be the greatest event in all of Egyptian history

"This is consistent with history books which place the earliest Jewish inhabitants in northern Egypt at about 650BC—six hundred years after the alleged Exodus."

A body floating in the canal

"Yet, that is not why I brought you here."

He waited for eye-to-eye contact. "Last month, Pasquale was found floating in the canal that runs behind your hotel.

"Pasquale...?" It was a new name to me.

"Brother Amedore. The inquest determined he had drowned. Piccolo had an autopsy performed. No water was found in the lungs; he was dead when thrown in the water. There was hemorrhaging in the brain; he had been clubbed. Piccolo's suspicions were sound.

179

"You're suggesting the Vatican took out Pasquale because the Israelites had never been in Egypt?" I hinted at the ridiculous. "It shouldn't be that much of a surprise the Israelites were not in Egypt.

"Television takes us into scores of tombs exhibiting thousands of figures and never is there any hint of the Israelites. If there was any trace of the Israelites having been in Egypt, these entrepreneurs would capitalize on it as their market is a Judeo-Christian audience. It should be no surprise to the faithful Moses was telling lies."[4]

"It's not that. It's something else." He paused to emphasize the importance of what he was about to say. "The protestors, you passed on the train, are much more than union workers. They are trying to bring about a redistribution of wealth society here in Italy."

"Yes, I saw their signs, *'Equal Pay.'*" I agreed.

"A redistribution of wealth society is much more than equal pay" he corrected me. "It is communism. Today, Italy is on a fast track to becoming a communist nation sitting in the middle of Europe. Despite that electoral progression is moving overwhelmingly toward communism and socialism, the work is going too slowly for much of Italy's impatient youth. They have taken to the streets."

"Why doesn't Piccolo stop them?" I challenged

"Stop them? He and some of his priests have been leading them. So much so, the newspapers have tabbed the movement, *'the priest-worker revolution.'* He's been encouraging them to stand up for their rights. The protestors are overwhelmingly street orphans who have survived to adulthood. Having been deprived of education, they are made to work almost as slaves for a small pittance of their worth.

"Piccolo wants to bring an end to Moses' doctrine of bigotry—hatred of one's fellowman. Yet, above all, he wants to bring about a world in which every child has an equal opportunity to a good life including higher education to enable them to contribute to society.

"Christ's dictate of a redistribution of wealth society is the most explicit testimony of His ministry. He said it in so many different ways, if one could not get it in one way, one would be sure to get it in another way, *'Sell all that thou hast and give to the poor.'*[5] *'Lay not up for yourselves treasures upon this earth, where moth and rust doth corrupt. But lay up for yourselves treasures in heaven, where neither moth nor rust doth corrupt. For where your treasure is, will be your heart also...'*[6] *'It is easier for a camel to pass through the eye of a needle than it is for a rich man to enter the Kingdom of*

Heaven...[7] He rambled on and on until my eyes told him to stop.

"Like Marx, Christ condemned private property. So much so he required His disciples to give up all they owned and come follow Him. Peter gave up his fish nets. Christ dictated a redistribution of wealth society—communism—*'What is in this for others?'*

"Yet, today, those who pretend to be Christians prefer to think He didn't mean what He said. They prefer to think He had had too much wine the night before He said these things—things he said every day of His ministry. Christ was an alcoholic so to speak.

"They prefer to live in their world of capitalism. All they have to do is get down on their knees at night and go to church on Sunday.*"*

"Yes," I agreed. "I have often thought of what would this first century man who preached *'sell all thou hast and give to the poor'* think if He were to stroll into the Vatican today. If he were to take the first pew in St. Peter's and watch a deranged madman dressed up in women clothes of silk and satin prancing about an altar of marble and gold drinking His blood from a diamond studded chalice? What would Christ think of a mob of ghoulish zombies lining up in a cannibalistic ritual to get a taste of His flesh? What would He think if he stopped in the Raphael bathroom with its magnificent trappings on the second floor of the Papal Palace on His way to meet the Pope if, God forbid, He had to relieve Himself? What would He think...?"

Jack retook the floor. "Ten years ago when the Communist Party in Italy reached double-digit electoral progression, Richard Nixon, then Vice President, established Operation Gladio—a covert army of former Nazis—to keep communism out of Europe. Communism in Italy was particularly dangerous to him as, unlike Russia, Italy is a free democratic society. The growing success of communism was the will of the people. If it were successful in Italy it would spread rapidly in Europe and eventually to the Americas—the world would become a redistribution of wealth society as Christ had instructed.

"Shortly afterwards, in 1960, Nixon lost the presidency to John Kennedy—a democrat—an advocate of a redistribution of wealth society. Kennedy was followed by Johnson—too, a firm believer in a redistribution of wealth society. Until recently, Operation Gladio—unsupported by American presidents—remained dormant. During this time, the Communist Party of Italy has grown to very much more than simply double-digit progression in the polls.

"But, today, Nixon is president. Someone who is convinced

society can be driven only by greed. Someone who believes it is fair some children are born into immense wealth while others are born into immense poverty.

"He has stepped up his war against communism and supplied Operation Gladio with hundreds of millions of dollars and weapons and ammunition caches together with instruction to terrorize the Italian people and turn its mindset against communism."

"You're suggesting Nixon killed Pasquale?" I shivered.

Jack didn't bat an eye. "Operation Gladio did the job."

"But, why Pasquale …?" I started.

Jack cut in, "Pasquale was Piccolo's man-on-the-job organizing youth in the Veneto country. He was becoming much too visible and a threat to American interests here. He had to be taken out. Colombo has lost several others…"

"Colombo?" My ears perked up.

"Giovanni Colombo," troubled I'd never heard of him.

"When Paul—the Archbishop of Milan—became Pope in 1965, he replaced himself in the heart of industrialized Italy with Colombo together with the commission to lead Italy into a more just society.

"Paul's commission was much more than a covert instruction to one man. Two years ago, Paul issued his decree *Populorum Progressio*.[8] He established certain basic rights of man including the right to a just wage and the right to fair working conditions and the right to join a union. Paul ignited the priest-worker revolution.

"Italians remain among the most devout Catholics in the world and it has been Colombo and his lieutenants who have preached Christ's message from the pulpit that the Italian socialist-communist parties have attained an overwhelming plurality in the polls.

"Piccolo is Colombo's right-hand man. Together with Aldo Moro they are the driving force in Italy, actually in all of Europe, behind Paul's encyclical to bring about a day when everyone has enough.

"More recently, Paul expanded his encyclical into Latin America and other impoverished parts of the Catholic world.

"There, the press has tabbed it *Liberation Theology*. Here, we call it *the Priest-Worker Revolution*. Both movements, led by clergy, are carrying out Paul's encyclical to bring about a free communist society—a redistribution of wealth society as the will of the people.

"Nevertheless, Piccolo called Paul and told him of the autopsy findings. A half-dozen unwed mothers had been living in the castle bedrooms. Because of the impending danger he relocated them to other buildings. Now, the rooms are occupied by guards Paul sent up from the Vatican. One accompanied you on the train from Venice.

"Strange. I didn't notice…"

He cut me off, "Another was the gardener in the castle courtyard.

"Gladio is likely to continue picking off those in the ranks. If Gladio were to take out Colombo or Piccolo, it would yield much more than a footnote in the world press. Yet, we are all in danger. Even Paul, himself, must taste his porridge suspiciously each day."

He paused briefly and started up again, "Nevertheless, in case something happened to us, Piccolo feels someone should know. Someone who it is reasonable to believe will be around at the end of the century and could bring an end to the world of greed we live in as quickly as one turns off a faucet. That Piccolo, long after he is gone, perhaps, long after I am gone, will carry out his father's order, 'You must find the strength to do what you have to do to bring about a day when all men accept each other as equal.'

I stopped him, "But me? How could I possibly accomplish such a thing? I will probably be a 'nobody' at that time."

He didn't give up, "You will do it in the same way every other 'nobody' has accomplished his or her objectives. The same way Mark and his contemporaries accomplished their objectives."

"Mark and his contemporaries?" I added a question mark.

"Yes, like the evangelists wrote of Christ generations after His time." He paused and raised his voice, "You, too, will write a book."

"But I don't know how to write a book," I told him.

"You will write a book, for each and every one of them!"

My mind drifted back to yesterday, to that time I had taken the pledge in the cemetery at Milan, *". . . my solemn promise to carry out that sacred pledge for each and every one of them. That what they dreamed of, those things they willed to be, will come to be, for each of them, and for me, and for you, and for all humanity!"*

The factory

Getting up, he patted me on the shoulder, "Enough said. Let's go to lunch. Vittorio Veneto is smack in the middle of Italian wine country. I will take you to a sidewalk cafe where the food is terrible, but what counts most, the wine is marvelous."

We wound down around the mountain and strolled along the seminary. "This is our crown jewel. It is what makes Vittorio Veneto such an important post. It was Piccolo who made it that way."

We headed down a cobblestone street and passed a clock tower. At its base was one of those gelato stands one sees all over Europe. Jack said, "There are ten million of these stands in the world. This one is in first place. We will stop here on the way back."

"Not many people," I thought. Each one, some walking, some running, and a few on bicycles, had obviously been there all their lives; a hundred, perhaps two hundred Italians, and I.

As people looked at me, I relished my individuality. Each one said "Hi Jack" in perfect English despite that Jack could speak perfect Italian. Each of them had an expression of great respect and admiration and awe, as if Jack were some kind of a God.

1 *Mathew 19*

2 The story '*The Shovel and the Ribbon*' in the author's book of short stories '*Let's All Get Behind the Pope*' recreates Bishop Luciani's effort to build the clinic.

3 *Genesis*

4 The last alleged apparition to Moses was the taking of the Ten Commandments on Mount Sinai on the Sinai Peninsula. Late in the twentieth century, when hundreds of archeological expeditions by the Vatican and other Christian churches confirmed the Israelites had never been in Egypt and the 40 year wandering had never taken place on the Sinai Peninsula, dozens of peaks in the Mid East were renamed 'Mount Sinai.' Preachers since claim the taking of the Commandments took place on these various mountains. The official position of the Catholic Church today: the taking of the Commandments took place on a mountain in Eastern Turkey and not on the Sinai Peninsula. Jack's declaration "The Israelites were never in Egypt." would not be as startling in today's world where people of average intelligence know the Israelites were never in Egypt. There is not a Jew in Israel today who goes to Egypt to trace his or her heritage. All Bibles printed before 1881, specifically number the Israelites as six hundred thousand men and their women and children—generally placing the Israelite population that crossed the Red Sea at over two million. Most current Bibles drop the phrase '*and women and children*' to reduce the number to six hundred thousand. The King James Bible drops the number entirely. Modern films reduce the number to a few dozen in order to get around the archeological fact the Israelites were never in Egypt. Book and films depict literally millions of hieroglyphs—not a single Hebrew symbol or figure has ever been found among them.

5 *Mathew 19*

6 *Mathew 6*

7 *Mark 10*

8 Paul issued his encyclical '*Populorum Progressio*' on March 26, 1967. It sparked the worker's revolution in Italy which led to the Communist Party rise in the polls in the seventies. The cover quote is taken from Paul's edict and it established what would have been the scope of John Paul's papacy.

Photo Egyptian Hieroglyphic - *author*

The author is a scholar in Egyptology and has spent much time in Egypt. Through the intercession of the Cairo Museum he has gained access to tombs off limits to the general public

Chapter 20

Albino Luciani and General Patton

"It is our differences that have built us into the great nation of one that we are. There should be no room here for preachers and politicians who would choose to use them to divide us."   General George Patton

We took a table outside a restaurant where the street formed a wedge with its neighbor, one of those they try to duplicate in the big cities with little success. Heeding Jack's advice, I decided on bread, cheese and fruit. He doubled the order.

Shortly, the waiter returned and spread an assortment of breads, cheeses and fruits. In the center he placed a crystal clear bottle of wine set in chopped ice. I was about to get a taste of the afterlife.

Reaching for the bottle, Jack poured our glasses properly half full of this memory—this wine of the Gods—which is still with me today. Like any other close friends, who hadn't seen each other for a number of years, we started to chat about the good old times.

Alas, I asked, "You sure are popular. Just being a seminary priest gets you that?"

"It has nothing to do with that," he answered. "It is owed entirely to something else."

A thousand 'hellos'

"My uncle was in the military during the world war. He held two purple hearts and a dozen other enviable decorations. In a heroic action he was hit in North Africa and was hospitalized for six months with serious liver damage. He was nominated for the *Medal of Honor*, but instead received a *Silver Star*.

"He was hit again, this time paralyzed from the waist down. He was hit by friendly fire when he placed himself between his own men and twenty-eight Italian school children to alert them they were about to fire on the children. It happened just outside Milan.

"He was nominated for the nation's highest award. Because it had occurred toward war's end and helped to heal the wounds of war

185

and since it had been witnessed by so many, we were certain this time he would reap the honor that had escaped him in North Africa.

"Wow. He won the *Medal of Honor!*" I exclaimed

"Not quite," he corrected me. "This time they gave him the *Distinguish Service Cross*, the nation's second highest award."

"But, I don't under…"

He cut me off, "The *Distinguished Service Cross* is awarded for risk of life *'not quite'* justifying the *Medal of Honor*. The *'not quite'* in my uncle's case was determined the same way as was the case of many other candidates who were passed up for the highest award."

"How's that?" I queried.

"During the world war, *'not quite'* was most often defined as being soldiers of color and of ethnic backgrounds including Asians. In my uncle's case *'not quite'* meant something else."

"Something else?" I repeated.

"My uncle was gay. Because his life seemed wasted he felt he could be a martyr for the cause. Foolishly, he announced he was gay while the matter was pending. He told my mother his admission of his homosexuality took much more courage than when he had placed himself before the firing squad to protect the children. He hoped he could attract national attention but he didn't attract a fly. All he did was to deprive himself of the nation's highest military award.

"Nevertheless, this is why I am a celebrity in these parts. This is why wherever I go I get a thousand 'hellos.' People believe some of my uncle's courage has rubbed off on me.

"Back then, homosexuality was not the type of thing his family wanted to talk about, much less see spread across the front page of the local newspaper. In fact, it still isn't today."

"So, the Army threw him out?" I presumed.

"No. There was no policy restricting homosexuals from serving in the armed services. Many gay men and women served honorably through the years. There was no box to check, no problem.

"When you have a real war, one in which you are fighting for survival, one doesn't stop to sort out what the preacher considers to be morality.

"That he didn't attract a fly was not entirely true. He drew an official reprimand from Eisenhower; something General Patton, my uncle's commanding officer, tried to block.

"My uncle relished it. He saw it as a victory; he had drawn the attention of Ike, himself."

"So how is he now? Certainly he could do something now, being a war hero," I offered.

"He isn't," he replied, "A couple of months after receiving the award he died from a liver infection related to his earlier injury that was brought on by his confinement to bed."

"...a new different of courage..."

"Only his father flew to Italy. His mother was too distraught. His father told my mother the army provided full military honors for him. There was speculation General Patton, who happened to be in the area at the time, would attend.

Although several hundred villagers attended, he didn't show up. In fact, not a single officer showed up despite that my uncle held one of the nation's highest awards. Yet, someone else did show up."

"Someone else?" I queried.

"Yes, Piccolo. It is not by mere chance I managed to secure an assignment here as an instructor in this remote Italian seminary and eventually grew so close to my patron. Piccolo had officiated at my uncle's interment. Yes, I groomed myself for the assignment going so far as to earn a PhD in psychiatry and becoming fluent in Italian. But, the only reason I got the job was because Piccolo had rendered my uncle's eulogy.

"At the time, Milan was conservative and no local priest could be found who was comfortable in officiating at the ceremony. The archbishop reached into the Veneto country. The choice was the revolutionary and outspoken young priest from Belluno.

"As I said, the army provided full military honors for my uncle. A lance corporal showed up heading up a detail of four soldiers, three with rifles and one with a bugle. Piccolo doesn't remember too much of what he said, other than he had ended his string of prayers with an embittered comment, '*It is the soldier who shed his blood on the field of battle and not the preacher who cowers in his pulpit, who should determine who should or should not be free.*'

"The detail raised their rifles and fired off three volleys over the heads of three hundred villagers and the man with the bugle did the best he could with the taps.

"Three volleys for a man who gave his life to save twenty-eight children. Yet, military rules call for nineteen volleys for political appointees of a president. It kind of tells one how America thinks.

"Anyway, as the crowd started to move away from the grave, a strange thing happened."

"A strange thing?" I repeated his statement as a question.

"Yes, an olive green military sedan, one of those with the big bubble fenders one often sees in the movies, entered the cemetery and moved along its outer perimeter and came to rest in the roadside along my uncle's grave. A young soldier got out of the front seat and opened the rear door. An army officer of about sixty stepped out.

"When Patton reached the gravesite he introduced himself to Piccolo and my uncle's father as if the rows of stars on his shoulders could not have conveyed the message. A light rain was falling from darkened skies and one could imagine hearing the firing of artillery shells in the distance though there was nothing there.

"Patton told them, speaking decisively and pausing on each syllable, as if he was addressing Congress, 'At West Point, there are many courses, one learns many things. One learns the history of war, one learns the purpose of war, one learns the strategy of war, one learns the struggle of war, one learns the noise of war, one learns the horror of war, one learns the victory of war and one learns the hopelessness of war. Yet the most important course one takes is taken on the great battlefield itself. That course is called *courage.*

"'This is the difference between Ike and myself for Ike has never taken this course. Never once in his lifetime has he carried himself into battle, into the pit. Not once in his lifetime has he pulled the boy out of the mud and searched for where the mud left off and the blood began. Not once has he reached for the final pulse of this thing called life. Never, not once, has he given himself the opportunity to realize this great prize we know as *courage.* His only experience in battle has been in his textbooks and in his toy soldiers and in his toy tanks and in his toy ships that he moves about on his great table of war. Like the preacher in the pulpit whose only time in battle has been in the atrocities of the ethnic cleansing wars in his scripture.'

"With a great tear forming in the corner of his eye, Patton placed his hand on my uncle's father's shoulder and told him, 'I apologize for Ike's action. It does not speak for me, does not speak for those who fought alongside your son, does not speak for America.

"'Your son has won for all of us, this thing called *courage.* This

188

thing called *courage* that I, too, have sought many times. That I, as a commanding general, would place myself upon a tank at the forefront of battle in open line of enemy fire and with artillery shells bursting all about me, I too, have craved for the taste of this thing *courage*. Yet, even I have yet to realize its dream.

"'Yesterday, I assigned my most courageous and most highly decorated officer to represent your son's fellow soldiers here today. Yet, I found that officer had failed in his duty by delegating his sacred responsibility to a subordinate.

"'Not because he had more important things to do, but because he didn't have the *courage* to be here—a different kind of *courage*, a greater kind of *courage*. He was afraid of what the press might do to him, of what his fellow soldiers might do to him, of what his family might do to him, of what America might do to him.

"'Your son had that kind of *courage*. He wasn't afraid of what the press might do to him. He wasn't afraid of what the army might do to him. He wasn't afraid of what his family might do to him. He didn't care what America might do to him.'

"The general then stepped a few paces to the left and placed his hand on the shoulder of the adjoining tombstone, the one marked *Anthony Jackson, Bronze Star.* 'Even today the *Christian right* continues to segregate and persecute blacks, many of whom have also shed their blood on the great battlefields of this war.'

"He placed his hand on the shoulder of the next stone, the one marked *Patricia Wilde, Bronze Star.* 'The world will never know of her valor, will never know of her bravery, will never know of the things she did for freedom. All that evidences she had ever been, is this small white granite stone and the marks upon it.'

"Freedom without equality is not what it pretends to be . . ."

"The general then turned toward the crowd and raised his voice, *'After this war is won, after the final volleys are fired, after the smoke clears and the tears begin, America must fight a new kind of war and that war will be fired by a new kind of courage.*

"'This war will win for America and all mankind this thing called freedom. But that war, the war within, will someday win for America the great prize of equality for all men and women, something this war cannot do. For freedom without equality is not

what it pretends to be. The diamond would be made of paste.

"'It is our differences that have built us into the great nation of one that we are. There is no room here for those preachers and politicians who would choose to use them to divide us.

"'Today men and women of great courage are engaged in this great war which will soon crush the enemy from without, but it must take many more men and women of still another kind of courage, a greater kind of courage, to rise up and crush the enemy from within. Only then, would these brave men and women not have died in vain. Only then, will the diamond, this thing one calls freedom, be real.'[1]

"As he climbed into the car, Patton turned to my uncle's father, 'I have been proud to have had your son serve in my army here.' Looking up, 'He is proud to have him in His army, today.' A tear dropped onto his cheek. He nodded to his driver. They were off.

"Yet, you're right. If my uncle were alive today, he could do something; perhaps not much, but something. In fact, all the other homosexuals who hold high military awards including many who hold the *Medal of Honor* could do something."

I interrupted him, "I thought they weeded out the gays in awarding the *Medal of Honor?*"

"The great majority of gays remain in the closet today, even more so was the case then. In the war, four hundred congressional medals were awarded. If one plays the percentages, this would mean about thirty to forty of them are held by truly homosexual men. But of course, like my uncle most did not survive. But if a few of them who did survive were brave enough to come forward, it would stop much of the preacher's bigotry in its tracks. But, as my uncle said, that would take a greater kind of courage than did his action in 1944 when he stood before the children.

"This is what Patton was referring to when he said *'It must take many more men and women of still another kind of courage, perhaps even a greater kind of courage, who must rise up and crush the enemy from within.'* Celebrities who make public their sexual orientation serve as great role models for gay youth. Bring it out in the open and the stigma will disappear overnight. As you know in the fifties, this is what brought an end to the stigma of born-out-of-wedlock children, something the Vatican has never accepted."

With a gesture of reverent solemnity, he stretched out his arm. He pulled back his sleeve to display his watch. On one side on the band was welded a small heart pendant with an image of George Washington on a purple background. On the opposite side of the face of the watch was welded a Silver Star. "The *Distinguished Service Cross* and the others are with him. They are in the great cemetery at Milan. Yet, there is something more.

"Three years ago, Piccolo used his influence with Aldo Moro who was then Prime Minister. In 1965, at the grave with twenty-three of the surviving children looking on, on behalf of my uncle I accepted the citation from Moro that is on Piccolo's office wall."

Leaving some of the wine in order that we could find our way, I settled up with the waiter and we started back. Stopping at the gelato stand, I followed his lead, "One of these, one of these, one of these and one of those." As we walked away, I wondered how the finest gelato in the world could have found its way so near to its finest wine. At the end of the street, he went one way, and I the other. He called out after me, "Dinner is promptly at seven."

As I walked back to the hotel, it ran over and over again in my mind, *"To carry out that solemn promise, to answer that fervent prayer, to carry it out for each and every one of them, that what they dreamed of, those things they willed to be, will come to be, for each of them, and for me, and for you, and for all humanity!"*

Author comment: Patton and Luciani shared an interest in the possibilities of reincarnation something they often discussed until Patton's untimely death. On Christmas day 1945, Luciani eulogized Patton in the Duomo at Belluno,

> *"I remember them all*
> *Many names, many faces*
> *Many times, many places*
> *Many ups, many downs*
> *Many smiles, many frowns*
> *Many struggles, many dreams*
> *Yet always, me!"*   *Albino Luciani*

1 *Affria Italiani* 31 Mar 44. Milan Italy 29 March 44. General George Patton. Albino Luciani, who had officiated at the same ceremony, quoted Patton's remarks on October 17, 1973 in a sermon in the Basilica San Marco in Venice—author's file. The unitalicized remarks are to the best of Albino Luciani's recollection as he related them to the author.
2 Albino Luciani, Milan Italy 29 Mar 44. He repeated this many times during his ministry

Chapter 21

The Mud in the Street

"When I was a teenager, my father made me promise I would live my life in imitation of Christ. I have kept that solemn promise. Each time the fork in the road has come up, I have asked myself, 'Now, what would Jesus have done in this case?' I have often pondered the possibility as to how much better the world would be if everyone were to do this..."

Albino Luciani

I found myself in an ancient room of stone. Its focal point a pair of bottle-bottom leaded glass windows peering out through ornate iron grates. Though their opaqueness obscured the view, it was clear what they were looking at—the surviving ruins of the castle walls.

The old stone floor with its centuries of wear was every bit as cold as it seemed to be. A beautiful antique sideboard of mellowed wood ran along the wall opposite the windows.

Just above it, an aging, colorful, tapestry of princes and paupers blanketed the wall. At the far end of the room a giant oil painting in a gold encrusted frame depicted Christ's miracle of the loaves and fishes. I correctly assumed it was another Titian.

A huge black iron cauldron hung in front of walk-in fireplace cut into the ancient stone exactly as it was on the day it had been forced into retirement by the stove that stood in the kitchen off to one side.

In the center of the room was a carpet of extraordinary value. On it stood four richly carved chairs which clashed with the table they surrounded—one of those cheap enameled tables of the forties. Four chairs that would easily draw five thousand dollars each at auction, hemmed in a table that would go for five dollars in a yard sale.

"One of his first visitors from Rome was Bishop Caprio. When he came into the dining room and he saw the table was gone he thrust his arms into the air like a man out of his mind. He ordered Piccolo to stop this madness, *'Sell all that thou hast and give to the poor.'"*

"He built the orphanage I passed with money he got for a table?"

"No," he corrected me. "He built that one with money intended to build a church. The day he took up residence here he received a letter from a terminally ill man. Lacking heirs, the man offered to leave his fortune to build a church dedicated to Christ the Savior.

"Piccolo went to visit the man the next day and asked him to leave the money to build an orphanage instead of a church. The man held his ground and demanded the great church be built.

"Having exhausted every possible alternative, Piccolo reached into his hip pocket and played his trump card, one he often used to get his way. *"When I was a teenager, my father made me promise I would live my life in imitation of Christ. I have kept that solemn promise. Each time the fork in the road has come up, often only minutes apart, I have asked myself, 'Now, what would Jesus have done in this case?'* He then asked the man, *"Now, what do you think Jesus would do in this case?*

"A week later, the man took a shovel and broke ground for the orphanage, one designed for infants who otherwise would have been aborted. He was buried a month later in a nearby cemetery. A granite marker was placed on his grave by the grateful bishop of Vittorio Veneto, *"Each day he breathes new life into the world."*

"As long as a child lacks a roof over his or her head and has not enough to eat, not a block of stone will be laid to build a church. Not a stone has been laid to build a church in the diocese since he came here. Likewise, should he rise to the papacy, not a single stone will be laid to the honor and glorification of God in the Catholic world until every child has a roof over his and her head and enough to eat.

"Before he came here it was commonplace on Sunday to see a hundred orphans gathering in the street in front of the church; most of them out-of-wedlock, others emotionally or physically impaired, retarded, missing limbs, deaf or blind and of other deformities.

"Their only possessions were the tattered and torn rags they wore, mostly covered with mud in the spring and fall and frozen with flakes of snow in the wintertime. Then there were the tin cups they held in their hands. Most of the parishioners would sneak around to the rear entrance of the church in order to avoid them.

"When Piccolo celebrated his first Mass here, an overflowing crowd came from miles around. When they showed up at the church on January 11, 1959, much to their surprise there wasn't an orphan to be seen. Some remarked *'It is about time someone cleaned up this mess.'* For the first time in years, they were able to ascend the steps and enter through the main entrance of the church. Yet, when they entered the church they got the biggest surprise of all.

"There on the end of the first pews hung a small sign, *'Riservato ai bambini speciali di Dio' 'Reserved for God's special children.'* Lined up, row after row, were orphans gazing at the magnificent altarpiece. His first words to his new congregation were, *'Christ picked me up from the Mud in the Street and gave me to you.'*

"*'Mud in the Street'* was an expression used by church goers in referring to street orphans. That he had come from the *'mud in the street,'* fired rumors he had been born out of wedlock. Since bastards cannot be ordained, his enemies demanded he be defrocked.

"When the situation started to get out of hand, the Archbishop of Venice published a marriage certificate proving Giovanni Paulo Luciani and Bartolomea Tancon, had wed a year before his birth.[1]

"Nevertheless, this good man has picked up thousands out of the *'mud in the street'* since and given them their rightful place in society; thus his leading role in the priest-worker movement.

"Piccolo has performed a miracle here in the Veneto country. When he got here, the congregation thought all they had to do was go to church to be saved. Now they think much differently. Piccolo has created an army of people who are trying to help each other.

Capitalism and Charity vs. Communism

"When a child reaches his or her sixth birthday, the child gets a big party and everyone brings them gifts. This teaches the child from the start; gimme. How wonderful it is to get. Conditioning the child with greed——Moses' teachings in the Old Testament.

"Not here in Piccolo's world. In the days leading up to one's sixth birthday, the child is busy making small craft items. When the day arrives, everyone except the child gets a gift. Conditioning the child how wonderful it is to give——Christ's teachings in the Gospels.

"Each time the fork in the road would come up for each of them in the past, they would ask themselves, *'Now what is in this for me?'* Now they ask themselves, *'Now what is in this for others?'*"

I shot him a dreadful look. "But, you are talking Marxism. We know that doesn't work. Society can only be driven by greed."

He decided not to challenge me. "We shall see. We shall see."

He tipped forward one of the chairs. "The chair you are about to occupy has held many others. On its back were aging brass plates.

194

Leo XIII 11 November 1879	Paul VI 23 December 1963
Pius X 2 January 1904	Paul VI 23 March 1964
Benedict XV 24 June 1904	Paul VI 22 July 1964
Pius X 23 September 1906	Paul VI 16 March 1966
Pius XI 22 September 1923	Paul VI 16 October 1966
Pius XII 2 February 1943	Paul VI 2 March 1967
John XXIII 22 January 1959	Paul VI 24 December 1967
John XXIII 14 July 1961	Paul VI 22 July 1968

Puzzled, I asked, "Why has Paul been here so often?"

Jack replied, "Here in the remote foothills of the Alps, is the only place Paul can get away from it all. Even at Castel Gandolfo, he is in the public eye. He holds his summits here—summits on poverty.

"He wants to rid the world of poverty. The only way to do that is Marxism—a redistribution of welfare society—an evil word in the west. Meetings must be kept secret—here is the perfect place.

"Almost every cardinal of the world's pockets of poverty has been here—Africa, India, Latin, Central America, you name it...

"There are two possible solutions to poverty.

"The combination of *capitalism* and *charity*—the wealth a few can accumulate is unlimited. The poor are dependent on compassion.

"Paul and Piccolo are convinced the combination of capitalism and charity cannot work. After centuries of trying it hasn't worked. Fifty thousand children literally starve to death each day.

"Even Christ knew voluntary charity would never work, *'You will always have the poor, and you can help them whenever you want to...But, you will not always have me.'* [2]

"But, Paul and Piccolo know what will work—a society that affords each child an equal opportunity at education to enable each of them to make their maximum contribution back to society.

"In their world, *charity* would no longer be a voluntary function of the individual. It will be an involuntary function of society. The rich will be taxed to help the poor. Unlike the Soviet Union, their vision is for a democratic-Marxist society—the will of the people."

I winked a wink of doubt.

He looked me square in the eyes, "They will change the will of the people when they are six years old."

1 *Veneto Nostro* 7 Feb 59
2 *Mark 14* Mark who wrote the 1st Gospel spoke of Christ as a man and not as a God. Thus, we have *'You will not always have me.'* In Mark, three times, Christ denies he is God. One always has God.

195

Chapter 22

The Winning Card

"Religion is a business in which entrepreneurs capitalize on man's tendency to believe in ghosts to accomplish political convictions."[1]

Albino Luciani

Footsteps coming down the stairs interrupted our thoughts.

As if not a moment to lose, the bishop sat down and rather than saying grace, picked up his wine glass and offered a toast to Christ. He had barely finished when he reached across for the rolls. Jack quickly followed with the meats and vegetables. We were off.

Jack offered, "Lucien wants to be certain he's playing with a winning ticket."

Piccolo looked across at me, "I have a winning ticket for you, the winning card. Guaranteed, guaranteed to win. No doubt about it."

Reaching for the truth, "Who is it? Is it Christ? Is it Allah? Is it Buddha? Is it Brahma?"

Much to my surprise, "None of them." Pointing to his temple, "It's here. All you have to do is do what it tells you to do. Always do what is right. Always do what this," again pointing to his temple, "tells you to do. You do that, and that alone, and you're going to be in the winner's circle. Let there be no doubt about it."

"But, how can you tell which religion is right?" I persisted.

"If you are strong enough to do what I just told you to do without any outside help, then that should be enough for you. In that case you would be dealing directly with your maker. But if you need a go-between—more cards—you need religion—the business Jack and I are in. Yet, the winning card is not which religion is the true one. It is what I have just given you. The only purpose of religion is to help you play," again pointing to his temple, "the winning card."

"Yet, you raised the question: How does one prove Catholicism, Protestantism, Judaism, Islamism, Buddhism, Hinduism or Taoism is the true religion? The answer is simple, one doesn't. It can't be done. It can't be proved. Yet, what one can do is prove a particular religion is not the true one. Let me give you an example of how this

196

works, one cannot prove the true religion, yet, one can prove a particular religion is not the true religion."

The 'expert' said so—it must be true

"In Paris, where Modigliani had worked, a sculptured head was recovered by divers from the canal that ran behind the artist's house. On the assumption the work may have been executed by the master, it was brought to the attention of a local curator who believed it could be an original work. It was subsequently examined by experts recognized as the world's foremost authorities on Modigliani and it was found that it had, indeed, been executed by the great artist.

"A local hippie challenged the find. Although the hippie had no credentials for making his claim, the experts saw it as an opportunity to gain publicity for the find. They arranged a live debate between them and the hippie on television. The debate was widely publicized and the press made the hippie out to be a kind of fool.

"The hour long debate allowed for a ten minute summary at its end for each of the parties. Although the hippie had disclosed serious flaws in the experts' analyses, their immense credibility in the field of art enabled them to seal their claim as being sound. It was clear to all viewers the hippie really didn't know what he was talking about.

"The hippie got his ten minutes. He said something the art world has never forgotten, *'No one, not all the experts on this stage or all the experts in Europe or, for that matter, all the experts in the world can prove any work of art is an original executed by a particular artist. Yet, one can prove, a work is not authentic.'*

"To the astonishment of all, he ran a film of himself sculpting the head. He closed with, *'The only way one can tell one is truly in possession of an original work of art is to watch the artist create it, watch him complete it, have him sign it and take the work and place it in a safe to which only one knows the combination.'*

"Religions are like works of art. When you believe one is the true one, you are relying entirely on the expert, the credibility of the preacher who really doesn't know anymore about it than you do. To put it bluntly, you are relying on your own gullibility.

"The only way you can know a particular religion is the true one is to have been there. In the case of the Christian, this means to have been there in the Sinai Desert when the Burning Bush—God—spoke to Moses. In the case of the Muslim, it means to have been there upon the winged horse when the Angel Gabriel took Mohammed to meet this same God in the heavens. In the case of the Mormon, it means to have been there at the edge of the pond when two Gods— God the Father and Jesus—appeared together to Joseph Smith.

"Otherwise you are relying entirely on what someone said to someone else, who in turn passed it on to someone else, for all time. As my father told me, in those days, as in these days, men had great motive to lie in these things for if they convinced their fellowman they had talked directly with God, it would make one a great and wealthy man. Most of all, it would give one unyielding power over the minds of men. After all, one's words come directly from God.

"This includes Moses, Constantine, Mohammed and Smith and all the others who claimed to have talked to God. It also includes present day preachers who earn their livelihood this way, a few of which are trying to make this a better world to live in, but most of which get their kicks out of wielding power over the minds of men. So weakened is man by his mortality he blindly pays the preacher for his salvation, despite the fact the preacher knows no more about the possibility of an afterlife than he does. He's never been there."

. Other hippies run their films

"Yet, as with art, it is possible to tell a certain religion is not the true one. We see this happen every day. As more and more scientific facts become available, more and more do we question the prophet and more and more is his credibility eroded.

"Today, no one doubts the hippie's testimony, because we now have the facts. Yet, when he made his claim, no one believed him, not a soul. The credibility regarding the Modigliani sculpture was entirely with the so-called expert.

"Likewise, when Darwin and Einstein first made their claims, no one believed them, for the credibility was entirely with the so-called expert—the preacher. Many thought Darwin and Einstein insane.

"Darwin had proposed we had evolved as apes before the time of the first excavations of prehistoric fossils and the development of modern genetics which later proved his hypothesis.[2]

"Whereas, Darwin spoke of things that could readily be seen— the resemblance of man to his fellow higher primates, Einstein spoke

198

of things one could not see. He claimed everything from the air one breathes, to the hardest substance known—diamond—is made of moving particles—infinitesimal specs of energy which he claimed were the most powerful forces in nature and from them had grown all living creatures and the world they lived in.

"The marble floor beneath us is bits of empty space—atoms—which are traveling at placements which give the illusion of solidity. Our bodies are made up of identical atoms which are traveling at different placements which give the illusion of more porous objects. What's more, he claimed infractions of space hold them together—everything, not only the planet earth, has a center of gravity. [3]

"When Darwin and Einstein proposed their theories as to how we all came about, very few believed them. They obviously didn't know what they were talking about. What they claimed contradicted what the experts were saying: God created Adam and Eve as adults.

"Like the hippie in the case of his make-believe Modigliani, both these men have now had the opportunity to have run their films.

"In the case of Darwin, archeology and more importantly genetics have proved his theory beyond a shadow of a doubt.

"In Einstein's case, photographs of an eclipse of the sun proved his theory to his fellow scientists.[3] For the common man, today's microscopes are able to magnify millions of times—one can see this tiny bit of energy he spoke of—the atom—the most powerful force in nature. For those having no access to powerful microscopes, the splitting of a single atom at Hiroshima should have done the trick.

"So now, Darwin and Einstein, too, have had their time before the cameras. What they proposed as theory is now very much fact.

"Einstein's theory, as to the origin of man, is more devastating to Christianity's fundamental unit of creation—*Adam and Eve*—than is Darwin's theory of evolution. Einstein proved the egg came first; God did not create man and woman as adults. Einstein proved the fundamental unit of creation was an infinitesimal speck—the atom—which gave birth to all living things and the world they live in."

I agreed, "You're right. Darwin's theory of evolution is not quite as devastating as the preacher has the loophole of claiming God created Adam and Eve as caveman and cavewoman."

"Not so," he corrected me. "The Old Testament is an unbroken genealogy from Adam directly to Christ: '*Adam, Seth, Enos, Cainan, Mahalaleel, Jared, Enoch, Methuselah, Lamech, Noah, Shem,*

199

Arphaxad, Salah, Eber, Peleg, Reu, Serug, Terah, Abraham, Isaac, Jacob, Judas, Phares, Esrom, Aram, Aminadab, Naasson, Sakmon, Booz, Obed, Jesse, King Solomon, King David, Roboam, Abia, Josaphat, Joram, Ozias, Joatham, Achaz, Mahasses, Amon, Josias, Jechonias, Salathiel, Zorobable, Abiud, Eliakim, Azor, Sadoc, Achim, Eliud, Mattham, Jacob, Joseph, the father of Christ.'

I shot him a questionable glance.

"I was a Straight-A seminarian," he explained. "Regardless, the chain is unbroken. The Bible gives the precise age at which all but three of them sired his firstborn. It also gives the age of death of each of them. One knows who was whose father and who was whose son all the way from Adam to Christ. *'Adam begot Seth who begot Enos... who begot Jacob who begot Joseph—the father of Christ.'*

"In ancient times, with no social practices restricting age at which one could sire one's firstborn, the average generation length was under seventeen. The mathematical calculation 55 generations multiplied by 17 is 935 years or 929BC for Adam and Eve.

"Bibles tell us differently. Those patriarchs who lived between 3100BC—the time of the first pharaoh—and 1400BC—the time of Moses—lived to an average age of 273. Conversely, the average lifespan of the pharaohs, for the same period, was 33 and the oldest, Ramesses II, lived to the extraordinary age of 86.

"The patriarchs who came earlier—4000BC to 3100BC—lived even longer, Adam living 940 years. Adam was still alive when the Pharaoh Naumer established the Egyptian Empire in 3100BC.

"When the Bible was first put together in a single volume, the authors realized, if these patriarchs had lived normal life spans, it would place the time of Adam and Eve sixteen hundred years after the pyramids had been built. Because the genealogy from Adam and Christ was unbroken, adding patriarchs was not an alternative. The only option was to add extraordinary lifetimes to the early patriarchs to push the date back to 4000BC—acceptable then, but not today—we know mankind goes back tens of thousands of years before that.

"There is no wiggle room here. The integrity of the Bible rests on the fact Adam and Eve were created around 4000BC—the reason no preacher will budge from that date—his credibility is at stake.

"Regardless, when Darwin and Einstein came along, the preacher would show up in the courtroom. Armed only with his immense credibility, he would win every time.

200

"But where is he today? He is not there. He is not there because he knows the 'hippie' now has his film. Darwin and Einstein now have the facts. They will make mincemeat of him.

"Religion is like a work of fine art. One might be an expert in religion. Another might be an expert in fine art. The preacher is the expert in religion. It is his job to win the credulity of his customers so they will respond with their faith and ultimately with their dollars.

"The dealer is the expert in fine art. It is his job to win the credulity of his customers so they will respond with their awe and ultimately with their dollars.

A better way

"Yet, there is a more reliable way to determine a religion is not the true religion than scientific disclaimer." My ears perked up.

He answered my ears, "The Winning Card!

"Let us consider Mother Church. The thesis of canon law is *'Some children are born better than others and are entitled to more.'*

"Without delving into the handicapped, the remarried, certain ethnic groups, transgenders, morphodites, homosexuals, born-out-of-wedlock children and others deprived of basic rights under the laws of nations by Mother Church, consider the plight of the little girl.

"Canon law conditions children from an early age little boys are better than little girls. Only a little boy can grow up with the power to change a piece of bread into the body of a God—unless, of course, he happened to have been born-out-of-wedlock.

"It doesn't take scientific disclaimer to determine one is not dealing with the true religion here," pointing to his head. "Common sense tells us, if we are all children of the same God, all children are created equal. Mother Church has gone astray here. Some children are not born better than others. Yet, these things can change. It is possible to change the Church back to what Christ had intended."

He paused for a moment to emphasize his summarization, "It is possible to change Christ from what Mother Church has made Him out to be—a piece of bread in a cup—to *'What is in this for others.'*

"Yet, there is a more telling reason one knows the Church as it is today is not the true Church Christ spoke of in the gospels. In *Matthew,* Christ explicitly defines his Church, *'When thou prayest, thou shalt not be as Hypocrites are; for they love to pray standing in*

201

the synagogues and in public places, that they may be seen and heard of men. Verily, I say unto you, They have their reward in this life. But thou, when thou prayest, enter into thy closet, and when thou hast shut thy door, talk to me in secret; and verily, I say unto you, Ye will have ye reward in my Kingdom. When ye pray, use not vain repetitions as the heathen do; for they think they shall be heard for their speaking in public places... '[4]

"Christ tells us His Church should not be the public display we have made of it in the west. He tells us our relationship to God is a direct and sacred one and not the business we have made of it—the definition of religion in all communist societies.

"Roncalli said it best, *'His Church is not in buildings of wood and stone... it is in your heart. It is in your compassion for others.'*[5]

"Roncalli?" I scratched my head.

"Yes, Roncalli... John XXIII," he smiled at my ignorance.

"Regardless, religion is not God. It is what ancient and medieval men of motive defined as God in order to accomplish political goals. Today it continues to be a business which entrepreneurs capitalize on man's tendency to believe in ghosts to accomplish political convictions.

"Yet, the definition of God, religion vs. atheism, is quite similar. Both religion and atheism agree the ground beneath us and the air around us and the space beyond us—actually the composition of all atoms to the core of the earth to the infinity of the universe—is God. That religion decrees God is the air around us is readily seen in that all religions claim God keeps His eye on each of us at all times—a must for preachers to accomplish their political objectives.

"Yet, religion goes a step further. It claims this composition of atoms 'thinks' the way we do. It tells us the composition of these atoms is mentally a human being—a Supreme Human Being.

"Scripture claims God made man in His image. Yet, if one relies on common sense, man created God in his image. Even the most gullible of Christians today know that God did not create Adam and Eve as adults. For Darwin and Einstein now have the facts."

He answered my unasked question. "Besides, there would be no point to it. Both religion and atheism agree 'God' created the parts—the atom—from which everything grows. It would make no sense to make each one of us individually. What's more, if God made each one of us individually He would create each of us as adults. What's more, He would create each one of us as perfect adults.

"It is most likely the true God is the God we know as a matter-of-fact gives us life—the *God of Nature*—the God of my atheist father. Studies have shown children who grow up outside religion grow up free of prejudices instilled in children by preachers and are more likely to follow Christ's instruction, *'Love Thy Neighbor as Thyself.'*

"It is that my father was an atheist that made him a true follower of Christ. Also true, as you know, of Karl Marx," he smiled.

"My father knew if Christ actually performed the miracles said of Him, though a common man, He would be a historical figure like many other common men, like Fulton, Edison, Einstein, Tesla and others who have left their miracles behind.

"It was that my father saw Christ as a man, and not as a ghost, that enabled him to see past the mythology of Christ to the reality of Christ. Although he did not believe a man lived who had performed the miracles that are said of Him, my father did believe good men had written the gospels—men who wanted to do away with the evilness Moses and other ancient ghosts had left behind. My father's convictions are well founded. They are historical fact."

"Historical fact?" I pondered.

The Quest for the Historical Jesus

"The Quest for the Historical Jesus[6] begun by Reimarus in the eighteenth century and followed by a long progression of the world's leading theologians and historians. It was finally put to rest by Nobel Laureate Albert Schweitzer in 1905, clearly establishing the gospels as theological and not historical documents.

"The consensus of these scholars—among the most brilliant men who ever lived—clearly established Christ a theoretical figure and not a historical figure. Christ was not a man, but an ideology.

"This is still true today. Despite centuries of investigations, no leaf left unturned, no one has ever found the scarcest bit of evidence Jesus Christ ever lived. That is, a man who performed the thirty-five miracles He is said to have performed.[7]

"This does not conflict with faith. There is no school of theology in the Catholic world that recognizes Christ as a historical figure. Schools of theology teach faith. They do not teach history. Christ is a matter-of-faith—not a matter-of-fact. No pope or theologian has ever challenged Schweitzer's conclusions.

"Conversely, no history book mentions Jesus Christ. If it were possible to attend in one's lifetime all the history classes of all the universities in the world since the beginning of time one would never hear the words, 'Jesus Christ.' Yet, we have the remarkable phenomenon Jesus Christ is believed by half the western world to have been the most important historical figure who ever lived.

"One will learn of the Pharaoh Naumer followed by a long line of others all the way down to Cleopatra. Along the way one learns of people like Homer, Aristotle, Plato, Alexander, Confucius, Buddha, Tao, Caesar, Diocletian, Constantine, Mohammad, Genghis Kahn, Guttenberg, Galileo, Da Vinci, Michelangelo, Magellan, Columbus, Napoleon, Fulton, Washington, Lincoln, Pasteur, Bell, Edison, Salk, Darwin, Einstein, Lenin, Tesla, Hitler, Churchill and millions of others—the overwhelming number of which were born as common men, but, one will never hear the words, 'Jesus Christ.'

"There is no better example of the confusion of faith and reality than we think of Jesus Christ as a man who actually lived and think of Sherlock Holmes as a man who never lived, whereas just the reverse is true.[8]

"All western religions thrive on the tendency of the population to believe in ghosts. The religion one pays depends on which ghost one believes in. The 'Burning Bush' which spoke to Moses was followed by a succession of two dozen other ghosts appearing to various prophets, each one contradicting what the others had to say which came before it—the reason the Bible is selective reading—one can support whatever one has to say on either side of the aisle.

"Strangely, this 'ghost' who claimed to be the God of all of us never appeared to more than one of us at a time. There was no independent witness to any single one of these ghost's testimony.

"The only thing that separates the Bible from *Jack and the Bean Stalk, Snow White and the Seven Dwarfs, Cinderella* and *Goldilocks and the Three Bears* is the phrase *'God—a ghost—spoke to…'* which preface each storyteller's testimony. Otherwise, it is just a fairytale.

"Yes," I agreed. "This afternoon, Jack and I concluded Moses lied when he told his many tales."

'I am the Lord thy God…'

The bishop looked at his protégé as if he had missed the lesson of the day. He then turned back to me.

204

"Moses was not lying. He did not lie when he claimed a ghost—a burning bush appeared to him. He didn't lie when he claimed to have taken the Commandments on Mount Sinai. He didn't lie..."

"He didn't lie?" I looked at Jack.

The bishop responded, "Moses, himself, is a fictional character.

"Today we know the stories Moses is said to have told are fiction. Today, we know the Israelites were not in Egypt at his early time, so we know the stories of the Ten Plagues, the Exodus, the Red Sea Miracle and even the Ten Commandments were fiction. One knows the earth is round and rotating around its sun and is not the flat center of the universe the God of Moses claimed it to be."

"How can one tell that? None of us were there." I corrected him.

"That his stories are fiction tells us Moses, himself, could not possibly have written them. Had he written them at his time, people would have known—as we know today—they were fiction.

"Had he written he had led two million people out of Egypt and parted the Red Sea and drowned the Egyptian army together with its pharaoh, the people of his day would have known he was writing fiction because they would have known the Jews had not been in Egypt and the Egyptian army and its pharaoh were very much alive.

"No, the stories were first told at least a few generations after his alleged time, more likely, centuries after his alleged time, probably around 650BC when the history books place the first Jews in Egypt.

"The culmination of all of Moses' stories is the taking of the Promised Land. They were fabricated by Hebrews with motive of territorial expansion who wanted to convince future generations God gave the rich land on the banks of the Mediterranean Sea to them. As we know today, it worked—much of the western world is convinced God gave that land to the Jews."

I looked at him as if I had just awakened from the dead.

He smiled and pointed to his temple.

Allowing several minutes for the awakening to take hold, "There is nothing wrong with children believing in ghosts before their sixth birthday. But, when one carries it beyond the world of *Goldilocks and the Three Bears* and claims this ghost or that ghost dictated some kinds of people are better than others and are entitled to more, men and women of good conscience" pointing, once more, to his temple, "must intervene and stand up for what is right.

"It follows we have the evangelists—from the other side of the aisle—who wrote of Christ as much as a century after His time.[9]

"A century after His alleged time?" I questioned.

The Mythical Christ

"Although we do not know when the gospels were written we do know the earliest date each of them could have been written because each of them mentions historical events.

"The *Gospel of Mark* speaks of the destruction of the Temple of Jerusalem (70AD), so we know it could not have been written before 70AD. *Matthew* and *Luke* were written after 85AD as they speak of events which did not occur until that time. For this same reason, the *Gospel of John* could not have been written before 95AD. Although the gospels were most likely written long after these times, we know they could not have possibly been written before these times.

"To see this clearly, one must consider what has survived." He stepped to the sideboard and retrieved a sheet of paper.

History	period written of	Earliest possible date [10]	most probably date [10]
Mark	24-27AD [9]	70AD	100AD
Matthew	7BC-27AD [9]	85AD	105AD
Luke	7BC-27AD [9]	85AD	110AD
John	24-27AD [9]	95AD	125AD

Oldest surviving gospel manuscripts

Ca. A.D.	150	200	250	300	350	450
Base:			←papyri------parchment→			
Mark			b		c	d e
Matthew			b		c	d
Luke			b		c	d e
John	a		b		c	d e

a = tiny fragment of a part of a verse is the oldest surviving gospel manuscript. Not possible to determine 2nd vs. 3rd century papyri, the speculation this could be as early as 150AD is based on handwriting comparisons prevalent at the time

b = sporadic verses considered unreliable as they contain countless scribal errors

c = Vaticanus substantial manuscript held by the Vatican

d = Sinaiticus complete manuscript of the gospels held by the British Library

e = Alexandrinus partial manuscript held by the British Library

"Conservative scholars claim the scrap dated as early as 150AD proves the gospels were written before then. It supports conservative historians' claim the gospels were written late in the first century.

"Middle-of-the-road historians place their authorship in the early to mid-second century. No historian places authorship of the gospels prior to the earliest possible historical dates (70-95AD). All agree on the order which the gospels are written: Mark-Matthew-Luke-John.

"Seminaries get around history by claiming the evangelists, being guided by God, were able to predict these historical events and wrote them into the record. Thus we have the widespread misconception the evangelists followed Christ around with notebook and pen.

"Regardless, *Mark* includes Christ's ministry, miracles and the *Resurrection*. *Mark* speaks of Christ as *'Son of Man.'* In *Mark*, three times Christ denies He is God. *Mark 10, 'Jesus said unto him, Why callest me good? There is none good but one, And that one is God.'*

"Consistent with his use of *'Son of Man'* Mark does not mention the *Virgin Birth*—a requirement of divinity in Greek mythology.

"The most credible of the gospels—*Mark*—the only gospel that could have possibly been written by a man who could have possibly witnessed Christ's ministry—clearly denies Christ is God.

"We know Mark was not a direct witness to the events he speaks of or he surely would have told us so. What is more revealing is that he does not cite other witnesses. Mark does not disclose his sources.

"From the beginning of time all nonfiction writers have divulged their sources. The difference nonfiction vs. fiction is one has sources and the other doesn't. There is only one possible explanation why Mark did not disclose his sources."

"Possible explanation?" my ears perked up.

"He had no sources. Mark was writing fiction."

He paused for a moment or two, the time it took for the hairs to curl up and down my neck and run up and down my back.

"Middle of the road historians place the writings of Mark, the first gospel, in the second century because if he had written as early as 70AD, a few could have been alive who had been alive in Christ's time. They would have not known of a man who performed the miracles he spoke of. Christ performed some of His miracles before thousands of people in Nazareth, a town of ten thousand.

"How can you be so sure Mark wrote the first gospel?"

207

"*Matthew* and *Luke* plagiarize *Mark* and add the concept of the *Virgin Birth*. Had Mark plagiarized the others he surely would not have omitted the most fundamental aspect of Christ's divinity—the *Virgin Birth*. Mark wrote the first gospel. Bibles place *Matthew* first so that the New Testament begins with the birth of Christ.

"*Matthew* and *Luke* are direct plagiarisms of *Mark,* copying it in many cases word-for-word, taking care to change only the phrase *'Son of Man'* to *'Son of God.'*

"Yet, even Mathew and Luke don't claim Christ is God. The early pharaohs, Plato, Aristotle, Alexander the Great and the Caesars were recognized as *'Son of God'*—a step up from man, but not God.

"Yet, a half century or so after *Mark,* in which Christ explicitly denies He is God, *John* explicitly declares Christ is the same God as God the Father. *John 10, 'I and my Father are one.'*

"In *Mark*—the only gospel written by a man who could have possibly been a witness to Christ's ministry—Christ denies He is God. Yet, a half century later, by most accounts, Christ changes His mind in *John* and declares He is God; a gospel written by a man who could not have possibly been alive at Christ's time.

"Most bizarre, unlike Mark, Mathew and Luke who do not claim to be direct witnesses and do not otherwise divulge their sources, John—who wrote his gospel more than a century after Christ's time—claims to be the disciple John who walked at Christ's side.

"John lies in the very first verse of his gospel."

Mark	a few miracles and the resurrection. Christ is not God - Son of Man
Matthew	adds a few miracles and Virgin Birth. Christ is Son of God – not God
Luke	adds a few miracles and Virgin Birth. Christ is Son of God – not God
John	Declares Christ is God. The Son and the Father are one.

The Reasonable Christ

"Yet, it is reasonable to believe a man was crucified for radical ideas about the time claimed by the evangelists in the gospels.

"It is reasonable to believe a man spoke out against the evils of the Hebrew God. In addition to saving the occasional damsel in distress—*"He who is without sin cast the first stone"*—His ministry centered on the establishment of a redistribution of wealth society—communism—which, by itself, may have ended in His demise.

"As we do today, Christ lived in a capitalistic society, one driven by greed. He would have been a threat to the rich and powerful at the top that controlled the minds of the masses at the bottom.

"Christ was the Karl Marx of the first century.

"Nevertheless, it is not reasonable to believe a man performed the miracles attributed to Christ for if He had fed four thousand Jews with seven loaves of bread and a few fish as Mark had claimed, and five thousand more with five loaves of bread and two small fish as John had claimed, the Jews would have known He was God.

A Greek God

"Yet, what has survived suggests something more.

"*Resurrection* and *Virgin Birth* are divinity in Greek mythology, not Hebrew mythology. Moses does not provide for resurrection *'Dust thus art, to dust thou will return.'* The Jews have no afterlife.

"In Greek mythology, Zagreus dates back a thousand years before Moses. A tablet in the British Museum reads *"Zeus, King of Gods, speaks, 'Hail thy offspring who come upon thou without lust ...Hail thou who has been counted among thieves and murderers... suffered and death ...Thou wilt become God from man and rule eternal life.'"*[11]

"Zeus sends His Son to save the world from sin. Zagreus, Son of Zeus, is born of a virgin—'*without lust,*' a requirement of divinity in Greek mythology. When sent to earth, Zagreus is tried as a criminal by His chosen people—the Titans—who who tear him apart.

"In resurrection, Zagreus reincarnates as Dionysus who comes to rule the universe as Christ will come to rule in Christian mythology.

"It follows we have the prophesy of the coming of Christ, a thousand years after the time of Moses in the book of Isaiah, *'The God of Isaiah speaks, Behold, a virgin shall conceive and bear a son, and call his name Immanuel...He hath poured out his soul unto death; and he was numbered with the transgressors; and he bare the sin of many, and made intercession for the transgressors.'*[12]

"All that has survived—both in ideology and documentation—is powerful evidence the Greeks wrote the gospels. Mark, Matthew, Luke and John were Greek. Every single surviving manuscript predating the sixth century is written in Greek. Not the tiniest scrap predating this time has ever been found in the Hebrew language."[13]

The finale

He paused a long while to let us catch up. He nailed the lid shut.

"Once more, *'religion is a business which entrepreneurs capitalize on man's tendency to believe in ghosts to accomplish political convictions.'*

"Preachers are little more than politicians who use what ancient political giants wrote in books to accomplish political objectives.

"To one side, we have those who created the fictional character of Moses to foster a society in which *some children are born better than others and are entitled to more.* To the other side, we have those who wrote of Christ to foster a society in which *all children are created equal and are entitled to an equal share of the pie.*"

He paused that we would remember it all the days of our lives.

"On Napoleon's tomb is engraved, *'Man's only immortality is what he leaves behind in the minds of men.'*

"True, not only of men, but also, of Gods."

Both Jack and I gave him a questionable look of apprehension.

"It makes no difference whether or not Christ ever lived or whether or not He performed the miracles that are said of Him. What is important of any man, even one who claimed to be God, is not so much His life on earth, but rather what He left behind—like Tao, like Buddha, like Mohammed, like Lincoln, like Einstein, like Edison and all the others who have come before and after Him.

"What is important of Christ's life is not His life on earth, not the miracles He is said to have performed, not His death on the cross, not even His ascension. Like any God, or for that matter, any man, all that counts is what He left behind, *'Love thy Neighbor as thyself.'* The fundamental truth Mark, Matthew, Luke and John left behind.

"These things we have talked of may seem devastating to religion as we know it today. Yet, from these few truths will one day emerge a new kind of religion, one no longer based on the hatred and greed of ancient men, but one based on the fundamental truth all children are created equal and are entitled to their fair share of the pie."

He stopped. He asked me. "Where do you go from here?"

"To Rome, St. Peter's. Then, back to the grind in the states."

He offered, "I could make arrangements for you to stay in one of the Vatican apartments but I don't think you would feel comfortable there. Not far from St. Peter's is a little pension. You will feel less ecclesiastical there." He took out a card and scribbled on its back.

210

He retrieved a second card and scrawled on its back, "When you visit the Vatican, find the office of Paul Marcinkus. It is in the Palace of the Holy Office opposite the Papal Palace on St. Peter's Square. He was here just this past week. We were discussing the pros and cons of merging the parish banks with Banco Ambrosiano.

"I am sure he will be happy to arrange to have someone give you a tour of the gardens—maybe even the Papal Palace, itself.

"Thank you," this man with the perpetual smile added, "You have enlightened me and given me good substance for my infallible sermon on the mount." Getting up, he stopped at the sideboard and picked up a few pieces of stationary headed *Vittorio Veneto.*

He answered my unasked question. "Notes of what we have talked of today. Shot for the cannon. See you on the battlefield." He headed for the stairs. I followed him with a puzzled look.

He looked back at me, "The enemy, preachers who prey on the weakness of the minds of men."

Smiling after him, "You can count on me, I will be there."

As the bishop's footsteps faded up the stairs, Jack explained, "Forgive him. He retires at precisely nine o'clock and is up at four. Even if the Pope was here, he would do the same thing."

"Wow, up at four. He must sleep all afternoon."

"He has no idea what a nap is. I will walk you to your hotel."

1 *Messaggero Mestre* 12 Sep 61
2 Darwin published his thesis *The Origin of Species* in 1859. The first Neanderthal fossil was discovered in Germany in 1856 but it was thought to have been a modern man until thirty years later its origin and age was determined.
3 In 1919, observation of a total solar eclipse of the sun proved Einstein's theory everything has a center of gravity to the scientific community. For simplification, the text speaks of the atom as the fundamental unit of creation, yet, the atom, itself, is made up of sub-atomic particles
4 *Matthew 6*
5 *Messaggero Mestre* 25 Dec 57 Basilica di San Marco Angelo Roncalli—John XXIII
6 *'The Quest of the Historical Jesus' Schweitzer Internet and libraries*
7 Following Schweitzer's *'The Quest of the Historical Jesus' there began a second search in which believers search for some scant evidence such a man ever lived. Included is the Shroud of Turin, the first century box alleged to contain the bones of James, the alleged tomb of Jesus, etc.*
8 Arthur Conan Doyle based his character *Sherlock Holmes* on Eugene Francois Vidocq—a French thief turned detective who first developed the analysis and deduction techniques exploited by Doyle. See the story *Quest for the Historical Holmes* in the author's book: *Let's All Get Behind the Pope...*
9 Herod died in 4BC. Allowing two years for the killing of the firstborns Christ was born in 6 BC or earlier with conception year earlier. He could not have died later than 27AD.
10 Most history books cite later dates. Some cite the earliest possible dates 70AD – 85AD – 95AD
11 Clay tablet dated 2253BC *Story of Zagreus Dionysus* in the British Museum
12 *Isaiah 7*
13 that Christ's conception so closely mirrors that of Zagreus is powerful evidence *Isaiah* was added in the Greek translation the *Septuagint* in 253BC. The *God of Isaiah,* aside from offering redemption, like Christ who would follow Him, contradicts the God of Moses in most everything He has to say.

Chapter 23

To the End of Time

"In revealing the dark secret that must haunted him all his life, Gregoire forces the transformation of Christianity."   Toby Johnson , *White Crane Journal*

It was sheer silence as we walked along the stone walls of the seminary and wiggled our way down through the village streets.

Jack broke the quiet of the night. "For the Church to survive into the twenty-first century it is imperative it change from the church it has been—one based on the make-believe world of yesterday—to a church built on the real world of today. If it fails to make this transition, it will cease to exist." I shot him a questionable glance.

"When a child is taught in history class the Eskimos migrated across the Bering Peninsular in 10000BC and taught in Bible class God created Adam and Eve in 4000BC he or she begins to see the light. Today only the dimmest of children accept the story of Adam and Eve. Even fewer of them believe a Burning Bush ever talked to Moses in the desert. To children these are fairytales.

"How long do you think it will take for the average six-year old to figure out that had Moses written, at his alleged time, he had led two million people out of Egypt and parted the Red Sea and drowned the Egyptian army together with its pharaoh, the people of his day would have known he was writing fiction? How long will it take the average six-year old to realize this thing we think of as God the Father in the western world is nothing more than a figment of the imagination of men who lived long after Moses' alleged time?

"How long do you think it will take the average six-year old to realize had Christ actually performed the miracles attributed to Him, the Jews would have known He was God? How long do you think it will take them to wonder why the gospels were written so long after Christ's time? How long do you think it will take them to wonder why Matthew waited a hundred years to create the story of Christ's conception and birth? How long do you think it will take them to find the indisputable results of the *Search for the Historical Jesus* on the Internet? How long do you think it will take them? How long?

212

"Angelo Roncalli once said, *'A church that rises from specters will soon dissipate into the specters which gave birth to it. If we are to have a true church it must be built on truth, not on myth.'*[1]

"John XXIII," my mind connected the name.

"*'Myths,'* John once said, *'are devastating to true religion. We can fool half of the people half of the time, yet, the half we do not fool will eventually wake up the half we do fool.'*[2]

"As science continues to advance it will eventually destroy the myths the Church is built on. Until recently most people believed in ghosts. After all, if ghosts do not exist, when one is dead, one is dead. Man's immortality rests entirely on his belief in ghosts.

"But, today only half the people believe in ghosts. This is quite visible here in Europe where, more and more each day, Catholics are waking up and realizing the Church is based on myth. Europeans, like other first world countries, are leaving the Church in droves.

"Yes, third world countries, which remain deeply immersed in disease, poverty and starvation imposed upon them by the Church, remain vulnerable to the magician's wand."

The awakening

"Yet, in a few years, today's third world countries will become first world countries and their populations will no longer respond to tales. Children will realize—like *Snow White* who came after him—*Moses* is a fictional character created long after he is alleged to have lived. They will begin to realize when they line up to eat the body of their God they are lining up to eat a piece of bread. As John said, *the Church will dissipate into the specters which gave birth to it...'*

"We must change the basic ideology of the Church from what it has become: *Some children are born better than others and are entitled to more* to the fundamental truth *all children are created equal and are entitled to basic human rights and opportunity.*"

He stopped. I stopped with him. Reaching over, he grasped me by the shoulders and riveted my eyes with an unfathomable stare, "If Piccolo does not live to complete his mission, you will write your book. You will destroy the mythical Christ the Church is built on and in its place establish the fundamental truth of Christ, *'Love thy Neighbor as Thyself.'* Such a church will last to the end of time."

213

The making of a pope

Silence prevailed for awhile broken only by the rhythm of our steps. This time, I broke the quiet of the night.

"'Infallible.' Piccolo used the word 'infallible' in referring to his 'sermon on the mount.' Does he really think he will succeed Paul?"

Jack countered, "He knows he is going to be the next pope.

"Paul visited here the week before he issued his decree banning contraception. When he made the ruling, Piccolo followed almost immediately with his public letter calling for modification of it.

"Paul's ruling was inconsistent with his papal platform—to rid the world of poverty. After all, the ban on contraception is the driving force behind poverty. Yet, Paul left the door open…"

I asked with my eyes. "He refused to invoke papal infallibility. Paul made the most important decree of his papacy as a man and not as a pope. He intended the ruling be changed by his successor. In the meantime he left the door open for one to make up one's own mind.

"If he intended it be changed by his successor, why did he make the ruling to begin with? Why did he instruct Piccolo to challenge it?

"He made it for an entirely different reason.

"In a single swoop he made contraception the number one issue of the election which will choose his successor. A third of the voting cardinals are from third world countries where the contraception ban is the driving force behind poverty, starvation and disease—though conservatives they will vote for the man most likely to repeal it. In instructing Piccolo to challenge his ruling, Paul made him that man."

We stood in front of the hotel—a southern hotel there in the most northern part of Italy. He spread his arms and clasped them around me. He held me there for the longest moment of my life. He stepped back. The last time I saw him—the last time I saw him, alive.

And, Piccolo? Well, that was the last time I saw him, too. Yet, I have never forgotten him. No, I have never forgotten him—partially, because of his perpetual smile, but, mostly, because of his toes.

1 *Messaggero Mestre* 17 Oct 55
2 *Messaggero Mestre* 12 Jan 57

214

Chapter 24

The Scene of the Crime

He found himself sitting in a tailor shop, one of those reserved for kings.

There was a large sewing machine of the latest vintage. A ruffle of white satin flowed from its center as if a bell had rung and the seamstress had gone out to lunch. On a table, just off to one side, were a half dozen or so rolls of satin, all of the very same shade of white.

Then there was the gold. It was wound up on spindles lined up at one end of the sewing machine. A dozen or so golden sentinels watchfully guarded a grand catafalque of white.

To the other side, rose a towering mirror with its edges heavily encrusted in gold.

A platform stood before the mirror. There was a slight indentation at its center and a haze rising above it as if a ghost were standing there.

It was flanked by a half dozen or so breast dummies each wearing a part of some form of dress. One was all dressed up. All dressed up just short of holding the Eucharist in its hands. It even wore the papal miter.

The breast dummies were all of one size. Just a month earlier they had been of another size. He knew in just two weeks time they would be of still another size.

Only he of all of mankind knew this.

For only he could make them change.

Rome

The pension Piccolo recommended was near the Roman Forum, about a fifteen minute walk from the Vatican. I spent three days enjoying the traditional tourist rendition of Rome before finding my way to the Palace of the Holy Office.

I handed Piccolo's card to the guard at the entrance and he directed me to a corridor where I handed it, again, to a receptionist who sat before two intricately carved doors.

Marcinkus came out to greet me. Much to my surprise, instead of assigning a subordinate, he took me around the Vatican grounds himself. Best of all he took me into the Papal Palace. The Apostolic Palace includes dozens of buildings, thousands of rooms, hundreds of stairways and elevators. But, in the case of the Pope, one has to concentrate on that building which houses the Papal Apartment.

As palaces go, it is not a particularly large building. As palaces go, it is not a particularly beautiful building. That is, from the outside. If located in the downtown section of a midsized city, one could easily mistake it as a retired department store.

It is a perfectly square freestanding sixteenth century building, which facade faces St. Peter's Square. It is only four stories high but because of the immense ceiling height—thirty feet on each floor—it is as high as is a modern ten-story building.

The ground floor serves as the base of the building and houses the central bank of the Vatican—the Patrimony of the Holy See.

The palace consists only of the top three floors which are referred to as the first, second and third loggias of the palace; yet, they are the second, third and fourth floors of the building.

On the facade side the windows are ten across. They measure eight feet wide and twenty feet high. At the time, there were two glass panels that opened inward within each frame protected by two outer wooden louvered shutters that opened outward.

Paul VI had heavy draperies hung on the windows which were kept closed. He preferred air-conditioning. John Paul I had the draperies removed as they interfered with his opening the windows. He preferred the fresh air.

Of all the places I had the opportunity to visit in Vatican City I remember most vividly my visit to this important building. It is quite different from all the others for the interior of all the others, from St. Peter's, to the Sistine Chapel, to the Apostolic Library, to the Gallery of Maps, to the Vatican Museum, were very much the same. No matter where you went you were roofed in by an endless array of frescos which in turn were hemmed in by heavily encrusted frames of gilt and gold. If someone were not there to tell you where you were, you would never know where you were. But the Papal Palace is much different. You knew where you were.

Swiss Guards flanked the great studded bronze door which marks the papal entrance to the building. They, like most of the Swiss Guards, are perpetual; they are always there.

One enters into a long white marble corridor running to the rear of the building. The floor is marble, the walls are marble, even the ceiling is marble. The ceiling is arched and the walls are lined with ancient sconces which at one time held gas lamps, candles and other primitive lighting and are now outfitted with electric bulbs. Ashen remains darken the walls just above the sconces.

Although the Vatican contains the largest collection of ancient sculpture in the world, not a statue is to be seen. There is no carpeting here. One walks on the same white marble floor others have walked on for centuries past—through a beautiful white marble tunnel. A few hi-backed chairs ran along the wall and a mahogany desk greeting me as I entered the building.   A guard sat there.

I was required to sign in and asked for my passport. Marcinkus was permitted to enter on sight.   He told me persons of rank and those who cared for the papal household were not required to sign in; they were free to come and go as they pleased. This included maintenance workers who lived elsewhere in Vatican City.

Toward the far end of the corridor was the only hint of sculpture, an arched framework of cherubs which housed a grand white marble staircase leading up to an imposing door—this one more golden than bronze. Above the door was the papal coat of arms, also in gold.

A Swiss guard stood at the golden door.

He pressed a button and the door slid open. We followed him into what appeared to be a small vestibule. Yet, as we entered, I realized we were not in an apartment at all, but in an elevator. Here the stark white marble had come to an end and the gold and the frescos began.

I looked up at the ceiling and if it were not for the size of the elevator I would not know where I was. For there were the frescos of the heavens above, which to the eye of the novice were every bit as magnificent as were those which looked down from the ceiling of the Sistine Chapel. I touched its shimmering white marble walls because they were so perfectly pristine I thought them artificial.

I asked the bishop jokingly if this elevator also went down. He was quick to respond that this particular elevator only goes up. He joked there was another one at the other end of the building that went down—it serviced the basement and the first, second and third floors of the building that housed the Vatican bank and some of the Curia but not the fourth floor—the Papal Apartment.

It was a short ride. Exiting the elevator, I heard water gushing in the distance as if someone had left water running in a giant tub. Above our heads, a striking blue and golden leaded glass skylight peered down on the elevator which resembled an ornate golden birdcage sitting on the white marble floor—its golden dome cleverly concealing its mechanisms. Just to our left, a grand white marble staircase was crowned by a matching skylight of leaded glass.

Marcinkus told me the stairway was there to permit one to go from floor to floor without using the elevator. In the days before elevators it had been all that was there.

A Swiss guard sat in front of a towering heavily draped window at a desk—a match of the one that was on the first floor. I mentioned to the bishop they must have gotten two for the price of one.

Marcinkus told me, "A changing of the palace guards takes place every three hours, as the clock strikes twelve, three, six, nine and then twelve again. A guard has no authority to leave his post no matter what the needs. Not even a trip to the restroom is permitted.

"We are in the Papal Apartment. We call it the *'third loggia.'* Its nineteen rooms occupy the entire top floor. Six people live here, the Pope, his valet and the four nuns who run the place."

He pointed to stairs just behind the guard. "This leads to the attic. The Pope's secretaries have their rooms there. There are two dozen other attic rooms, a few of which from time to time are occupied by nuns, and the others are reserved for cardinals should the need for a conclave arise—the ones they paint horror pictures of in the press."

Turning from the guard, he opened a beautifully carved door with angels at its top poking spears down toward demons at its bottom.

As we entered, though there was no one there, he whispered, "This is the Pope's chapel. It is restricted to male members of the clergy living in the building." I later learned when Luciani arrived he extended this privilege to anyone who lived in the building including the nuns, a policy that was reversed when John Paul II took over.

Luciani never said Mass here. Rather he would assign the task to young priests who were studying in the seminary and serve as their acolyte. He would kneel before the priest, a practice which caused the priest to tremble. He would tell the young man, *"You must not be afraid. In the eyes of Christ, all His children are equal."*

The chapel ceiling boasted a magnificent blue, red and golden leaded glass rendering of *The Resurrection.*

The room was entirely of marble. It was as if we were enclosed in a giant sarcophagus. Running along either side were golden wall sculptures—*The Stations of the Cross.*

Ten rows of four beautifully carved red velvet chairs with matching kneelers—two on each side of the aisle—ran the chapel's length. Up front, directly in the center facing the altar was the Pope's throne—*The Lord's Prayer* carved in Latin on its black leather back.

A life-sized figure of Christ on a wooden cross set before a huge slab of copper colored marble served as a backdrop to the altar.

As we returned to the rear of the chapel, three beautiful arched stained glass windows rose up from the floor. I asked Marcinkus if they were by Chagall as they were predominately blue and reminded me of the ones at Chartres. He told me they were by someone else, someone whom I had never heard of and no longer recall.

He took me to a corner. A half-dozen or so golden chalices sat on a small table. "There are more than five thousand of these in Vatican City. Many are studded with diamonds, rubies, emeralds and pearls. Any one of them could buy the building we are standing in."

To one side of the windows was a small door. "The chapel is built here on the roof—an addition to the original building."

A well manicured roof garden ran toward the front of the building where it took a right turn through a tunnel of overhead latticework laced with vines which ran along the front of the building and then took another turn toward the rear of the building where it took one last turn which dead ended at the side wall of the chapel.

A metal box was affixed to the wall. "This is a part of a system that controls the roving night guard. He carries a key and must clock in at specific times and places or an alarm will go off in the control station. This guard has no usual schedule and can show up anytime.

"There are boxes located throughout Vatican City. In order to reach this one, the guard must pass by the guard at the apartment entrance and pass through the chapel onto the roof—places the apartment guard is not permitted to go lest he abandon his post."

As we retraced our way back to the door it was clear the only access to the apartment from the roof was through the chapel door.

Marcinkus told me, "The garden encloses the Cortile de Sisto V Courtyard which patio is on the first floor of the palace."

Returning to the apartment we passed by the guard and headed down a marble corridor. The sound of water gushing grew louder as we headed down its length. Like the one on the first floor, it was lined with bulb-outfitted ancient wall sconces. It was roofed in by an arched ceiling which rose at its pinnacle thirty feet above us.

Unlike the ground floor, it was air-conditioned. Marcinkus told me during the reign of John XXIII a service building was added along the rear of the palace building and the adjoining building of San Damasus together with units which cooled all three floors of the Papal Palace and the corresponding floors of San Damasus.

The addition housed a fire escape and elevator which entrances were concealed behind the altar in the chapel. It had a ground floor entrance which access was limited to Swiss Guards and maintenance workers. Yet, anyone coming from the service building would have to pass through the chapel and by the papal guard to the apartment.

We proceeded past two sets of wide open doors on our left—a vast room lined with provincial furniture—mostly hi-backed chairs arranged in a half-dozen sitting areas. "This is the salon—the papal living room—the reason the doors are always open."

Further down we came to a set of richly carved doors on our left. "Here is the office of the Pope's secretaries. Like those of the salon, its windows look out on the Tiber. It includes a small makeshift operating room where Paul had his prostrate operation. It still serves that purpose for men-of-the-cloth living here or God forbid, should any of them leave here, for embalming.

← ← ← ←

<u>Pope's bedroom & bathroom - secretaries' office - salon - guard</u>
↓ River Tiber ↓

We came to that point at which the corridor led to two beautifully carved mahogany doors as if they would open to a magnificent cathedral.

"Here are a pope's private rooms. If you were to turn the doorknob, it would open to an anteroom set up as a study in front of a towering

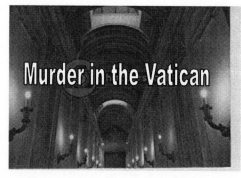

window overlooking the square. There are no locks on any of the

220

doors in the Papal Apartment. After all, everyone lives in the same house. A guard once stood to the right of this door, less than twenty feet from where the Pope sleeps. He became a cost reduction when modern technology moved in."

"Modern technology?" I repeated in a question.

"Yes, in 1960, a communication system was installed in the papal quarters. Until then, his only communication with the outside world was a phone and a cord that hung over his bed."

←   ←   ←   ←

mother nun - valet quarters - pope's library & study & bedroom

↓ St. Peter's Square ↓

We took a right-turn along the corridor which ran along the front of the building where we came to the valet's apartment and fitting rooms. Marcinkus told me, "By trade he is a tailor, a dress designer responsible for the design and coordination of the Pope's wear.

"If we were to enter and pass through his reception room and open a door at its far end, we would find ourselves surrounded by silk and satin in a tailor shop. His windows look onto St. Peter's Square. His secretaries and valet have the most frequent interaction with the Pope—the reason they are located so close to him."

We reached the corner of the building, "Now we come to where the women of the house live. In Vatican City, men outnumber women by twenty to one. Here at the top they outnumber the men.

"This door opens to the rooms of the mother nun who runs the place. She looks out at St. Peter's and the San Damasus Courtyard."

There appeared a white marble life-sized statue of the Blessed Mother at the far end of the corridor set in a fountain which explained the running water I heard when the elevator door had first opened. He took particular note to tell me this was a dead end.

"Down here on the left are the private rooms of three of the nuns who care for the residence. Each has a small sitting room, bedroom and bath. They do the cooking and housekeeping for the men of the cloth who live on the three floors of the Papal Palace."

↑ San Damasus Courtyard ↑

mother nun qtrs - three nuns qtrs - dining room - kitchen - statue

→   →   →   →

He opened a set of doors. "This is the papal nutrition center."

An aging wooden table was surrounded by a dozen chairs. An old sideboard stood off to one side and a ragged rug hung on the wall at one end. At the far end was a door that led to the kitchen.

This remained precisely the layout and occupants of the Papal Apartment on the night of John Paul's death. When John Paul II took over, he hired a world-renowned chef and added a state-of-the-art kitchen. The nuns were relocated to the attic.

Marcinkus went on, "Directly under the quarters of the mother nun and those of the valet is the apartment of the Secretary of State and the Pope's public office which overlook St. Peter's Square.

"Directly under the Pope's bedroom is the apartment of the Dean of the College of Cardinals and beneath the secretaries' office and the salon are the apartments of the Undersecretary of State and the Foreign Minister who has the privilege of living here only because his offices—the Council of Public Affairs—are on the first floor.

"There is a conference room on the first floor where they discuss the problems of the Church, or should I say, where they figure out how to avoid the problems of the Church," he laughed.

Later the bishop described the Pope's private rooms. He looked up from St. Peter's Square and pointed to the windows. He read them from left to right, "These three windows, third, fourth and fifth from the right hand corner of the top floor, front the Pope's private library located directly above his office which is on the second floor—two of the largest rooms in the building—sixty by forty feet. Dignitaries who visit the Pope in his private quarters find themselves in this room. Its focal point is Da Vinci's *Ascension,* one of the most valuable paintings in the world.

"The window second from the upper right hand corner is his private study. Had we opened the doors to his chambers we would have entered into this room. It is set up as a reception area with an antique desk and chairs. This room serves as a vestibule to his library to one side and his bedroom to the other. There is a sixteenth century bathroom here used by visitors. There is also a door to his secretaries' office which allows him direct access to his secretaries without going out into the main corridor.

"The window at the top right corner is the Pope's bedroom.

"Just around the corner, on the side that overlooks the Tiber, are two more bedroom windows and a third window which fronts the Pope's private bathroom.

"His private bath, as large as is a typical living room, in sharp contrast to the rest of the palace, is modern and has all of the amenities one associates with marble bathrooms found in the luxury suites of five-star hotels including whirlpool jets in an oversized tub and a huge marble shower. Its fittings are entirely solid gold. Until 1965, the space it now occupies was used as a private dining room."

When John Paul moved in he had exercise equipment installed including a bench press and a treadmill in this bathroom which he had brought with him from Venice.

Nevertheless, Marcinkus told me, "It is these three rooms, which is the private domain of the leader of the largest church in the world." He described the bedroom in such great detail if a roach had been sitting on a windowsill he wouldn't have missed it.

The scene of the crime

"As one enters the bedroom, one passes by a massive mahogany armoire which houses the Pope's everyday attire—his regal attire is stored in the valet's quarters down the hall. There are no closets in the Papal Apartment, as it was built long before the time of closets.

"In the corner, to the right of the window that looks out onto the square, is a white marble statue of Christ by Bernini fronted by a red velvet kneeler. A perpetual red votive candle burns before the statue.

"In the corner to the other side of the window is a sitting area—a sixteenth century sofa and matching chairs share an overly ornate coffee table. On a side table is a white antique Italian phone.

"The bed is dominated by a bronze headboard. At its top center is a solid gold crucifix flanked on either side by threatening feline gargoyles which protect the Pope from evil spirits while he sleeps. The papal bed is outfitted with new mattresses as each changing of the pope takes place, yet, the headboard has remained the focal point of the room since the nineteenth century when elevators made possible the move of the papal residence to this building.

"A red velvet bell cord hanging just above the pillows is wired to the guard's desk at the entrance to the corridor which leads to the chambers. If pulled it would ring loud enough to wake the dead.

223

"At one time, this was the Pope's only contact with the outside world when he was sequestered in his own little corner of the world. But, as I have already pointed out, in the middle of the twentieth century modern technology stepped in.

The strange set of circumstances that caused three men to sleep
in the great bed in the Papal Apartment in the fall of 1978

"Nightstands flank either side of the bed.

"The one on the left serves as a communication center—a row of buttons drive an intercom. There are buttons to the guard, to his secretary's offices and bedrooms, to the valet's rooms and one that rings in both the kitchen and bedroom of the mother nun. Another is wired to the Secretary of State's office and bedroom.

"One more. A red button—the one reserved for emergencies. It activates a flashing red light in the corridor outside his quarters and buzzes at the guard station at the entrance to the Papal Apartment."

This is the bedroom as it was the night of John Paul's death. There was an electronic unit which allowed him access to six people—his secretaries, his valet, the nun who ran his household, his secretary of state and the guard who sat at a desk just eighty feet from where the Pope sat up in his bed reading his papers.[2]

Only five of these were in the Papal Palace on the night John Paul died as the valet was away in connection with a death in his family. Yet, not one of the other five heard a ring.

Then there was the bell cord—rarely used. Yet, had he pulled it, everyone in the building would have heard it ring.

Pope Villot

Marcinkus also took me on a tour of the second and third floors of the palace. As we passed Jean Villot's quarters he told me at one time a proposal was made to move the Secretary of State's quarters to a more remote part of Vatican City, particularly, in that Villot was both Secretary of State and Cardinal Camerlengo.

The term of the Secretary of State comes to an end when a Pope dies. Yet, upon a Pope's death he forms a commission in overseeing the election of a new pope together with the Cardinal Camerlengo.

During the interim period, although their primary duty is to guide the conclave, the two have the full authority and responsibility of a pope. If an election were to stalemate for months, together they would have the power—should the need arise—to make changes to doctrine. This includes the authority to change the rules of election.

Jean Villot was only one of two cardinals to ever jointly hold both the Cardinal Secretary of State and Cardinal Camerlengo positions demonstrating the extreme confidence Paul had in him.[1] Technically, Villot reigned as Pope five days longer than John Paul as he was the interim Pope between Paul VI and John Paul and again between the two John Pauls—thirty-eight days in all.

Following the assassination attempt on John Paul II in 1981, the Secretary of State's rooms were relocated elsewhere. Today, for security purposes, where a pope sleeps is not public knowledge. Yet, the assumption is he still sleeps in the corner bedroom.[3]

The bathrooms on the lower floors were bathe in gold, among them the *Raphael Bathroom* with trappings worth a king's ransom.

I had lunch with Paul in a garden restaurant. I told him of the great white wine Jack and I had enjoyed that afternoon at the village wedge café in Vittorio Veneto. He told me he had been there too. "As we priests change wine into the blood of Christ, so, too, does the little wedge café turn common wine into the blood of gods."

As we walked back to his office, he told me I now knew more about the layout of the Papal Palace than the CIA and KGB combined. That was the last time I saw him.

Those inside the palace

On the night of John Paul's death, besides the Pope there were six people in the Papal Apartment—the perpetual guard at its entrance, the mother nun together with the three nuns who slept along the San

Damasus Courtyard side of the building and the Pope's secretary Lorenzi who was sleeping in the secretaries' office while his attic rooms were being painted. The only private rooms unoccupied were those of the valet who was away on funeral leave.

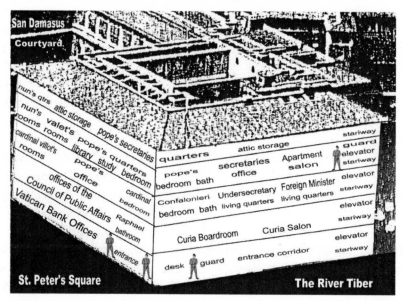

Other than these, anyone gaining access to the Pope's bedroom, whether one came up the stairs or elevator or the fire escape through the chapel or down the attic stairs would have to pass by the guard.

On the floor below were sleeping three prelates of Mafia families: Carlo Confalonieri, Agostino Casaroli and Giovanni Caprio.[4] There was a fourth, the French cardinal, Jean Villot.

John Magee was in his attic room up over the pope's bedroom accessible only by stairs in full view of the guard who sat at a desk at the entrance to the apartment. Three additional nuns were sleeping in rooms in the attic on the San Damasus side of the building.

This gives us another falsehood in the corrected Vatican release of October 10, 1978, "*We wish to correct our statement it was the Pope's secretary Magee who discovered the Pope's body. The Pope was first discovered by the nun who delivered his coffee at the usual time. When she sensed something wrong she summoned Magee...*'

In order for the nun to summon Magee—who she barely knew—she would have to pass by Lorenzi who she had lived with for two years and by the guard in a time of emergency—a Swiss guard, in

226

addition to being a human fighting machine is a paramedic.

Those outside the palace

Could anyone outside the palace gained access to the bedroom?

For my knowledge of the interior of the palace I must draw entirely upon my visit forty years ago, as they certainly wouldn't let me in there today. Yet, my recollection of its exterior is much more recent. When I first suspected murder a few years ago, I scoured the possibilities as forty years ago there was no need for possibilities. I took one of those helicopter tours over Vatican City.

As the helicopter passed over the rear of the building I struck on what I thought was much more than just a possibility. I slipped the pilot twenty dollars and asked him if he could make a closer pass. He told me he would not go closer but that he would go around once again. He pointed to two guards who were stationed atop the roof of the service building that adjoined the rear of the palace.

He told me the tripods outside the shack were not telescopes. They could take down a helicopter in seconds. He was right. As we made the pass both guards moved toward the tripods. I asked him if they had been there when the Pope died. They were added after the assassination attempt on John Paul II.

When we came out over the side of the building I noticed a row of iron fixtures running from the ground at the rear corner of the building to the fourth floor. There were a few more that ran along the top floor to the Pope's bedroom. A similar row of fixtures ran along the sides of the second and third floors of the building.

At one time a catwalk extended from these windows to a fire escape which ran down the rear of the building. They had been painted to blend in with the building. Yet, they were there.

I had to be certain the fire escape was not there in 1978.

The cards in the souvenir shops had only recent photographs of the building, so for a day or so I toured bookshops in Rome. Finally, in a little shop on the Via Pomezia I found an old picture book of the palace dated 1963, the year Paul was elected. Although one would have to look for it in order to see it, as it blended into the building, the catwalk ran right up to the Pope's bedroom window.

They had been retained it as a secondary means of escape when the service building had been added. This made sense as the corridor running through the apartment was a dead-end and smoke coming from its entrance would block one reaching the exit in the chapel.

I had a momentary rush of adrenaline and despair. If the catwalk had been there the night John Paul died, anyone had the opportunity to commit the evil deed. Luckily, I found other pictures dated in the early seventies. The fire escape was gone. We can eliminate it as a means of access. Yet, one must still consider the roof.

The roof of the building adjoins the roof of San Damascus and its roof adjoins the roof of the next building and so forth.

Anyone gaining access via the roof would have had to pass by the guard. Yet, the roof slants outward toward the perimeter of the building at an angle not that sharp a man could have moved about it without risk of falling off. It is possible for someone to have climbed down to the edge of the roof and to have thrown something into the Pope's window—a distance of thirty feet. Yet, it is not reasonable to believe one could have done this as the roof over the Pope's rooms is in full view of the square, we will resolve this as we go along.

Regardless, we can conclude for now only six people had direct access to John Paul the night he died—the mother nun Vincenza, the three nuns, the Pope's secretary Lorenzi and the apartment guard.

Eight others would have had to somehow elude the guard— Casaroli, Caprio, Confalonieri, Villot on the floor below and John Magee and the three nuns sleeping in the attic above.

The valet, as we have said, was away on funeral leave.

1 Cardinal Pacelli (Pius XII) also held both titles

2 At the time, there was an identical electronic console in the Pope's private library.

3 During the death watch of John Paul II in 2005 world television focused on a lighted window second from the right. There was no light on in the room in which John Paul had been found dead. This would suggest the bedroom in which the pope now sleeps is today on the San Damasus side of the building— formerly a nun's quarters—out of direct line of fire from the square and surrounding buildings.

4 Casaroli and Caprio were cousins in the Gambino family. Confalonieri was of the Mafia family of his name. In 1990, when Casaroli and Caprio retired, John Paul II severed the Vatican's relationship with the Mafia. The reason no cardinal has ever officiated at a Mafia family funeral since.

Photo caricature three popes in bed is by Ben Vogelsang – author's property

Photo Papal Apartment Shutterstock photo

Diagram of the Papal Palace is the property of the author

Chapter 25

Testament to Murder

"Hickory Dickory Dock..." Agatha Christie

I have promised some scenarios as to what caused three men to sleep in the great bed in the Papal Apartment in the fall of nineteen hundred and seventy-eight. Here they are for you to choose from— all of the possible ways in which the Pope could have died.

To begin with, we must separate the facts, from the probabilities, from the possibilities, from the rumors. That we will do now.

There is one circumstance of his death agreed to by all witnesses including both Vatican releases, the nun who found him, both his secretaries, the embalmers and all others brought to his room, *"The bed lamp was on and he was sitting up in his daytime clothes wearing his glasses reading papers held upright in his hands."*[1]

The embalmers told ANSA, the reputable Italian wire service, when they first viewed the body the papers were upright in his hands and he was wearing his glasses. Yet, when they took possession of the body, the papers and glasses were gone.[2]

Yet, this is the starting point for any investigation as the position the body was found is the only known circumstance of his death.

There is no heart attack, no matter how massive, which would not have allowed John Paul time to pull the bell cord or press a service button to summon help. Or, for that matter, a heart attack so painless it would have left him sitting up in his bed with his papers still held upright in his hands. Unless, of course, if one accepts the Vatican hypothesis, *"...he was able to retain papers upright in his hands in the midst of a massive heart attack by the grace of God."*[3]

It does not take a world-renowned cardiologist to tell one this. Any imbecile would know it. Yet, most Catholics believe the 33-day Pope died of a heart attack so massive he was unable to pull the cord or press a button, yet, so painless he was able to retain the position he died in sitting up in bed holding his papers upright in his hands.

This tells us something else killed him. Something so sudden he was unable to reach for the cord which hung a few inches from his right shoulder or press an emergency button an arm's length to his left. So painless he was able to retain papers upright in his hands.

The anatomy of death

How did John Paul die? There are only four ways anyone can die. One dies of natural causes. One commits suicide. One dies of accident. One is murdered. There are no other ways one can die.

Just what are the possibilities in John Paul's case?

Natural causes

That the Pope did not die of a heart attack does not necessarily mean he could not have died of some other natural cause.

Here we have powerful evidence that points to only one possible natural cause. The position which he was found points to a cause of death both instantaneous and painless—otherwise he would have reacted to the pain and dropped his papers. The only natural cause that can result in instant death without pain is stroke.

There are two kinds of fatal stroke—intra-cerebral and ischemic.

An intra-cerebral stroke or cerebral hemorrhage—bursting of blood vessels—can kill one instantly. Yet, it can be ruled out as it is accompanied by enormous throbbing head pain which would cause him to drop his papers. We can eliminate this as a cause of death.

Conversely, an ischemic stroke—usually blockage of the carotid arteries carrying oxygen to the brain—is painless. Yet, an ischemic stroke is not instantaneous. It graduates through the body from top to bottom. It takes several minutes and often hours to progress.

Early warning signs are dizziness followed by numbness in the face, loss of speech, unable to grasp with either the left or right hand. Even a massive bilateral stroke—infinitely rare—in the first minutes affects only one side of the body, which would have allowed him to sound the alarm with the other side—unless, of course, he had been sleeping. Yet, we know he was awake and reading. He would have had more than enough time to have acted.

What makes stroke a long shot in the Pope's case is his relatively low blood pressure—as surefire a prevention of both heart attack and

230

stroke that exists.[4] Blood viscosity is instrumental to stroke. We do know his viscosity level was at normal levels as it had been tested in his physical exam a few months before.[5]

Yet, what nails the lid shut on the supposition the Pope died of stroke is the doctor who pronounced him dead.

Doctor Buzzanetti did not suggest stroke. In the case of an unwitnessed death, it is possible for a doctor to examine the conditions a corpse is found and eliminate stroke as a possibility whereas it is not possible to eliminate *'myocardial infarction'* or, for that matter, *'pulmonary embolism'* as a possibility without autopsy.

If the corpse had showed any signs symptomatic of stroke, the doctor certainly would have struck on it. Particularly in that it would have headed off all of the rumors that have surfaced since. But, he did not. So one knows John Paul did not die of stroke.

Even without medical expertise everyone who went to the room knew he had not died of stroke—the reason why stroke has never been a consideration in all the investigations of his mysterious death which have been spent since—he was awake when he died.

Myocardial Infarction vs. Pulmonary Embolism

Here again, as we have many times before, we must dispel the myths. The first release claimed the Pope had died of *'myocardial infarction to the heart.'* After this was widely disclaimed by the medical profession, the second release did not claim a specific cause. What is did do was claim the Pope had been suffering of *'swollen feet'* to plant the seed an embolism had killed the Pope.

In 1984, David Yallop published *In God's Name* and, in 1987, John Cornwell published *A Thief in the Night*. These bestsellers still reign today as the premier books of John Paul's death.

Both these men are reputable world-renowned journalists.

They both interviewed the same witnesses of the Pope's death. Yet, they came up with entirely different conclusions.

Lorenzi	told Cornwell John Paul had experienced chest pains at 8 o'clock whereas he had never mentioned them to Yallop or to anyone else for nine years.[6]
Magee	told Cornwell John Paul had experienced a *'choking'*

231

	pain at 4 o'clock whereas he never mentioned it to Yallop or to anyone else for nine years.[7]
Vincenza's	witness in Yallop's book was the most damaging to Cornwell's conclusion John Paul could have died of natural causes.[13] Yet, by providential coincidence she had died in the meantime and was unavailable to Cornwell who discounts her witness in Yallop's book as *'delusions of an old nun.'*[12]
Embalmers	the day of the pope's death, embalmers told ANSA—Italy's most reliable wire service—they were picked up about 5:30 AM. They changed their story in 1987 for Cornwell saying they were picked up a bit later and performed a light embalming before 11AM.[2]
Lina Petri	told Cornwell *"The manner of his death is consistent with pulmonary embolism…One is not aware of death in embolism…"* Though contradictory to the Lorenzi-Magee's testimony the Pope had experienced *'pains,'* Cornwell based his conclusion on this hypothesis—John Paul died of pulmonary embolism.[8]

At the time, a doctor could speculate embolism may have killed him because science did not know what it knows today. Today, one will not find a cardiologist in the world who has known a patient to be unresponsive to the trauma of death in pulmonary embolism.

Even the American cardiologist, Dr. C. Francis Roe, the 'expert' witness Cornwell bases his conclusion on, tells Cornwell *"I've seen many embolism deaths. Yet, I've never seen any of them die unresponsive to what was happening to them."*[12]

Eye embolism vs. pulmonary embolism

Lina based her theory on an incident that had occurred in 1975.

Yallop and Cornwell interviewed Dr. Rama who treated Luciani for what was thought to be a clot in the left retina. The condition was treated with aspirin and mild medication and the result was quick and recovery of vision was complete and had never reoccurred.

232

According to Dr. Rama's testimony Luciani's viscosity level was normal—the reason he was not put on the anti-coagulant Warfarin.

When I talked to Luciani's doctor Da Ros after the Pope's death I asked him why Luciani's physical exams included ultrasound and viscosity testing? This seemed strange to me, as this kind of testing was done only when a clotting problem is suspected. I assumed Da Ros had made it a part of his exams because of the 'eye' incident.

He told me it had nothing to do with it. Though he avoided the word 'hypochondriac,' he told me Luciani was overly concerned with his health and made use of every available test. Ultrasound and viscosity had been a part of his exams for a decade or more.

Da Ros told me to think an eye embolism could develop into a massive pulmonary embolism would be as much as to think a man died of pneumonia because he sneezed on a single occasion a few years ago. Though both clots, one has very little to do with the other.

A retina embolus originates in the throat and is microscopic in nature whereas a pulmonary embolus generally originates in the legs and is enormous in nature. A pulmonary embolism that blocks the pulmonary artery—an inch and quarter in diameter—can be as big around as a man's thumb and a foot long.[9]

It would not take a world-renowned cardiologist to tell one that a massive pulmonary embolus could not develop in the human body instantly when the patient has had no history of it. Also, that it could move from the legs through the heart to the lungs without the patient being aware of it. Again, one can draw on common sense.

This is precisely the position of the medical community today, though both clots, one has very little to do with the other.[9]

Yes, had Luciani died of a clot to the brain—a microscopic clot that comes up from the throat—one might relate it to the retina problem. Yet, as we have just demonstrated, this was not the case.

This is consistent with a study involving twenty-five hundred patients who succumbed to pulmonary embolism, not one had a history of retina blockage. Yet, another study which examined fifteen hundred patients who had died of cerebral hemorrhage disclosed three percent had a history of retina blockage.[10]

Low blood pressure, heart attack, embolism, anticoagulants

233

When Yallop and Cornwell wrote their books, low blood pressure was thought to be a contributing cause to myocardial infarction and pulmonary embolism.[11] Yet, today, low blood pressure is known to be as surefire prevention of heart attack and embolism that exists.[4]

In the case of a massive myocardial infarction—heart attack—one that kills quickly—there is a strangulating pain in the heart, like a 'charley horse' to the heart. For those who don't already know it, the heart is technically a muscle. Death occurs in minutes.[4]

In the case of a massive pulmonary embolism—one that kills quickly—a sharp piercing stabbing pain to the lungs is followed by a period of painful shortness of breath, in turn, followed by a period of palpitations—rapid beating of the heart—ending in cardiac arrest.[4]

In a massive embolism, death normally occurs within an hour or two. There have been rare cases where death occurs in minutes, yet, these have been limited to patients being treated for the condition.[4]

Yet, Lina Petri's testimony is important in determining the truth.

Again, when one investigates the possibility of murder, one must consider not only the evidence that is there, but also the evidence which should be there, and is not there.

As we have said, in Hercule Poirot's *Hickory Dickory Dock* we have the footprints which should have been there and were not there. In Sherlock Holmes' *Silver Blaze* we have the dog which should have barked and did not bark. In the *Swiss Guard Murders* we have the commander's weapon which should have been there and was not there. In the case of the *33-day Pope,* we have the alarm clock which should have rung and did not ring. In the case of *Lina Petri,* we have the testimony that should be there and is not there.

In her testimony to Cornwell, she speaks of retinas and swollen legs of elephantine proportions to support her theory of embolism. She speaks in speculations and implications and innuendos. She 'thinks' he may have been on anticoagulants.

Yet, there is something that should be there, but is not there. She tells us what she 'thinks.' She does not tell us what she 'knows.'

Lina Petri was, by all accounts, the closest family member of the Pope. So close, she had visited him a number of times in his brief papacy. So close, she had been the first of the family at his bedside.

What's more, she was a physician.

To 'think' he could have been on anticoagulants and she not have not 'known' of it would boggle the imagination. After all, it would

234

be no secret, many people would have known of it. At the time, anticoagulants, still true today, required weekly visits to a hospital or laboratory for viscosity testing.

Warfarin, the common anticoagulant of 1978 as it remains today, is a dangerous drug and requires ongoing testing lest one risk bleeding to death internally.

It is well known, during his papacy he was never examined by a physician other than Dr. Da Ros, the pharmacy never issued him a prescription of any kind, and had he showed up at the Vatican clinic every week we certainly would have heard about it by this time.

We also know from Dr. Da Ros' testimony to the press, viscosity testing had not been a part of the three visits he made to the Papal Palace during John Paul's papacy.[15]

Lina is not an impartial witness. As a surviving family member, particularly one so close to him, in the Cornwell testimony, she was at the mercy of John Paul II. She would do anything he asked of her. Like his other surviving kin, Lina's driving ambition for her beloved uncle rests entirely with the sitting Pontiff—sainthood.

For this reason today, clergy books and websites are designed to destroy the controversial life of Albino Luciani and bury the truth of his death. The Vatican is calling the shots. It holds the cards.

"...upright in his hands."

Yet, concerning the most critical piece of evidence determining the question of murder vs. natural causes, all parties agree.

Both Vatican releases were explicit the *'Imitation of Christ* (1st release) and *'the papers'* (2nd release) were *'upright in his hands.'*[1&3]

John Magee, in the testimony he gave Cornwell, is explicit in his description of the body, *"...there he was, propped up with pillows, his papers still erect in his hands, his face turned to the right, with his spectacles on, he looked intent on what he was reading."*[12]

Magee agrees with Sister Vincenza's description as released by ANSA—Italy's most reputable wire service—the day the pope was found dead, *"...The light was on. He was sitting up in bed in his daytime clothes reading papers held upright in his hands. He was looking in my direction. I greeted him, 'Good morning.' He held to a mime position as if deeply involved in what he was reading..."*[12]

Lorenzi told Cornwell he took the papers from the Pope's hands. "'...He was sitting up in a position like this.' Lorenzi imitated a typical reading position pushing his glasses slightly down on his nose... 'The light by the bed was on. One would never guess he was dead. The sheets of paper were upright...That is, they had not fallen... I, myself, took the papers out of his hands...'"[12]

It has been well documented Lina Petri spent a half-hour in the room with her uncle before the embalmers took charge. She detailed her description to Cornwell which agreed with that of Lorenzi, Magee, Vincenza and all the others bought to the room. "It was as if he was smiling at me. His face showed no sign of suffering...there was something very strange. He was wearing his daytime clothes...if in bed why was he wearing his daytime clothes? ...His sleeves were all torn. Why should they be torn like that? I wondered..."[12]

Lina does not mention the papers as she viewed the body five hours after it had been found and they had already been removed.

One can trust these descriptions as all of these witnesses were at the mercy of John Paul II. Vincenza, Magee and Lorenzi were clergy and Lina depended on the sitting Pontiff for her uncle's sainthood.

None of them mention vomit which erases the digitalis-Effortil myth which in her testimony she refers to as 'a crackpot idea.'[12]

As already pointed out, Dr. Da Ros had denied having prescribed Effortil.[14] What's more, the Vatican pharmacy testified it had not issued prescriptions of any kind to John Paul.[12]

Fifteen years later, Da Ros crushed the rumor of 'swollen legs of elephantine proportions.' He spent the Saturday afternoon before the Pope's death with him and assured the press the Pope had never suffered from swollen feet either during of before his papacy.[15]

Regardless, who took the papers from his hands is immaterial. What is important here is that all parties agree they were upright.

You will not find a cardiologist in the world who would testify in a court of law today that John Paul could have died of myocardial infarction or pulmonary embolism and not have dropped his papers.

John Paul II personally met with John Cornwell and approved those interviewed. One can speculate Magee, after nine years, added 'pain' to the soup as part of his being made a bishop as a prerequisite to the Cornwell interviews. One can speculate Lorenzi, after nine years, added 'pain' to the soup as a part of his special allegiance to a reigning pontiff required by his order of the Don Orione Brothers. As Lorenzi told Cornwell, *"I have taken a vow of obedience. I do anything I am told."*[12] One can speculate Lina Petri gave her 'expert' testimony to pave the way for Luciani's sainthood in a conservative church——the reason why others who knew him tend to annihilate the controversial life of Albino Luciani today. One will never know.

Yet, what one does know is John Paul did not die of heart attack or, for that matter, pulmonary embolism. As we shall see, he died of a more deadly malady...the collaborating and politicking of men.

It is not important to know who took the papers from his hands. All that is important is who put the papers in his hands. Who put the papers in his hands is the same person who placed the glasses on his nose. Someone who did not know he did not require them to read.

Suicide

Next, we have suicide. That he did not pull the cord or press a button could have been intentional on his part—true if suicide had been his intent. There is only one method of suicide that would have not left evidence of foul play for those who found him—poison.

Only two poisons result in painless, instantaneous or close to instantaneous death, strychnine and cyanide—the reason they have found their way into mystery novels.[19] Strychnine can be eliminated as it results in massive convulsions for a few minutes before death— it would have never left him in the position he was found.

Cyanide concealed in food would take several minutes, as much as an hour, to kill him. Yet, biting down on a cyanide capsule would kill him almost instantly as in a gaseous form it is deadly. When one bites down on the capsule the gas attacks membranes cutting off oxygen flow almost immediately. Yet, had this been the case, he would have required an accomplice. Death occurs so suddenly it is impossible to swallow the capsule. No capsule was found.

Yet, what closes the lid on suicide is motive. Here was a very purposeful man who had worked all of his life to attain the position he now found himself in. Now he had the power to right the wrongs of the past, to bring an end to bigotry once and for all. Now he was in a position to bring an end to poverty and starvation in the world.

That he would take his own life on the very brink of the realization of his lifelong dreams makes no sense at all.

What's more, one has the testimony of Dr. Da Ros. It boggles the imagination to think a 'hypochondriac' would take one's own life.

Accident

Again, the position of the body is the clue.

If you can come up with an accident that could have left the body in the position in which it was found you are much more a Sherlock Holmes than I. For certain an accident was not involved.

Unless, he had been killed by an accident caused by someone's negligence who, in covering up, sat him up in the position found. This would be true if Lorenzi had accidentally killed his master.

Lorenzi? Why Lorenzi?

Of all the men in the world, other than the guard, he was the only one who had unlimited access to the Pope throughout the night. In his case, he would not even have to pass through the main corridor, as a door connected the secretaries' office directly to the papal study which annexed the papal bedroom. Let us consider the possibility.

Dr. Da Ros was emphatic that the only prescription he had issued Luciani still active at the time of the Pope's death was for treatment of the adrenal cortex. The injections were given twice a year— toward the end of March and toward the end of September.[15]

Although not required for the medicine involved one normally refrigerates injection vials. It is likely they were stored in the kitchen refrigerator with other medicine of members of the papal household. Cardinal Confalonieri stored his insulin in this refrigerator and one of the nuns who suffered from a thyroid condition also stored her medicine there. There may have been others. One will never know.

One might assume Vincenza gave the injections. Yet, that they were given in the area of the buttocks it is unlikely a nun would have had the Pope drop his pants. They were most likely administered by his secretary Lorenzi whom he had brought with him from Venice.

It is possible Lorenzi unknowingly injected the Pope with a lethal substance—he had mistakenly taken the wrong vial. If this had been the case, it would explain many circumstances surrounding the death of the 33-day Pope.

It would explain why the Pope was dressed in his daytime clothes as the injection would have been given shortly after he retired at 9:30 the evening before—it would make no sense John Paul would awaken Lorenzi at four in the morning to give him an injection.

It would explain why Lorenzi told Cornwell nine years after the Pope's death John Paul had experienced chest pains whereas he had not mentioned pain to anyone else for nine years. [6]

It would explain why Lorenzi has repeatedly denied the Pope was murdered when he has no other way to know this.

It would explain why Lorenzi has repeatedly told the press John Paul wanted to die, as to suggest he was suicidal. For example, his testimony in Cornwell's *A Thief in the Night*, *"He was constantly talking of death, his papacy would be a short one. John Paul told me, 'The type of rest I would like is for a good and quick death.'"*[12]

It would explain the missing slipper socks which Lorenzi may have used to wipe the tinge of blood an injection would leave.

It would explain why the alarm clock did not go off. It had never been set to begin with.

It would explain why the Pope was sitting up reading with his glasses on with papers held upright in his hands. It would make sense for Lorenzi to sit the Pope up reading papers to give the impression he died while reading the evening before. Otherwise Lorenzi alone would have had to dress John Paul in his bedclothes.

Yet, if he staged the body for the nun to find in the morning, why place the glasses on its nose. Of all the people in the Vatican, he and Vincenza would have known John Paul didn't need them to read. Yet, he may have been clever enough to have done this to place suspicions away from him in the event foul play was suspected.

It may be the notes held in his hands were, indeed, listings of cardinals to be removed from office as the rumors had suggested—composed and staged by Lorenzi to cast suspicions toward others.

Yet, there is an inconsistency in this supposition. It conflicts with the embalmers' claim *'the body was warm.'* A corpse will usually fall from 98.6 to its environmental temperature in about 8 hours after death. Yet, there are factors which can slow the rate of cooling.

We know from the nun's testimony, though dressed in daytime clothes, the bedclothes were pulled partly up over him which could have warmed the body surface. Body fat, some foods and certain toxic substances can greatly slow the rate of loss of body heat.

Yet, we are talking here of the chance of a snowball in hell. That these conditions could have misled the embalmers is highly unlikely.

Then again, it may be the nun Vincenza did ask the Pope to drop his pants. She gave John Paul the injection. She accidentally killed the Pope. In her case, she could have given him the injection when she delivered coffee—consistent with the embalmers' claim he had not been dead for more than an hour or two.

The argument against this is that being a small woman she would have had difficulty maneuvering the body into position. Also, in her subsequent actions she never tried to cover up for murder. In fact, it was her unwavering witness through the years which supports much of the investigation that continues to go on today.

Regardless, this is all speculation. One will really never know.

One has to assume Lorenzi or someone else accidentally killed the Pope at the exact moment in history his enemies both inside the Vatican and across the pond wanted him dead. This is unfathomable chance of coincidence. Yet, it remains a possibility that someone accidentally killed the Pope and covered up. For this reason, though a long shot, one must keep it on the table.

A possible alternative is Lorenzi did not accidentally kill the Pope. He was unknowingly an accomplice to murder. He thought he accidentally killed the Pope and staged the cover up, whereas, as a matter-of-fact, someone else had tampered with the vials.

The hole in this theory is that anyone tampering with the vials would have no way of knowing Lorenzi would cover up the deed. Had he not covered up there would surely have been an autopsy.

Regardless, in conclusion, we have no chance of natural death or suicide. Though there remains a remote possibility of accident and cover up, we know, with a reasonable degree of certainty, John Paul was murdered. There are no other ways one can die.

Murder

Yet, just how was he murdered? How does one kill a pope?

To answer these questions, we must first clear up some loose ends—the time of death for example. Yes, let us take the time to close the door on that one.

All the witnesses agree he retired shortly after nine o'clock.

If one believes the doctor who declared him dead, the Pope died before midnight.[1] If one believes the embalmers—*the body was still warm*—he died in the early morning hours.[2]

At first, this discrepancy in testimony as to when the Pope had died—the doctor versus the undertakers—was widely reported in the press. Since it seemed immaterial the press dropped it as an issue.

Today, we know the time of death is quite material as it answers many questions including the most puzzling of all. How could he be dressed in daytime clothes and still be reading at midnight? As we have said before, if one intends to read oneself to sleep, one will first don one's bedclothes and climb in between the sheets.

It would mean the Pope had risen at his usual time, of about four o'clock, turned off the alarm, completed his morning toilet, dressed for the day, and sat himself up in his bed reading while he waited for the coffee knock on the door—just as the nun had assumed.

If the embalmers were right—embalmers have more experience than do doctors in examining recently expired corpses—this would mean the Pope may have died as late as four-thirty in the morning.

In that the night had been chilly and the windows were open would further substantiate the embalmers claim the Pope could not have been dead for much more than an hour as the chilly air would have accelerated the body's cooling.

To fix the time of murder, one must consider motive. Would the embalmers have had any reason to lie? At least to this author, they would have had no reason to have lied. It is reasonable to believe influenced by John Paul II nine years later they changed their story for Cornwell that they had arrived after dawn and not before dawn—a story contradicted by the Vatican motor pool records.[21]

Yet, would the doctor have had motive to lie? Would Cardinal Villot, who issued the press release the Pope died before midnight, have had motive to lie? The answer is a resounding "Yes."

There would be nothing unusual about embalming eight hours after death because Italian law which prohibited embalming earlier than twenty-four hours after death did not apply in the Vatican.

But, it would be highly unusual to have embalmed immediately after death—particularly, to have roused the embalmers at five in the morning when the body would not lie in state until noon.

It makes all the sense in the world that Villot and the doctor lied about the time of death to place considerable time between death and the embalming to avoid suspicion of poisoning. Yet, Villot erred by including in the release he had performed the last rites, when it was known no priest would do such a thing over a cold corpse.

The Vatican implied time of death unimportant, *"It is immaterial when the Pope died; all that matters is he was found dead."*[3]

The Vatican made this statement because it knew the time of death was material to the possibility of foul play.

Had the Pope died before midnight, as the doctor claimed, foul play was unlikely; but, if he had died early in the morning, as the embalmers claimed, the likelihood of foul play was almost certain.

It may be Villot knew the Pope had died before midnight. Either Lorenzi or Vincenza or someone else involved in an accident had confided in him. Or could Villot have been involved in a conspiracy to murder his boss? We will examine these things as we go along.

"Light...by the grace of God"

"...The light was on ..."[1] tells us much more.

The police in the square had taken note of John Paul's practice to leave his windows open as his first few evenings in the palace were hot and uncomfortable. Paul, before him, on hot nights would have the windows closed—he slept in air conditioning. John Paul was a fresh air fiend—he preferred to sleep with the windows open.

So much so, they had a pool going—with the nights growing colder as to when the Pope was going to close his windows. They were certain the Pope's light was not on at three in the morning as it was at that time the changing of police in the square took place and they would check the windows to see if anyone had won the pool.[17]

The press took his open windows as symbolic of his papacy. *"He will open the windows of the Church and let in the 'free' air."*[16]

Regardless, had the Pope's light been on all night it would have surely been reported in the news. There were times Paul's light had not gone off until after 2 o'clock in the morning—always reported in the newspapers the next day. Also, hundreds of tourists roam the square at night and the papal bedroom is a focal point not only from the square but from the surrounding district as well.

There was no notice in any newspaper the Pope's light was on all night. On the other hand, several newspapers reported the next day the Pope's light came on at about its usual time.[17]

'Its usual time,' had been so unusual it had become a topic of conversation. For fifteen years during the reign of Paul VI and for five years during the reign of John XXIII and for nineteen years during the reign of Pius XII the light would go on about six o'clock.

On the day following Luciani's election the light came on at four o'clock. Even for a man-of-the-cloth, he was an early riser. That he was on-the-job at four o'clock was widely reported in newspapers.[18]

We know from the police in the square the light was not on at three in the morning. Early-rising Romans who habitually checked the Pope's windows testified his light came on at its usual time. So we have the fact, *the light was not on all night. Either the Pope or someone else turned it on at about 4 o'clock in the morning.*

That the light was not on all night does not destroy the 'Lorenzi' scenario as a possibility, as he would have turned it off before midnight. He would have done this because he knew that when the police in the square noticed the light on all night they would surely notify the Swiss Guard in the Vatican to investigate.

This would have been true of anyone who may have killed the Pope before midnight—they would have turned the light off and returned before dawn to turn it back on as to not arouse suspicions. It is also true of anyone who may have killed him before four o'clock in the morning—they would have turned it on at its usual time as not to arouse suspicion. Sufficient light to commit the deed would have come through the windows.

The great weight of evidence, the testimony of the embalmers and that the light came on at 4 o'clock in the morning tells us John Paul was murdered sometime before 4 o'clock in the morning—with a reasonable degree of confidence between 3:30AM and 4:00AM.

To this day, the official position of the Vatican remains, the Pope died before midnight and the light was on all night—by chance the police and the crowds who roam the square at night and those who lived in surrounding buildings had not noticed it had been on all night. Perhaps, too, *"by the grace of God."*

Now, let us consider the possible instruments of murder.

Poison

There is the supposition John Paul was poisoned at dinner. In the alphabet of poisons from A to Z one can conceal in food or drink,

243

there is not one which allows the victim to go unscathed for hours and suddenly result in instant death. This includes everything from cyanide to the deadly Barbados nut.[19]

We can eliminate slow-arsenic poisoning as, as in Paul's case, he would have been too ill to continue his office for weeks.

We have already eliminated the digitalis-Effortil myth.

Creatures

A killer can kill in one of two ways. He either performs the deed himself or he employs another person or creature to carry out the deed. Let us first eliminate the possibility of a creature.

Other than poison, animals leave physical signs of destruction.

There are snakes which incisors are so fine they might not have been detected by the embalmers. The puff adder has incisors so fine that unless the victim actually sees the snake strike, he may not be aware he has been bitten. It has venom so powerful it results in near instant paralysis which could be consistent with how the body was found. Yet, being a large snake, it is easily detected under covers.

Yet, there exists no creature so poisonous it kills instantly. All of them allow, at the very least, a few minutes to seek help.

An exception is the giant golden scorpion. The pale yellow scorpion kills more people on a per-capita basis than does any other creature on earth because it lives in the desert where few people live. Yet, it injects very little venom which allows one time to seek help. On the other hand, a mutation of the pale yellow species, the giant golden scorpion injects enough venom to kill ten men on the spot.

In 1975, Bishop Casaroli was one of two dozen survivors on a French Carousel jet which crashed in the Moroccan Mountains killing over a hundred passengers. While awaiting rescue crews, two of the survivors were killed by this predator.

Because of this coincidence, in earlier editions of *Murder in the Vatican,* I examined the possibility John Paul may have been killed by a scorpion. Many came away with the conviction a scorpion had killed the Pope. So, I am guilty of creating a few myths myself.

My success in creating such a myth was made possible partially because scorpions kept by Casaroli in the miniature desert in the gardens at the Castle Gandolfo disappeared shortly after John Paul's death. Yet, it is likely the bishop removed them to avoid rumors arising than it was they had actually been involved in the deed.

If one considers the remote possibility someone came from the roof of the adjoining buildings and threw something down into the open window, of creatures, a scorpion would make the most sense as scorpions are instinctively attracted to human body temperature— the reason desert campers are warned never to sleep on the ground.

Yet, there is a more compelling reason to exclude creatures.

It would be a poor choice of other available methods.

It involves chance and would require removal of the creature after the deed. If one was talking fiction, it would be a good choice. But, in the case of a real life murder, particularly one involving a head-of-state, it does not pass the test of common sense.

Guns, knives, smothering with pillows

In the covert murder of a pope, one does not resort to poisons, creatures, or, for that matter, knives, guns or blunt instruments. Since the eleventh century all popes have lay-in-state on an open catafalque. One must take care not to damage the face or hands. If a pope lay in state in a closed casket it would rile up more than rumor.

Two things suggest how John Paul was murdered. The position the body was found and the embalmers did not detect violence.

We have explained the position of the body. We have examined every possible way he could have died and none of them would have left the body in the position it was found. So we have a third fact, *someone sat him up in bed in his daytime clothes with his glasses on reading papers held upright in his hands with the light on.*

Cornwell's *A Thief in the Night* offers an interesting hypothesis to explain the position he was found which would be consistent with his having died of natural causes: *"Magee noticed light coming from beneath the bedroom door at about eleven o'clock at night and entered to investigate. He found the Pope dead on the floor. He roused Lorenzi and the two spent the night reminiscing about the Pope. They dressed him in his daytime clothes reading for the nun to find in the morning."*[12] Lorenzi and Magee deny this in his book.

Yet, if the pope had died of natural causes, foul play or any other cause we know this to be a fact, *someone sat him up in bed in his daytime clothes with his glasses on reading papers held upright in his hands with the light on.* For none of these could have left him in the position he was found. We know this for another reason, John Paul, himself, would have never placed the glasses on his nose.

Cornwell, seals his case John Paul died of *'pulmonary embolism'* with Magee's testimony the Pope spent two hours walking in the salon that afternoon to help his swollen feet—a condition mentioned in the Vatican release which we know today he did not suffer from.[15] Even if he did suffer from swollen feet, it does not take a doctor to tell one the worst thing for swollen feet is to walk on them.

In his testimony to Cornwell, the newly appointed bishop Magee not only claims the Pope walked for two hours the afternoon before his death, but on every afternoon of his papacy, *"Every day, through those thirty-three days, he walked on the roof for two hours."*[12]

Dr. Da Ros would confirm this in his interview with Andrea Tornelli many years later. Because the Vatican was more confined than Venice, he had advised the Pope in addition to his morning exercises to walk a couple of hours at a brisk pace each day.[15]

Two hours, at a normal walking pace, or a moderate exercise pace, is eight miles a day. How many people walk eight miles a day and suddenly succumb instantly to a sudden circulatory condition?

After nine years of silence, Lorenzi would add *'chess pain'* to the soup. Magee would verify the Vatican's claim of *'swollen feet.'* Lina Petri would shout *'pulmonary embolism.'* 1, 2, 3, case closed!

Regardless, concerning the embalmers did not detect physical signs of violence—there are limited methods which would not leave visible evidence: asphyxiation, gas and lethal injection.

One might imagine a methanol, ethanol, chloroform or other chemical saturated gauze or sponge held over the face. Although these chemicals can be fatal, there is not one among them which does not leave a lingering odor for hours particularly in bedclothes.

There are some odorless deadly gases like nerve gas. Yet, there is not one of these deadly chemicals if applied in this fashion that would not kill everyone within the room not wearing a gasmask.

Finally, one could imagine an odorless lethal gas seeping into the room. Someone could had come from another building and thrown a gas grenade down into his window from the roof above. Yet, his two cockatiels remained alive in their cage in the corner of the room.

Who killed the Pope and how?

246

How the Pope was killed tells us who killed the Pope and vice versa. For example, if digitalis or other ingested poison was involved one knows an amateur killed the Pope. Conversely, if professional killers had been employed, it tells us how the Pope was killed.

It may seem more sinister and sell many more books to think of disgruntled old men of the Curia spiking the Pope's soup. Yet, this is not how popes are murdered in a modern era.

When one considers the murder of a head of state—in this case a controversial and dangerous man in the eyes of his enemies—there is no sensible alternative other than to engage professional killers.

David Yallop's bestseller *In God's Name* concludes *'Whoever killed Albino Luciani was no amateur.'* We take no exception to his conclusion. John Paul was murdered by professional hit men. This narrows the instrument of death to lethal injection.

This also narrows the search for the killers, something we will talk about in what is yet to come. Of Gladio, Condor, the Mafia and all the other killer organizations operating in Italy at the time, only one had a physical presence in the Vatican in the fall of 1978—P2

Regardless, when *'no trace of foul play'* is a necessary ingredient in the recipe for murder, this is the choice of professional killers.

The perpetrators would have no room for error. Lethal injection requires someone from the medical or scientific communities and/or professional killers. It requires professional expertise.

One has to employ a toxin which will stop the heart instantly to avoid struggle. Such toxins are not readily available. One has to know how much of the toxin to inject. One has to know where to inject it. For example, 10ccs of potassium cyanide injected directly into the Vargas Nerve will result in instant paralysis and death.

One would avoid a toxin having the properties of an element which would assay of foul play as one could not guarantee autopsy would be performed. Canon law clearly allows for autopsy of a pope or cardinal when murder is suspected.[20]

Elements can assay of foul play centuries after death. Practiced killers would have surely avoided employing an element. If John Paul's tomb was opened today it may not yield evidence of foul play. On the other hand, as we shall prove, if one were to exhume Paul VI's tomb today, it would wobble the Vatican Empire.

Lethal injection is the only method of murder consistent with the known facts of the case. A needle leaves a tiny mark. If wiped of the tinge of blood, it would not have been noticed by the embalmers.

Lina Petri told Cornwell *"his sleeves were all torn."*[12] The extent of the damage made clear by her use of the word *'all.'*

Few popes go about in ragged clothes. He may have gotten away with it as a bishop and as a priest—but not as a pope.

It suggests a struggle took place possibly while he was wearing his daytime clothes—those he was found in. Although I do not agree with Lina's 'opinion' as to the cause of her uncle's death, I don't believe she lied. She would have had no reason to have lied.

If he had struggled, an injection could have left more than a tinge of blood—more than could be swiped with an inch square cotton pad a killer would bring along. The killer may have reached down by the side of the bed and picked up one of the white slipper-socks to clean excess blood, he would have been a fool to leave the other behind.

Sleeping?

We have already determined the position he was found—*sitting up in his daytime clothes with his glasses on reading with papers still upright in his hands*—was staged by the killers.

Let us examine the possibility he was attacked while sleeping. There were no locks on any of the doors in the Papal Apartment. Anyone eluding the guard at its entrance and gaining access to the apartment had free access to the Pope's bedroom.

Lethal injection of a hostile victim requires a minimum of two people—one to hold the victim and the other to make the injection. This would be true whether he was awake or sleeping.

The *'torn sleeves'* is consistent with either hypothesis—if he had been awake and dressed in daytime clothes or if he had been asleep in his bedclothes. If he had been in his bedclothes, he would have had to have been redressed in his daytime clothes. One is not likely to tear a sleeve when dressing oneself, yet, this can often occur when pulling clothes onto a rigid body, particularly delicate pope sleeves.

Why would the killers dress him in his daytime clothes?

The answer could have been to place the time of death after he retired the previous evening sometime before midnight. This would support the early morning embalming. This would be true only if Cardinal Villot who ordered the early embalming had been involved.

Yet, it is more likely they would have dressed him in his daytime clothes to give the impression he had risen at his usual time, turned off the alarm, turned on the light, completed his toilet, dressed for the day, and sat himself up in bed reading while he waited for the coffee knock—just as the nun who found him had assumed.

The Catholic world believes the police and crowds who roam the square at night and those who lived in surrounding buildings had not noticed the light had been on all night *"by the grace of God."*

It believes scores of early risers in the surrounding buildings who told the press the pope's light came on at its usual time, lied.

That he was wearing his glasses points to someone who did not know he did not require them to read—a professional killer. That they disappeared suggests an accomplice—an insider involved in a conspiracy. Someone who came to the room—realizing a mistake had been made—confiscated them. According to all those brought to his room, including both Vatican releases, the Pope was wearing his glasses. Yet, by the time the embalmers took charge they were gone.

We have resolved Lorenzi took the papers from his hands. Could it be he took the glasses at the same time? One will never know.

The watch

Finally, we have the watch he had been fumbling with at dinner. *"It was of such an unusual design, it looked like it had come out of 'Dr No.'"*[13] The watch, no one knew where it came from.

There is the possibility it had been set for the time of death. A spring mechanism released a needle at the wrist and instant death.

The CIA has a unit that does nothing but develop contraptions of this sort. One does not have to depend on *'Dr No.'*

This may have left the body in the position it was found. One could say if it had been set for a few minutes before the nun showed up with coffee, it could explain why he was in his daytime clothes.

Yet, the watch, at most, could have rendered him immobile to facilitate the killers' transgression. It could have never done the job by itself. For it could have never placed the glasses on his nose.

Unless, of course, it did come out of *'Dr No.'*

Final tally

When all is said and done, it is reasonable to conclude the Pope was killed by lethal injection shortly before four o'clock in the morning and at least two people were involved in the evil deed—people who did not know he did not require his glasses to read.

One hears many stories. One hears, on the one hand, there was no embalming—the nuns, Magee and Lorenzi readied the body for viewing at noon, going so far as to place the jaw in a sling to correct twisted features to suggest heart attack. If true, they did a good job. Six hundred thousand mourners passed by the body on an open catafalque and not one of them noticed a contorted face at all.

On the other hand, Vatican motor pool records show a van was dispatched at 5:23AM on the morning of September 29, 1978 to pick up the Signoracci brothers from the nearby school of medicine.[21]

In addition, Mario de Francesco who interviewed the embalmers and the embalmers, themselves, have never changed their story in the press, *'He had not been dead for more than an hour or two.'*[22]

We may never know who placed the spectacles on the man who did not need them to read? Who turned the light on which was not on all night? Who turned the alarm clock off which did not ring? Who dressed him in his daytime clothes? Who gave him the watch which ticked the time of death? Then again, was the watch set for the time of death? Who took the scorpions, the spectacles, the slippers socks and the watch? Who took the time to methodically destroy all nine copies of his will?

Yet, one thing we do know. It was not John Paul. For he would have never placed the glasses on his nose.

This good man was killed by lethal injection administered by paid professional killers. Yet, how did they gain access to the Pope that night without passing by the guard?

More importantly, who called the shot? His enemies inside the Vatican? His enemies across the pond? A combination of these?

We will prove these things in what is yet to come.

Yet, we will never know who called the shot in Vincenza's case. Her witness in David Yallop's *'In God's Name'* is most critical to his conclusion the pope was murdered

Had she been alive in 1987, and, unlike Magee, Lorenzi, the embalmers and others, not been persuaded to change her testimony, John Cornwell could have never written his book.

David Yallop's *'In God's Name'* was published on June 1, 1984. Within a week the world learned a pope had been murdered.

Vincenza was the leading lady on Yallop's stage. Reporters were lining up to reap the scoop of the century. Yet, she was not there.

Sister Vincenza Taffarel was found dead in her bed as the cock crowed in the wee hours of the morning of June 17, 1984.[23]

Nevertheless, before we go on, let me tell you of what became of Jack. Yes, whatever became of my good friend Jack?

1 Composite of Vatican wire release, *La Osservatore Romano* and *Vatican Radio* 29 Sep 78

2 *ANSA* Mario di Francesco's interview with the embalmers—the Signoracci brothers 29 Sep 78

3 *Vatican Radio* 10 Oct 78   A composite of what was announced by *Vatican Radio* and what was published in *La Osservatore Romano* is used to describe the corrected release of 10 Oct 78

4 *Medical dictionaries dated after 2000* or search *Internet: 'heart attack stroke blood pressure"*

5 *Messaggero Mestre* 14 Oct 78

6 Lorenzi gave this testimony to reporters after Cornwell wrote his book in 1987 to help the Vatican refute Yallop's 1984 proof the Pope had been murdered. One has to wonder why he waited nine years to give this very critical testimony. See www.johnpaul1.org for film clip of Lorenzi's press report. Lorenzi was 39 when the Pope died. He is obviously in his 50s in the film. Lorenzi does qualify his claim of 'pain in Cornwell's book, *"I am a member of the Don Orione Brothers who take a vow of special allegiance to the sitting Pontiff, I do anything I am told."*

7 Lorenzi claims *'chest pain'* (heart attack), Magee claims *'choking pain'* (pulmonary embolism). Magee hints the pope was taking anticoagulants. Not true per Dr. Da Ros, *"I was astounded when I heard them make these affirmations"* Il Giornale *Andrea Tornelli* 27 Sep 03. This is confirmed by Dr. Rama, the doctor who had treated him for his retina in 1975, *"His viscosity was normal. There was no need for anticoagulants. The condition was alleviated by mild medication relaxing the blood vessels."*

8 Even at the time it was known a massive pulmonary embolus could not form without the patient being aware of it. She cleverly only 'alludes' the pope was being treated for a clotting problem. If he had been treated for such a problem, she surely would have known of it and told us so.

9 *Mosby's Dictionary of Medicine* or any AMA approved medical dictionary dated after 2000.

10 *JAMA* Jul 94 *'Pulmonary Eyebolus?'British Medical Journal* Aug 99 *'Keep an Eye on the Brain.'*

11 *Medical dictionaries dated before 1980: 'heart attack stroke blood pressure"*

12 reprinted from *A Thief in the Night* John Cornwell 1987

13 *ANSA News Service* 30 Sep 78 *'Sister Vincenza'*

14 *Messaggero* Mestre 14 Oct 78

15 *Il Giornale Andrea Tornelli* 27 Sep 03

16 *La Stampa* 5 Sep 78

17 *La Repubblica* 1 Oct 78

18 *La Repubblica* 2 Sep 78

19 *Deadly Doses* Serita Stevens or search Internet or libraries: 'poisons'

20 *Catholic Encyclopedia Second Edition*

21 *La Stampa* 2 Nov 78

22 *ANSA* Mario di Francesco's interview with the embalmers—the Signoracci brothers 29 Sep 78

23 *La Repubblica* 18 Jun 84. Cause of death was not released.

Chapter 26

The Murder of Jack Champney

Jack went from the mountain diocese to Milan where he served under Cardinal Colombo until 1975 when he was moved to the Vatican and assigned to the council which examined spiritual events.

When Luciani was raised to the papacy, Jack was assigned the task of quelling uncertainties of those Curia cardinals expected to lose their jobs.

On the second day following John Paul's death, a small notice appeared in a Rome newspaper. Its translation,

"The body of a hit-run victim dressed in a yellow shirt, tan shorts and white bucks was found on the Viale Vaticano near the Vatican Museum entrance this morning. Police are looking for witnesses of the incident and someone to identify the man who is believed to be an American tourist in his thirties."

...halfway between a *Silver Star* and a *Purple Heart*

As I drove into the funeral home parking lot, I thought of my last visit with Jack, one of the few times I had seen him since the day he had stood at the pinnacle of secondary school life rendering the coveted address on graduation day. Perhaps, he should have used the words Lincoln had used so modestly at Gettysburg, *". . . the world will little note, nor long remember what is said here . . ."* Unlike Lincoln, Jack would have been telling the truth.

I thought of Jack's letter in which he had told me of John Paul's talk with the Curia cardinals just a week earlier, *'...Mother Church will cease to be the cause of many of the world's problems and rather will begin to be the answer to them.'*

As I stood before him, I couldn't see him, for the mutilation had been much too terrible to allow the body to be viewed. As I began to realize he was now still, I recalled what he once was and I prayed he had had time to have completed his work. At the same time, I thought of Piccolo and I knew he had not had time to complete his work—which has caused me to write this book.

As I reached over and lay my hand on the lid of the coffin just above his heart to confirm to myself this was forever goodbye, a tear came up out of my heart and started from the crevice of my eye and crept toward the lid. I glanced, first, to the right, then to the left, and, again, to the right, and, finally, to the left, once more. I held it there hovering on the edge of the cliff.

Turning to the audience, a wave of applause moved forward in muffled cries, in sighs of desperation and hopeless sobs. I went to the one who sat in the front row and introduced myself and told her of a part of my life which had been a part of her son's life.

She reached into her purse and brought forth a small package. Placing it in my hand, "Jack told me if anything was to happen to him he wanted you to have this. We gave it to him for his ordination, the most important day of his life."

Later in the funeral home parking lot, I looked at the package.

It was postmarked *Centrale Poste de Roma* and dated a few days before the Pope's death. As it had never been opened, Jack had undoubtedly called his mother sometime between then and now.

I was puzzled it was not postmarked *Poste Citta del Vaticano,* as had been true of his correspondence to me through the years. I unwrapped it and opening a small box, I found it was six o'clock, exactly halfway between a *Silver Star* and a *Purple Heart.*

A strange coincidence

A couple of weeks after Jack's funeral, a package arrived in the mail. It, too, was strangely postmarked from the *Centrale Poste de Roma*. There was a note bearing the letterhead, *L'ufficio della Segreteria di Stato Vaticano*. It was signed by Jean Villot.

Enclosed was the above news clipping and a small booklet black pockmarked leather and engraved in gold, *'The Vatican, 1978.'*

There is nothing of great interest—a daily reminder. There was one meeting with Cardinal Confalonieri, the longest reigned cardinal and, therefore, Dean of the College. There were one, two, three meetings with Agostino Casaroli. There had been another with Jean Villot who had been good enough to have sent me the notebook.

Jack also had a meeting in Genoa with Cardinal Siri. There was a notation Casaroli and Caprio had attended the same meeting. It struck me as odd two bishops would travel two hundred miles to meet with a man of the rank of a simple priest, when they could have met with him anytime in Rome by just walking down the hall.

A second notation cleared the matter up. Jack had run into Cardinal Wojtyla, the Archbishop of Krakow, who was exiting the cardinal's palace as he arrived. Casaroli and Caprio had traveled to Genoa to meet with Wojtyla. It was coincidental with Jack's visit.

Yet, I wondered what could be so important that would cause the Polish cardinal to journey seven hundred miles back to Italy to meet these men when just two weeks before he had spent ten days with them at the conclave that had elected John Paul?

I assume they were meeting to plan the strategy as to how the conservative *right* was going to survive under the liberal papacy of John Paul. Or, perhaps, they were just planning the next conclave.

In retrospect, there would be nothing wrong with leaders of the conservative *right* to plan the strategy for the next conclave just as there would be nothing wrong for the leaders of the progressive *left* to plan strategy for the next conclave.

What was unusual about this meeting, if it was indeed held to discuss strategy of the next conclave, is that the reigning pontiff was still alive. As a matter-of-fact, no one would have guessed—no, not in a million years—John Paul would be dead in three weeks time.

Yet, there is nothing in the press to link this gathering to a conspiracy to murder John Paul. Also, the particulars of a conspiracy can be handled by phone and other means, it is not necessary to meet face to face. Also, these men were friends, and may have been doing not much more than vacationing together.

The last item in the booklet was dated the day John Paul was found dead. It was addressed to me, most likely why Villot had mailed the booklet to me as he had circled it in red.

"Lucien, His brother Edoardo. It was no accident. It was murder."

This would haunt me for years. John Paul's demise had never been considered an accident and his brother Edoardo was very much alive. In fact, shortly after John Paul's death, I had been granted an interview with Edoardo Luciani for a fee of only two hundred bucks.

1 Other than of an Italian newspaper, source is unknown. The clipping was in the Villot package

Chapter 27

Motive and Opportunity

"Sadly, Giovanni, when we have finally finished our work, and everyone has enough, there will always be those who want too much!" Albino Luciani

This past summer, as I had done so many times before, I traced my patron from the village of Canale d'Agordo to Belluno, then on to Vittorio Veneto, then on to Venice and, finally, on to Rome.

I carried in my hand a copy of *Murder in the Vatican*.

No matter where I was, in a park, in a pub, in a store, in a coffeehouse, I was approached by Italians. Each one laughed, *"You're not telling us anything we don't already know."*

It is a rare Italian who doesn't know John Paul was murdered. What's more, they didn't have to wait six years for David Yallop's *In God's Name* to tell them. The events of the time did that for them. Yet, their commonality ended there.

Those in the liberal north claimed he had been murdered for ecclesiastical reasons. He would fuel the emerging social evolution of contraception, feminism, genetic research, ecumenism, divorce and remarriage, single parenthood and even gay liberation.

Yet, in conservative Rome most were of another opinion. They believed he was murdered to protect the regency of the papacy, something they agreed with and therefore looked the other way. The Roman prefers not to give up his king.

John Paul would not only shed his regal robes and the Vatican treasures but would annihilate much of the ritual of the Church. He would pull them up off their knees chanting vain repetitions to their gods and put them to work helping others—a threat to those who really believed they could walk to heaven on their knees.

In any event, most Italians thought the perpetrators came from *inside the Vatican.*

Across the pond

Few Italians recognized the murders of Aldo Moro, Paul VI and John Paul I—in rapid consecutive order as if a machine gun had mowed them down—had brought an abrupt end to what until then had been the rising success of communism in Europe.

There is the old adage when one is in the forest *'one cannot see the forest for the trees.'* The people of Italy had been at the heart of the communist movement in Europe. A movement which at the time threatened the stability not only of Europe and Latin America but the capitalistic world the United States and Britain thrived in. Could it be few Italians considered the order may have come from the other side of the pond because *'one cannot see the forest for the trees?'*

Regardless, in the case of murder, one must first consider motive, for this is the most basic requirement of murder. In fact, it is the only absolute requirement of murder. What's more, it is the most telltale evidence of murder. Once the super sleuth determines 'why' one was murdered, one has the murderer. Does one not?

So let us take these one by one. Let us give them each a chance.

Ecclesiastical motive

When one is dealing with men who would kill for doctrine one is dealing with men of faith, not men of reality. They live and die for what they believe in. When Luciani was elected much of what his ecclesiastical enemies stood for had come to an end and handwriting on the wall was telling them even the positions of rank in the Church many of them held were also about to come to an end.

Yet, what gives ecclesiastical motive such great credence in John Paul's case has been the Vatican's methodical destruction of the controversial man he actually was and the fabrication of the man it has made him out to be. That it has gone out of its way to destroy the ecclesiastical motive for murder is compelling evidence its leaders believe—or perhaps know—the plot came from within the Church. Yet, just what made this man so dangerous to his enemies?

Luciani was not a great orator. Never did he speak in encyclicals deeply steeped in canon law or ancient and medieval theology to hypnotize his congregation. Never did he tap the scholarly voice of his intellect or academic acclaim to mesmerize his listeners. Never did he drive his listeners to dictionaries. Never did he raise his voice in towering eloquence. Never did he rock the chandeliers.

Yet, what he did do—from the time he challenged his teacher at the minor seminary at Feltre to the time he chatted with the boy Daniele in his final public audience the day before he was found dead, was reach the most brilliant of scholars and the slowest child in the same sentence and be understood by both.

This is what made him so dangerous to his enemies. Unlike his ecclesiastical adversaries who with intimidation and philosophical innuendos preyed on their gullible congregations, he spoke in simple conversation everyone could understand. What's more, all of what he had to say made sense. It made sense because, unlike his peers who entranced their audiences with the make-believe world of yesterday, he spoke of the real world of today.

Regardless, ecclesiastical motive, to say the least, would have been widespread. Any man-of-the-cloth who had an intense passion to resist change would be on the list.

Those who knew of his loathing for Moses would be on the list. Those who could not accept the Israelites had never been in Egypt would be there too. Those who feared he would reduce Moses to a fairytale someone once told would be there also.

Most dangerous of all, there were those who feared he would destroy the idolatry of Christ and restore the ideology of Christ. He would pull the crucifixes down off of the walls and drag their spellbound spectators up onto their feet and put them to work helping others. He would change the Church—he would change the world—back to what Christ had intended.

He would expose the modern myths of Lourdes and Fatima and the Shroud and others like them.

Too, there would be those who enjoyed spending their Saturday afternoons listening to the sins of the flesh of eight, nine and ten year olds and teens. These were also about to end. Particularly, high up on this list would be those Vatican cardinals who took pleasure in hearing the confessions of the beautiful Maltese altar boys.[1]

Most numerous of all, would be those who didn't want to give up their pretty dresses and pomp and ritual. These men in women's clothes would be threatened by his warning, "...*We, the clergy and our congregations, who substitute regal attire and gold and pomp and ceremony in place of Christ's instruction, who judge our masquerade of singing His praises to be more precious than human life, will have the most to explain.*"[2]

257

Then there were those who feared the threat he posed to the regency of Rome—the Vatican Museum, the Sistine Chapel, the Castel Gandolfo and other royal assets of the Vatican Empire, including possibly Vatican City itself might be liquidated to help the poor. He would turn the property in the center of Rome—among the most valuable real estate in the world—over to developers and establish modest quarters in the countryside.

There were those who believed the Church could not survive without its monarchy, something John Paul was bent on destroying. Those who believed it is the regency of the papacy that controls the populace—in spiritual matters the people need a king who lives in a palace. There was consternation among many a pope with a Christ-like image would be unable to rule—the Church would fall to ruin.

Most of all, when one considers ecclesiastical motive, those who were in high positions and controlled the ecclesiastical destiny of the Church and were about to lose their jobs would top the list.

Men who thought morality—*right from wrong*—was defined by sex. Men who thought there was something wrong with sex—so much so they believed it made them holier-than-thou to give it up.

As a seminarian, as a young priest, as a bishop and as a cardinal, he had many times told his audience, *"We have made of sex the greatest of sins, whereas, in itself, it is nothing more than human nature and not a sin at all."* Until now, he had been just another man-of-the-cloth talking through his hat. Yet, if he were to utter this same sentence as Supreme Pontiff, it would change the definition of morality in the Roman Catholic world, it would become canon law.

In a single a swoop he would destroy the ecclesiastical position of *right wing* factions in the Church who waged an ongoing war against born-out-of-children, women parity, contraception, genetic research, sanctity of remarriage, homosexuality, transsexuality, and a host of other issues driven by the natural biological composition of man.

The Last Supper [3]

So there were many inside the Vatican who may have had a motive to kill this pope and there are others outside the Vatican we will speak of. Yet, when one considers opportunity the list narrows; there were a limited number of people who had access to John Paul's chambers on the night he died.

In addition to those who were in the Papal Apartment—the four nuns and Lorenzi—we must consider those who lived on the other floors as they may have eluded the guard. There were eight in all.

Cardinal Villot, Cardinal Confalonieri, Bishop Casaroli and his cousin Bishop Caprio lived on the floor below the Papal Apartment. These were the Cardinal Secretary of State, the Dean of the College of Cardinals, the Foreign Minister[4] and the Undersecretary of State.[5]

Paul's secretary John Magee, who was serving in transition, had his rooms in the attic just above the Pope's bedroom. Three other nuns also had their rooms in the attic.

All except one of these arrived in the dining room at about seven-thirty the evening before the Pope's death. Confalonieri didn't show up. He had left a message with the guard he wasn't feeling well and would be retiring early.

Other than the Pope, there were twelve at dinner: the secretaries Magee and Lorenzi, Villot, Casaroli, Caprio and seven nuns. It was that the valet was away on funeral leave that made for the hallowed count. Also, Paul's second secretary Macchi, though he would show up to help out with the mail during the day, had been relocated elsewhere n the Vatican to make room for Lorenzi.

Again, we have to dispel rumors. Some authors imply Luciani brought the Guzzo brothers from the Veneto region to live with him in the Papal Apartment. Whereas these brothers were bought work in the apartment they lived elsewhere in Vatican City. They had their rooms in a small building near the Vatican supermarket.[6]

Regardless, with women among them, this gathering was a bit different than those who had gathered at another table two thousand kilometers away and two thousand years before, yet, nevertheless, every bit as clandestine—perhaps, a traitor or two among them.

John Paul arrived early. Concerned for the aging Confalonieri, he asked Sister Regina to bring the cardinal a bowl of soup.

He pointed to a chair as each of the others came into the room.

As the last one took a seat, Sister Regina came back into the room. John Paul asked her how the cardinal looked.

"He looked suspicious," she joked. "He made me taste the soup."

Everyone roared. The aging cardinal did not approve of Luciani. He also knew it was that he and seventeen others had been prevented from casting their votes by Paul who had excluded those over eighty from the voting conclave that had made Luciani a pope.

The soup had been sent by the man the aging cardinal considered his greatest enemy, John Paul. Reared in a Mafia family, he would have been a fool not to have required the nun to taste the soup.

Confalonieri had a long association with the press. It may be providential coincidence more than he envisioned anything would happen to the new pope, when Luciani was elected, he referred to him as the *'August Pope.'* When Luciani lived into September, he referred to him as the *'September Pope.'* If he were to survive into October, he would have to rename him again—the *'October Pope.'*

It was an austere room to say the least. It had poverty written all over it. It was John Paul's favorite room in what was otherwise a lavish palace of feather pillows and golden vessels and priceless works of art. He felt most at home here. It reminded him of when he had grown up in an impoverished village in the Italian Alps.

Its walls were graying and its unadorned windows looked out over the courtyard. There was an old table as one might find in a workshop. It was made of old planks of wood set upon two beat up wooden workhorses. Although its surface was worn from time there was no significant damage except for a few old stains here and there. It was the kind of thing that would be the first thing one would throw out once one would climb out of the cellar of poverty. Twelve rickety chairs surrounded it, that is, to the extent it is possible to match a few old planks of wood. An old rug hung on one wall.

Everyone in the household had a secret, a secret they kept to themselves. John Paul did not know of this secret. If he knew of it, this room would suddenly become much less a home to him.

The table he was about to sit at was a first century piece of oak taken out of an eighth century monastery and would easily reap ten million dollars at auction. The old rug which hung on the wall could easily garnish a few million more. It was the carpet that had lain in the church which once stood where St. Peter's stood now. Any one of the chairs could easily be traded in for a new Mercedes.

John Paul and twelve at supper

Sister Maria Elena sat at the head of the table. Who's she? She was the nun one would pass scrubbing the floors in the palace halls. At the other end sat Sister Vincenza, the mother nun. Most of the men present were not happy about it. Yet, they had to put up with it.

They did not understand this man who would have a simple maid at the head of his table. It was not necessary they understand him. All that was necessary was that he understood himself.

Magee and Lorenzi were bringing out the breads, the meats and the vegetables. The other men at the table cringed a bit, wondering when it would be their turn to take up the role of servant.

One of the nuns started to get up. John Paul motioned her to sit down, "You have worked all day. I have not done much more than talked." He disappeared into the kitchen and returned with a pitcher of water in one hand and a bottle of wine in the other and went around the table filling glasses.

The Pope gestured to Sister Maria Elena to begin grace.

In the fifteen years of Paul VI's reign, and in the five years of John XXIII's reign, and in the nineteen years of Pius XII's reign, and in the fifteen years of Pius XI's reign, and in the eight years of Benedict XV's reign, and in the eleven years of Pius X's reign, and in the twenty-five years of Leo XIII's reign, only two people had ever said grace in this room; the Pope, and in his absence, the Cardinal Secretary of State. What kind of pope was this who would have a mere woman, a scullery maid, lead the prayer?

The conversation was light. The Pope was laughing and joking.

He toyed with his new watch as does a boy with a gadget he found under a Christmas tree. Macchi had delivered the watch to the pope—it had arrived by special post that afternoon.

At quarter to nine, Casaroli said he had an appointment and left. It was likely he had no appointment at all; it was obvious he wanted to get out of helping with the dishes. He had done the same thing the evening before and the one before that and the one before that. He even carried a briefcase to cover for his leaving early. He just did not intend to yield to this latest rule of the house.

Concerned with Confalonieri's illness, John Paul asked Sister Genevieve to drop in on the cardinal and see if he needed anything. As she left the room, he winked after her, "Tell him Sister Regina couldn't make it, she has been taken to the hospital..." He drew another round of laughter, this time followed by a bit of applause.

He vanished into the kitchen together with the nuns. The others lingered at the table, chatting away. Just before nine, Caprio claimed to have an appointment and left. He, too, carrying a briefcase.

Villot joked with Magee and Lorenzi, "He must be training these nuns to be altar girls." He liked the idea a pope would do these things. What he didn't know was that John Paul was not training them to be altar girls. He was training them to be priests. It was likely Casaroli and Caprio had already guessed this.

Mother Vincenza and the other nuns remained finishing up in the dining room. The men followed the Pope down the corridor and stopped outside his door chatting a bit before retiring. A phone rang in the secretaries' office and Lorenzi left momentarily to answer it. Returning, he nodded to his boss, "Cardinal Colombo."

Villot went down the hall and past the guard and down the stairs. Magee, followed by a trilogy of nuns, went down the hall and past the guard and up the stairs to the attic above.

John Paul disappeared into the office—for the last time.

The next day the cardinal of Milan would give the press the last words of his long time ally in the war on poverty, *"Sadly, Giovanni, when we have finally finished our work, and everyone has enough, there will always be those who want too much!"*

Those in the Papal Apartment

When one considers those who had unlimited access to the Pope's bedroom that night, one is narrowed to six people, Lorenzi who slept in the secretaries' office while his rooms in the attic were being painted and the four nuns who slept along the San Damascus side of the building, and the guard, himself.

Anyone coming from the floor below or from the attic above would have had to have passed by the guard who was stationed at the entrance to the Papal Apartment.

To seal our conclusion—the Pope was murdered by professional killers by lethal injection—we must eliminate these six who shared the rooms with John Paul. So let us look at these six, these six who were in the Papal Apartment on the night of John Paul's death.

The guard

There was the guard who sat at the entrance to the apartment in full view of the elevator, the staircase leading from the lower floors, the chapel door and the stairs leading up to the attic. This could be either of two guards or both guards who rotated the post that night.

It is possible that either of these guards could have entered the Pope's bedroom during the night. If anyone chanced by, of course, the guard's absence would have been noticed. There was always the chance the rotating-guard might show up on his random rounds.

One has to consider the guards because according to reports[7] the Vatican police assigned one of their men to the 3-6AM post in the Papal Apartment when the guard normally assigned the post fell ill.

One has the providential coincidence a human fighting machine of the Swiss Guard—in the optimum of good health—would fall ill, without foul play being involved in his illness, at the precise moment in history a Pope is murdered. Yet, there has survived no record to suggest foul play in the case of the displaced guard in the press.

The Swiss Guard is very limited in number—at the time one-hundred-and-twenty. These are entirely committed to assigned posts. There are no spares. In those very rare instances a guard falls ill or for some other reason is unable to fill his post, the vacancy is filled by the Vatican police which supplement the Swiss Guard.

As a rule, Vatican police recruits are on loan from the Swiss Army—young officers who aspire to the Swiss Guard. It is normally a requirement one serve a brief apprenticeship with the Vatican police sometime in the years preceding induction into the Guard.

The police, if called upon, fill off-hour spots that are away from the general public as they do not wear the attire of the Swiss Guard. If a vacancy occurs in a daytime shift, a guard is reassigned from a nighttime post which is away from the public eye and his nighttime post is filled in turn by one of the Vatican police.

It is not unusual for a rookie to be assigned the post closest to a pope in the wee hours of the morning because it is the furthest from the public eye. This does not endanger a pope as there are three perpetual seasoned guards at the palace entrance on the ground floor.

In the case of guards, like any other suspect, one has to consider motive. The only motive a guard might have would be promise of rank or money. Although a long shot, it is one we must consider.

If the rookie guard who was assigned to the post closest the pope had been part of a conspiracy, the deputy commander who assigned the guards would have had to have been involved. Yet, it is possible most any cardinal or bishop could have influenced this officer, particularly, one who might become Secretary of State—the position the Guard reported to—if anything happened to John Paul.

Although second in command, it is rare for a deputy commander to succeed to the top job, commander of the Swiss Guard. Yet, the promise may have been made in exchange for his cooperation.

Ronald Buchs, the deputy commander at the time of John Paul's death, acceded to the top job, but not until 1982 when the incumbent commander fell ill and died.

Though a pope has unilateral authority to make any changes he sees fit, not being a political appointee, no pope has ever replaced the commander of the Swiss Guard upon taking office.

The promise could have been made the deputy commander would accede to the post when the incumbent commander died or retired.

We will leave this for the mystery buffs for now. Yet, we will come back to it a bit later.

The nuns

Next, we have the nuns.

Vincenza certainly had the opportunity to have committed the crime at any time during the night. She, as we know, knocked on the door at four-thirty in the morning and discovered him dead. To wake the Pope she did not have to pass by the guard.

Could she have had a motive? One must assume most anyone could have a motive. Again, there could have been promise of rank or money. Perhaps, more likely in her case, the threat of harm or death to a loved one if she did not comply.

Vincenza had served Luciani for twelve years. Luciani was the closest person to Vincenza in the world. It is likely if anyone had threatened her, he would have learned of it. Yet, it could be she gave him the shot in the rear. One will never know.

How about the other nuns? They must have fallen in love with this man. He was the first pope to demand they join him in the papal dining room. Until then, they had been confirmed to the kitchen. What's more, they could for the first time pray to their God in the Pope's chapel rather than just scrub its floors for their male masters to walk on. The nuns would be at the bottom of the motive list.

The valet

We know from newspapers the valet was on leave in connection with a death in his family. His stepbrother had fallen from a sixth floor balcony in Arezzo just south of Florence. Unwitnessed, police could not determine whether it was accident or suicide.[8]

Nevertheless, if the valet had returned that evening, he would have had to have passed by four guards. We know this did not happen as the palace guards were scrutinized by the press the next day in connection with rumors of foul play that surfaced.

This is how we know today who was in the Papal Palace that night and who was not. For this we must give thanks to the rumors.

Just about every reporter in Italy was trying to land the scoop of the century. At first, because poison was thought to have been the culprit, they concentrated on who had access to the dining room and the kitchen and who did not. In that the Pope died so suddenly, they turned their attention to those who had access to the Pope's bedroom and who did not. For much of this information they scrutinized the guards who had been on duty the night the Pope died. Unfortunately, the rookie guard assigned to the post closest to the Pope seemed to disappear into thin air—reporters were unable to track him down.

The guards themselves believed the rumors to be true and were carrying on their own investigations. After all, they had experienced a laughing, joking, vibrant man one day and a corpse the next.

Nevertheless, the record is there in the microfilm today. One knows who was at dinner that night and who was not and when they arrived and when they left. One also knows who was sleeping in the Papal Palace and where they were sleeping the night the Pope died.

Though opportunity is not possible in the case of the valet, one has to consider motive. Was there a motive in his case? Not much, but it was there, yet, perhaps, not enough to justify murder.

It is not possible to replace a papal valet in the short term as he is the busiest man alive. A pope's vast wardrobe must re-sized. Yet, in the longer term, this pope who would do away with the regency of the papacy would bring an end to his recognition in the world of fashion; it would destroy it. It would destroy all he had worked for.

Yet, if one considers opportunity he would be at the bottom of the list, for had the valet been seen in the building it most certainly would have been reported in the press.

In retrospect, the valet did not gain by the Pope's death as John Paul II eventually replaced him with Opus Dei member Angelo Gugel—who contracted leading fashion houses for the papal attire.

Lorenzi

Finally, one must consider the secretary Lorenzi. Other than the guard he was the only man who had unlimited access to John Paul's bedroom that night. Motive in the case of Lorenzi could have only been personal. To see this one has to step back a few years.

At Vittorio Veneto, Vincenza[9] as head of his household oversaw office duties assisted by nuns and students from the seminary. Yet, he had Jack and others, who politically astute, could intelligently discuss the ongoing war between the *right* and *left*.

In Venice, he had a new political soundboard, Mario Senigaglia. Senigaglia was the man he used to get his most prolific message to his flock, *"We have made of sex the greatest of sins, whereas it is nothing more than human nature and not a sin at all."*

Two years before Luciani's election, Don Diego Lorenzi came into his life. Lorenzi had no interest in politics. It remains a mystery today as to why Luciani picked him. Lorenzi was an angelic looking young man to say the least. It may be that Luciani chose him for the innocence he projected. It was partially for this reason the press tabbed him *'the pope's widow'* after John Paul's death.

Nevertheless, without political interests, Lorenzi could have murdered his patron only for personal reasons.

It was Lorenzi who Vincenza first fetched upon discovering the body. It was Lorenzi who sent the nun to fetch Doctor Buzzanetti who lived in a remote part of the Apostolic Palace.

Normally one would call the doctor. There was a phone in the bedroom. It may be he did not know the doctor's number. Yet, the guard at the top of the stairs certainly would have had the doctor's number and could have made the call. Nevertheless, according to Vincenza and his own testimony, the nun ran to fetch the doctor. This allowed him to be alone with the body until the others arrived.

Lorenzi would have first called Villot on the bedside intercom as upon a pope's death the Camerlengo is the first one summoned.

One does not know if Villot told him to notify the embalmers or if Lorenzi acted on his own. Yet, it is unlikely Villot would have given such an order without first seeing the body.

It is possible he called the embalmers on his own to tell them to get ready, as Villot did not arrive until 5:20 and the motor pool records show a van had been dispatched at 5:23 to the nearby school of medicine to pick them up. Also, the record shows the van returned at 5:53 so they must have been dressed for pickup at about 5:35.

That he may have alerted embalmers at an early hour on his own suggests he suspected foul play as embalming masks the evidence of poisoning. Yet, if he thought the Pope may have been poisoned, why did he years later claim the Pope had complained of chest pains the night of his death? If he thought the Pope had died of a heart attack why did he order the embalmers so early in the morning?

It might be he had given the Pope the injection with the wrong vial he had taken from the papal refrigerator and knew embalming would destroy evidence that an autopsy otherwise would detect.

He certainly would assume autopsy would be performed as John Paul was relatively young and in good health and it was no secret he had many enemies both inside and outside the Vatican who wanted him dead. Then again, it could have been prearranged Lorenzi was to call the embalmers on finding the corpse. One will never know.

In retrospect, we know Lorenzi did not gain in rank from the Pope's death as he has never been made a bishop. As he explained to Cornwell when after nine years of silence he suddenly added 'John Paul's pain' to the puzzle, *"I am a member of the order of the Don Orione Brothers. I have taken an oath of special allegiance to an incumbent pope, I do anything I am told."*

The only possible motive in Lorenzi's case would have been jealously. Maybe John Paul was considering retaining him to handle the paperwork and considering another for the top job. A pope's first secretary is his press secretary—a job Lorenzi was not particularly qualified for. I leave that one for the dreamers, too.

Yet, that he was the only man other than the guard with free access to the Pope that night and considering some of the actions he took on his own at the time and since, he must remain on the list. He would have had the opportunity to commit the deed anytime during the night and have had time to clean up any lingering evidence when the nun went to fetch the doctor between 4:45 and 500AM.

267

He would have placed the glasses on the nose, to cast suspicions away from his own involvement.

Those in the attic

Magee and three nuns slept in the attic.

We have already eliminated the nuns. Yet, could Magee have eluded the guard? Could he have possibly had a motive?

Magee had served as first secretary under Paul VI and was still serving as first secretary under John Paul. This is seen that he served as spokesman for the papacy following the Pope's death. He also continued as first secretary under John Paul II.

For those who think Lorenzi held the post, Magee retained the first secretary's apartment above the Pope's bedroom. Lorenzi was headed for the second secretary's apartment over the Pope's study.

Yet, it was expected he would be replaced. Something he looked forward to. Magee wanted to return to pastoral work in his native Ireland. More than anything else in the world he wanted to become a bishop. Perhaps, end up his days as Primate of Ireland.

If Magee was involved in John Paul's death it has escaped this author. He did not gain in ecclesiastical rank as a result of the Pope's death. He remained in the same job for two years under John Paul II when he was transferred to pastoral work. It makes no sense it had been John Magee who had paved the way for Cardinal Wojtyla's rise to the world's stage. Not enough for this author to implicate him in the murder of the Pope. Yes, if Magee had been named a cardinal, like others we will talk about, one might think otherwise.

One has to consider opportunity. Magee could have thrown something down into the Pope's bedroom which was directly below his rooms. Yet, the attic windows are small and open at an angle of three or four inches at the most. Also, the walls are almost two feet thick which makes the sill two feet across. Not possible. Yet, he may have eluded the guard. If so, he would have had to elude him twice, as he would have to return to the attic after committing the deed.

Although the events of 1978 don't seem to implicate him in the murder itself; the events of 1987 do implicate him in the cover-up.

As we have said, in 1987, John Magee was likely made a bishop as a prerequisite for his testimony in the Vatican's cover-up book *A Thief in the Night*. Magee's testimony dramatically contradicted his testimony of 1978 and is instrumental to John Cornwell's conclusion the Pope died of a pulmonary embolism.

Those who lived on the floor below

It is also possible John Paul may have been murdered by one of those who lived on the floor below who may have eluded the guard.

First, there was the secretary of state, Jean Villot.

John Paul's election had come as a blessing to him. Villot was a liberal particularly open to changing doctrine. As a result, during his tenure most of the Vatican cardinals had not accepted him as their leader. He had no ecclesiastical motive to have killed the new pope.

When one considers succession as motive in a pope's death, the secretary of state would normally be at the top of the list as in modern history the incumbent has often succeeded to the top job. However, in Villot's case, he was a liberal and, unlike Luciani, not a popular one. He would have never garnished the vote.

Although short of retirement age and in impeccable health, Villot wanted to live out his years teaching in the Gregorian University in Rome. Actually, he wanted to shed his robes and live in Rome.

Although John Paul had reaffirmed his appointment as secretary of state immediately on taking office it had been part of a blanket confirmation of all the cardinals as cardinals

It was no secret at the time Cardinal Benelli of Florence, who had played such a major role in Luciani's win, would get the job.

In retrospect, this is obvious as Benelli and not Villot had spent much of the thirty-three days of John Paul's papacy involved in the audit of the Vatican bank including the IOR, activities which would soon report to him as secretary of state.

Yet, some suspicion surrounds Villot as he was responsible for much of the misleading information including both press releases which caused the rumors of foul play to flourish. We will get to that as we go along. Yet, for now, concerning motive and opportunity, Villot would rank relatively low on the list. He had nothing to gain and much to lose. What's more, like Magee, he would have had to have eluded the guard, not once, but twice, as he would have had to have returned to the floor below after committing the deed.

Next is Cardinal Confalonieri. The layout of his rooms was similar to that of the Pope's rooms directly above, except that he did

269

not occupy the huge space beneath the Pope's library. Instead he had a sitting room under the Pope's bathroom. He slept thirty feet below where the Pope sat up dead in his bed that fateful morning.

Everything John Paul stood for was Confalonieri's enemy. Yet, considering opportunity, he like the others who lived on this floor would have had to have passed by the guard twice.

Next is Casaroli, also, high on the motive list—a bit about his record, his aspirations, his ambitions, his hopes and his dreams.

It was not his objective to rise to the papacy. Yes, the desire was there, but he knew that being the extreme ultraconservative he was, he would never muster the vote of any of the moderates or liberals needed to win the papacy. His lifelong ambition lay in locking up the number two spot, secretary of state. Yet, in recent years his hopes had dwindled into sheer fantasy rather than ambition.

During the sixties, Casaroli's influence on Paul had made many men cardinals. So much so, it was expected his name would head the list in each succeeding consistory. His influence on Paul had been so great it had driven doctrinal changes, some of which Paul would live to regret and never forgave him for. Midway through his reign, Paul started to ignore him. Casaroli knew as long as Paul lived he would never be named a cardinal, much less secretary of state.

When Paul died, his dream once again became an ambition, to be named a cardinal and succeed to the secretary of state position, the Vice President of the Roman Catholic Church.

Of course, in Casaroli's case, had advancement to the secretary of state position been the motive for murder, it would have had to involve three murders, as three men considered to be in good health at the time had to die in rapid consecutive order to have allowed him to succeed to secretary of state, Paul VI, John Paul and Jean Villot.

In retrospect, today, one knows, this is exactly what happened.

Also, there was a nasty rumor Casaroli would be replaced as foreign minister with a moderate, someone who could better work with communists to work out solutions. If John Paul was to live another week, much less another month, Casaroli would not only be blocked from going up the ladder, he might go down the ladder.

Like Confalonieri, he would have had reason to have hated the new Pope. But the problem was opportunity, as he lived on the floor below. He would have had to have passed by the guard, not once, but twice. He goes partway up the opportunity ladder.

Innocent until proved guilty

A bishop who had read *Murder in the Vatican* called me and told me he had been a seminarian at the Gregorian University in Rome and was living in the Vatican the night the Pope died. He told me Casaroli treated everyone beneath him as if they were dirt under his feet; he considered himself to be a prince among princes of the Church and was always dressed in elaborate attire.

"On that morning, we peons gathered in a cafeteria. There was no reason to believe anything had been involved other than murder. John Paul had been a raging locomotive just the day before on a rapid track to rid the world of poverty and now he was dead.

"The conversation quickly centered on Casaroli.

"If those present had been a jury, he would have been put away for life. Yet, this was probably because we hated him so much more than that we had any evidence which would stand up in court.

"Yet, his ambitions to be secretary of state were so intense they fit in with murder. Yet, we were confused because the incumbent Jean Villot, like John Paul, was in enviable good health. Not one of us would have guessed he, too, would be dead in such a short time.

"Yet, we acquitted Casaroli on the grounds that in the second conclave Benelli would certainly succeed to the papacy and that would mean curtains for Casaroli..."

Regardless, he was surprised I considered Casaroli a suspect, as all others who had written about the Pope's death had ignored him. To be honest, I didn't consider him a viable candidate for the electric chair until I was more than two years into my investigation.

Finally, we have Bishop Caprio. He would most likely move up in the Vatican bank structure if his cousin were to go up the ladder. Casaroli and Caprio were of the Gambino family, the most powerful Mafia family and the largest private contributor to the Church, the reason why they had risen to the Episcopate to begin with.

Having spent the past decade as secretary-treasurer of the Vatican's central bank, his ambition was to become chief financial officer of the Church—Prefect of Economic Affairs.

Yet, if one considers Caprio as a suspect, it would have required four murders, as four men had to die in rapid consecutive order to

271

have allowed him to succeed to his goal, Paul VI, John Paul, Jean Villot and Egidio Vagnozzi the sitting Prefect of Economic Affairs.

In retrospect today, one knows, this is exactly what happened.

Like the others who lived on the lower floors, both Casaroli and Caprio would have had to pass by the guard twice. Although low on the opportunity ladder they go high up on the motive list.

Let's rank these candidates as to how they size up:

	Motive	Opportunity
Absolute	Casaroli and Caprio Confalonieri	Guard(s) Lorenzi The four apartment nuns
Possible	Guard(s) The valet Lorenzi	Magee Casaroli and Caprio Confalonieri The three attic nuns Villot
Remote	The nuns Magee Villot	The valet*

* Only thru an intermediary, not in the Papal Palace the night the Pope died

Let us list the approximate order of events:

Dinner	7:30PM
Pope retires	9:30PM
Pope dies of heart attack per the Vatican release	11:00PM
Police in the square check pope's windows and light is not on	3:00AM
Pope dies according to embalmers	3:30Am-4:15AM
The clock set for 4:15AM is turned off	4:00AM
The bedroom light is turned on	4:00AM
Vincenza discovers John Paul	4:35 AM
Vincenza fetches Lorenzi sleeping next door	4:40 AM
Lorenzi sends Vincenza to fetch the doctor	4:50 AM
Lorenzi calls Villot and Magee on the Pope's intercom	4:50 AM
Lorenzi calls embalmers to get ready for pickup	4:55 AM
Lorenzi calls motor pool to send a van to pick up embalmers	5:00 AM
Magee who was sleeping in the attic arrives	5:10 AM
Villot arrives and performs the last rites	5:20 AM
Motor pool dispatches van to pick up embalmers	5:23 AM
Confalonieri, Casaroli, Caprio arrive	5:25 AM
Doctor Buzzanetti arrives and pronounces him dead	5:30 AM

Embalmers arrive	5:45 AM
Pope found dead by Magee per the Vatican release	6:30 AM
Official press release of the Pope's death	7:30 AM
Lina Petri views the body	9:00 AM
Embalmers remove body to operating room in salon	9:30 AM
Villot seals the Pope's quarters	9:45 AM
Embalmers complete light embalming	10:30 AM
Embalmers interviewed by ANSA	11:00 AM
John Paul lies in state in St. Clementine Chapel	12noon-7:PM
Vincenza's comments reach the press	2:00 PM
The nuns, Lorenzi and Magee are sent on sabbatical	5:00 PM
Embalmers complete full embalming	9:00 PM

One more suspect

We will consider others who had motive. Yet, before we leave the Episcopate, there is one more suspect one must consider—the one who benefited the most by John Paul's death.

Although it is an unpopular thing to say, to ignore Karol Wojtyla as a suspect in this case would be to eliminate the youthful husband of an aging wealthy heiress as a suspect when he is the beneficiary of a *'one-hundred-million-dollar policy.'*

For an unknown reason something goes astray in the intellect of the public when it comes to evaluating motive in the commission of an autocratic crime. Any detective will tell you the person having the greatest motive, the one who gains the most, is found guilty of the crime of murder nineteen out of twenty times—the reason one concentrates one's investigation on those with the greatest motive.

Yet, when a crime is committed in the public forum not many consider motive in their speculations—John Kennedy, for example.

It was widely known his vice president, Lyndon Johnson, had an intense craving to be president. He had prepared himself all of his life for the job only to have the prize taken from him at the wire by the upstart senator from Massachusetts.

Johnson knew he would never be president. He knew the more successful he was in his job the more successful would Kennedy be in his job. If John Kennedy was successful, the nation was looking at a quarter-century of Kennedys as his brothers Bobby, the attorney general, and Teddy, a senator were coming up right behind him.

Yet, in Kennedy's murder, no one ever considered the man who had the most to gain to be suspect despite the fact that out of fifty

273

states the murder happened to have occurred by coincidence in Lyndon Johnson's home state where he knew everyone from government officials to business magnates to mob bosses to the shoeshine boy on the corner. This included Jack Ruby, the man who killed Oswald who allegedly killed Kennedy. With a simple phone call Johnson could have set it up. The public accepted it was a rare coincidence the murder took place in the only state in which the vice president had any likelihood at all of pulling such a thing off.

Karol Wojtyla also benefited by this phenomenon, the public's tendency not to consider the one who has the greatest motive. Unlike Johnson, whose motive would have been limited to one of personal gain, the motive in Wojtyla's case would have been one of principle, that kind of motive which causes great men to kill great men.

There was no gain in principle in Johnson's case as he shared the same ideologies as Kennedy. He could have achieved his ideological goals even if Kennedy had lived. In retrospect, it was Johnson who eventually brought Kennedy's dreams and aspirations to fruition.

Ecclesiastical motive for murder

The Polish cardinal ponders his future

When Hitler lost the war, Karol Wojtyla lost much of what he dreamed of, and now that Luciani had risen to power, the rest of his ambitions were about to come to an end. During the war, Wojtyla and Hitler shared the same objectives the reason Pius XI had united the Vatican with the Nazi movement in the German Concordant of 1934. This does not mean, in itself, Pius, Hitler and Wojtyla—were bad men. At the time, that is the way most good Christians thought.

in the wake of Luciani's election

Yet, there was a difference between these men. Hitler would achieve his ends through annihilation. Wojtyla would achieve his ends through political means. The results can be equally devastating. It makes no difference whether a child dies in a concentration camp or whether he dies of starvation or AIDS in a third world country.

Regardless, if one considers the assassination of world leaders, the weight of them have been ideologically motivated. Great men do not kill great men for personal gain. They kill them for principle, to permit the enactment into society of their own ideologies.

Notwithstanding their opposing positions on other aspects of the social revolution—feminism, remarriage, gay liberation and so forth, their disparity on contraception, by itself, could have done the trick.

One will never know what the 33-day Pope would have achieved concerning his ecclesiastical ambitions. Yet, only an imbecile could view the actions he took during his brief reign and not conclude he was on a fast track to rid the world of poverty. He could have never done this without first removing the driving force behind it—the ban on contraception.

If one is a pro-life extremist as Wojtyla was—believed God has preselected the sperm and egg that will eventually become a human being—the murder of John Paul I was not only a good thing to do, it was a holy thing to do. In Wojtyla's mind, Luciani was a baby killer.

Luciani threatened to make the 'pill' the mainstay of family life to control the world's population and rid it of poverty and starvation. Worse yet, he would make condoms available to teenagers to avoid untimely pregnancies and prevent the spread of disease—syphilis and gonorrhea in first world countries and Ebola in Africa.

To underline how ingrained this thinking is in men like Karol Wojtyla and Joseph Ratzinger, in March 2009, Benedict XVI visited countries so heavily infected with AIDS that pregnancy invariably produces an AIDS child born only to live an unspeakable life and die an unspeakable death. He told them to use a condom was mortal sin.

According to Christian scripture ensoulment takes place at birth, the reason why no church baptizes before birth.[10] *Jeremiah* could not have made it more clear, *"I knew thou before thou wast in the belly and I sanctified thou when thou camest out of the womb."*[11]

To Wojtyla and Ratzinger quality in this life is immaterial—it is none of their business. Their business is the afterlife. In their minds, this life is as a grain of sand on the vast beach of eternity.

In the case of Luciani, the emphasis was on quality of life in this life—acceptance of what is given one in this life and not lust for more. According to Christian doctrine, Wojtyla and Ratzinger are the 'good guys' and Luciani is the 'bad guy.'

We are speaking of the most fundamental difference between the preacher on the *right* and the preacher on the *left*. The one on the *right* really believes in the afterlife and the one on the *left* does not.

The extremist on the *right* believes in ghosts while the extremist on the *left* does not. He believes rising from the dead is nothing more than an idea someone came up with hundreds of thousands of years ago to capitalize on man's mortality and take advantage of others.

Those on the *right* believe this life is a grain of sand on the vast beach of eternity. Quality of life in this life is immaterial. To impede the union of a particular sperm and a particular egg which God has predetermined to be a human being from being born is to deprive it of eternal life—the most fundamental goal of Christian belief.

Regardless, in conspiring to murder John Paul, Karol Wojtyla would have a clear conscience as he went about his holy day-to-day business—he would have rid the world of a baby killer and not only preserved the ensoulment of billions of children, he would have saved countless others from eternal damnation as those adults who followed Luciani's rules for the pill would certainly lose their souls.

So the Polish cardinal did have clear motive to have conspired to murder his predecessor since the latter threatened his ecclesiastical destiny. What's more, unlike Johnson, his motive would have been one of principle, that which causes great men to kill great men.

In addition to motive of principle, in Karol's case there would have also been personal ambition. He never concealed his ambition to accede to the papacy. As we have said he campaigned ten years for it visiting just about every city where a voting cardinal lived.

If one considers the history of the courts, as we have said, nineteen times out of twenty times the person having the greatest motive for a capital crime is found guilty.

Karol Wojtyla goes to the top of the list. The reader is reminded of the sacred code of the tribunal, *'innocent until proven guilty.'*

1 *Kullhadd* 13 Jul 93
2 John Paul I public audience 27 Sep 78
3 Details of his last dinner a composite of *La Repubblica* 3-5-16 Oct 78
4 The official title of the Foreign Minster was Secretary of the Council for Public Affairs
5 The official title of the Under Secretary of State was Substitute for General Affairs. Under Paul VI, Villot had no financial acumen; he appointed Benelli and Caprio to oversee banking activities
6 *La Osservatore Romano* 8 Sep 78 *'Papa porte Guido Gian Paulo Guzzo dal paese del Veneto'*
7 *La Osservatore Romano* 30 Sep 78 *La Repubblica* 3 Oct 78 *La Stampa* 8 Oct 78
8 *La Nazione* Florence 28 Sep 78 *'Edoardo Calo'*
9 This is still true today, a nun serves as the bishop's secretary in Vittorio Veneto
10 Late in the twentieth century Canon was issued to consider *baptism by desire* to cover unborn children, yet, it remains a matter of 'hope' and not a matter of 'faith'
11 *Jeremiah 1* consistent with Adam's creation in *Genesis,* ensoulment takes place at birth.
Photo Karol Wojtyla *Associated Press* 2 Sep 78

Chapter 28

A Conspiracy Buff's Delight

There is a more concrete reason than ecclesiastical motive and personal ambition to include Karol Wojtyla among our suspects.

First, let us, once and for all, clear up the delusion concerning interim counts in a papal election.

Books, motion pictures and even newspapers, in sensationalizing an election, report counts of the interim ballots in dramatic fashion.

Concerning the conclave which elected Luciani, one newspaper reported, *"On the first ballot Pignedoli led with forty-one votes, Siri had nineteen, Suenens had thirteen...On the second ballot Luciani had come into the pack with fourteen, Suenens had advanced to twenty-seven..Pignedoli had all but dropped out of the race..."*[1]

Another newspaper gave this account, *"Suenens and Siri came out of the gate neck-and-neck with thirty votes each with Pignedoli close behind with twenty-two...Things remained relative stable for the next two ballots and then on the fourth ballot Luciani suddenly made his move and came from behind to take the roses."*[2]

Still a third newspaper captured the imagination of its readers, *"A thirty-to-one shot Baggio came out of the gate with forty votes with the rest of the field spread out behind him..."*[3]

Dozens of others reported vastly different accounts. The reason for this disparity is because no one outside the conclave knows.

I have said this before, and because it is paramount to what we are speaking of here, I will say it again. If a cardinal discloses anything that goes on within a conclave he excommunicates himself. No cardinal has ever revealed anything that goes on in a conclave.

Yes, as we have said, after a cardinal dies, an author might claim the cardinal had confided with him before his death and write a book to capitalize on the suckers. Yet, no media has ever published what a cardinal might have said of a conclave while he was still alive.

Until John Paul's election, the final count was obvious as all elections had been announced as unanimous. When Luciani failed to gain a unanimous vote, it caused a problem—the Curia could not use the word 'unanimous.' A decision was made to reveal the count: ninety votes—the only time the Vatican released a specific number.

With this exception, no responsible newspaper has published the number of votes a candidate received. For example, in Wojtyla's election in October 1978, The Washington Post reported, *"It is not known how many votes the new pontiff received as this information is restricted within the conclave."* The Associated Press and the New York Times wire service reported this identical wording.[4]

Yet, we, too, have been guilty of this kind of sensationalism. We have mentioned, from time to time, Luciani won the election with seventy-five votes. An assumption based on what is known today of the cardinals who participated, yet, never released by the Vatican.

Regardless, since Luciani did receive ninety votes on the final count one knows twenty-one remained cast against him. Although no one really knows who retained these votes one does know they were cast for someone whose mindset was fixed against repeal of *Humanae Vitae*—the major issue of the election. Otherwise they would have certainly been yielded to Luciani on the final count.

It is not only against conclave rules to announce interim counts to the public but prior to 1996 when John Paul II made changes to the rules, interim counts were not announced to conclave cardinals.

To the extent the seating arrangement discussed in Chapter 11 is true—the leading cardinal was placed in the center chair on the St. Peter's side of the chapel, the runner-up in the chair directly opposite him, and the one receiving the next largest number of votes to his right, and so forth—so the cardinals knew who was running first, second, third, etc., yet, as successive ballots were cast, none of the cardinals knew the number of votes cast for candidates.

The counters

Of course, someone had to know because someone had to count the votes. When one considers Cardinal Wojtyla's involvement in a conspiracy involving the death of John Paul I, this is a critical point.

In 1978, although the rules specified three counters, only two were chosen. Only these two and the Cardinal Camerlengo were allowed in the room where the counting takes place.

The counters—scrutinizers as they were called—were selected by an open vote of the cardinals, making them the most influential members of the conclave as these two were the only two who—knowing how the interim voting was proceeding—could steer either side to victory. For this reason, they traditionally held extreme political positions, one coming from the *left* and the other coming from the *right,* to avoid giving one side an unfair advantage.

Leon Suenens, a liberal, and Karol Wojtyla, a conservative, were the two counters in the conclave that elected John Paul I.[5]

They were the only ones who knew the results of each ballot as the election progressed. This included the Camerlengo Villot, who though present, was not permitted to know the results of interim ballots until the counters had come up with a winner. At that point, the Camerlengo would recount the ballots and a winner declared.

In the 1978 elections, the ballots together with the counters' tallies were burned after each count was completed and no record was permitted to be retained. If no candidate received the required number of votes a chemical was added which produced a puff of black smoke from the Sistine Chapel signaling the vote had failed. If a winner was declared the papers were burned with straw to produce a puff of white smoke signaling a new pope has been named.

In 1975, because of rumors of conclave leaks—never proved—Paul VI tightened up the rules which made the 1978 conclaves the most guarded in history. For example, until then, others than voting cardinals were allowed in conclaves including pages and medical aides. In 1978, only voting cardinals were allowed in the conclave and guards were placed outside the doors of the Sistine Chapel.[6]

As mentioned in Chapter 11, in 1996, John Paul II made changes to the rules which greatly reduced the secrecy of elections—each cardinal in addition to writing his choice on a slip of paper and placing it into the chalice would announce the name of the cardinal he voted for—materially diminishing the influence of the counters.

Yet, this is important if a conspiracy had been involved in the case of John Paul's death, either of these two counters would have had to have knowingly or unknowingly participated in it. These were the only two who were in a position to tell what would happen in a successive election. They were the only two who knew who the twenty-one votes withheld from Luciani had been cast. They were the only two—knowing the interim counts in the first election—could successfully strategize a successive election.

The conspirators, if there were any in the death of John Paul, would have had to assure themselves another liberal would not win in a successive election. Otherwise they might be as well off with

Luciani. The only way they could be certain of this was to consult with Wojtyla, as Suenens was a liberal. What's more, they would have had to have consulted with him while John Paul was still alive.

There was virtually no change in the number of voting cardinals in the two elections of 1978. Luciani and one other cardinal had died in the meantime. However, the other cardinal, having fallen ill en route to the first election, had not voted in that election.

Also, Cardinal Wright, who had been ill and therefore confined during the first election and was therefore unable to vote, showed up in a wheelchair for the second election. The number of cardinals remained the same at 111 with Wright replacing Luciani.

Since a cardinal cannot vote for himself, this may have tilted the balance a bit to the *left*, yet, the political balance in the second conclave remained the same as it had been in the first conclave. The cardinal who would have been elected in the second conclave would normally have been the same cardinal who would have been elected in the first conclave had Luciani not been a factor in that election—someone fairly close to Luciani in ideology. One might put men like Benelli, Suenens, Colombo or Willebrands at the top—men who like Luciani could attract those in the middle. Yet, this was not the case. Instead, a conservative won the second election.

In retrospect, the election that elected John Paul II was flawed. Suenens and Wojtyla should have been eliminated as candidates as they were in a position to have lobbied the second election in their favor as they knew how the voting had gone in the first election.

The counters in the first conclave should have been disqualified as candidates in the second conclave because one was dealing with the same constituency in both elections. John Paul II was elected in a tainted process; having been one of the counters in the previous election a month earlier, he had an unfair advantage over the other candidates. Yet, one also knows it is a little late to demand a recount.

Nevertheless, if a conspiracy was involved in the death of John Paul—not known to be a fact—either Wojtyla or Suenens had to have been consulted concerning the question: *Which cardinals does one go after to get them to change their votes?* Of all we know of these two men, the finger points only to Wojtyla.

This does not mean the Polish cardinal would have necessarily been involved in a conspiracy as conspirators could have drawn this kind of information out of him without him being aware of just why they were asking such questions.

Yet, if a conspiracy had been involved in the murder of the 33-day Pope, this did take place. What's more, it took place while John Paul was still alive.

'The Unknown Pope'

John Paul I, was billed in the world press as a moderate—one who had an open mind to changing canon in those cases where it imposed unfair restraint upon the everyday lives of innocent people.

The Philadelphia Inquirer reported, *"Cardinal Luciani's election is a signal to the world that the Church is steering a course from the traditionalists who say the Church is changing too fast toward the progressives who say it is advancing to slowly."* [7]

nside: The Football Guide; Phils win

Philadelphia Inquirer

Sunday, August 27, 1978

's Cardinal Is the Pope; the Name John Paul I

Moderate selected quickly

Yet, one must keep in mind, not much was known of him outside of Italy. He had been tabbed *'moderate'* by the world press on what had reached the world press—the times in Belluno he had been caught baptizing illegitimate children, his order to hospitals in the Veneto to admit partners of homosexuals to intensive care units, his public letters opposing the ban on contraception, his position on the innocence of sex, and his courageous defense of the world's first artificially inseminated child just a month before his election.

Not much was known of this man from Venice.

The Washington Post billed him as *'The Unknown Pope.'* A few papers went to the *left* and tabbed him a 'liberal' and few went to the *right* and tabbed him *'a conservative with an open mind to changing doctrine in those cases it it is unfair to some kinds of people'*—as the press had billed both John XXIII and Paul VI when elected.

Conversely, Wojtyla, when elected a few weeks later, was billed as a *'theological conservative.'* This is demonstrated by his papacy. He changed doctrine only in those cases forced on him by society.

For example, because of confusion caused by his predecessor in the case of Louise Brown, shortly after his election, he reconfirmed Pius' decree prohibiting genetic research. What's more, he did it in a way that questioned the ensoulment of artificially inseminated children in the same way doctrine had once denied the ensoulment of out-of-wedlock children. In 1984, public pressure forced him to modify the doctrine recognizing all children have souls.

Yet, for those who knew Albino Luciani, those within Italy and the voting cardinals, the man from the Venice was much more than a moderate. He was a progressive. For those who really knew him, he was a monumental progressive.

How the game is played

Although a liberal can make headway in the moderate ranks, the middle is not fertile ground for a conservative. A conservative by nature does not believe in change.

A moderate has broken from his ecclesiastical past concerning one issue and remains firm on all other issues. A liberal is one who has broken from his ecclesiastical past on a number of issues.

The vote of a moderate can be gained by a liberal if the voting cardinal is willing to accept some of the other issues the liberal candidate stands for in order to gain the change in the doctrine he wants repealed. But a moderate would never vote for a conservative because he would know that if a conservative were elected the change in doctrine he, himself, sought would never come about.

A moderate who wanted a repeal of *Humanae Vitae* and stood steadfast on all other issues might vote for a man like Luciani who also supported genetic research and women equality. The voting cardinal would accept the changes in what he felt were lesser issues in order to gain for himself what he felt was the major issue.

Regardless, in 1978, which cardinals made up the moderates?

There were those who wanted the Church to loosen its ropes on celibacy, homosexuality, remarriage and women in the Church. Yet, none of these was the major issue in the first conclave of 1978.

Humanae Vitae, the edict prohibiting the use of contraceptives, was this issue. It was this issue, and this issue alone, that marked the difference between a moderate and a conservative; the moderate sought repeal of the doctrine and the conservative did not.

Wojtyla's position concerning this issue had been made clear.

It had been spread across Europe when the proclamation was being drafted. *"No use of contraceptives regardless of spread of disease, poverty and starvation."*[8] He had been the loudest voice in the days leading up to the election against repeal of the doctrine.

This suggests it may have been Wojtyla and not Siri who retained the twenty-one votes withheld from Luciani—cardinals frozen in their convictions. After all, the media which guessed Siri retained these votes knew no more about what goes on in a conclave, than does the preacher about the afterlife—it has never been there.

We have *The Times* article, *"...Cardinal Villot approached the cardinal in the center seat. Directly opposite him was Karol Wojtyla of Poland..."*[9] If the supposition concerning the seating arrangement is valid, then Cardinal Wojtyla, and not Cardinal Siri, as the pressed had guessed, was the runner-up in the first election of 1978.

Regardless, who retained these twenty-one votes is immaterial to the conclusions which follow. Yet, this is precisely how Luciani had gained the moderate vote in the first election of 1978. Publicly, he had been the loudest voice concerning repealing the doctrine.

A few months before the decree, he had sent a public letter to his superior Cardinal Urbani of Venice, *"I recommend the anovulant pill developed by Professor Pincus be adopted as the Catholic birth-control pill."*[10] A week after Pope Paul issued the doctrine, Luciani challenged it *"Some accommodations for artificial birth control must be made within the confines of the Church."*[11]

Now we have come to a most remarkable conclusion.

Not only does a conservative win the successive election, but one who held stark ideological differences from those in the *middle* and those on the *left* concerning the most important campaign issue of the time. How is it possible the same cardinals elected the man most likely to repeal *Humanae Vitae* in August and turned around in October and elected the man most likely to hold the status quo?

In winning the second election, it is clear Wojtyla gained the lion's share of the votes in the *middle* as he could have never gained those on the *left*. He did not gain the moderate vote on his promise to repeal the doctrine prohibiting contraception for this was at the core of his ecclesiastical existence. Just how did he muster the votes of those in the middle? We will answer that question as we go along.

In retrospect

Beyond motive and opportunity, one has another measure of who may have been involved in murder. I call it 'in retrospect.'

The astute detective concentrates his investigation on those who have the greatest motive because nineteen out of twenty times the one who has the greatest motive is found guilty of murder in a court of law. He does not ignore the youthful husband of the aging heiress who is beneficiary to a *one-hundred-million-dollar-policy*.

Yet, if one considers John Paul II having been involved in the murder of his predecessor, one is dealing with scant evidence.

One is limited to the coincidence two of the six men—cousins in the Gambino family—who shared the Papal Palace with John Paul the night he died were elevated by John Paul II shortly after he became pope and by another coincidence these happened to be the two bishops he met with in Genoa three weeks before John Paul's death. We have the notice in a Genoa paper, *"September 13 1978, Cardinal Wojtyla arrived last night at the airport. He will spend the week with Cardinal Siri at his residence. Bishops Casaroli and Caprio arrived by train this morning from Rome to visit with the Polish cardinal."*[14] Keep in mind, CIA affiliate Cardinal Cody had spent the previous week with Cardinal Wojtyla in Krakow.

Neither one of these promotions was an everyday occurrence.

A few months after John Paul's death, Jean Villot suddenly took ill and died. Agostino Casaroli was raised past two hundred others who outranked him to *Secretary of State*, the second ranking office in the Roman Catholic Church.[13]

So as not to draw the wrath of those who were in line for the job, or, perhaps, not to avoid arousing suspicion, it was announced the appointment was temporary on the guise to give the Pope time to decide who was best qualified for the job. A few months later John

Paul made the appointment permanent and at the same time he made both Agostino Casaroli and Giuseppe Caprio cardinals.[13]

Soon afterwards, for reasons we will discuss, he elevated Caprio to *Prefecture of Economic Affairs*—Chief Financial Officer of the Roman Catholic Church.[13]

About the same time, for reasons we will also discuss, Joseph Ratzinger was raised to the most powerful ecclesiastical post in the Church, *Prefect of the Congregation of the Faith.*[14]

Yet, it is the strange promotion of these four men to the four ranking positions in the Roman Catholic Church that could possibly link John Paul II to a conspiracy to murder his predecessor and, of course, the providential coincidence a number of men known to be in good health died in rapid consecutive order to make it all possible.

Nevertheless, it is a incredible coincidence Karol Wojtyla picked up the proceeds of the *one-hundred-million-dollar policy*, Agostino Casaroli picked up the proceeds of the *seventy-five-million-dollar policy*, Joseph Ratzinger picked up the proceeds of the *fifty-million-dollar policy* and Giuseppe Caprio picked up the proceeds of the *twenty-five-million-dollar policy.*

It is something more than a remarkable coincidence that one of two cardinals who had counted the votes in the previous election, of one hundred and eleven cardinals, won the next election—one of two cardinals in the first conclave who could successfully strategize the second election in his own favor won the next election.

"A funny thing happened on the way to the conclave..."

We have left open the door as to the astonishing phenomenon the same constituency of cardinals elected a liberal in one conclave and in the very next conclave made a complete about-face and awarded the prize to a conservative.

It had, on the one hand, elected a man who had ordered hospitals within his jurisdiction to admit long term partners of homosexuals into intensive care units and, on the other hand, elected a man who warned of the intrinsic evils of homosexuality.

It had, on the one hand, elected a man who had been understanding of divorce and remarriage and, on the other hand, elected a man who had condemned the practice.

It had, on the one hand, elected a man who had taught all his life *"We have made of sex the greatest of sins, whereas it is nothing more than human nature and not a sin at all"* and, on the other hand, elected a man who thought there was something wrong with it.

It had, on the one hand, elected a man who just a month earlier had told the world *"I have sent my most heartfelt congratulations to the parents of the little English girl whose birth took place artificially..."* and, on the other hand, elected a man who had condemned the same little girl as *"...a child of the Devil."*[15]

It had, on the one hand, elected a man who revered women, *"God is more our Mother than She is our Father"* and, on the other hand, elected a man who required the solemn oath of all of his candidates for the *red cap, "I promise to oppose the elevation of women in the Church for the rest of my days."*[16]

Yet, most remarkable of all, it had, on the one hand, elected a man who had publicly objected to the doctrine *Humanae Vitae*—the major ecclesiastical issue of the time—and, on the other hand, elected a man whose efforts had helped make it possible.

How did Karol Wojtyla possibly gain the votes in the middle?

We know he did not waiver on the issue of *Humanae Vitae* as the doctrine has never been changed or, for that matter, modified.

If he did not buy the votes of those in the middle with a tradeoff of ecclesiastical doctrine, how did he possibly gain them?

Could it be he bought them with the only other thing that buys votes? He bought them for cash?

Could it be Christ changed His mind? Could it be the greatest liberal the world have ever known appeared to the voting cardinals in the second conclave and told them to vote for a conservative?

Could it be they voted for the Polish cardinal because they thought he would look pretty in a white satin gown?

You've got it—none of these.

John Paul I drew a huge roar from the crowd in St. Peter's Square in his first public words as Supreme Pontiff of the Roman Church, *"A funny thing happened on the way to the conclave..."*[17]

Consider the major issue in the first conclave.

Two-thirds of the cardinals were from first world countries which were totally ignoring *Humanae Vitae* and practicing planned parenthood. If Karol Wojtyla was elected, according to canon law, their congregations would be condemned to live in a perpetual state

286

of mortal sin for the rest of their natural lives. What's more, they would live out their supernatural lives burning in hell for all eternity.

One-third of the cardinals were from third world countries whose congregations adhered to *Humanae Vitae*. They would be looking at decades of poverty, starvation, disease and death.

One would wonder how Wojtyla could have possibly gained a single vote, let alone the overwhelming plurality he needed to win.

Something happened that caused these men to change their minds—something that made the Polish cardinal the overwhelming choice in the second election whereas he may not have been a factor at all in the first election.

Something that did not take place on the spur of the moment midway in the conclave as one might be led to believe. *A funny thing happened on the way to the second conclave of 1978.* We will get to that *'something'* before you turn the last page in this book.

Yet, for now, as we proved conclusively in Chapter 11—*How a Pope is Elected*, the cardinals knew who they were going to vote for—Wojtyla—before they entered the second conclave of 1978 just as they had known who they were going to vote for—Luciani— before they entered the first conclave of 1978.

John Paul II was not chosen by Christ.

Like John Paul I before him, he was chosen by the politicking and collaboration of men. Perhaps, even the murdering of men.

Shall we see? We shall see. Yes, we shall see…

1 *Il Foggio* 29 Aug 78
2 *La Stampa* 29 Aug 78
3 *L'Espresso* 30 Aug 78
4 *Washington Post* 27 Aug 78. *New York Times,* on strike at the time was limited to wire service
5 *L Osservatore Romano* 27 Aug 78
6 *L Osservatore Romano* 25 Aug 78
7 *Philadelphia Inquirer* 27 Aug 78
8 *Dziennik Polski* 3 Jan 68
9 *The Times* London 29 Sep 78
10 *Veneto Nostro* 21 Apr 68
11 *Messaggero Mestre* 28 Jul 68
12 *The Times* London 17 Oct 78
13 Benedict XVI Wiki and biographies
14 *Genova Secolo XIX* 13 Sep 78
15 Agostino Casaroli – Giuseppe Caprio biographies
16 Benedict XVI biographies
17 *Polityka* 21 Jul 78
18 *Baltimore Sun* 22 Feb 01 - *Washington Post* 22 Feb 01
19 *The Times* London 29 Aug 78

Chapter 29

The Murder of Paul Marcinkus

"You don't run money through war-ravaged parts of the world unless you intend it remain there."

Paul Marcinkus

It would seem we have narrowed the choice down to those from the lower floors who attended the last supper who might have hid in the valet's rooms. Both Casaroli and Caprio left dinner early.

The guard on the 6PM to 9PM shift would have seen them arrive and assumed they had left during the 9PM to 12PM shift and the guard on the 9PM to 12PM shift would have never known they had been there. The guard on the 6AM to 9AM shift who would see them leave in the morning would assume they had arrived on the 3AM to 6AM shift when the clamor had begun.

For the mystery enthusiast, Casaroli carried a briefcase in which he could have concealed most anything, including one of his little 'friends' from the miniature desert at the Castle Gandolfo.

A conversation with Paul Marcinkus

In the fall of 2005, Paul Marcinkus, who had been working as a common priest in Sun City Arizona, picked up a copy of *Murder in the Vatican* in a Phoenix bookstore.

It was that he recalled the young man he had once taken around the Vatican grounds, rather than anything in the book, he called me.

Yet, he told me, "Although I had suspicions in Paul's death, I have nothing to add to what you have found in the papers concerning John Paul. Yet, the Vatican's refusal of autopsy has always haunted me. I was surprised one was not performed, especially when Benelli and Felici wouldn't let up in their demands for one.

"One thing I can say for certain, in no way did this man break under the weight of the papacy as one would want one to believe. From beginning to end, he was a fireball who drove many of us to break under the weight of our own jobs. There has been no time in my life which I looked forward to the comfort of my bed at night.

"Yet, if John Paul had indeed fallen victim to foul play, I do not agree only these few had the opportunity. If members of the Vatican hierarchy had been involved, they had available means to employ professional hit men rather than involving themselves.

"In 1978, about fifty Freemasons were working as maintenance workers in Vatican City. Some of these were members of the *right wing* terrorist group P2. They often worked in the Papal Apartment and could come and go as they pleased.

"They could have concealed themselves in the valet's quarters during the day and waited their chance. The only other private rooms not occupied at night were the dining room and kitchen which were often raided through the evening hours and the salon which doors were always open. The secretaries' office was occupied by Lorenzi."

"Yes," I told him, "It was a godsend the valet's brother happened to have died just two days before John Paul's death."

"If P2 was involved," he corrected me, "it was no godsend.

"If someone planned the murder of John Paul, they would have had to vacate one of the apartments. The valet's rooms were best suited as his fitting room was twice removed from the corridor door. They were also the rooms closest to the Pope's quarters.

"This doesn't mean your 'friends' Casaroli and Caprio could not have been sharing the valet's rooms that night, just that they would have been fools to have committed the deed itself.

I asked, "Where did the $1.3 billion go?"

No response.

I followed, "Surely as president of the Vatican bank…"

He cut me off, "I was never president of the Vatican bank. As you know when you toured the holy grounds, the bank is on the ground floor of the Papal Palace. My office, as president of the IOR, was across St. Peter's Square in the Palace of the Holy Office.

"It was that I, as head of the IOR, negotiated the so-called scandal transactions that the IOR became known as the 'Vatican Bank.' Yes, I deposited the money in the IOR account in the Patrimony, but that's where I left off. The Patrimony took over from that point forward. The courts that investigated the scandal tell you that…"

"Nevertheless, you were involved. Surely you must know what happened to the …"

He hesitated as if he were about to confess to murder. Then he answered my question. *"You don't run money through war-ravaged parts of the world unless you intend it remain there."*

For a time, Paul Marcinkus had been one of the most powerful men in the Church. He had spent his life in the public spotlight and had relished attention. Yet, for the last fifteen years of his life, he lived in seclusion in Sun City Arizona. I asked him why?

He told me why. Something I will not tell you.

That was the last I heard from him.

The following day, I searched the library microfilm for notice of the 'accidental' death of the valet's brother. I ran into another twist of fate. The thirty year old had fallen from his sixth floor balcony in Arezzo south of Florence. By coincidence, Opus Dei member and Grandmaster of P2, Licio Gelli, had his villa in Arezzo.

Finally, a light went on 'upstairs.' It had not been John Paul's brother 'Edoardo Luciani' Jack had referred to in his note, *"His brother Edoardo. It was not an accident. It was murder."* It had been the valet's brother, 'Edoardo Calo,' Jack had referred to.

The murder of Paul Marcinkus

In June 2005, members of the Sicilian Mafia were brought to trial in Rome for the murder of Roberto Calvi.[1] Early in February 2006, the Rome court filed papers in a United States federal court in Phoenix intending to extradite Paul Marcinkus.[2]

Marcinkus' testimony would be damaging not only to defendants in the trial but more so to P2 and Opus Dei who many believe had lured Calvi to London on the guise of a loan to get him out of his predicament and murdered him. Yet, that an extradition would be successful was questionable as Marcinkus had immunity from Italian courts granted by John Paul II and protected by the Lateran Treaty.

On February 21, 2006, the Archdiocese of Phoenix reported Marcinkus had been found dead in his home. A sealed casket sat upon the altar in St. Clement of Rome Church in Sun City Arizona. Though pestered repeatedly by reporters, the Archdiocese refused to disclose the cause of death. Cause of death remains unknown.[3]

In 1984, David Yallop published *In God's Name* in which he incriminates Marcinkus in the murder of John Paul. He did such a riveting job most of those who have written of this subject since have incorporated his thesis into their work—Marcinkus was part of a conspiracy to murder John Paul because the audit the pope ordered would have uncovered Marcinkus' role in what eventually exploded in the press as *The Great Vatican Bank Scandal.*

As we shall see in what is yet to come, the Vatican bank scandal did have much to do with the Pope's demise. Yet, the conspiracy to murder the Pope involved much more than just the bank scandal.

As we shall see, the results of the audit of the bank ordered by John Paul did not incriminate Marcinkus, it vindicated him. Up to the time of the audit, the 'shady deals' he had been involved in under Paul VI had been not much more than good business. Yet, one might take some exception to affairs like the IOR guarantee of Sindona's acquisition of the Franklin National Bank which money ended up in Somoza's pocket regardless of Richard Nixon involvement.

Regardless, it was the 'shady deals' he was about to be involved in under John Paul II which would bring him down.

Knowing he had done nothing wrong up to that time, John Paul's audit would have brought an end to the rumors he was engulfed in at the time. Something one knows, in retrospect today, it did do.

What's more, Marcinkus was a liberal and a supporter of the emerging social revolution. From an ideological point of view he would have welcomed John Paul's papacy. Yet, as an American capitalist of the first rank he would have had serious concerns about the new Pope's war on poverty and how he was going about it.

That he played a major role in carrying out the bank scandal is a historical fact. Whether or not he was involved in the plot which led to the scandal is up for grabs. The events—which we are about to disclose—would acquit him on grounds of more than reasonable doubt in any court of law if charged with the bank scandal murders.

It is my judgment he got caught up in the surreptitious dealings which led to the scandal because of the position he held and the rising threat of communism in Europe and Central America and felt it his duty to squelch the fire. This is demonstrated by his guarantee of the Franklin Nation Bank deal years before which money went to curb the *revolution of the poor*—communism—in Central America.

1 *La Repubblica* 6 Oct 05
2 *The Arizona Republic* 9 Feb 06
3 *Sun City Daily News* 21 Feb 06

Chapter 30

The Swiss Guard Murders

"The Pope's Conscience"   Alois Estermann, The Swiss Guard

Regardless, the Marcinkus encounter left me with two thoughts.

One that has much to do with what we are talking about here. Members of P2 concealed themselves in the valet's rooms the night of the murder. Tried criminal cases tell us P2 had an arsenal of professionally trained killers some of them living in the Vatican.

This eliminates other groups including the Mafia were known to have had no professional hit men in the Vatican at the time.

David Yallop's *In God's Name*—concludes P2 killed John Paul. *Murder in the Vatican* takes no exception. This does not tell us who called the shot—just who pulled the trigger.

The other thought is no more than conjecture on my part and may or may not have had anything to do with what we are talking about here. Yet, no book dealing with *Murder in the Vatican* would be complete without it. Could the rookie guard assigned to protect John Paul at the moment of his death have been Alois Estermann?

Who is Alois Estermann?

Alois Estermann was a young officer in the Swiss Army who served his apprenticeship with the Vatican police in the fall of 1978 and later joined the Swiss Guard under the reign of John Paul II. He would rise rapidly through its ranks to the very top.

In the mid-1970s, Alois had enlisted in the Swiss Army. At about the same time, he became a member of Opus Dei, the clandestine cult which was at the time financing Karol Wojtyla's rise to power.

Although officers in the Swiss Army are fluent in Swiss, French, German and Italian, Estermann was also fluent in Scandinavian and Eastern European languages. It was that he was a linguist that made possible his rise to the pinnacle of his profession.

His ability to speak Polish led to assignments in both Warsaw and Krakow. It could have been at that time he made the acquaintance of

Karol Wojtyla. We don't know this to be a fact, but we do know he spent much of 1977 in Krakow. It may have been through his membership in Opus Dei Estermann gained the acquaintance of the Archbishop of Krakow—again, possible, but not known to be a fact.

What is known is that he was a twenty-three year old officer in the Swiss Army serving an apprenticeship with the Vatican police in the fall of 1978. There is no record the Archbishop of Krakow used his influence to get Alois this assignment at this particular time.

Also, it is not known if Estermann was the guard assigned to the post closest to John Paul the night of his death. Even if this is true— Estermann had been that guard—it does not necessarily mean he played a role in the Pope's death.

Yet, from the time of Wojtyla's election in 1978 through the end of 1979, Alois was involved in laundering drafts and documents through Scandinavian banks to Eastern Europe, rumored—not proved—to have been linked to *The Great Vatican Bank Scandal*.[4]

The following year, Estermann was inducted into the Swiss Guard as the personal bodyguard of John Paul II. In the picture to the right, Estermann is the young man at top center cradling the wounded pontiff in the 1981 assassination attempt in St. Peter's Square.

Alois quickly became the closest confidant in the Pope's life, so much so, he was nicknamed in the Swiss Guard as *"The Pope's Conscience."* The relationship of Estermann and John Paul II was welded together during the years he served as the Pope's personal bodyguard, sharing rooms on trips to scores of countries and dozens of ski lodges. After, the assassination attempt on the Pope's life, security measures required John Paul II's personal bodyguard share his rooms whenever and wherever he traveled.

While still in his twenties, Estermann married a woman in her thirties, also a member of Opus Dei. In fifteen years they had no children which gave rise to rumors of homosexuality; the marriage had been one of convenience.

In 1989, Estermann was promoted to Deputy Commander and assumed operational command of the Swiss Guard. He was 34, the youngest to ever hold the position.[1]

Cedric Tornay

In 1995, young attractive Cedric Tornay came into his life. Rumors of an affair surfaced when Tornay became a regular visitor at the Estermann apartment and Estermann made Tornay a non-commissioned officer ahead of others in line. The embers of rumor were further stoked by an incident that took place in February 1998.

Swiss Guards, when not on duty are permitted to go out on the town (Rome) but are required to return to the barracks by twelve midnight. Not to return by midnight normally meant a guard met someone in a bar and slept over. Before Estermann took operational command, guards were severely reprimanded for breaking curfew. Estermann did away with the practice and it is largely for this reason he was so well liked by the rank and file guards.

On the evening of February 25, 1998 Tornay broke curfew—slept over in Rome. Estermann issued an official reprimand. It was this action that locked in rumors of a personal relationship between the two; Estermann was enraged Tornay had cheated on him.

Swiss Guards are recruited between the ages of 19 and 25. They must be Swiss citizens of the Aryan race and have completed basic training in the Swiss Army and cannot be born out-of-wedlock. A few, like Estermann, aspire to be career guards while most, like Tornay, intend to complete a three-year tour and leave to seek other employment; the experience is attractive to employers. In addition to the reprimand, it was rumored Estermann threatened to withhold the Benemeriti Medal awarded for honorable service to Tornay.

Regardless, a short time before, the commander position in the Guard had opened up. According to Swiss Guard code an absolute prerequisite for the job is nobility and Estermann had been born into a working class family. Cardinal Secretary of State Sodano, to whom the Guard reported, conducted a six month search for a replacement finally narrowing his choice to a Swiss Army colonel.

Before Sodano could make his move, on May 4, 1998, John Paul II, set aside the code, and elevated Alois Estermann to Commander of the Swiss Guard. Sodano was infuriated with the Pope's action. Yet, there was much greater alarm concerning Estermann than was simply his role in protecting the Pope.

Marcus Wolf, Deputy Commander of Stasi—the East Germany communist organization—attests Estermann had been a Stasi agent for years.[2] While a Stasi agent, Estermann had emerged more than just *'The Pope's Conscience.'* Estermann had become the Pope's chief advisor, particularly concerning humane issues.

Curia cardinals viewed Estermann as taking advantage of John Paul's growing senility, particularly as it concerned matters of the poor. There was a growing danger Stasi's communist ideology would find its way into canon law. Estermann was not only a concern within the Vatican. He was equally a concern of the CIA across the pond in McLean Virginia. The anti-communist pope, it had put into the job twenty years before, was growing, as each day passed, more and more compassionate for the poor.

The Murders of Alois Estermann and Cedric Tornay

La Repubblica 5 May 98 *"Estermann, who had been appointed yesterday as Commander of the Swiss Guard, was found dead in his apartment after neighbors investigated a loud dispute. The bodies of Mrs. Estermann and Cedric Tornay were found on the floor. All three had died of gunshot wounds…According to Vatican sources Tornay's body was found sprawled atop his service weapon, a 9mm service pistol. Six shots had been fired. Tornay's pistol was found empty. No other weapon was found at the scene."*[3]

On hearing the news, a nun who cared for the papal household told a reporter, *"I can't imagine there was anyone in the Pope's life dearer than Alois; he looked at him as his own son. John Paul was a regular visitor in the Estermann apartment next door to the Palace. His Holiness was devastated when he heard the news."*[4]

John Paul II grieves over Estermann's coffin

A few years later upon John Paul II's death, another nun told the press, *"It was after Alois was murdered John Paul's health spiraled downward. Up until then, the Holy Father had shown some senility but was in excellent health. One of the most terrible things that can befall one is to lose one's offspring. It was solely the Holy Father's conviction in the afterlife that got him through that difficult time."*[5]

The apparent murder-suicide came two days before the annual assembly of the Swiss Guard in the San Damasus Courtyard. A few hours before the murders—the Vatican reported—Tornay had given a colleague a suicide letter he asked to have forwarded to his mother.

Subsequent investigation revealed Tornay had not given the letter to anyone as no one could be found to validate the claim. Also, she received the letter by mail. Most anyone could have mailed it.

In 2005, Tornay's mother, in the interest of clearing her son's name, brought the case to trial in a Swiss court. She presented the court with handwriting analysis and a mountain of other evidence proving the letter had not been written by her son.[6]

It is not unusual that Tornay's service weapon was found at the scene as all members of the Swiss Guard are required to keep their pistol fully loaded and on their person at all times. Should they leave the Vatican grounds, they check weapons at the gate, unless they are on duty in Rome.

What was unusual is that Estermann's pistol was not found at the scene; he, too, was required to keep his pistol perpetually in his presence. Estermann had at least two pistols—the standard issue SIG Sauer 9mm pistol as did Tornay and a ceremonial pistol, a Swiss Army SIG 49 6mm weapon, an auxiliary issue for ranking officers of the Swiss Guard.[7] Neither weapon was found in the apartment.

The report that six shots had been fired and the gun was empty evidently came from a novice who assumed all handguns—like most revolvers—hold six bullets. However, the cartridge in a Swiss Army SIG 49 9mm pistol holds nine (9) 9mm shells. Nine shots had to have been fired or the gun could not have been empty.

Tornay's mother presented the Swiss court with results of an autopsy which proved among other things the exit wound in the skull was 7mm; it could not have been caused by a 9mm pistol.[9] Since an exit wound is slightly larger than an entrance wound, it was most likely caused by a 6mm pistol. Also, Tornay's two front teeth had been knocked out, as if someone had shoved the gun into his mouth. He would not have broken his teeth if he had shot himself.

Swiss Guards found blood in the unpaved cellar of an adjoining building. This raised speculation Tornay had been killed in the cellar and his body planted in the Estermann apartment to stage the murder-suicide. [8]

The woman who lived upstairs heard the commotion and came down to investigate. She found the Estermanns in pools of blood and checking for pulse found them warm to the touch.

She turned her attention to Tornay who lying face down with no blood visible, she thought he was still alive. Yet, when she turned him over his mouth was caked with dried blood and the front of his clothes covered with dirt. Having just felt the Estermanns pulse, she was surprised Tornay was cold to the touch.[11] She also told the guards there had seemed to be as many as a dozen shots.

It was that the guards had made this discovery in the adjoining cellar and that the bodies of the Estermanns were warm but that of Tornay was cold that caused them to believe there had been foul play in Tornay's death; one of their finest had been framed

They demonstrated their conviction of Tornay's innocence two days after the murders at the annual assembly of the Swiss Guard. In his honor they left the place, where Cedric Tornay would have otherwise stood, vacant.[9]

Highest ranking Opus Dei member and Cardinal Secretary of State, Angelo Sodano took charge of the case. He refused the offer of investigating teams of both the Italian police and Scotland Yard. He placed a gag order on all Vatican personnel and channeled all communication through the former roommate of Josemaria Escriva, Navarro-Valls—Director of the Holy See Press Office.

Valls, the second ranking Opus Dei member, issued an immediate statement, *"a fit of madness caused Tornay to commit the murder-suicide."* This remains the official Vatican position today.

Vatican release *L' Osservatore* 5 May 78 *"At about 4pm last evening a triple murder was discovered in the flat of the commander of the Swiss Guard. Estermann's wife was the first to be discovered. She had been shot. Further inside, in the sitting room, Estermann was found shot through the cheek and the neck. Nearby Lance Corporal Cedric Tornay was found slumped over the gun that had killed all three. After having killed the Estermanns, he had put the gun in his mouth and fired. A neighbor upstairs heard shouting and came downstairs to investigate. Cedric Tornay's revolver was empty No other weapon was found in the apartment."*[10]

Vatican release *L' Osservatore* 8 May 78 *"Tornay arrived at the Estermann apartment early the evening of May 4, 1998. Enraged over having been left off the list of those to receive the Benemeriti medal, he shot Commander Estermann twice while he was on the telephone. He then turned the gun on Estermann's wife Gladys Romero and fired a third shot which missed and killed her with the fourth shot. He then knelt down and turned the gun on himself."*[11]

The Vatican has no in-house homicide or forensic expertise. If there had been an intimate relationship between Estermann and Tornay—though the strongest of dozens of rumors not known fact—lovers do tell each other secrets. It may be Estermann told Tornay something he knew of either John Paul I's death endangering both their lives. Many people have fallen victim to murder for nothing more than they knew too much about murders and related events.

The extreme closeness of Tornay and Estermann is demonstrated in that Tornay was the officer assigned by Estermann to the post closest to John Paul II. It could be his own familiarity with the Papal Apartment may have prompted Tornay to pester Estermann with questions of the 33-day Pope's mysterious death.

Yet, what is important here is: Was Alois Estermann the rookie guard assigned to the post closest to John Paul I the night of his death? Did his influence with John Paul II end in his own demise?

In that, ranking Opus Dei officers refused to take the Italian police and Scotland Yard up on their offer and instead sealed the case from the public raises some questions.

Was Opus Dei involved in the Estermann and Tornay murders?

Was the CIA involved in the Estermann and Tornay murders?

Were both Opus Dei and the CIA involved in the Estermann and Tornay murders?

Were Opus Dei and the CIA involved in John Paul's murder?

Shall we see? We shall see. Yes, we shall see.

Autopsy

The Vatican has a record of not ordering independent autopsy[12] in the case of mysterious deaths within its walls.

This was true of the Swiss Guard murders and it was also true of John Paul I. One might understand this in the case of John Paul where there were no physical signs of violence and one may have wanted to cover up the possibility of murder. Yet, it staggers the imagination, Sodano and Valls would not want to get at the truth in the case of the Swiss Guard murders which were obviously murder.

One might wonder why it follows this practice particularly in that it invariably leads to rumors which otherwise would never arise.

In connection with the Swiss Guard murders the only conceivable explanation seems a Scotland Yard investigation would lead to Opus Dei or the CIA or both had called the shot.

In the case of John Paul, if Villot was certain the Pope had not been murdered, he certainly would have ordered an independent autopsy for this would have brought an end to the rumors. Villot either knew foul play had been involved or at the very least suspected it. One has to wonder for what other reason an autopsy was not performed in the case of John Paul I. Particularly, in that ranking cardinals led by Benelli and Felici demanded it.

Except perhaps, that an autopsy was also not performed on Paul VI, who had died just a month earlier, also presumably of a 'heart attack.' Although Pope Paul, unlike John Paul, had some health problems, including having had a prostate operation ten years earlier, he had no history of heart disease, none whatsoever.

One would wonder what were the circumstances of his death—the mysterious death of Pope Paul VI. To best understand the circumstances of Paul's death, one must first understand the circumstances of his best friend's death—Aldo Moro.

1 *Poteri Forti* by Ferrucio Pinotti
2 Alois Estermann *Wikipedia* and other biographies
 La Repubblica 5 May 98
4 *La Repubblica* 5 May 98
5 *La Repubblica* 4 Apr 05
6 *Biel Bienne* 9 Jan 05
7 *Swiss Guard Code*
8 *La Repubblica* 11 May 98
9 *L' Osservatore* 8 May 78
10 *L' Osservatore* 5 May 78
11 *L' Osservatore* 8 May 78
12 According to the Vatican autopsies were performed on the Estermanns and Tornay which determined they died of gunshot wounds. The autopsy of Tornay's body ordered by his mother was possible when she stole the body from a Swiss morgue

Photo John Paul assassination attempt *Associated Press*
Photo John Paul prays over Alois Estermann's coffin *Associated Press*

Chapter 31

The Murder of Aldo Moro

The opening and closing bits of satire in the following chapter is used only to demonstrate how the CIA operates under its charter.

9:00AM January 30, 1976. McLean Virginia[1]

It was his first day on the job. He swung around and looked up,

Mission

We are the nation's first line of defense.

We go where others cannot go and accomplish what others cannot accomplish.

We carry out our mission by conducting covert operations at the direction of the president to preempt threats against the United States of America.[2]

"There is something wrong here." He read it again. "Something wrong." He scratched his forehead, "Something very wrong."

"Yes…" his eyes caught the phrase, *"…at the direction of the president…"* He laughed.

Footsteps crept up behind him. Robin carried a small box. Placing it on the desk with one hand, she laid a small white card in front of him with the other. She gave him a glancing smile as she disappeared out of the room. He read the card,

George Herbert Walker Bush
Director of National Security
The United States of America

Turning, he looked back up at the wall. *"...at the direction of the president..."* He laughed again.

"Threats," the word caught him.

There were hundreds of them.

What's more, there were hundreds of niches in the CIA scattered around the globe that took care of them. People, who he, much less the president, would never know who they were, or for that matter where they were, let alone know what they were doing.

Each of them going about their sacred trust conducting ongoing covert operations to preempt threats against the United States, endless myriads of independent death squads commissioned by various directors and presidents all the way back to when Harry Truman had first established the CIA in 1947.[2]

To some extent these are killer organizations. Yet, they rarely pull the trigger themselves. They have a bottomless barrel of money to pay others. The CIA has established links to many *right wing* killer outfits in the world. In a split second, the top agent of any one of the subversive units of the CIA can dispatch a code and preempt most any threat to the United States. A sitting president rarely knows of their existence, let alone of their activities.[2]

Except for the appointment of a few at the top, the CIA is not a partisan organization. When a new president takes office he usually appoints his choice to the director position. The director, in turn, might appoint a few to the top jobs. But the buck stops there.

A newly appointed director does not clean house. As a matter-of-fact, according to its charter imposed upon it by Congress, a newly appointed director can't clean house lest he imperil the security of the nation. Actually, he wouldn't know where to begin. No one, including its leader, has any idea how many employees are in the CIA. This is the authority of Congress and a matter of national security. The number is usually placed between twenty and forty thousand, but, as a matter-of-fact, no one knows—a reason why the CIA is funded by two dozen other government organizations and lacks an identifiable budget.[2]

Again, he looked back up at the wall, *"... at the direction of the president..."* and laughed again.

His eyes focused once again on the word *"threats."*

There were only two which he, himself, would ever have to deal with. There was the emerging threat of the Arab world and there was the ongoing threat of communism.

He had important partners in each of these jobs. In the case of the Arabs, Israeli Intelligence headed the list. Then there were the French, British, German, Australian intelligence operations and dozens of others scattered around the globe.

When it came to communism, the list was shorter. As long as he would sit at this desk, he would have ongoing communications primarily with two people. There was the Director General of the United Kingdom's Secret Intelligence Service, Michael Hanley. More than any other nation, the United Kingdom most closely shares the capitalistic convictions of the United States.

More importantly, was the Vatican—the world's greatest enemy of communism and the redistribution of wealth society it demands. The Vatican is the most powerful force on earth driving a rich and poor society. The Roman Catholic Church thrives on poverty.

The common fundamental mission of communism, from Christ to Marx and Lenin to postwar Italy and Central America to modern day China, has been to annihilate poverty in the world. If this were to happen, the Church would lose most of its congregation.

The closer one is to the ground, the more vulnerable one is to vendors of the supernatural. The closer one is to starvation, the more vulnerable one is to vendors of the supernatural. The closer one is to death, the more vulnerable one is to vendors of the supernatural. The Roman Catholic Church is the *Wal-Mart of the Supernatural World.*

Poverty stricken people are uneducated and will believe most anything one tells them. Prosperous people are educated and will not believe anything that does not make rational sense. As one knows, today, very little of what the Vatican has to say makes sense. That is, in first world countries.

302

Yet, in third world countries, all the Vatican has to say makes sense. In the most heavily AIDS infected areas of Africa, believers won't use a condom despite the inevitable risk of spreading AIDS and inviting a pregnancy which will invariably produce an AIDS child, born to suffer an unbearable life and die an unspeakable death.

On this frigid January morning as he gazed out toward the frozen Potomac, George Bush's concern was not so much what was going on in Russia, as what was going on in the Vatican, particularly as it concerned itself with America's neighbors to its immediate south.

One could ask why the poor in Central America, who outnumber their ruthless dictators ten-thousand-to-one, have never overthrown them to bring about a more equitable society? Why have they stood aside for years and allowed their children to literally starve to death?

The answer lies in Rome. Popes of the twentieth century have historically fed them faith rather than food. Priests and bishops traditionally allied themselves with the rich, often wining and dining in their mansions; actually, they lived in mansions themselves.

Priests, monks and nuns, if caught sympathizing with the poor, were quickly defrocked by the ruling pontiff. The message from Rome: *"that your children starve to death is God's will."*

However, the newly appointed CIA Director was confronted by a new kind of pope. From the start, Paul had been sympathetic with the poor. His doctrine *Liberation Theology*—feed them food rather than faith—was beginning to take hold in Central America. Paul's Marxist principles were threatening the stability of those countries neighboring the United States endangering the security of the nation.

To make matters worse, Paul had, just the month before, made the renegade priest, Oscar Romero, bishop of Santiago de Maria. There were rumors Paul would soon make him an archbishop and perhaps even Primate of Central America. If that were to happen, only God knew what would follow.[3]

Nevertheless, in Paul, the poor now had a Pope who was telling them to share in God's wealth is His will. Embers of communism were glowing in America's backyard. Paul was becoming more and more dangerous to the security of the United States.

"My God," he dreaded the thought. "If the poor overthrow the rich in Central America, it will soon spread to all of Latin America and eventually back to the United States."

Bush was equally concerned with what was going on in Italy. The objective of the recent union of Moro's Christian Democratic Party and the Italian Communist Party was a society that affords every child an equal opportunity to make its contribution back to society.[4]

Moro would tax the rich to educate the poor through the college years. He would force the rich to help the poor. In Bush's mind, Moro, not the Soviet Union, was the world's greatest threat to the free capitalistic tenet on which the United States had been founded.

"Worst of all," he dreaded the thought, "Moro and the Italian Communist Party have a clear fidelity to free elections. Recent polls have them all but wiping out the opposition in the upcoming election. More dangerous, they embrace emerging social movements including contraception, planned parenthood, feminism, controlled abortions, divorce, remarriage, single parenthood, gay liberation and a general trend away from a Vatican controlled state."[4]

His mind drifted back to the days, his father, Prescott Bush, Managing Director of the Harriman Bank, had financed Hitler's rise to power—going so far as to continue to finance the German Army after the United States entered the war. George was eighteen when the feds seized his father's bank under the *Aiding the Enemy Act*.[5]

In order to avoid being drafted as a foot-soldier against his father's ally on the Western front, George enlisted. Through his father's influence, he got into Naval Aviation School and served in the Eastern Theater. Two years later, he would ignore the sacred marine code—the captain is the last to leave the ship—and bail out of his TBM Avenger and leave his crew behind to perish in the sea.[6]

He thought of Hitler's *New World Order* declaration the day he became Chancellor of Germany, *"The National Government must preserve and defend those Christian principles upon which our nation has been built which define our morality and family values,"* which had been adopted as its primary mission by his Republican Party in the United States.[7]

"My God," he thought to himself, "if the polls are right and the Communist Party achieves a majority in the Italian Parliament, it will spread rapidly through all of Europe. It will be the beginning of the end of all family values in the Western Hemisphere."

He knew how the success of the Communist Party in Italy had come about. Paul had done nothing to stop it. In fact, at times, he had done much to encourage it. His decree of Populorum Progressio in 1967 had ignited the priest-worker revolution led by Luciani in

Venice and Colombo in Milan, men who had been reared by atheist social revolutionary fathers. Together they had led the *revolution of the workers* which had evolved into the socialist movement in Italy which had eventually given rise to the Communist Party in the polls.

What's more, two years earlier, in December 1973, the American Psychiatric Association adopted the resolution homosexuality is a matter of instinct and not a matter of mental illness.[8] Paul not only failed to condemn the declaration, he accepted it. So much so, rumors flourished as to his own sexual orientation.[9]

"Yes," he gazed down at the plain white card on his desk. "It will be the end of all family values in the Western Hemisphere. Paul is becoming more and more dangerous to the security of the United States of America. It is my duty, my sworn duty, to stop him."

The equivalent of the CIA Director in the Vatican is the Vatican Foreign Minister. Like the CIA Director in the United States, he has a similar mission—stamp out communism.

At the time, Agostino Casaroli, Bishop Agostino Casaroli, was the Vatican Foreign Minister.

9:35AM Jan 30, 1976. Papal Palace, Rome

Casaroli swiveled around in his chair and looked up at the wall,

Mission

We are the Vatican's first line of defense.

We go where others cannot go and accomplish what others cannot accomplish.

We carry out our mission by conducting covert operations at the direction of the pope to preempt threats against the Sovereign State of the Vatican.[10]

305

"A two-headed eagle," he thought. The one on the left keeping a watchful eye on the West and the other keeping a watchful eye on the East—each one knowing exactly what it was looking for.

On that chilly morning in January 1976, the eagles didn't have to look far. The greatest threat of communism in the Western world loomed just outside the Vatican walls. Italy was about to become a communist state.

Casaroli's eyes focused on the phrase, *"... at the direction of the pope..."* He laughed.

He read it again, *"...at the direction of the pope..."* He laughed again. His coffee spilled onto his lap.

The phone rang. He picked it up. It was George Bush...

Aldo Moro

A short time before the death of his lifelong friend Paul VI, former prime minister and leader of the Christian Democratic Party, Aldo Moro, turned up in the trunk of a car on Via Caetrina.[11]

Moro had emerged as the great enemy of the Vatican and the United States. He had been methodically going about changing the mindset of the Italian population—leading the people away from the Church and the rich and poor society its doctrines demanded.

Moro was encouraging citizens to ignore the Vatican's ban on contraception and use their judgment as to how many children they can afford. He had become the leading proponent in encouraging the use of contraceptives, not only as a means of birth control but as a means of curbing disease; syphilis and gonorrhea had been running rampant among teens.[12]

It had been his lobbying, much to the consternation of the Curia, which made contraceptives legal in Italy in the first place. When the *religious right* tried to push a bill through Parliament requiring a warning label on contraceptives: *"Use of this product will cost you your soul,"* Moro not only killed the bill, he pushed through another bill which—to the horror of fundamentalists in the Vatican and the United States—made them available to teenagers.[13]

Moro was also lobbying abortion be made legal in order that it could be better controlled by the state as it was resulting in unnecessary mutilation of women and often death. He knew that being illegal, it resulted in countless abortions that otherwise might be prevented by the state; implementation of *Roe vs. Wade* in 1973 which legalized abortions in the United States had reduced abortions overnight from over three million to less than a million a year.[14]

In legalizing abortion, the government sets the rules under which abortions can take place. For example, in the United States, third-term abortions are limited to cases in which either the mother's life is threatened or the child would be born severely physically or mentally impaired. In 1978, in Italy, driven by the Vatican's policy banning contraception, abortions were exceeding a million a year—a country one-sixth the size of the United States.

Much to the chagrin of the Curia, Moro was embarrassing the Church by demanding it make sexual education more explicit and easier to understand in the curriculum of its schools. Perhaps, worst of all, he was encouraging homosexuals, even transsexuals, to stand up for their rights. He was riling them up.[15]

Yet, most dangerous of all, on the heels of the 1976 election, he had united his Christian Democratic Party (38.8% of the vote) with the Communist Party (34.4%) positioning communist ministers to take control of Italian Parliament.[16]

Karol Wojtyla, anti-communist archbishop of Krakow, called the union, *"An engine of destruction of all moral values in the western world."*[17]

From the other end of Poland, Boleshaw Filipiak, pro-communist bishop of Gniezno and longstanding archenemy of Wojtyla, called the union, *"The embryonic beginning of a more just world."*[18]

Regardless, on March 10, 1978, Moro announced he would move communist members into control of Parliament on March 16th, an authority given him by the combination of the *Historic Compromise* and the results of the 1976 election. Italy was about to become a free communist nation sitting in the middle of Western Europe.[19]

Moro was not only the most influential man in Italy, he had rapidly emerged as the most influential man in all of Europe. The threat of communism loomed over Europe.

A quiet morning [20]

Early on the morning of March 16, 1978, Eleonora Moro sat pensively at one end of the breakfast table while her husband scoured through a stack of newspapers at the other end. She thought back a couple years to when she and her husband and four children had lived in freedom, back to those days when their lavish estate was a paradise with views as far as the eye could see.

Now she lived in a fortress.

All she could see when she looked out of her windows were the blank stucco walls of the buildings that surrounded the modest fifth floor penthouse she now found herself living in. Moro had selected the building because those facing it had no windows.

On the floor beneath her, two dozen armed guards were either sleeping, readying themselves for the night shift, or getting up to the light of day. Two more were on the roof above, armed with surface-to-air missiles should a low flying aircraft threaten the building. It was as if she had moved into the Castel Gandolfo, except the guards were not dressed in the elaborate garb of the Swiss Guard.

Outside the walls enclosing the building, a line of cars was forming as if a funeral procession was about to begin. Yet, these cars were not loaded with flowers and dressed-up mourners. Instead, they were loaded with more armed guards who would guarantee Aldo's safe travel to his office and the safety of Giovanni, the last of their live-in children, as he made his way to school.

Speaking of the Castel Gandolfo, it was there it had all began two years before. When, at the request of Paul VI, Aldo spent a week at the papal residence within the ancient fortress.

She thought they would spend the time reminiscing about the good old days. Like the time, she had told Aldo his first and only son was on his way. Of that time, Aldo had suggested they surprise his *uncle* and name the boy after him. So it was the infant was baptized Giovanni Montini Moro by Paul who, at the time, was Giovanni Montini, Archbishop of Milan.

She knew something must have gone terribly wrong that week for shortly afterwards Aldo united his Christian Democratic Party with the Communist Party in his *Historic Compromise.* He began to move the people away from much of the ideology of the Roman Catholic Church. After that, Aldo never met with Paul—at least as far as she or anyone else knew.

Paul's favorite son and chosen successor Cardinal Luciani and the man Paul had picked to succeed himself as Archbishop of Milan— Giovanni Colombo—had something to do with this strange turn of events. They had been involved in that clandestine meeting and she believed it had been their strategy to unite the two parties in the *Historic Compromise* to give them time to iron out their differences.

Nevertheless, it was then the threats began—the anonymous death threats to Aldo and his family. For the most part, Aldo ignored them.

Then one day a threat came from across the pond—America. The next day Aldo hired an army of armed guards and moved his family out of the sprawling suburban estate she had once lived in happiness into the fortified prison which she now found herself.

Yet, on the other hand, she knew Paul and Aldo were constantly in touch with each other. It was she who approved the household phone bills for payment. Each week Aldo would make calls to Paul as if he were trying to reconcile himself with the Pope. She knew he must have been making some headway, as the calls were quite lengthy. Paul had not been hanging up on him.

There was something strange about the order of the calls. They followed a geometrical pattern on consecutive days of the week. If one week's call was at 8 o'clock on Monday, the next week's call was at 9 o'clock on Tuesday, and the following week's call would be made at 10 o'clock on Wednesday, and so forth.

It was as if Aldo knew at these particular times the calls would go directly to Paul without being routed through his secretaries, as if to keep the matter of their possible reconciliation a private one between them. None of the calls were made by Paul as to leave no evidence of their communicating in the Vatican records.

Nevertheless, she missed Paul. It was a rare day in summer or winter the reigning pontiff would not show up at the Moro estate and spend the afternoon playing with the children and chatting with those who were lucky enough to get invited for the day. Yet, since she had moved her family here, Paul had never come to her prison.

Yet, the void had been filled by Cardinal Giocomo Violardo, a frequent visitor to the guarded penthouse in the sky. Giocomo, who held a doctorate in civil law from a Rome university, was how Paul kept his fingers on what was going on in Parliament. The cardinal had powerful influence with devout Catholics in the House of Representatives—votes which Aldo often needed to lock up his agenda—the reason he and Giocomo had grown so close.

Eleonora had no idea Giocomo's visits were about to come to an end. The following morning, his body would be found at the bottom of staircase in a remote corner of the Vatican bank.

Regardless, it was that morning she decided to ask Aldo, just what was the story? She had noticed the phone calls and she wanted to know if he had made progress with Paul. She asked the question.

He took her by the hand and led her to an overly-stuffed wingback chair which looked out of an enormous picture window. One that, in her memory, at one time had enclosed a beautiful blue pond hedged in with the greenery of weeping willows which had served as a home for swans. But now, all she could see, on this magnificent spring day, was the sun bouncing off a blank browning stucco wall.

"Paul also has his walls. But, in his case, the walls are built of flesh and bone and mostly of the minds of men. Unlike concrete, it will take much longer to tear them down. Only we here on the outside can help Paul tear down his walls. It is important his walls not know they are being taken down from the outside."

That is all he told her. He smiled and kissed her lightly on the cheek and left her there in the chair. He headed for the door. That was the last time she saw him.[20]

[20] *'A Quiet Morning'* is a part of Eleonora Moro's court testimony in the Moro trial July 1982

The kidnapping of Aldo Moro

Moro set out from his self-made prison with a half-dozen security guards in two cars for the last time. The cars turned onto the busy Via Fani and moved at a whisker above medium speed.

Suddenly, the car directly in front of Moro's car slammed on its brakes. Moro's car crashed into its rear. The car with his bodyguards slammed into the rear of Moro's car, pinning it between the two.

The incident took place in front of the Café Randolfo on the south side of the avenue. Immediately on impact, nine men and one woman dressed in the uniforms of the Italian airline Air Alitalia emerged from behind the bushes which hemmed in the sidewalk café with automatic weapons. When all was said and done, all of his bodyguards were dead or mortally wounded. Moro was whisked away in a three-car convoy escorted by two motorcycles equipped with police sirens. He was never seen alive again.[21]

An hour after the siege, Prime Minister Andreotti—expected to lose the upcoming election to Moro—addressed a shocked nation,

"This is obviously the responsibility of the Red Brigades. Under no circumstances will we negotiate with terrorists."[22]

Andreotti's message confused the Italian people. Why would a *left wing* terrorist group, that, up until that time, had kidnapped thirty-two others all prominent *right wing* leaders, suddenly change its direction and kidnap someone from their own side of the aisle?

Andreotti was right. Shortly, the press received calls from people who claimed to represent the Red Brigades. The ransom demands included a payment of three billion lire—five million dollars—and the release of fifteen Red Brigades' members who were awaiting trial for resisting arrest in a political rally.

At the time, there were twenty-three Red Brigades' members serving life sentences for capital crimes. It made little sense the Brigades would seek the release of members who had not yet been convicted and who most likely would be released in the short term and allow the state to retain others for the rest of their lives.[23]

Eyebrows were raised as to how Andreotti knew the kidnappers were the Red Brigades before they had identified themselves. Yet, that they identified themselves should have set off a bell by itself.

Though the Brigades had been brought to court and convicted of other kidnappings and murders they had never before identified themselves as the perpetrators in order to protect themselves in the event they were brought to trial.

Had the kidnappers not identified themselves, it would have been assumed a *right wing* terrorist group, most likely Operation Gladio, was involved, as Moro was a prominent *left wing* leader.

Though involved in dozens of abductions, the Brigades had not previously committed a capital crime in a kidnapping. The gangland style of the attack was more characteristic of Operation Gladio and other *right wing* terrorist groups than it was of the Red Brigades.

The event had been witnessed by two hundred, several of whom knew members of the Brigades. Yet, no one recognized the attackers described as being in their forties and fifties. The Red Brigades was a youth organization, almost entirely in their teens and twenties.[24]

There remained the question, of the rich and powerful, Moro was the most heavily protected. Why take unnecessary risk in abducting him. Why not kidnap an easier target.

It would seem if the Brigades desired release of prisoners they would have abducted children or other relatives of *right wing* Prime

Minister Andreotti who had little protection. Andreotti would have released the prisoners and paid the five million dollars on day one.

If the motive had been release of prisoners, why kidnap the greatest enemy of Prime Minister Andreotti who as head of state was the only person in Italy empowered to pardon prisoners. All of Italy knew Moro was Andreotti's greatest adversary. The Brigades would have known their demands would never be met.

Despite these glaring inconsistencies, without other leads to go on, the police concentrated their search entirely on the Red Brigades.

The rise of communism in Western Europe

To determine who murdered Aldo Moro as well as most of the others we have and will talk about in this book, one must understand what was going on in Europe and Central America regarding the rise of communism in the western world as a free democratic society.

We will get to Central America soon. Now we will cover Europe.

In the aftermath of the war, Italy and Spain emerged as sitting ducks for communism. The Italians had suffered under the *Hitler-Mussolini-Fascist* regime and were prone to turn to the other extreme. The Spanish had suffered under the *Franco-Escriva-Opus Dei-Fascist* regime and were more and more finding their salvation in communism. These were two of the most Catholic countries in Europe and their populations were fed up with the remnants of fascism the Vatican continued to impose on them.

Yet, the threat of communism in Western Europe was not taken seriously until 1958 when the Communist Party in Italy achieved a recognizable level of electoral progress. Immediately following the 1958 election, the CIA and British Intelligence, through NATO, established Operation Gladio—a *right wing* terrorist militia with a mission to keep communism out of Western Europe.

Gladio remained relatively dormant until late in the 1960s when developments in northern Italy—*the priest-worker revolution*—gave it the foe it had been established to defeat. [25]

The common objective of Aldo Moro, the Christian Democratic Party, the Italian Communist Party and the Red Brigades was to create a society that affords every child an equal opportunity to earn his/her share of the pie, with an emphasis on education, to enable each of them to make their maximum contribution back to society.

Communism in Italy then was not in the pure Marxist/Christ-like sense of the word—all God's province is to be divided up equally. It intended only to impose heavy taxation on the rich to give equal opportunity to the poor, again, with an emphasis on education.

It was not a pawn of the Soviet Union. Unlike Stalinism, the Italian Communist Party had a clear fidelity to democracy and free elections; it was how it had come to power in the first place.

The wave of terrorism in Italy

The wave of terrorism that engulfed Italy in the 1970s had its roots in the 1960s.

On March 26, 1967, in his encyclical—*Populorum Progressio*—Paul condemned private property—the distribution of the world's goods and resources should benefit all rather than few.

He defined the inalienable economic rights of man. Among these were the right to a just wage and the right to fair working conditions and the right to join a union. He specifically defined what was not the inalienable right of man, '...*It is the inalienable right of no man to accumulate wealth beyond the necessary while other men starve to death because they have nothing.*'

Thus began the *priest-worker revolution.*

The student movement took to the barricades and other social protagonists emerged to make their mark in the political arena. The factory worker class demanded fair wages for all. Communism has long been tagged by the opposition *right* to be synonymous with *revolution of the poor* in third world countries. In postwar Italy's case, it extended to *revolution of the workers.*

The revolution was particularly strong in the northern industrial areas of Venice and Milan. The Archbishops of Venice and Milan, Luciani and Colombo, not only supported the worker's cause, they had risen up as leaders of it. Paul VI—often tabbed a communist—had by design placed these champions of human justice in these heavily industrialized areas.[26]

Luciani had a personal motive for supporting the uprising. Many of the workers were orphans who had survived to adulthood. Regardless, it was from this unrest in the northern factories emerged the *left wing* terrorist group that today we know as the Red Brigades.

313

For much of Italy's youth the movement was going too slowly. The **Red Brigades** was a *left wing* Marxist youth group which sought to accelerate the movement toward a more just society through terrorist activities. It followed a pattern of high profile kidnappings of the rich and powerful who were using their influence to impede the progress of communism in Italy. Among those it kidnapped were executives of factories, magistrates including Genoa Judge Mario Sossi, industrialists including Vallarino Gancia and even NATO generals. It financed itself with ransom money following a precise pattern: If the ransom was paid, the victim was returned. If it was not paid, the body of the victim was returned.[27]

While its members were repeatedly brought to trial in connection with the string of bombings that terrorized the Italian population in the 1970s, no Brigades' member was ever convicted of any of them. An indisputable record of court decisions stand as historical proof the Red Brigades had no involvement in the wave of bombings that terrorized Italy in the 1970s.

The Brigades had no motive to terrorize the general public. After all, the population was very much on its side as demonstrated in the elections and the polls. The mission of the Brigades was solely to terrorize the rich and powerful who were restraining the population's movement toward communism as it was defined at the time in Italy—a society that affords every child an equal opportunity to make his or her contribution back to society.

Major players in terrorism in Italy

Operation Gladio: *right wing* covert military operation established by the CIA and Vice President Richard Nixon in Europe in 1958 with a primary presence in Italy and Spain with a mission to stamp out communism—*revolution of the poor*—in NATO countries.[28]

In tried criminal cases, its members were convicted of more than half of the bombings and assassinations that terrorized Italy in the 1970s. Its members were primarily anti-communist fascist dissidents and former Nazis. It was financed principally by the CIA.[29]

Ordine Nuovo: Italian *right wing* neo-fascist organization which carried out a series of bombings in the 1970s in protest of the communist movement in Italy. It financed itself by carrying out covert activities and providing expertise to Operation Gladio.[30]

Avanguardia Nazionale: Italian *right wing* neo-fascist terrorist organization linked to Operation Condor and Operation Gladio. It financed itself by carrying out blackmailings and other undercover activities and providing expertise to both these organizations.[31]

Operation Condor: Chilean based *right wing* covert operation organized by the secret service of the Condor Countries of South America including Argentina, Chile, Uruguay, Paraguay, Bolivia Brazil, Ecuador and Peru in the mid-70s—all countries ruled by extreme *right wing* military dictators—countries which would fall to communism should Paul's *Liberation Theology* and subsequently John Paul's *Liberation of the Poor* take hold in Central America.

In 1976, CIA Director George Bush annexed Condor into the CIA's family of covert operations and extended its operations into Central America. Later he extended it to Italy when convictions of Operation Gladio' members in connection with bombings had weakened its effectiveness. Bush stepped up operations of Operation Condor in Central America when the renegade priest Oscar Romero was made a bishop by Paul VI in El Salvador.[32]

Propaganda Due commonly known as **P2:** *right wing* clandestine Masonic Lodge operating in Italy and inside the Vatican in the 1970s. It had an army of professional hit-men, some working as maintenance workers in the Vatican. Several of its members were brought to trial and convicted of assassinations and bombings in Italy in the 1970s. It financed itself by carrying out covert activities including capital crimes for anyone for cash which eventually made its leader, former Nazi Licio Gelli, one of the richest men in Europe. Much of its revenues came from the CIA. Actual court convictions establish P2 as the No. 2 killer organization in Italy in the 1970s.[33]

Opus Dei: *right wing* cult founded by Jose Maria Escriva which together with the Franco regime terrorized the Spanish people for decades. Its mission is to control the moral pulse of the world through control of the papacy and judicial branches of nations.[34]

These *right wing* organizations and others like them shared the CIA-NATO-Gladio anti-communist strategy which had been set into motion immediately after Richard Nixon took office in 1969.

The CIA-NATO-Gladio strategy was to carry out a wave of bombings and assassinations in Italy designed to turn the mindset of the Italian people against communism. An instrumental part of the plot was to plant incriminating evidence to frame the Red Brigades and turn the people against communism.

There were other *right wing* terrorist groups operating in Italy at the time, but the CIA's Operation Gladio allied itself with Ordine Nuovo and Avanguardia Nazionale because these organizations had recognized forensic and explosive experts who could be called upon to lock up convictions against the Red Brigades. Gladio allied itself with P2 insofar as covert executions were a part of the game.

The scheme started out with a bang in December 1969 with the bombing of Piazza Fontana—a Milan bank—leaving 17 dead and 90 wounded, followed by a wave of terrorist activities thru the 1970s cumulating with the August 1980 bombing of the Bologna train station leaving 92 dead 300 wounded.[35]

When the reign of American *right wing* terrorism in Italy came to an end, 491 innocent civilians were dead and over four thousand permanently maimed—the American government made the Italian people pay dearly for voicing their opinion in free elections.[36]

This CIA strategy—to terrorize the Italian population and frame the Red Brigades and turn its mindset against the youth group and communism—was exposed in the courts many times.

On May 31, 1972, a car-bomb in Peteano killed three policemen. A circled five pointed star—the symbol of the Brigades—had been scrawled on the hood of the demolished car. Members of the Brigades were brought to trial.

A casual film taken by a tourist introduced by the defense showed Vincenzo Vinciguerra of Avanguardia Nazionale scratching the Brigades symbol on the hood of the car.[37]

Court proceedings proved Marco Morin of Ordine Nuovo, an explosive expert in the Italian police, deliberately provided false expertise in testifying explosives used were the same as those used by the Red Brigades. Other expert testimony demonstrated the explosives were clearly C4, a NATO explosive. The bomb material had, in fact, come from a CIA-Gladio arms dump in Verona.[37]

The court found that *right wing* organizations Ordine Nuovo and Avanguardia Nazionale had collaborated with Operation Gladio and Italian Counter-Intelligence in the attack. Together they engineered the Peteano terror and wrongly framed the Red Brigades.[37]

Although members of the Red Brigades were brought to trial on incriminating evidence found at the scenes, always accompanied by a circled five pointed star, in every case, the evidence was proved to have been planted and no member of the Red Brigades was ever convicted of a bombing of a public facility in the 1970s in Italy.[38]

On the other hand, many Brigades' members were convicted of capital crimes in connection with kidnappings of the rich and powerful. In all, at the time of the Moro kidnapping, the Red Brigades' assassination toll had reached twenty-two.[38]

Those organizations convicted in tried criminal cases of the terrorist bombings of the 1970s in Italy: Operation Gladio 53%, Operation Condor 7%, Ordine Nuovo 13%, P2 Masonic Temple 19%, Avanguardia Nazionale 5%, others 3%.[38]

Friends in terror

How these *right wing* organizations operated in harmony is best demonstrated by the interrelationships of some of the players.

Agostino Casaroli was a longtime friend of Licio Gelli, founder of the clandestine Masonic Lodge, Propaganda Due (P2), and Jose Maria Escriva, founder of Opus Dei. On August 6, 1966, Casaroli had been inducted as a Freemason in a Zurich branch of P2 Lodge No. 041/1. He was also believed to be a member of Opus Dei.

As Foreign Minister with a focus on communism, Casaroli spent much time at the 'front' in Poland. It was he who served as the link between the Polish Cardinal of Krakow, Karol Wojtyla, and Opus Dei which eventually made possible Wojtyla's rise to the papacy.

He also introduced Karol Wojtyla to Licio Gelli. It was that Wojtyla and Gelli were avid skiers which molded their friendship. According to Wojtyla's secretary, Stanislaw Dziwisz, John Paul II took more than a hundred ski vacations during his papacy, most of them to a ski lodge in the Abruzzo region owned by Gelli.[39]

Among other convictions involving the Bologna bombing and other terrorist activities, in April 1998, Licio Gelli and Jose Mateos were brought to trial in connection with the Vatican bank scandal. The prosecution proved they had conspired with the Vatican, Opus Dei and Central America factions in creating the scandal. Sentenced to twelve years, Gelli disappeared on the eve of his imprisonment.[40]

Opus Dei established a substantial treasury after the war when, in its alliance with Franco, it was paid handsomely for arranging the escape of Nazi war criminals through Madrid to Argentina. By 1950, it had emerged as a major investment house in Europe.[41]

The Opus Dei-P2 alliance went back to the 1940s when Escriva and Gelli were a part of the Franco regime. Many of their members were officers of both organizations. For example, Jose Mateos was treasurer of both organizations. Many of their business dealings were in unison dealing with the same commodities and the same banks.

For this reason, it is logical to conclude Opus Dei was involved in the bank scandal and the murders surrounding it. Yet, unlike P2, which officers were convicted of the crime, Opus Dei officers were never brought to trial as they had been immunized from Italian courts by John Paul II's authorization of the Prelature of Opus Dei effective the day before Banco Ambrosiano went under.[42]

The CIA and the Pope

In 1975, George Bush's nomination for the CIA-Director position caused a furor in Congress. He was suspected of having been a subversive agent in the CIA in the early 1960s.

In 1966, District Attorney Jim Garrison presented vast credible evidence linking Oswald—the man who pulled the trigger in the Kennedy assassination to the CIA. Among other things, he proved the CIA paid for a trip Oswald had made to the Soviet Union.[43]

In Bush's CIA-Director confirmation process, Senator Byrd of Virginia asked him, *"Where were you on November 22, 1963?"*

"I don't remember," replied Bush. To this day, Bush holds to his story, he doesn't remember where he was. Today, we know George Bush was in Dallas on the day Kennedy was killed.[44]

Whether or not the future president had been in Dallas that fateful day is immaterial. After all, he lived in Texas a few hundred miles away. What caused a problem was he couldn't recall being there.

Father of George Bush, Prescott Bush, is shown here with his protégé, Richard Nixon. George Bush, in turn, became Nixon's protégé. John and Robert Kennedy's murders made possible Nixon's return to the political arena. Neither he nor Bush would have ever risen to the top had the Kennedy brothers lived as the nation was looking at a quarter-century of Kennedys.

Nevertheless, today, the CIA is positioned to assassinate many heads of state and others who might surface at any time as a threat to the security of the United States on a moment's notice. This includes a sitting president. It also includes a sitting pope.

The CIA agent-unit commissioned to take out a pope should a pope threaten the security of the United States was established by George Bush in 1976 when Paul's pro-communist principles were influencing the rise of communism in Europe and Central America.

Through Agostino Casaroli, Bush engaged Licio Gelli's Masonic Lodge P2 which members were working in the Vatican. This could have only intended to add the papacy to the CIA hit-list as CIA's Operations Gladio and Condor already had Italy and all of Western Europe covered. Gladio and Condor had no presence in the Vatican.

Illuminati News reports the Bush-Gelli deal involved a CIA payment of $10 million/month to P2 by the CIA from mid-1976 until the pro-American anti-communist Pope Wojtyla took office in October 1978. Regardless of the *Illuminati* reporting, subsequent events are clear testimony such a deal was made. [45]

Bush would eventually get some of the money back.

Gelli was the largest contributor to Bush's campaign for president in 1988. Gelli, when questioned concerning his trips to the Bush Kennebunkport compound, denied having a personal relationship with Bush. He explained his visits as being a matter of business.

Licio Gelli, Grandmaster of the Masonic Lodge killer organization Propaganda Due (P2) and major contributor to the Bush campaign, stands with Bush as he is sworn in as President of the United States in 1989. There are also pictures of Gelli standing with Reagan-Bush

as they were sworn in as President-Vice President in 1981

The Bush family and the Vatican

It was probably because of the coincidental relationships of their fathers with Adolf Hitler—Prescott Bush as his financier and the senior Ratzinger as his bodyguard at Eagle's Nest—George Bush and Joseph Ratzinger struck up an endearing relationship.

In 1999, Bush's son Neil and Joseph Ratzinger co-founded the *Foundation to Promote Ecumenical Understanding.*"[46] The president's other son Jeb Bush was the official representative of the United States at the 'coronation' of Benedict XVI in 2005.

Casaroli and Caprio retired to a villa outside Naples on the same day in 1990. In his last act as Vatican Secretary of State, Casaroli visited Bush in the Oval Office in October 1990 and had dinner with Bush and Gelli the following evening at the Vatican Embassy.

The Holy Alliance

The Holy Alliance is believed to have had its origin in a meeting between CIA Director George Bush and Cardinal Wojtyla during the latter's July through September 1976 tour of the United States.[47]

No one knows what the future president and future pope talked about during the time they spent together, yet, history tells us they most likely strategized their rise to the pinnacles of their respective worlds. CIA Director Bush would do everything in his power to move Wojtyla into the Papal Apartment. Wojtyla, in turn, would openly endorse Bush's rise to the Oval Office. As a sweetener, Bush would stack the U.S. Supreme Court with devout Catholics.

At the time not a single Catholic was on the Supreme Court as less than one-fifth of the American population was Catholic.

In retrospect today, this is what happened. In the following election, for the first time in history, a pope endorsed a presidential ticket by attacking the Reagan/Bush opponent Jimmy Carter.

The Reagan-Bush-Bush presidencies have appointed a wave of Catholics to the Court. In a nation overwhelmingly protestant and non-denominational, today, six Roman Catholics control the nine-judge court. Even those nominated by Reagan-Bush who failed to be endorsed by the Senate—e.g. the controversial nominee Robert Bork—were stanch Roman Catholics. The court is today entirely a Judeo-Catholic body which had its upbringing in Mosaic Law.

United States Supreme Court Religious Affiliation

Catholic	Jewish
Roberts	Breyer
Scalia	Ginsberg
Thomas	Kagan
Alito	
Kennedy	
Sotomayor	

Scalia and Thomas are openly members of Opus Dei. Roberts and Alito are believed to be members of the clandestine cult.[48]

More importantly, in that Bush and Wojtyla emerged as the key principals in the Iran-Contra Affair and the Vatican-Contra Affair of the 80s, it is reasonable the ideology involved in the Vatican bank scandal was conceived in this covert meeting. The following year—1977—Bush would chair the First International Bank of Houston which had branches in Panama where the money disappeared.

Nevertheless, the *Moses/Hitler/Franco/Escriva/Opus Dei/Fascist* ideology that terrorized the world in the 1940s continues to live on. Joseph Ratzinger, whose father moved his family from their ancestral home in Western Bavaria to the Province of Traunstein to gain employment in Hitler's regime which caused Joseph to serve in Hitler's personal scout troop, controls the moral pulse of the most powerful nation on earth. Mostly made possible by another man—George Bush—whose father financed Adolf Hitler's rise to power.

So we have connected a few dots for you. Dots which make the world go round. We will connect many more as we go along.

Preamble to the Moro murder

That the CIA strategy to terrorize the Italian people and turn them against communism had failed was demonstrated by the results of the 1976 election: Christian Democrats 38.8%, Communists 34.4%, Socialists 15.8%, Proletarians (blue collar) 8.0%, Republicans 3.0%. Except for the tiny fraction garnished by the Republican Party, the vote was entirely on the *left*. Although each party had individual opinions as to how it would go about achieving its objectives, they all had one goal in common: a redistribution of wealth society—communism—*a society that affords each and every child an equal opportunity to make his or her contribution to society.*[49]

321

A change in strategy

When Aldo Moro enacted his *Historic Compromise* which united his Christian Democratic Party and the Communist Party giving the coalition an overwhelming plurality in Parliament, the CIA strategy shifted from terrorizing the rank-and-file population, to eliminating the leaders of the pro-communist movement in Europe.[50]

The period 1976-78 witnessed a growing alliance of Moro's Christian Democratic Party and Berlinguer's Communist Party. It also witnessed a growing personal relationship between Moro and Berlinguer—their families pestered by reporters while vacationing together on the Aegean coast and the Island of Corfu.[51]

Aldo Moro's intent to bring communism into Europe was not a secret he shared only with Enrico Berlinguer. It was widely known throughout the world. This has been widely recorded in the world press in criticism levied at Moro from his *right wing* enemies.

George Bush, a steadfast republican who spent a lifetime making the rich richer and the poor poorer, called the union *"...a greater threat to the free world than is the Soviet Union."*[52]

George Bush had been *"born with a silver foot in his mouth."* He had been born into immense wealth. He knew what wealth could bring. He had been brought up in the lap of luxury, gone to the best schools and had used his family's industrial and political power to rise to the top. Communism—a redistribution of wealth society—was his most bitter enemy.

Secretary of State Henry Kissinger reacted even more fiercely to Moro's action, *"I believe the advent of communism in these (Italy and Spain) European countries is likely to result in a sequence of events in which other European countries will move in the same direction... the Communist Party has emerged as an effective vehicle for developing jobs and providing education for the common people and this endangers our free capitalistic society... If communism takes hold in Italy, NATO would collapse and the United States would be dangerously isolated..."*[53]

In a follow-up, Kissinger pinpointed his position, *"Domination by Moscow is not the issue. Communist control of Italy and Central America is the issue... It would have terrible consequences for the United States and it is today the number one threat to its national security and must be dealt with accordingly."*[54]

Referring to Operation Gladio and other anti-communist terrorist organizations operating in Italy, *"It is clear anti-communist forces within Italy are paralyzed by the success of the Communist Party in the polls and will be unable to stop it... A clean external amputation is preferable to internal paralysis..."*[54]

One can only surmise *"external amputation"* meant assassination of Aldo Moro by a foreign power. What else could have it possibly meant? Aldo Moro, who had risen as the most influential man in Europe, was clearly the 'link' between communism and Europe. Remove the 'link' and communism in Europe would fail.

Two weeks before Moro's abduction, US Ambassador to Italy Richard Gardner released an official statement from the United States Embassy in Rome, *"Moro is the most dangerous force in the history of the Italian political scene."*[55]

A few days before the kidnapping when it became known Moro would move communist members into control of the House of Representatives, John Killbrick, British Ambassador to NATO, *"The presence of communist ministers in the Italian Parliament pose a serious threat to the security of the alliance of the free world."*[56]

On the afternoon of the kidnapping, from the other side of the aisle, reacting to Prime Minister Andreotti's claim the Red Brigades had abducted Moro, *left wing* General Benigno Zaccagnini, President of the Italian Senate, pointed his finger directly at the United States and Britain, *"This kidnapping is clearly a part of a plan by foreign interests aimed at upsetting the new Italian majority. It has nothing to do with the Red Brigades."*[57]

The Bush-Casaroli-Kissinger-Gardner fears were well founded. Unlike all other countries communism had invaded in the past where it was faced with the insurmountable hurdles of immense poverty, poor education and relentless revolution, Italy was a thriving stable democracy. As a matter-of-fact, it was free elections that had moved the country toward communism to begin with.

Bush, Casaroli, Kissinger and Gardner were terrified communism would succeed in Italy for it would certainly follow quickly in Spain where it had already reached double digit electoral progress. It would eventually spread to all of Europe.

It was the *Historic Compromise* of 1976, more than anything else, that caused Moro's name to move up to the top of the CIA hit-list.

It was his impending threat to move communist members into

control of the House of Representatives that pulled the trigger.

The plot to assassinate Aldo Moro

To understand who murdered Aldo Moro one must first consider motive. The greatest motive to have carried out the murders of Moro and others on our list was shared by a coalition of three states: the Vatican, the United States and Great Britain. These three shared a common motive: Stamp out a common enemy—communism.

In this context, the key players in a conspiracy involving an assassination of any foreign leader or person would be the CIA, British Intelligence and the Office of the Vatican Foreign Minister— the Vatican counterpart of the CIA. In the case of a NATO nation, a conspiracy to assassinate a citizen would be most effective if it included the Intelligence operation of the targeted state—in Italy, at the time, Italian Counter-Intelligence.

This was particularly true in Moro's case, as Italian Counter-Intelligence had raided dozens of Red Brigades' hideouts through the years and had storerooms full of items seized in the raids which could be planted to frame the Red Brigades. It also had several buildings in Rome where Moro could be retained which would escape a controlled search for the former prime minister.

The coalition of these foreign states had a more than willing partner in Giulio Andreotti, the incumbent Italian prime minister. Andreotti had spent a lifetime fighting communism and condemned the *Historic Compromise* from the day Moro made it public.

In addition to his hatred of communism, he had a personal motive for wanting Moro out of the way. The *Historic Compromise* had given Moro an overwhelming plurality in the upcoming election; Andreotti was about to lose his job.

Italian Counter-Intelligence reported directly to Andreotti and the extent of its search for Moro could be restricted by him. The prime minister took a hardline approach and not only refused to pay the ransom money but refused to enter into dialogue with those who held Moro. Dialogue alone can often lead to where the victim is held whether or not the calls are made from the site. Perhaps, Andreotti didn't want anyone to know where Moro was being held particularly if it had been within the Italian Counter-Intelligence network. He knew dialogue would be a monologue with himself.

Why Andreotti refused dialogue with the terrorists in Moro's case is no mystery today. Three years later when his friend Ciro Cirillo was kidnapped he took no hardline approach at all; he paid ransom on demand. In Moro's case, he would not even engage in dialogue.[58]

The murder of Carmine Pecorelli

To give some credence that leaders of free nations, let alone CIA directors, have the capacity to kill. In November 2002, former Prime Minister Andreotti was convicted in a Perugia court of having ordered the assassination of Carmine Pecorelli and was sentenced to 24 years. He was later pardoned by the Supreme Court of Cassation because of his public service.[59]

Pecorelli was a maverick journalist and editor of *Osservatore Politico*. In a cryptic article, in May 1978, a week after the Moro murder, he established a credible connection between Operation Gladio and the CIA and Andreotti and the Moro murder.[60]

Early in 1979, Pecorelli gained important contacts within Italian Counter-Intelligence. His colleagues testified he had been working on an article which would expose *"The Role of the United States and Italian Intelligence in the Moro Murder."* He was assassinated on March 20, 1979; his house ransacked and the office of his journal *Osservatore Politico* destroyed by fire. What Pecorelli knew about CIA, Operation Gladio, P2, Italian Counter Intelligence and Giulio Andreotti's involvement in the Aldo Moro murder died with him.[60]

"A clean external amputation..."

In CIA headquarters in Virginia, the strategy of framing the Red Brigades for the bombings, having been exposed many times in the courts, had not only failed, it had moved the populace further to the *left*. In 1976, as we have said, the vote all but annihilated the *right*.

Moro had emerged as a monumental progressive threatening to drive communist ideology into Italy's ruling coalition. It was the sworn duty of the CIA to stop Aldo Moro.

Yet, the rapid succession of court proceedings in Italy had not only cleared the Red Brigades of involvement in the bombings; it had clearly established *right wing* terrorist groups had repeatedly tried to frame them. This tied the hands of the CIA and Gladio. An assassination of Moro could not be blamed on the Brigades as the populace would know the true perpetrators. If a car bomb was used to assassinate Moro and a circled-star scratched on its hood, it would point to the CIA and Operation Gladio and not the Brigades.

Hence, in planning a Moro assassination—*a clean amputation*—the possibility of framing the Red Brigades was out of the question.

Or was it?

A new strategy

The Red Brigades did have a long record of kidnapping the rich and powerful and holding them for ransom. Moro certainly fit that mode for he was both rich and powerful. Yet, there was the problem he was on the wrong side of the fence. The others victimized by the Red Brigades were *right wing* enemies of the socialist-communist movement. Moro was its greatest ally.

Court trials had clearly defined the pattern of the Red Brigades: Kidnapping of high profile figures. If the ransom was paid the victim was returned, if not paid the body was returned. Regardless of the victim's wealth, the ransom was always set at about $5 million.

Operation Gladio and its allies in the underground terrorist world of Italy had no record in the courts of ever having kidnapped their victims. In retrospect today, it would seem the CIA struck on the idea of following the pattern of the Red Brigades. It would kidnap Moro and hold him for ransom of $5 million and plant incriminating evidence sufficient to indict and convict the Red Brigades. It would include in the ransom demands, the release of Brigades' members being held on non-capital charges, to seal the case against them.

More importantly, in that only Prime Minister Andreotti could pardon prisoners, this would preclude a third party from meeting the monetary demands. The CIA would instruct Andreotti not to engage in dialogue with the kidnappers less it might accidentally lead to where Moro was being held—either in the United States or British Embassies or by Italian Counter-Intelligence.

Yet, the CIA had the problem Moro and the Brigades shared the same ideology. Whereas his *Historic Compromise* in 1976 may have been met with some apprehension in the Brigades, when it became known prior to his kidnapping, in the spring of 1978, Moro would move communist ministers into control of Parliament, it was met by much celebration within the ranks of the Red Brigades. It would make no sense a *left wing* communist terrorist organization would murder the man who was about to make Italy a communist nation.

For this reason—most critical to the operation—Moro was not to be harmed in the abduction. Had he been killed in the abduction, the finger would have pointed directly at Gladio and the CIA. That his driver sitting next to him and six armed bodyguards were killed and Moro untouched points to a highly precisioned SWAT team—characteristic of Operation Gladio.

When Moro was abducted he was not on his way to his office. He was on his way to the Italian House of Representatives; he was about to move the Communist Party into control of Parliament that very morning. He had the authority to do this vested in him by the 1976 election which he had put on hold with the *Historic Compromise*. [61]

If Moro had completed his journey to Parliament that day, Prime Minster Andreotti would have lost his authority, as Moro's coalition of the Christian Democratic Party and the Communist Party would have not only controlled three-quarters of Parliament, it would have controlled Andreotti's cabinet as well. The timing of the Moro kidnapping to the exact point in time the Communist Party would enter into controlling majority in Italy was no coincidence.

The Moro trial

Regardless, four years later in 1982, Mario Moretti and the Red Brigades were brought to trial for the alleged kidnapping and murder of Aldo Moro. Although nothing was ever proved, Moretti and twenty-two others were convicted. In its judgment, the court relied entirely on the testimony of ten Red Brigades members who turned state's evidence in exchange for lighter sentences. Not the slightest link of Moretti and his followers was made to the Aldo Moro murder despite that the trial spanned a year-and-a-half.

A mountain of conflicting evidence was presented by the defense.

Brigades' members who testified against Moretti claimed Moro had been held outside the city although they did not know where. Yet, the red *Renault 5* Moro's body was delivered in had been stolen from a building only six miles from where it had been found.

The car had been serviced the day before and the speedometer reading noted by the garage showed the car had moved only fourteen miles. If it had gone outside the city it would have traveled a minimum of thirty-two miles at the nearest point. The police determined Moro had been shot after he was placed in the trunk as several bullets passing through the body had lodged in the trunk's walls; he could not have been transferred from another vehicle.[62]

Had the car traveled directly from the point of theft to the United States Embassy and then to the Via Caetani where it was found, it would have moved twelve miles. Yet, avoidance of roadblocks set up by police could have caused it to detour. Of course, there were hundreds of other buildings in the same area this would be true of. In fact, had Moro been held by Italian Intelligence, the agency had two buildings within the limits—one a high security retention center. The court did conclude Moro had been held inside the city.

The defense introduced the court transcripts of a mall-bombing that had occurred a year after the Moro murder. Two Alitalia Airline pilots—members of Operation Gladio—had been convicted in the case. The two, serving five year sentences, were questioned about the theft of the Alitalia uniforms used in the Moro kidnapping. Both prisoners denied involvement. Of course, if they had been involved in the Moro murder, they would be looking at life sentences.[63]

A *Brigate Rosse* backdrop in a photo of Moro released by his captors was questioned. Comparison of the photo with a banner seized in a raid of a Brigades' Bologna flat two years before the kidnapping proved they were the same banner. It was found to be missing from the Italian Counter-Intelligence criminal evidence inventory in Rome. It would have had to have been obtained by someone in the Italian Counter-Intelligence headquarters.[64]

Although not one of the two hundred witnesses of his kidnapping identified any of the defendants, bullets extracted from Moro's bodyguards and the kidnapping scene—NATO 5.56 mm—proved M-16s available only to U.S. armed forces—Operation Gladio—had been used in the abduction. Yet, the 9mm pistol later used to execute Moro was a commercial weapon available to most anyone.

On July 19, 1982, Moro's wife Eleonora testified in the open court, *"In recent years, Aldo had been threatened dozens of times. Yet, it was on the morning after Kissinger's threat that Aldo took security measures. We moved from our estate into the well fortified building on the Via Forte Trionfale; bodyguards occupying the floor directly beneath us. The windows were sealed in with bulletproof glass and wire mesh. It was like being locked up in a high security prison. It was terrible,"* she told the court. *"I couldn't even open a window. Nevertheless, after that, Aldo, I and Giovanni never left the apartment without a half-dozen heavily armed guards."*[65]

Asked what the American diplomat had told Moro, *"It is one of the few occasions my husband told me exactly what had been said to him. So I have always remembered it. I will repeat it now: 'You must abandon your policy of bringing these (communist) political forces in your country into coalition, or you will pay dearly for it.'"*[65]

When her testimony appeared in the press the next day, Kissinger denied having made such a threat despite that his past press releases attacking Moro and the *Historic Compromise* certainly confirmed it.

As a precaution, she and her son Giovanni were shown dozens of photos by Aldo's guards. The pictures were mostly members of Operation Gladio, Ordine Nuovo and Avanguardia Nazionale. When shown a photo of Licio Gelli of P2, the guards told her, *"'We have reason to believe, not only Aldo's life is in danger, but that of Pope Paul as well. This man has people living in the Vatican.'"* She told the court, *"We had no fear of the Red Brigades. Although we did not agree with their activities, they were very much on our side."*[65]

Although she did not name a name, Eleonora testified in her opinion she was certain, Aldo's kidnapping and murder had been ordered by *"a high ranking United States official."*[65]

In the Moretti trial, the prosecution presented no forensic evidence linking Moretti to the crime and the weapon was never found. In that the court could not determine where Moro had been held, it had no hard evidence connecting Moretti and the Brigades to the crime. All it had was the testimony of ten turned-state's witnesses who had no idea where Moro had been held.

Despite the lack of evidence and Eleonora's testimony and the Kissinger threats in the world press, Moretti and twenty-two others were found guilty on all counts.[66]

Eleonora's testimony and the lack of evidence and the fact that Moro and the Brigades were on the same side of the political arena caused most Italians to view the conviction with the same sort of skepticism as was the *Warren Commission Report* viewed in the John Kennedy assassination in the United States. To the rank-and-file citizen, it made no sense the Red Brigades would murder the man who was about to bring its dreams to fruition.

A year-and-a-half and a hundred thousand pages of testimony failed to determine where Moro was held captive.

The prosecution went so far as to offer absolute immunity to any Brigades member, including those charged in the capital crime itself, who could disclose the location of the *People's Prison.*

The hunt

To understand this more clearly one must consider the extent of the search for Moro. The entire Italian army reserve was activated. Every house and building inside and outside of Rome was searched. Roadblocks were set up throughout the city. Every vehicle entering or leaving the city and many moving within the city were searched. No leaf was left unturned.

In addition to police, many citizens in Rome involved themselves in the search; each one keeping an eye on the goings on in-and-out of newly occupied houses and apartments. Prime Minister Andreotti labeled the place where Moro was held as the *People's Prison,* despite that the people overwhelmingly supported Moro. In all, the search spanned fifty-four days. Not a trace of Moro could be found.

There were only three places in all of Rome that were immune to search: the Vatican, foreign embassies and any building(s) the Italian Counter-Intelligence designated as off-limits.

It is not likely Moro was held in the Vatican. It would not have been possible to get his body riddled with bullets out of the Vatican gates without notice of the guards who during Moro's incarceration searched every vehicle entering and leaving it. Yet, the Vatican was within the fourteen mile radius.

Concerning embassies, several embassies waived immunity and invited police to search their facilities; the United States and British embassies were not among them. Even Paul VI waived immunity, yet, he could not get Andreotti to search the Vatican grounds.[67]

The aftermath – Judge Casson's findings

In court actions led by Judge Casson in 1990, General Giandelio Maletti, Chief of Italy's Intelligence unit SID, testified he had collaborated with the CIA and its affiliate Operation Gladio in ordering many of the terrorist activities in the 1970s. Maletti told the court, *"The CIA wanted to create an Italian nationalism capable of halting what it saw as a dangerous slide to the left and for this purpose it employed right wing terrorism to change the mindset of the Italian population. American taxpayers paid the salaries of thousands of Gladio members and other right wing terrorists and provided them with what was, at one time, 139 caches of weapons and explosives strategically placed throughout Italy."*[68]

Maletti was among dozens of Italian Intelligence officers found on a list of 962 members of P2 seized in the 1981 raid of Gelli's villa. Examination of the list by Judge Casson's court determined that Richard Nixon's National Security Advisor Henry Kissinger had *'authorized (paid) Licio Gelli to add 400 high ranking Italian and NATO officers into his Lodge in 1969.'*[69]

In addition to Maletti, the Chief of the Italian Military Secret Service and the Chief of Italian Counter-Intelligence were also on the list. All three were double agents drawing salaries from both Italian and American taxpayers. The latter were also subpoenaed by Judge Casson and they confirmed Maletti's testimony.

Three of the magistrates who had presided over the Moro trial were found to have been on the list. To make matters worse, the list had been discovered before the Moro trial and this information had been withheld by Italian Intelligence from the Moro trial of 1982.

Vincenzo Vinciguerra of Avanguardia Nazionale, who was serving a life sentence for the Peteano bombing, testified *"Ordine Nuovo, Avanguardia Nazionale and other prominent right wing terrorist organizations had cooperated with Operation Gladio and the Italian military secret service to terrorize the general population and frame the Red Brigades to destroy the political left in Italy."*[70]

By midsummer 1990, Judge Casson's findings flooded the press. Confronted by the scandal, former Prime Minister Giulio Andreotti addressed a Parliamentary commission on August 3, 1990 and owned up to his involvement with the CIA and Operation Gladio in the 1970s. He provided a document to the Italian Senate on November 9, 1990 formally recognizing the existence of Gladio. He testified that the United States and other capitalistic countries including Great Britain had been behind the bombings of the 1970s.

He quoted and agreed with General Zaccagnini, President of the Italian Senate's remark the day of Moro's abduction, *"This is clearly a part of a plan by foreign interests aimed at upsetting the new Italian majority. It has nothing to do with the Red Brigades."*

Andreotti's document detailing CIA and Gladio involvement in the terror of the 1970s—*'The Parallel SID - Operation Gladio'*—was published by the Italian magazine *Panorama* it in its entirety.[71]

On Casson's findings and other revelations in the 1990s, despite serving six consecutive life sentences, Moretti was freed in 1998. [72]

If one ignores motive, it could have been Mario Moretti who pumped ten bullets into the blanket covered body of Aldo Moro in the trunk of a car on the morning of May 9, 1978. If one considers motive, the CIA pulled the trigger, at the very least gave the order.

That it was Aldo Moro's *Historic Compromise* that led to his demise is demonstrated by the final act of his kidnappers.

The body of Aldo Moro was found in the trunk of a car on the Via Caetani precisely 1,757 meters from the front door of the Christian Democratic Party headquarters in one direction, and precisely 1,757 meters from the front door of the Communist Party headquarters in the other direction.[73]

The funeral of Aldo Moro

Representatives of nations from around the globe poured into Rome for Aldo Moro's funeral. Henry Kissinger was among those representing the United States.

Deeply emotionally drained, yet strong and unyielding through his hour-long eulogy, the eyes of the pro-communist pontiff Paul VI came to rest in a threatening stare on Giulio Andreotti and Henry Kissinger who sat together in the first row, *"...The extremist believes he can halt the carriage of change. But, there are too many wheels. Take one away and another will rise up to take its place. His is a futile struggle. He has no purpose and he has no place in time. No place in humanity. No place beyond humanity..."*[74]

9:00AM May 14, 1978. McLean Virginia[75]

On the other side of the pond in CIA headquarters in McLean Virginia, a bushy eyebrowed man took up the morning edition of *The Washington Post* and read, *"...Take one away and another will rise up to take its place."*

332

He mumbled to himself, "Henry was wrong, *'Amputate the link and communism will fail.'*

He turned and looked up at the wall, *"...threats ..."*

He turned back to the desk, "The ball has shifted from the most influential man in Europe, to the most influential man in the world."

He opened a book. There was a list of names. He ran his pen halfway down the list and struck out the name, ~~Paul VI.~~

Returning to the top, he struck out the name, ~~Aldo Moro.~~

Beside it, he wrote the name, *Paul VI.*

1 Opening bit of satire is based on what is in fact CIA mission, employees, etc. *Wikipedia*
2 *CIA Charter*
3 *Oscar Romero Wikipedia* or biographies
4 Combined platform, Italian Communist Party & Italian Christian Democratic Party, 1976
5 *Prescott Bush   Wikipedia* or biographies.
6 In the inquest, Bush testified he thought his crew was dead. Yet, other members of Bush's squadron saw his radioman bail out but too late as the plane crashed into the sea. Through his father's influence he received The Distinguished Flying Cross.
7 *New World Order, 'Adolph Hitler Installed German Chancellor'* 1 Feb 33 Wikipedia
8 *New York Times* 16 Dec 73, 'APA removes Homosexuality from list of mental disorders
9 *L'Espresso* Mar 74
10 Mission of the Vatican Foreign Minister rephrased to mirror that of the CIA.   The eagle is satire.
11 *La Repubblica* 11 May 78
12 *Corriere della Sera* 27 Sep 76
13 *Affari Italiani* 22 Aug 76
14 *Statistical Abstracts of the United States* 1970-75
15 *La Repubblica* 10 May 77
16 *La Repubblica* 24 Jul 76
17 *Malopolska Silesia* 25 Jul 76
18 *Tygodnik Zamojsk* 26 Jul 76
19 *La Repubblica* 11 Mar 78
20 *La Repubblica* 22 Jul 82 (¹)
21 *The Times* London 18 Mar 78
22 *La Repubblica* 18 Mar 78
23 *The Times* London 19 Mar 78
24 *The Times* London 20 Mar 78
25 *Operation Gladio Wikipedia* or Italian history books
26 *IL Messaggero* 12 Feb 69
27 *Red Brigades Wikipedia*
28 *Operation Gladio Wikipedia* or Italian history books
29 *La Repubblica* 24 Oct 90 - *Corriere della Sera* 24 Oct 90 - *La Stampa* 24 Oct 90
   Article: *Prime Minister Andreotti—Gladio*
30 *Ordine Nuovo Wikipedia* or Italian history books
31 *Avanguardia Nazionale Wikipedia* or Italian history books
32 *Operation Condor Wikipedia* or Chile history books
33 *Propaganda Due P2 Wikipedia* or Italian history books
34 *Opus Dei Wikipedia* or Catholic history
35 *Piazza Fontana & Bologna Railway Station Bombing Wikipedia* or Italian history books
36 *La Repubblica* 24 Oct 90 - *Corriere della Sera* 24 Oct 90 - *La Stampa* 24 Oct 90
   Article: *Prime Minister Andreotti—Gladio*
37 *La Repubblica* 1 Jun 74 *Vincenzo Vinciguerra Peteano Bombing Wikipedia* or Italian history books
38 *Italy terror 1970s Wikipedia* or Italian history books
39 *A Life with Karol* Stanislaw Dziwisz

40 *Licio Gelli Wikipedia* or Italian history books
41 see Chapter *'How a Pope is Elected'*
42 see Chapter *'The Vatican Bank Murders'*
43 *Jim Garrison JFK Assassination Wikipedia* or American history books
44 Search Internet: *'Bush JFK Dallas'*
45 *Illuminati News* see also *'Licio Gelli' Wikipedia*
46 *St. Petersburg Times* 23 Apr 05
47 *Malopolska – Silesia* 27 Aug 76 *Le cardinal Wojtyla se rencontre avec le Directeur de CIA Bush.* Bush and Wojtyla met for three days Aug 26-28, 1976 in Washington DC.
48 United States Supreme Court *Wikipedia* or library
49 1976 Election Italy *Wikipedia* or library
50 *Historic Compromise Wikipedia* or library
51 *Telegrafos Corfu* 23 Jul 77
52 *Washington Post* 16 Aug 76.
53 *Covet Action Quarterly* Washington DC No. 49 Summer 94
54 *TIME What if Communists Win a Role?* 26 Apr 76
55 *L'Europeo* 1 Mar 78
56 *La Repubblica* 12 Mar 78.
57 *La Repubblica* 18 Mar 78
58 *Aldo Moro Wikipedia* see also *NATO's Secret Armies* Ganser pg 79
59 *Giulio Andreotti Wikipedia*
60 Carmine Pecorelli *Wikipedia* – see also Aldo Moro *Wikipedia*
61 Aldo Moro *Wikipedia* or Italian history books
62 *La Repubblica* 18 May 78
63 *La Repubblica* 12 Jul 82
64 *La Repubblica* 16 Jul 82
65 *La Repubblica* 20 Jul 82 and 21 Jul 82 ([2])
66 *Mario Moretti Wikipedia* or Italian history books
67 *La Repubblica* 22 Apr 78
68 *Guardian* 26 Mar 2001 & *'Giandelio Maletti Gladio' Wikipedia*
69 *La Repubblica* 5 Apr 1981 also NATO's Secret Armies p 74 Ganser
70 *La Repubblica* 14 May 84 *'Vincenzo Vinciguerra' Wikipedia*
71 *Panorama* December 1990
72 *Mario Moretti Wikipedia* or Italian history books
73 Aldo Moro *Wikipedia* & *La Repubblica* 10 May 78
74 *La Repubblica* 14 May 78
75 Closing satire

([1])*A Quiet Morning* is a part of Eleonora Moro's testimony of July 19, 1982 in the Aldo Moro trial..

([2]) In addition to being in the court's transcripts, Kissinger's threats have been widely published in books about the Moro murder including the bestsellers, *The Aldo Moro Murder Case* by Richard Drake 1995 (pg 85) and *Days of Wrath* by Robert Kat (pg xxiv). NATO's Secret Armies by Ganser pg79

Photo Peteano terror - *Associated Press 1972*
Photo Nixon-Prescott Bush - *Associated Press 1954*
Photo Bush inauguration – author photo
Photo Moro Banner – *La Repubblica 1982*

Author's note: in order to explain why the Red Brigades murdered Aldo Moro who was about to bring its dreams to fruition, it has been suggested by some that Mario Moretti was actually a Gladio officer who had infiltrated the ranks of the Brigades. This allegation has never been proved. Even if true it points to the CIA.

Chapter 32

The Murder of Paul VI

"We have fought the good battle. Let us finish the run!"   Paul VI

From the tower of strength he had been at Moro's funeral, in July of 1978, Paul was worn out. He was pale and lacked any semblance of energy. He had been taking uncharacteristic naps. They had begun shortly after Moro's funeral. It seemed the strain of losing his friend was too much for him. He agreed to take a rest at Castel Gandolfo.

There are five magnificent palaces including the papal residence within the retreat. Yet, the Castel, itself, is a part of the ruins of an embattlement built by Urban VIII in the seventeenth century to protect the city of Rome and St. Peter's—Castel Franco to the north, Castel Sant'Angelo to the east and Castel Gandolfo to the west.

Sitting high on a hill it keeps a watchful eye over St. Peter's. The basilica's immense dome can be viewed from its northern turrets.

To the west are the glistening waters of the Mediterranean, and to the east is a perfectly oval shaped blue lake set in a field of green trees. Off in another direction, one can view wooded slopes falling swiftly down to the gray murky waters of an ancient volcanic crater.

If one is privileged to witness the view from the papal rooms, themselves, one can see the Apian Way lined with towering trees on either side—soldiers standing at attention awaiting their emperor to proceed down between them. On a perfectly clear day one can follow them along the ancient viaduct all the way down to the Adriatic Sea.

Off in one direction one can see the low rolling Alban Hills. Off in another direction one can see still another lake edged in by the ruins of the palace of the Emperor Diocletian where Constantine—founder of the Roman Catholic Church—had played as a boy.

The world's most beautiful gardens are here too.

The architecture of the gardens is a composition of Italian, French, German, Russian, Chinese, Japanese, Indian, African, Australian and even American. Not even the Eskimo and Arab have been left out.

In one corner Arctic roses peek up from a carpet of tundra and just a few feet away flowering cactus bloom in a miniature desert of sand, as if one must watch for polar bears and scorpions at the same time.

The gardens are edged in by palm trees at one end and evergreens at the other. Even Christ would be at home here. There is patch of ground taken out of His hometown of Nazareth—this one fenced in to keep small children and stray animals out.

Its crown jewel is the striking plant Omithogalum Uumbellatum. Its flower, commonly referred to as the *Star of Bethlehem* because of its white star design, is as dangerous as it is beautiful. It has found its way into mystery novels. Its nut flavored bulb, easily concealed in nutty flavored foods, if ingested, results in respiratory convulsions culminating in death within a few hours.

It seems the only thing one cannot see, is snow.

The Godfather's last ride

In the still of the darkness of the evening of July fourteenth nineteen hundred seventy-eight, Paul left the Vatican for the last time. He warded off his secretary's offer of assistance as he climbed into the limousine that would take him to the papal retreat. Carlo Confalonieri, aging dean of the College of Cardinals, did take Macchi up on his offer as he struggled into the car next to the Pope.

The car was a black Mercedes from the pool of vehicles reserved for use by Vatican cardinals. He had chosen not to use the helicopter, which usually took him to the castle. He would go incognito this time by ground as if he knew of his fate; he wanted to be witness to the streets and the people of his beloved Rome for this last time.

Although decidedly slower than he had been at the time of Moro's funeral, there was little outward change in his appearance, except for a mustard-like tinge to his skin. His face looked like it was hewn out of yellow pine. It was flaking, as if God had used a chisel on him.

Jean Villot, his longtime friend and confidant had decided at the last minute to go along for a few days. He climbed into the car from the other side so as to wedge Paul in between the two of them. That Villot chose to go along was a break in protocol as the secretary of state usually remains in the Vatican when the Pope is away. Macchi took the jump seat in the rear compartment and John Magee, Paul's first secretary, slid silently into the seat next to the driver.

Though one was a pope, one a dean, one a cardinal, one a bishop, and one a monsignor; all five were dressed in black, solely in black.

Five men, six with the chauffeur, dressed in black suits with a half-dozen black boleros topping them off.

Except for the presence of Swiss Guards in their elaborate attire to either side of the palace doors, one would assume the Mafia was taking the Godfather for his last ride. As if a gangland episode was about to occur along the way; somewhere between here and there his body would be thrown out from the car, perhaps beneath a viaduct.

Particularly, if one were to notice a second Mercedes follow the first one out of the gates. Four more men in black suits topped off with matching boleros——Swiss Guards so as not to attract notice.

Yet, nothing happened along the way. Except for Paul's offer to share his cough drops, his only words during the short ride were, "Why do I tire so?" No one offered an answer. No one took him up on the cough drops either. After all, it was midsummer. He wiped his lips. A tinge of red spotted his white handkerchief.

"...to die like a cat or a dog."

Indeed, it was his last ride. Three weeks later, spiraling steadily downward, he was dead. The daily naps, progressing to all day sleeps to near coma, until the morning of the final day when he showed signs of recovery. Yet, early that afternoon he developed an acute respiratory problem and his blood pressure dropped dramatically.

As the Pope was obviously in his last hours, the 'heart attack' was announced to the press. His brother Senator Luigi Montini who had learned of his condition on the news was en route to Castel Gandolfo when Paul's pontificate came to its end.

Popes are not normally hospitalized—the privilege of royalty in Europe where the hospital packs up its bags and comes to them. This had been true when Paul had his prostate surgery ten years earlier; a small room in the secretaries' office was converted into a makeshift operating theater which remains today. Yet, in cases of serious illness, an intensive care mobile unit is usually summoned from Rome.

For some reason, Paul's physician never called for a unit. Not even after Paul had suffered the 'heart attack' with which he lingered for almost a day. This, despite that when the news reached Rome, an intensive care unit was offered by a hospital ten minutes away.

Actually, except for a consultation with an urologist in Rome, Dr. Fontana made no attempt to seek outside help although the Pope was critically ill. Also, no notice of his illness was released to the press or even his family until after he had suffered the presumed heart attack.

Members of the medical profession criticized this inaction. They questioned why Paul was not returned to the safety of the Vatican once it was known he was seriously ill. The Vatican, itself, had the equipment and personnel to have saved his life. When members of the press questioned the doctor as to why this was not done, the doctor responded the heart attack was sudden and by that time it was obvious Paul was dying. The doctor told reporters, until the last day, although very tired, Paul had not shown signs of serious illness.

Unbeknown to him, however, another member of the press was interviewing another witness at the same time. The mother nun told the reporter, *"The Pope had been bedridden for the past two weeks suffering from a high fever and had been slipping in and out of a coma since Tuesday night,"*—five days prior to the 'heart attack.'[1]

A second nun said she had been with the Pope when the attack occurred, *"He had eaten his cereal and juice that morning and it seemed he was getting better. Toward noon Cardinal Confalonieri began to say mass by his bedside and Paul interrupted him and completed the mass himself. We were delighted he was getting better.*

"In the early afternoon, we loaded his soup with vegetables. When I brought it to him he gobbled it up like he had been starving to death. He picked up the bowl of butternut pudding and was midway through it when he suddenly dropped the bowl onto the sheets and started choking and gasping for breath.

"At first, I thought it was that he had been eating too quickly. Then I realized what I was witnessing were convulsions. I ran out of the room and fetched Doctor Fontana. He examined Paul and told us it was just a matter of time. From that time on Paul gasped for breath as if each was his last; his chest rising and falling with each gasp."[2]

The press asked the nun if Paul had experienced pain and she told them he did not complain of any and his expression did not reflect pain. *"It was that he couldn't breathe. He was gasping for breath."*[2]

This led the profession to conclude Fontana had misdiagnosed the Pope's condition; respiratory failure without pain is not symptomatic of heart attack. This criticism by the medical profession was well founded as a common physician would have known this, much less a pope's physician. In fact, most laymen would have known it.

The nun who had the scullery duty of emptying the bedpan told a third reporter *"There had been nothing but blood in the pan for a week."*[3] Although bloody discharge from the bladder is a sign of serious illness, it has nothing to do with heart attack

An urologist in Rome confirmed the nun's story, telling still another reporter, he had been consulted by the Pope's physician earlier in the week concerning a bladder infection.[4]

When these conflicting testimonies were released the next day, editorials in Italian, French, UK and even American newspapers criticized this inaction on the part of the Pope's physician. Neither the doctor nor the Vatican ever responded to the criticism.

Dr. Sebastiano Caffaro, President of the Italian Medical Society, was particularly harsh. *"It is unbelievable a pope could be left to die without the care one would afford a cat or a dog."*[5]

The South African heart specialist Christian Barnard condemned Fontana's failure to call for an intensive care unit, *"If that had happened anywhere else in the world, the doctor would have been denounced by his medical association and found himself in court."*[6]

The Montini family, pestered as to why they were not kept informed of Paul's deteriorating condition, issued a press release, *"Whereas errors in judgment may have been made in connection with Paul's illness, we take no issue with the will of God."*[7]

The final vigil

At the time of Paul's death, there were two dozen people at Castel Gandolfo. At his bedside, were Dr. Fontana, Cardinal Confalonieri and two bishops—Caprio and Casaroli.

Outside in the hall was the Castel Director, Emilio Bonomelli, together with four nuns who cared for the papal residence and two monks who cared for the gardens. A ceremonial guard stood next to Paul's bedroom door. Elsewhere within the fortress were a half-dozen Swiss Guards and two maintenance workers who had been repairing the kitchen exhaust system that day.[8]

Caprio had arrived early in the morning just a few hours prior to the presumed heart attack—not unusual as he spent much of his free time at the Castel Gandolfo. An amateur botanist, he cultivated the Holy Land section of the gardens.

Cardinal Villot was not present. He had returned to the Vatican in late July. Yet, Paul's death came as no surprise to him as he had been summoned to Castel Gandolfo the day before to document Paul's elevation of Cardinal Yu Pin to Grand Chancellor of Eastern Affairs. He brought back with him Paul's last official words *"We have fought the good battle. Let us finish the run."*[9]

With the time between the rising and falling of his chest growing more and more apart, Paul died as if falling asleep——the slowing of his breathing broken only by the murmuring of prayers.

Arsenic poisoning

This is about as good a place as any to stop and talk about one of the culprits which weaves its way in and out of this book.

Slow-arsenic poisoning is not limited to mystery writers; it is a favorite of real killers. Available in many household chemicals, it is easily administered. Tasteless and odorless, it is easily concealed in food or drink. All one need do is go to a library and read a book.

More killings go undetected when arsenic is the instrument of murder than any other method. It results in symptoms characteristic of a wide range of natural illnesses and unless a doctor specifically suspects foul play it will go undetected.

For example, in 1970, a jaundiced skin man was admitted to a Chicago hospital complaining of tiredness, thirst, dehydration, sore throat, a pulmonary condition and urinary bloody discharge.

Test after test was done; the physicians were at a loss as to what was wrong with him. At a nursing station, one physician overheard students discussing the case. One, a mystery buff, joked, *"Maybe his wife in poisoning him."* The physician tested for arsenic. The results were positive. His wife had been doctoring his coffee.[10]

Initially there is jaundice, flaking skin, esophagus soreness and a bit of coughing up of bloody mucosa. It progresses slowly to a deteriorating condition accompanied by severe dehydration, swollen extremities and usually cumulating in pulmonary oedema.

Toward the end, there is a bloody discharge from the bladder——the most telltale sign of arsenic poisoning in a living person. In the end are convulsions and respiratory collapse. There is a peculiar odor in the corpse not easily erased by conventional embalming.[11]

The elderly are particularly vulnerable to slow-arsenic poisoning as many of its symptoms are compatible with advanced aging and death will come within a month or so whereas a younger person might survive six months or more with the same undetectable dosage.[12] Paul, at eighty, was a sitting duck for murder.

All of the conditions of Paul's death were symptoms of slow-arsenic poisoning, precisely the symptoms of arsenic poisoning, from the uncharacteristic naps, to the flaky skin, to the sore throat, to the bloody discharge, to the obnoxious odor his body gave off which delayed its viewing in St. Peter's by a day.

Paul lay in state for a day at the Castel Gandolfo where fans were installed to disperse the odor. After a second embalming he smelled like a flower and was moved to St. Peter's.[13]

The embalmers were questioned as to why the odor had been so pungent on the first day and had changed to that of a rose garden on the second day. They told the press that in preparing the Pope for the second viewing they had injected the body with perfume.[14]

That he developed a severe pulmonary condition when it seemed his body was fighting off the poisoning, a lethal dose may have been added to quicken the process. Yu Pin's elevation may have caused the perpetuators to speed his demise.

In that no autopsy was performed, no one knows what killed Paul, other than the medical community clearly established it was not a heart attack.

Dig him up

Much has been said to exhume the body of John Paul I. Yet, the circumstances of his death strongly suggest professional killers and lethal injection. With hundreds of toxins to choose from, it makes no sense professional killers would choose one which would survive today to assay of foul play as they would have no guarantee an autopsy would not be performed. Yet, in Paul's case, which is strongly suggestive of arsenic poisoning, traces of arsenic—an element—would survive in Paul's hair and fingernails today.

It may be that it was so widely known Paul suffered from swollen feet and died that prompted the Vatican to claim John Paul had complained of swollen feet, something we know today was not true. One will never know

A few weeks later [15]

On the other side of the pond in CIA headquarters in McLean Virginia, a bushy eyebrowed man took up the morning edition of The Washington Post and read, September 28, 1978, *"At a public audience today John Paul told a worldwide television audience '...It is the inalienable right of man to own property. Yet, it is the right of no man to accumulate wealth beyond the necessary while other men starve to death because they have nothing...'"*

He recalled Paul's last words at the Moro funeral, *"...Take one away and another will rise up to take its place..."*

He thought back to Kissinger's instruction, *"Amputate the link and communism will fail."*

He turned and looked up at the wall, *"...threats ..."*

He turned back to the desk, "The ball has shifted again, this time from the frying pan into the fire."

He opened a book. There was a list of names.

At the top of the list were the words, ~~Aldo Moro.~~

The name had been struck out and next to it had been written the name, *Paul VI.*

He took his pen and struck out the name, ~~*Paul VI.*~~

Beside it, he wrote the name, *John Paul I.*

Take particular note of footnote 12—the Fatima murders

1 *IL Messaggero* 7 Aug 78
2 *IL Messaggero* 7 Aug 78
3 *La Stampa* 8 Aug 78
4 *La Repubblica* 8 Aug 78
5 *Rinascita* 8 Aug 78
6 *Cape Times* 12 Aug '78
7 *Leggo* 28 Aug 78
8 *L'Osservatore Romano* 8 Aug 78
9 *L'Osservatore Romano* 9 Aug 78 Paul's last words to Cardinal Villot
10 *Deadly Doses* Serita Stevens *Chicago Tribune* 17 Jul 70
11 *Mosby's Dictionary of Medicine 7th Edition* or other medical dictionary approved by the AMA
12 In the Fatima murders discussed in Chapter 9, hospital records show that Jacinta Marto survived a hear and doctors were unable to diagnose her condition. A week before she died exploratory surgery of the chest cavity—pulmonary edema—failed to save her life. In that her brother Francisco was never hospitalized, less is known of his illness other than he survived six months. The only reliable record of his illness is his death certificate: *"cause of death: cystitis."* Cystitis is a medical term for bladder infection. Jacinta's death certificate cites 'urinary poisoning' as immediate cause of death.
Bloody discharge of the bladder is the most telltale sign of arsenic poisoning in a living person.
13 *L'Osservatore Romano* 8 Aug 78. Also: embalming Paul VI *Wikipedia*
14 *L'Osservatore Romano* 7 Aug 78 Yu Pin *Wikipedia*
15 Closing satire

Chapter 33

The Murder of Cardinal Villot

According to canon law the term of a secretary of state ends when the Pope who appointed him dies.

When John Paul I appointed Villot as secretary of state it was known the choice was transitional. At the time of his untimely death, the newly elected pope was in the process of replacing Villot with Benelli something both these men were looking forward to—Benelli looking forward to taking over management of the Church and Villot looking forward to teaching in the Gregorian University in Rome.

This was apparent as during John Paul's brief reign Benelli was deeply immersed in supervising the audit of the Vatican bank which at the time operated under the auspices of the Secretary of State. So it was no surprise John Paul retained the French cardinal at his side.

The surprise came when John Paul II rose to power. Instead of replacing Villot who stood for everything he was against, he retained Villot in the most powerful administrative position in the Church. Villot was in excellent health and short of retirement age and Benelli was no longer a part of the equation. Just why did John Paul II install this liberal cog in the conservative wheel of his papacy?

Could it be, if he were to replace Jean Villot with Agostino Casaroli immediately, it would have caused a furor among the two hundred cardinals and archbishops who outranked Casaroli? Could it be, had he replaced him with Casaroli immediately—one of three cardinals of Mafia families who shared the palace with John Paul the night he died—it would have raised suspicions of murder? Could it be, he needed time—not a lot of time, but some time—to ease his friend Casaroli into the job? Could it be, like Paul before him, Cardinal Jean Villot, too, fell victim to slow-arsenic poisoning?

A quiet ride

Regardless, a few months after Paul and John Paul's deaths, Jean Villot, jaundiced and skin flaking, was loaded into a black Mercedes at the rear gates of the Vatican. He, too, was taken for his last ride to Castel Gandolfo. He, too, was popping cough drops. He, too, would

343

suffer a 'heart attack.' Yet, he did not die at Castel Gandolfo.

His brother showed up at the retreat, Realizing Villot seriously ill, he ordered him moved to a Rome hospital, after which stay he was returned to the Vatican. Although the hospital cleared up a serious bladder infection, a few days later his blood pressure dropped and similar to Paul, he went into severe respiratory failure. Like Paul, he lingered for a few hours and died in the Vatican on March 9, 1979.

The strategy of Jean Villot

When one considers foul play in the death of Jean Villot, one is limited to his role in the events surrounding John Paul's death.

It was he, as interim pope, who released the statement John Paul died before midnight and had been found dead by his secretary John Magee at six-thirty in the morning. Also, John Paul held a book— *The Imitation of Christ*—upright in his hands.

Whereas, the Pope had undoubtedly died toward four o'clock in the morning and a nun had found him at four-thirty holding notes written on the stationary of Vittorio Veneto upright in his hands.

It had been Villot who summoned the embalmers at five in the morning. One might think he lied about the time of death in order to place time between John Paul's death and the embalming so as not to arouse suspicions of poisoning. Yet, today, one knows from the embalmers the embalming did not take place until after ten o'clock.

He lied about the time of death and roused the embalmers at such an early hour to arouse suspicion of poisoning—which we know, in retrospect, it did do. That he specifically included in the release he had performed the last rites—something he would have never done had the body been dead for six hours—seems to confirm this.

Villot was one of the most brilliant men in the Church. Six out of six mistakes in a brief release is not characteristic of a brilliant man.

It is obvious he made these 'mistakes' intentionally. He knew the press would interview those witnesses of John Paul's death just as they had interviewed those witnesses of Paul's death a month earlier. He knew the embalmers would tell the press they had been picked up at five-thirty which would conflict with the Vatican release the Pope had been found at six-thirty. He also knew the mother nun would confirm the discrepancy in time; she would tell the press she had discovered the Pope at four-thirty.

If Villot had not created the confusion that surrounded John Paul's death there would have been no investigation by reporters and all of the books investigating his death that have been written since would have never been written. This is especially the case, when one considers Villot continued to rile up the press.

He riled up the press by placing Vincenza, Magee and Lorenzi on sabbatical to remove their access—why remove the only witnesses of the Pope's death if the Vatican had nothing to hide?

What's more, he issued a corrective release more confusing than the original release causing the press to expand its investigation.

Speculation? Speculation turns to fact when one considers the papers. What Villot did with the papers John Paul held in his hands.

Villot destroyed them and their content has never been released. Content, which if made public would have brought an end to the most prolific rumor—John Paul held in his hands lists of cardinals to be replaced. Had their content been released it would have brought an end to the rumors and the case would have been closed.

Villot knew they were notes written while the Pope had been bishop of Vittorio Veneto. He knew that since they were not a roster of cardinals to be replaced if he were to release them it would have brought an end to the rumors. Yet, he destroyed them. He wanted the rumors to persist.

Villot acted in the way he did, not so much to protect Mother Church, but to create rumors that would trigger an investigation into the Pope's death—an investigation that was conducted by just about every reporter in Italy which is instrumental to this book.

As we have said, if one considers Karol Wojtyla and Agostino Casaroli as a suspects in John Paul's murder, it would have to have required three murders, as three men had to die in rapid consecutive order to have allowed him to succeed to the secretary of state position—Paul VI, John Paul and Jean Villot.

In retrospect today, one knows, that is exactly what happened.

There is a word for this: coincidence. There is another word for it: murder.

Chapter 34

The Vatican Bank Murders

In the 1970-80s, there were two fronts on which the CIA and the Vatican were confronted by communism as a free democratic society: Italy and Central America. If Italy fell to communism—a redistribution of wealth society—all of Europe would surely follow. If Central America fell to communism—a redistribution of wealth society—all of Latin America would surely follow.

One is not talking here of the Soviet Union.

The Soviet Union was never a free democratic society. It was an autocracy. More so, it was never a communist society in the true Marx-Christ sense of the word. It remained, from beginning to end, very much, a rich and poor society.

The communist movements in Italy and Central America for the most part rejected Soviet intervention. Although the Soviets courted revolutionaries in Central America with offers of arms, the insurgents had no intent of getting out from living under one regime, to end up living under another. The political ideology of the Soviet Union was never a formidable threat to the United States as being a tyranny it had the entire free world against it.

It was in those parts of the world communism was raising its ugly head as the will of the people which was so dangerous to the United States. As Kissinger warned *"Domination by Moscow is not the issue. Communist control of Italy and Central America is the issue. It would have terrible consequences for the United States and it is the number one threat to its national security…"*[1]

The two fronts in the movement toward a free democratic-communist society

346

When the Vatican bank scandal was first conceived, communism had already achieved electoral progress through free elections and the will of the people in Italy. In Central America, the poor were in the midst of a struggle against ruthless dictators to achieve free elections and a redistribution of wealth society—communism.

The Vatican Bank Scandal

Sensationalism and speculation in books and the press have left a smokescreen as to just what one is talking about when one speaks of *The Vatican Bank Scandal.* In a nutshell, the scandal involved the swindling of thousands of European investors out of $1.3 billion.

The money was raised by Banco Ambrosiano 1978-1981 on the guise the investments were guaranteed by the Vatican. Ambrosiano transferred the funds to its Nicaragua and Lima branches which, in turn, deposited it to the credit of the account of the IOR in APSA— the central bank of the Vatican—which, in turn, transferred it under the guise of loans to banks of Panamanian ghost companies and European offshore banks where it disappeared. In the end, the Latin America branches held $1.3 billion in worthless notes.

That most of the funds ended up in Panama suggests it was never intended to be returned to investors. Panama did not join the World Trade Organization until 1998. Monies flowing out of Panama were subject to restrictions its central bank would now and then place on them. Delays of weeks to months to up to a year were not unusual.

The playing field

The Patrimony of the Holy See (APSA), as it still is today, was recognized by the International Monetary Fund as the central bank of the Vatican.[2] All monies passing in and out of the Vatican had to pass through APSA. APSA—not the IOR as widely publicized— was the 'bank' which enabled Ambrosiano branches in Nicaragua and Peru to deposit funds in the IOR without going through the central bank of Italy. Likewise, APSA served as the vehicle for the IOR to get funds out of Italy to the Panamanian and European ghost conglomerates without going through the central bank of Italy.

The Patrimony and some of its representative accounts in 1978:

347

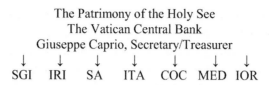

The Patrimony of the Holy See
The Vatican Central Bank
Giuseppe Caprio, Secretary/Treasurer
↓   ↓   ↓   ↓   ↓   ↓   ↓
SGI IRI SA   ITA COC MED IOR

SGI - Society General Immobiliare – controlled Vatican real property including properties outside the Vatican acquired under the Lateran Treaty including the Castle Gandolfo, Gregorian University in Rome and seventy embassies and other property in as many countries. Value considered upwards of $5.4 billion in 1978. The Church's field assets are owed by dioceses and are not owned by the Vatican.

IRI - Institute of Industrial Reconstruction - controlled Vatican interests in private companies reported to be upwards of $3.2 billion in 1978. For example, the Vatican was once the largest shareholder in Alfa Romero and Italian utilities.

SA – Special Administration - controlled Vatican interests in public companies through stock exchanges, reported to be upwards of $2.4 billion in 1978.

ITA - Italmobilaire – controlled its interests in banks. In addition to its substantial interest in Ambrosiano and many other banks, the Vatican had controlling interest in Provinciale Lombarda, Piccolo Credito Bergamasco, Credito Romagnolo, San Germiniano, San Prospero and San Paolo. 1978 value estimated at $3.8 billion.

COC - Vatican Museum – control of inventory/acquisition of Vatican treasures.

MED – control of media interests radio/tv and newspapers. Value prox $.9 billion. Controlling interest in *Il Gazzettino, Corriere delle Alpi* & scores of other papers.

IOR – Institute of Religious Works – funds would be deposited by orders and dioceses in foreign currencies and converted to Vatican lira which at the time traded at par with the Italian lira. It was that it had been set up as a clearing house for international transactions that positioned it to handle the mechanisms of the scandal transactions. Yet, as merely a depository and not a bank per se, it could not function as a bank outside the Vatican. It was that the IOR was the 'business' involved in the scandal transactions that it became known as the 'Vatican Bank.' The legitimate press often refers to it as the 'so-called Vatican bank' recognizing the Patrimony—APSA—as the bank which actually enacted the transactions.

The Institute of Religious Works (IOR), a depository for funds collected by Mother Teresa and other religious orders and 'Peter's Pence' and tourist revenues collected to support the lavish lifestyle of the papacy. Its residue—usually a deficit—was its deposits vs. the cost of maintaining Vatican City and its Rome properties.[3]

Bank of Italy, the central bank of Italy. With the exception of transfers in and out of the Vatican which was within Italy, all funds flowing into or out of Italy had to pass through this bank. It was this loophole in Italian monetary law which led to the bank scandal—the APSA/IOR functioning as an offshore bank in the center of Rome.

The Vatican Bank, in the *'Vatican Bank Scandal,'* the *'Vatican Bank'* refers to the joint activities of IOR and APSA. The IOR—Marcinkus—negotiated, contracted and guaranteed the transactions. APSA—Caprio—handled the money. The IOR was the business and the APSA—the Patrimony—was the bank involved in the scandal. The money flow and those involved in raising the money and those handling the technicalities of the banking transactions:

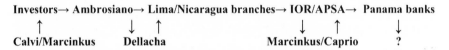

Investors→ Ambrosiano→ Lima/Nicaragua branches→ IOR/APSA→ Panama banks

Calvi/Marcinkus   Dellacha   Marcinkus/Caprio   ?

The Catholic Bank of Italy, Italy's largest bank had branches operating in every parish. Although they operated under the auspices of the Vatican, they were owned by the respective archdioceses.

Banco Ambrosiano, one of Italy's largest banks and Central America's largest foreign bank. 'Banco' in Italian = 'bench.' 'Banca' in Italian = 'bank.' 'Banco' in Spanish/Portuguese = 'bank.' Except for Ambrosiano, Italian banks are prefixed 'Banca.' It was founded as an international bank to service the huge Catholic Latin American population making it the natural partner of the Vatican.

Ambrosiano Group Banco Comercial, Ambrosiano Nicaragua based branch. Ambrosiano would raise money from unsuspecting investors and transfer it to this branch which in turn would deposit it in APSA/IOR which would transfer it—under the guise of loans—to Panamanian and European ghost companies where it disappeared.

Banco Ambrosiano Andino, in 1979, *left wing* Sandinistas took over Nicaragua and seized the Ambrosiano branch there forcing it to establish Ambrosiano Andino in Lima to handle future bank scandal transactions—deposits to the Vatican bank.

Players inside the Vatican

Giovanni Benelli, Florence Archbishop, As Nunciature Auditor to Latin America (1960-64) and as Substitute for General Affairs (1960-77) under Paul VI he had been involved in offshore Vatican banking activities for many years. [4] With Cardinal Vagnozzi he headed up the audit of the Vatican bank ordered by John Paul I.

Giuseppe Caprio, Substitute for General Affairs (1977-1981).[4] As Secretary/Treasurer of the Patrimony (APSA),[4] the central bank of the Vatican, he handled the technicalities of the transfers from the IOR account to the ghost companies where it disappeared.

Agostino Casaroli, Vatican Foreign Minister. The first 'bank scandal' deposit in the IOR account in APSA took place a week after he became Secretary of State. During the period of the bank scandal transactions, both the IOR and APSA operated under the office of the Secretary of State. After the scandal broke in the courts in 1981, the reporting status of IOR was changed directly to the Pope.[4]

Pericle Felici, Prefect of the Tribunal of the Apostolic Signatura and legal counsel to the papacy.[4] That he had served as legal counsel for banking activities under Paul VI and had been removed as legal counsel for banking activities under John Paul II made this astute lawyer suspicious which caused him to launch his own investigation of goings on in the Patrimony—the central bank of the Vatican.

Paul Marcinkus, President of the Institute of Religious Works. [4]

Jean Villot, He held the dual positions of Secretary of State and President of the Patrimony of the Holy See under Paul VI.[4]

Players outside the Vatican

Giulio Andreotti, political ally of Wojtyla, Casaroli, Caprio, Calvi, Gelli and Portillo. He was Italian prime minster in 1978 when the ideology which resulted in the bank scandal was conceived.

Roberto Calvi, President of Banco Ambrosiano a major investor in Central America which had in the 1970s funneled huge amounts to its dictators to suppress the *revolution of the poor.*

Graziella Corrocher, private secretary and bookkeeper of the scandal transactions and close confidant of Roberto Calvi.

Giuseppe Dellacha, Banco Ambrosiano executive who handled the technicalities of the transactions from Ambrosiano through its Nicaraguan and Lima Ambrosiano branches to the IOR/APSA.

Licio Gelli, Grand Master of P2. He was a major investor in Latin America, and had funneled tens of millions to its dictators to suppress the *revolution of the poor* to protect his interests there.

Alvaro de Portillo, Primate of Opus Dei which was a substantial investor in Central America, and had in the 1970s funneled millions to its dictators to suppress the *revolution of the poor.*

Michele Sindona, His first break came in 1957 when he won the favor of the Mafia Gambino family and managed its offshore heroin revenues. He educated the Vatican in offshore banking. In alliance with Ambrosiano, he was a major investor in Central America, and had in the 1970s funneled tens of millions to its dictators to suppress the *revolution of the poor* to protect his interests there.

Shady deals under Paul VI

One could write a book about the shady deals under Paul VI—many have—but they have very little to do with what broke in the press as *The Great Vatican Bank Scandal* in 1982.

Although the shady transactions under Paul involved some of the same people and established the international monetary mechanisms involved in the rip off of European investors which took place under John Paul II, they had nothing to do with the scandal per se.

To believe any of the transactions involved in the bank scandal which broke in 1982 occurred under Paul VI (1963-78) is to believe it took four years for highly competent investment houses to realize they had been ripped off. This is just not how the real world works.

There were one hundred and forty plaintiffs representing tens of thousands of investors involved in the courts that tried the scandal. To believe not one of them sensed something was wrong for more than four years does not pass the lowest hurdle of common sense.

To see this more clearly one must define precisely what one is talking about when one speaks of *The Great Vatican Bank Scandal.*

The scandal involved a rip off of $1.3 billion ($15 billion in today's dollars) from European investors in the period 1978-1982. Though it was the *straw that broke the camel's back,* the Vatican bank scandal was only a part of a much larger $3.5 billion 'black hole' in Banco Ambrosiano which brought it under in 1982.

Except for the $1.3 billion, most of the $3.5 billion shortfall had been built up in the 1970s when Roberto Calvi over-valued shares in his banks and acquired unsecured investments. Yet, there were some events under Paul VI that set the stage for the Vatican bank scandal--$1.3 billion—which took place under the reign of John Paul II.

For example, in 1969, Michele Sindona was recommended by the Gambino family to Giuseppe Caprio—a cousin in the family who had just been named Secretary/Treasurer of the Patrimony—APSA. Caprio hired Sindona to school the Vatican in offshore transactions. Because of the link of these two to the most powerful Mafia family in Italy, it was rumored the Vatican was laundering drug money.[5]

Dirty money would flow from eastern sources to the Vatican and then to Bellatrix and be returned as clean money from the Vatican to the account of the Gambino family in Ambrosiano in Italy. Yet, that the Vatican laundered drug money was rumor and never proved.

Another shady incident occurred in August 1971. Ambrosiano acquired a controlling interest in the Banca Cattolica del Veneto, the Catholic Bank of Venice, for $46.5 million—the price considered low as the Venice bank had assets of $700 million at the time.[6]

During the 1970s, Banco Ambrosiano acquired interests in other branches of the Catholic Bank of Italy at what were arguably low prices. Yet, these involved share-for-share exchanges in which the Vatican became the largest stockholder in Ambrosiano.

In 1972, Sindona, through the intercession of President Nixon, acquired controlling interest in the Franklin National Bank on Long Island. Two years later it collapsed. The courts determined Sindona siphoned off large sums of the bank's money to Somoza and other dictators in Central America to suppress the *revolution of the poor* there—the reason for Nixon's involvement. The Patrimony of the Holy See took a $40 million hit when the Franklin Bank went under to the extent IOR had guaranteed the transactions.[7]

In 1975, Paul Marcinkus became a board member of Ambrosiano Overseas Limited—a Nassau branch of Ambrosiano which began to route transactions through IOR/APSA to get them out of Italy.[8]

Courts determined, in a single transaction in 1978, $184 million was transferred from Gelli's account in Ambrosiano through Panama based Bellatrix earmarked for political purposes in Central America.[9]

In another transaction, Ambrosiano transferred funds from Gelli's account to Bellatrix which bought shares in a Rothschild bank. Calvi manipulated the value of the shares which resulted in a $142 million swell in Ambrosiano and an offsetting deflation in Rothschild.[10]

Courts determined Calvi siphoned off the Ambrosiano 'swell' to the dictator Somoza in Nicaragua and ruling regimes in El Salvador and Guatemala to suppress the *revolution of the poor*. It was this deal among others that caused some to believe Rothschild directors had been involved in the Calvi murder—never proved in the courts.[10]

Courts many times demonstrated that Opus Dei members Roberto Calvi, Licio Gelli, Alvaro de Portillo and Michele Sindona poured millions through shrouded activities into suppression of *revolution of the poor* in Central America in the 1970s. Being among its largest investors, stability of the region was vital to their interests.

Though these and other shady transactions that accounted for the lion's share of the $3.5 billion 'black hole' in Ambrosiano in 1982 took place under Paul VI, the Vatican had not been involved in them other than to guarantee some of them in exchange for commissions.

By the time Paul VI went to meet his Maker in 1978, the Vatican had become an important player in 'shady' international markets—borrowing, lending and taking in rich commissions as it went along.

The apples from the oranges

Yet, to understand *The Great Vatican Bank Scandal* one must first separate the apples from the oranges.

Whereas it is true the international mechanisms set up by Sindona in the 1970s were the same ones which eventually handled the bank scandal transactions, buying shares in offshore banks like Franklin National Bank and shady dealings in the Bahamas had nothing to do with swindling European investors out of hundreds of millions of dollars which resulted in the Vatican bank scandal a decade later.

To the extent the exchange of shares between Ambrosiano and the Catholic Bank artificially overvalued shares in Ambrosiano this would have been a part of the overall $3.5 billion 'black hole' found in Ambrosiano in the bankruptcy proceedings of 1982. Yet, they had nothing to do with the $1.3 billion swindling of European investors one speaks of when one speaks of *The Great Vatican Bank Scandal.*

Keep in mind, there was nothing illegal or immoral guaranteeing transactions of Ambrosiano. It was a matter of good business. As the principal owner of Ambrosiano, the Vatican was protecting its own interests. What's more, it earned rich commissions over the years which much more than outweighed the multi-million dollar hits it would take now and then when a deal went sour. As Paul Marcinkus once said, *"You can't run the Church on Hail Marys."*

Yet, after John Paul I was found dead, the Vatican would become involved in transactions so shady that all the king's men and all the king's horses have not been able to put them back together again.

The game

Thousands of books and articles written on this subject have left the reader engulfed in mystery as to what it was all about and the writer the expert as to what it was all about. The details of the bank scandal presented in banker-mumbo-jumbo fashion all mixed up.

Yet, one doesn't have to be a world-class banker to understand *The Great Vatican Bank Scandal*. One has to do not much more than view the events in the order in which they occurred.

Here for the first time, are all the events surrounding the bank scandal in the chronological order in which they occurred.

The scandal began and ended under the reign of John Paul II. [11]

It involved the raising of money from unsuspecting investors 1978-1981 on the promise their investments were guaranteed by the Vatican. By 1982, it culminated in a $1.285 billion shortfall which was part of a much larger $3.5 billion shortfall which brought down one of Europe's biggest banks, Banco Ambrosiano. [11]

The Vatican Banking Organization

Positions, incumbents and interrelationships[4] of those involved in Vatican banking activities when the game began in the fall of 1978.[4]

← = reporting status when John Paul II was elected

John Paul II ←Prefect Tribunal of the Apostolic Signatura   Cardinal Pericle Felici
↑
Secretary of State Cardinal Jean Villot ← Substitute for General Affairs   Caprio
↑
Prefect of Economic Affairs   Cardinal Egidio Vagnozzi
↑
President Administration of the Patrimony of the Holy See - APSA   Jean Villot
↑
Secretary/Treasurer of the Patrimony - APSA   Bishop Giuseppe Caprio
↑
President Institute of Religious Works - IOR   Bishop Paul Marcinkus

Concerning the mechanics of the bank scandal transactions two of these officers would have been directly involved—Paul Marcinkus and Giuseppe Caprio. Though it was possible for Marcinkus to deposit money in the IOR account, only Caprio could get it into the international market through the Patrimony—the central bank of the Vatican. None of the transactions could have taken place without the joint concurrence of Marcinkus—the man who ran the business—and Caprio—the man who ran the bank. When we speak of the bank scandal transactions we are speaking of the actions of these two men and, of course, Roberto Calvi and Giuseppe Dellacha who handled the technicalities of the related transactions within Ambrosiano.

Chronology of events

On August 27, 1978 John Paul I rose to the papacy.

On September 5, 1978, Metropolitan Nikodim—a pawn of the KGB—was led into the Pope's private study. A few minutes later he dropped dead after sipping coffee. Rumors of poison spread based on the supposition the CIA suspected the Pope was seeking Soviet arms for his *revolution of the poor* in El Salvador.

On September 5, 1978, CIA affiliate Cardinal Cody accompanied Cardinal Wojtyla to Krakow where they spent a week together. [12]

On September 13, 1978, the Polish cardinal Karol Wojtyla met with bishops Agostino Casaroli and Giuseppe Caprio in Genoa.

On September 24, 1978, John Paul changed the theme of the upcoming Puebla Conference in Mexico from *Liberation Theology* to *Liberation of the Poor* and announced he would preside over it. He praised those struggling for a better world in Central America. [13]

On September 27, 1978 John Paul, in a worldwide televised audience established the scope of his papacy, *"It is the inalienable right of no man to accumulate wealth beyond the necessary while other men starve to death because they have nothing."*

On the morning of September 29, 1978 John Paul was dead.

On October 17, 1978, John Paul II rose to the papacy. In one of his first public statements he condemned *Liberation Theology*. He warned radical priests and nuns—the principal inspirers of guerillas in Central America—to cease their support of the revolution.[14]

On October 30, 1978, the Pope removed Pericle Felici as legal counsel to the Patrimony restricting the scope of the Tribunal of the

Apostolic Signatura to canon law—a confusing move as Felici was a brilliant lawyer well versed in international monetary law.[15]

In November 1978, Calvi began raising money from investors on the promise their investments were guaranteed by the IOR. In 1982-84, Italian courts determined the first 'scandal' investment claimed by a plaintiff dated back to November 7, 1978.[16]

In mid-February 1979, Jean Villot, fell ill and died in early March of circumstances similar to those of Paul VI a few months earlier. Each man, vibrant and on the job, suddenly spiraled downward and three weeks later was dead. In the late stages, both men developed bladder infections from which they seemed to have recovered when on the last day they developed a sudden acute respiratory condition and died a few hours later. Unlike Paul's case, the younger Villot's death drew suspicions of foul play in local newspapers. [17]

Giuseppe Caprio had the unique privilege of having been the only person to have witnessed the deaths of both Paul VI and Jean Villot. In the case of Villot, Caprio had been the only witness. [18]

The Vatican bank scandal could not have taken place as long as Villot remained President of the Patrimony of the Holy See.

On April 28, 1979, Agostino Casaroli replaced Villot as Secretary of State and Giuseppe Caprio replaced Villot as President of the Patrimony of the Holy See—the Vatican's central bank. [19]

Eduardo Somalo was named Substitute for General Affairs. This position which had played a major role in banking activities under Paul VI in the persons of Giovanni Benelli and Giuseppe Caprio ceased to be involved in banking. Somalo had no interest in financial matters. His expertise was limited to doctrine. He would eventually accede to Prefect of the Congregation of Divine Worship.

At this early stage—before the Vatican bank would make its first move in what would eventually culminate in the bank scandal—John Paul II had materially revamped his banking organization.[4]

John Paul II
↑
Secretary of State Agostino Casaroli
↑
Prefect of Economic Affairs of the Holy See   Cardinal Egidio Vagnozzi
↑
President/Treasurer of the Patrimony – APSA   Bishop Giuseppe Caprio
↑
President of the Institute of Religious Works   Bishop Paul Marcinkus

Because there were thousands of legitimate transactions going on between Banco Ambrosiano and the Patrimony and the Catholic Bank of Italy at about the same time, the courts could not determine precisely when the first deposit in the Patrimony related to the bank scandal took place. They did determine the first significant deposit of 2.3 billion lire—about $3 million—took place on May 9, 1979. It was rapidly followed by others of millions of dollars each.[20]

Although the Prefect of Economic Affairs does not normally get involved in the day-to-day goings on in the dozen or so departments that report to his office, it became obvious Cardinal Vagnozzi was becoming aware of the surreptitious happenings going on around him when in mid-June 1979 he jokingly told a reporter, *"If one were to engage the entire armies of the CIA, the KGB and Interpol combined they would never be able to figure out how much money is involved here or where it is going."*[21]

The following week, June 30, 1979, he was made Chamberlain (Treasurer) of the College of Cardinals—a strange move as the incumbent Gabriel-Marie Garrone had not been in the job a year. Vagnozzi's office was moved from the Patrimony on the ground floor of the Papal Palace to the Government Palace where he became engulfed in managing properties of a hundred plus cardinals.[22]

Though he continued to retain his title as Prefect of Economic Affairs, he was rarely seen in the Patrimony again until late in 1980 in connection with an audit of the bank's records. Though the bank traditionally closed its books at the end of each calendar year, since the time of Paul VI, the Prefect personally conducted an audit every fourth year; audits had been performed in 1968, 1972 and 1976.

At about this same time in mid-1979, on the other side of the world, the Sandinista Liberation Front—a socialist-communist party which had grown up out of Paul's principle of *Liberation Theology* years earlier overthrew the ruthless Somoza regime in Nicaragua.[23]

In September 1979 the central bank of Nicaragua froze all money leaving the country. It also froze assets including manufacturing facilities and bank holdings of anti-revolutionary factions who had supported Somoza—Banco Ambrosiano was among them.[24]

On October 11, 1979, Ambrosiano opened a branch in Lima, Peru. From this point on the money was deposited in the IOR/APSA by the Lima branch and then loaned to the ghost affiliates.[25]

On October 16, 1979—a year to the day after John Paul II took office—the Lima branch made its first time deposits totaling $134.3 million in IOR/APSA which it transferred under the guise of a 'loan' to a Panamanian ghost company, United Trading Corporation.[26]

In mid-December, Cardinal Vagnozzi returned to the Patrimony on the ground floor of the Papal Palace to conduct the audit required every fourth year of APSA which included the IOR depository.

On the morning of December 26, 1980, Vagnozzi was found dead on the floor of his Vatican apartment.

It is not unusual for the Vatican not to disclose cause of death at the time of death. Yet, normally a few months afterwards for official reasons it proclaims the deceased died of a 'heart attack' or 'cancer' or... In Vagnozzi's case cause of death has never been disclosed.[27]

On January 30, 1981, Giuseppe Caprio was promoted to Prefect of Economic Affairs—Chief Financial Officer of the Church.[28]

On the same day, Secretary of State Casaroli replaced Vagnozzi as President of the Patrimony of the Holy See. One can only surmise this was to avoid anyone else learning of the scandal transactions.[28]

At this point, the transactions which would eventually culminate in the bank scandal were privy to only four men in the Vatican: John Paul II, Casaroli, Caprio and Marcinkus.[4]

Pope   John Paul II

↑

Secretary of State   Cardinal Agostino Casaroli

↑

Prefect of Economic Affairs of the Holy See   Cardinal Giuseppe Caprio

↑

President/Treasurer of the Patrimony - APSA   Cardinal Agostino Casaroli

↑

President of the Institute of Religious Works - IOR   Bishop Paul Marcinkus

Threads begin to unravel

In January 1981, the deposits of the Ambrosiano Latin American branches in the Vatican bank which in turn were transferred to the Panamanian ghost companies and European 'offshore' ghost companies had reached $1.2 billion of the $1.3 billion figure one speaks of when one says *The Great Vatican Bank Scandal.*

On March 17, 1981, police raided Licio Gelli's villa at Arezzo. In addition to finding a list of 962 members of P2, they discovered evidence Roberto Calvi had transferred hundreds of millions of dollars extracted from unsuspecting investors through the Vatican bank to Panamanian ghost companies in Central America.[29]

A few months later, the scandal transactions, as determined by the courts which tried the Ambrosiano downfall, had come to an end.

Deposits from the IOR/APSA to ghost affiliates
Total 1,285 million

Year		1979			1980			1981		
Quarter	2nd	3rd	4th	1st	2nd	3rd	4th	1st	2nd	3rd
	$156	$192	$298	$117	$178	$116	$98	$93	$37	$0

After a lengthy trial which persisted into the following year, Calvi was convicted of bank fraud and given four years and released on appeal. During the trial he was distraught and made no effort to defend himself. Asked by a reporter why he didn't defend himself, Calvi answered, *"I am in the service of someone on the other side of the wall."*[30] In Rome *'the other side of the wall'* is the Vatican.

During the Calvi trial, on September 26, 1981, for the first time in the history of the Church, a pope shed his civil title. John Paul II made Marcinkus President of the Sovereign State of the Vatican.[31]

This changed IOR's reporting status directly to the Pope. This has never been reversed. Today, the IOR no longer reports to the Prefect of Economic Affairs.

On November 25, 1981, Joseph Ratzinger was moved to the Vatican as Prefect of the Congregation of the Faith.[32] His office and that of Marcinkus——IOR——shared the Palace of the Holy Office.

Back in 1978, when the CIA and Opus Dei had wiggled their candidate into the top job, they felt secure for twenty-five years as the Polish Cardinal was only fifty-eight when elected.

In 1981, with the attempt on the Pope's life, assassination or even accident became a possibility. The CIA/Opus Dei coalition needed a backup on board should anything happen to the Polish Pope.

As the most powerful ecclesiastical voice in the Catholic world, Ratzinger masterminded the anti-*Liberation Theology* crusade and removed it from everyday life in Latin America to the history books.

Being a master of deceit, Ratzinger put together a razzle-dazzle platform designed to convince the poor of Latin America the concept of *Liberation Theology* was not only in conflict with the teachings of the Church—some children are entitled to more—but its promise of redemption was actually a restriction of opportunity for the poor.

By the end of the twentieth century he had silenced Leonardo Buff and other champions of *Liberation Theology* often referring to them as Marxists. In 2005, he added it to the vow required of candidates for the *'red cap,' 'I pledge to suppress the role of women in the Church, homosexuals, contraception, Liberation Theology...'*

Ratzinger took on the job of chief of propaganda in the Vatican not only in its war against *revolution of the poor* in Central America, but against *revolution of the poor* in Italy and Europe and anywhere else communism happened to raise its ugly head.

Regardless, Cardinal **Vagnozzi**'s death had left only two outside the Vatican banking inner circle who might have known of the *'shady deals'*—Cardinal Felici and his closest friend Cardinal Benelli. A blend of newspaper reportings took care of both of them.

"Cardinal Giovanni Benelli, once a leading candidate for the papacy, died two hours after he was removed from the hospital to his home yesterday afternoon. His death comes as a surprise a day after his doctor told reporters '...the cardinal is making good progress for recovery and should be released soon.'[33]

When criticized for having moved the cardinal, sources in the Vatican said Benelli, himself, requested he be removed from life support and returned to his residence. Yet, when asked, ambulance attendants said the cardinal was unconscious when moved.

Cardinal Secretary of State Agostino Casaroli—who happened to be in Florence—took immediate charge of the body and said there would be a three hour viewing of the coffin this morning in the Basilica di Santa Maria del Fiore. Following a funeral mass, Benelli will be interred beneath the floor of the cathedral this afternoon.

Factions in the Vatican complained as to why Benelli would not lie in state in the Vatican where he had served for ten years and was a friend of many of the Curia cardinals. Local sources complained of the brevity of the viewing, as it was customary bishops be viewed for three to five days to allow the congregation to pay respects.

The sixty year old Benelli had been in the process of lining up votes against the ratification the Prelature of Opus Dei. He told reporters just yesterday, he was anxious to get back to work.

360

Following the death of John Paul I in 1978, Benelli and Felici rose up as enemies of Opus Dei, so much so, they were labeled by the press, 'A twin-engine bomber headed for Monti Parioli.' Opus Dei headquarters is in the posh Monti Parioli district of Rome.

This past March, the bomber lost one of its engines when Felici— having just returned from Panama—presided over the Marian Congress. The cardinal had finished the consecration of the Mass and was in the midst of his sermon when he suddenly grasped his head and fell dead onto the podium.[34]

At the time of his death, the Vatican's chief legal authority, Felici was involved in investigating recent allegations that the coalition of Opus Dei and the Masonic lodge P2 had been involved in what has since exploded in the press as the Great Vatican Bank Scandal.

The twin-engine bomber headed for Monti Parioli is down. There are no survivors..."[35]

If Opus Dei had been brought to trial for the murder of these two men, any court would acquit the cult on the grounds of self-defense.

In the following spring when the extent of the bank scandal first became known, Marcinkus was harassed by reporters as to how this could happen. He slipped, *"I have told John Paul, if we continue to sweep things under the rug we will eventually trip over it."*[36]

Marcinkus became a prisoner in the Vatican. He was moved from his Rome apartment to the Vatican and was not allowed to go out of its gates until after the scandal was resolved in 1984. This not only cut him off from reporters, it protected him from being arrested by Italian authorities and brought to trial as a witness in the scandal.

On June 5, 1982, Roberto Calvi wrote a letter to John Paul II warning him of the imminent collapse of Ambrosiano.

The letter had the tone of *'every man for himself.'* Calvi warned in a threatening fashion, the Pope would have to resign unless he satisfied the demands of the investors.

A copy of the letter submitted as evidence in Italian court trials and widely published survives as compelling evidence Wojtyla and those supporting his papacy had involved Calvi in the conspiracy which led to the Vatican bank scandal—that Calvi had been assured if the 'deal' was uncovered prematurely, he would be made whole.[37]

Events which followed on the heels of Calvi's letter imply *right wing* forces in the United States, specifically the CIA, had been involved in the scheme from the start—the 'deal' had been a stop-gap measure in which the Vatican would finance the Contras through the Carter years. The CIA would step in and satisfy the debt before it went sour—consistent with that the CIA had joined *right wing* factions in the Church in electing John Paul II. Reagan was now president and had already taken up the cause for the Contras. It makes sense the Pope would have his hand out for the $1.3 billion.

The Holy Alliance

Two days later, on June 7, 1982, *Air Force One* landed in Rome.

For security reasons, the president's visit had been unannounced. Reagan had been critically wounded in an attempt the previous year and the Pope, himself, had survived an attempt on his life at about the same time. John Paul II and Ronald Reagan were sequestered behind closed doors in the Pope's private study for hours on the guise they were discussing Polish Solidarity. [38]

A president cannot pick up a phone and talk to a pope privately. White House phones are taped and there is no assurance they cannot be tapped on either end. The only way they can be guaranteed privacy is in person. Polish Solidarity—true of a myriad of other issues—could have been handled by phone. In fact, in its case, it could have been handled before worldwide television cameras.

No one knows what this president and pope talked about that day. What one does know it was not Solidarity or any other issue which could have been handled by phone or emissaries.

Some claim it was in this meeting the *Holy Alliance* was formed. The Pope controlled twenty percent of the votes in the United States where presidential elections are decided by one or two percentage points. John Paul II would support the Reagan-Bush campaigns by attacking their opponents. In exchange, Reagan/Bush would appoint a wave of practicing Roman Catholics to the Supreme Court. [39]

Yet, the timing of Reagan's visit to the precise moment in history the collapse of Ambrosiano became imminent and investigations by the courts were looming on the horizon is compelling, if not absolute proof, it had to do with the bank scandal.

No one knows what this president and pope talked about that day. Yet, what was taking place on the floor below tells one that.

Casaroli, Caprio and Marcinkus were meeting with United States Secretary of State Alexander Haig, CIA Director William J. Casey and National Security Advisor William P. Clark.[40]

Let us connect some dots here.

Alexander Haig had been NATO Commander (1974-79) during which time Giulio Andreotti's document *The Parallel SID* disclosed the CIA, NATO (Gladio) and Italian Intelligence had conspired in the terrorist activities in the 1970s in Italy intended to turn the mindset of the Italian people against communism. To the extent the CIA had been involved in the murders of Aldo Moro, Paul VI, John Paul I and some others we have talked of, Haig would have been the United States official intervening between the CIA and P2.[41]

Before being named to the NATO post, Haig, as Nixon's Chief of Staff, had met with Licio Gelli of the fascist P2 lodge conveying American funds to Gelli's plans for a new Italy. Gelli had the unique distinction of having served under all three fascist dictators. He had served as an Intelligence officer in Hitler's SS Guard, as a black coat under Mussolini and served in Franco's cabinet in Spain.[42]

William J. Casey was the same William J. Casey who would mastermind the Iran-Contra Affair just a few years later. [43]

William P. Clark was a former seminarian and a devout member of Opus Dei. In retirement, he built a chapel on his ranch. A statue of Saint Jose Maria Escriva adorns its altar.[44]

Nevertheless, this meeting—its participants widely named in the press—involved the three Vatican principals in the bank scandal and the three United States principals involved in the Contra war. This seems to confirm the president's trip had to do with the bank scandal as it related to the Contras in Central America. He did not want the bank scandal to break in the press as the Vatican-Contra Affair.

If this is true, and as the events of the time seem to say it is true, the $1.3 billion which disappeared in Central America had gone to the Contras. The Vatican had supported the Contras during the time (1979-1981) the American President Carter would not support them.

It makes sense *right wing* forces in the United States, particularly in the CIA, had been involved in the scheme to begin with. After all, they had made possible Karol Wojtyla's rise to the top. It makes all the sense in the world the Pope had his hand out for the $1.3 billion.

Reagan was now president and had already enticed congress to support the Contras. Though he did not give him the $1.3 billion, it may have been prearranged he would funnel through the CIA the $241 million which John Paul II would eventually satisfy his 'moral' obligation in connection with the scandal in 1984.

Regardless, a few days later, June 18, 1982, is the scene alleged by the film *Godfather III* to have occurred on the night John Paul I died four years earlier. Calvi had broken bail and left Italy. He was found hanging from a scaffold under Blackfriars Bridge in London.[45]

On the same morning, June 18, 1982, pedestrians found the body of Calvi's secretary and closest confidant—whatever he knew, she knew—Graziella Corrocher, splattered on the sidewalk beneath the fourth floor window of her office in Milan. Corrocher left a note in her typewriter Calvi should be *"twice cursed for the damage he did to the bank and its employees."* Although police were unable to determine who typed the note, they did determine it had been typed on another typewriter and then placed in her typewriter.[46]

The scandal broke on August 6, 1982 when Banco Ambrosiano filed bankruptcy.[47] Of its $3.5 billion 'black hole,' $1.285 billion was traced to money raised by Calvi from European investors which was funneled by Ambrosiano's Nicaraguan and Lima branches through IOR/APSA to ghost companies where it disappeared.[48]

On August 23, 1982, the Vatican announced John Paul II had *'authorized'* Opus Dei a Prelature of the Holy See effective August 5, 1982 immunizing its officers from Italian courts. The timing of the Prelature authorization to the day before the bank's collapse is compelling evidence the Pope knew officers of Opus Dei had been involved in the fraudulent deception of European investors—*The Great Vatican Bank Scandal*—and the murders surrounding it.[49]

The Pope was attempting to immunize those outside the Vatican including Andreotti, Calvi, Portillo and Gelli from Italian courts as they were known to be prominent members of the cult. He could not have been trying to protect those in the Vatican including himself, Casaroli, Caprio or Marcinkus as they were already immunized from the courts by the sovereignty of the Vatican via the Lateran Treaty.

On October 2, 1982, Giuseppe Dellacha, the Ambrosiano officer who handled the technicalities of the transactions from Ambrosiano to IOR/APSA was found sprawled across the sidewalk beneath his fifth floor window of Banco Ambrosiano in Milan.[50]

On October 12, 1982, capitalizing on the fact few cardinals spoke out in favor of the Opus Dei Prelature, Cardinal Benelli of Florence called for its ratification by the College of Cardinals setting the date for November 1, 1982.[51] As already pointed out, the sixty year old was in the midst of lining up votes against its ratification when he succumbed to a sudden 'heart attack' on October 26, 1982.[52] The Prelature was ratified by the College on November 28, 1982.[53]

By a remarkable coincidence, while the courts were in the midst of unraveling the mystery of the scandal the only persons still alive who had been involved in the scandal transactions occupied the four most powerful positions in the Roman Catholic world.[54]

All others, both inside and outside the Vatican, who could have known of the scandal transactions were dead.

By province of a more remarkable coincidence three of these had met in Genoa midway through the 33-day Pope's papacy—as we have said not necessary to conspiracy as such a matter could have been handled by phone or emissaries.

Yet, by province of even a more far reaching coincidence, two of these were 'sound asleep' in the Papal Palace the night of September 28, 1978 when John Paul I met his Maker.

John Paul II ← Paul Marcinkus   President of the Sovereign State of the Vatican
↑
Agostino Casaroli   Secretary of State and President of the Vatican bank
↑
Giuseppe Caprio   Prefect of Economic Affairs of the Holy See

~~Jean Villot~~	dead
~~Egidio Vagnozzi~~	dead
~~Pericle Felici~~	dead
~~Giovanni Benelli~~	dead
~~Roberto Calvi~~	dead
~~Graziella Corrocher~~	dead
~~Giuseppe Dellacha~~	dead

On the heels of court proceedings, in July 1984, John Paul II paid European investors $241 million through the Italian courts.[55]

1 *TIME* '*What if Communists Win a Role?*' 26 Apr 76
2 *The Patrimony of the Holy See Catholic Encyclopedia or Wikipedia*
3 *The IOR* or the so-called *Vatican Bank, Catholic Encyclopedia* 2nd edition or *Wikipedia*
4 Incumbents, descriptions and interrelationships of Vatican positions are taken from the *Catholic Encyclopedia 2nd Edition. Wikipedia* is fairly accurate as it is sourced from the *Encyclopedia*
5 *L'Osservatore* 19 Oct 69 *La Stampa* 23 Dec 69
6 *Il Gazzettino* 17 Aug 71 The decree of 'control' never disclosed. Third parties were involved

7 *Washington Post* 22 Feb 75

8 *La Repubblica* 17 Oct 75

9 *Washington Post* 15 Sep 78

10 *TIME-EUROPE* Oct 82

11 *TIME Europe* 82-84

12 *Malopolska Silesia* 7 Sep 78

13 *L Osservatore Romano* 24 Sep 78

14 *L Osservatore Romano* 19 Oct 78

15 It is not unusual for a pope to change the authority of a Curia post. E.g. in 2002 Joseph Ratzinger became Dean of the College of Cardinals and was elevated above the Secretary of State. The Dean of the College under Paul VI had been an honorary position assigned to the oldest cardinal.

16*TIME-EUROPE* 82-84

17 *NY Times* 10 Mar 79 *'Jean Villot'*

18 *NY Times* 16 Oct 05 *'Giuseppe Caprio'*

19 *L Osservatore Romano* 30 Apr 79 - *La Repubblica* 1 May 79

20 *TIME-EUROPE* 82-84

21 *La Repubblica* 17 Jun 79

22 *L Osservatore Romano* 1 Jul 79 *La Repubblica* 3 Jul 79

23 *NY Times* 20 Jul 79

24 *NY Times* 29 Sep 79

25 *La Repubblica* 14 Oct 79

26 *Wall Street Journal* 27 Apr 87

27*NY Times* 30 Dec 80 See *Catholic Encyclopedia Second Edition* for cause of death

28 *L Osservatore Romano* 31 Jan 81

29 *La Repubblica* 19 Mar 81

30 *La Repubblica* 25 May 82

31 *L Osservatore Romano*27 Sep 81

32 *L Osservatore Romano*26 Nov 81

33 There are a number of toxins which concealed in food or drink can induce 'heart attack' in a healthy person. See *Deadly Doses* Serita Stevens or Internet or library medical dictionaries.

34 The *Catholic Encyclopedia*, official record of the Church, records Felici's death as *"sudden and unexplained."* Methothianate mixed with a bit of alcohol results in a fatal brain hemorrhage about a half-hour after ingested—the time that had elapsed after drinking the wine in the consecration of the Mass. Canon law decrees sacramental wine must be alcoholic, a priest cannot substitute grape juice.

35 Composite of *NY Times, Washington Post, The Times- London, La Repubblica* 27 Oct 82

36 *La Repubblica* 30 Apr 82

37*TIME-EUROPE* 82-84

38 *L Osservatore Romano La Repubblica NY Times Washington Post The Times* 8 Jun 82

39 United States Supreme Court incumbents – see chapter *The Murder of Aldo Moro*

40 *L Osservatore Romano La Repubblica NY Times Washington Post The Times* 8 Jun 82

41 *Wikipedia* 'Alexander Haig' & see chapter *The Murder of Aldo Moro*

42*Wikipedia* & biographies of Licio Gelli

43*Wikipedia* & biographies of William J. Casey. Also, see Iran-Contra Affair

44*Wikipedia* & biographies of William P. Clark

45 *NY Times* 19 Jun 82

46 *La Repubblica* 24 Jun 82

47 *La Repubblica* 7 Aug 82

48 *TIME-EUROPE* 82-84

49 *L Osservatore Romano* 24 Aug 82 The official date of the Prelature is 28 Nov82 when the College ratified it. But, the legal date remains 5 Aug 82 the day John Paul II authorized it.

50 *La Repubblica* 3 Oct 82

51 *La Repubblica* 13 Oct 82

52 *NY Times* 27 Oct 82

53 *NY Times* 29 Nov 82

54 There were other rank and file personnel who were aware of the transactions but, as we will prove in the following chapter, they were not aware of their end purpose.

48 *TIME-EUROPE* 82-84

Chapter 35

The Vatican-Contra Affair

How is it possible the same constituency of cardinals elected a liberal in one election and just a few weeks later elected a conservative?

Nothing better demonstrates how the CIA functions independent of the president and congress than was its role in the Contra war.

Italian courts investigating the bank scandal determined that after President Carter cut off aid to the ruling juntas in Central America, the CIA began filtering money to the Contras through Ambrosiano.[1]

Another Italian court investigating the bank scandal disclosed the CIA circumvented presidential order when it funneled millions to the Contras after Carter cut off military assistance to the ruthless dictator Somoza for human rights violations in 1978.[2]

Still another tribunal investigating the scandal disclosed the CIA circumvented presidential order when it moved arms and money to General Romeo Garcia in Guatemala and Paz Garcia in Honduras after Carter cut off support to these ruling regimes.[3]

Conversely, presidents have often used the CIA as a vehicle to bypass congressional denial of funding of causes a president sees fit.

As world opinion turned against American intervention in Central America in the eighties, congress began to limit aid to the Contras in the war-torn countries of Nicaragua, Honduras, El Salvador and Guatemala and in December 1982 cut it off completely.

This set the stage for the Iran-Contra Affair in which Reagan by-passed the congressional freeze on aid to the Contras and directed the CIA to sell arms to Iran and transfer proceeds to the Contras to suppress the *revolution of the poor* in Central America. Reagan's popularity and advancing age saved him from impeachment. When questioned about the affair, he told Congress, *"I don't remember."*[4]

What happened to the $1.3 billion?

We have already set forth the supposition the $1.3 billion went to support the Contras in their suppression of the *revolution of the poor.* Now we will prove it. But, first we must dispel the rumors.

367

We have established those both within and outside the Church who were involved in the Vatican bank scandal. Yet, the scandal involved much more than individuals. It involved a conspiracy of nations—the United States and the Vatican in their war against communism—*revolution of the poor*. One can see this clearly when one considers what happened to the $1.3 billion.

Rumors the $1.3 billion went to fill the pockets of the civil principals involved are unfounded. That the money went to Polish Solidarity is inconsistent with the time of the bank scandal. That the money went to buy votes of third world cardinals—who voted for a liberal in the first conclave and voted for a conservative in the second conclave of 1978—is a weak guess at best. That the money went to the Contras to suppress the *revolution of the poor* in Central America is the only one that seems to make sense.

Yet, because the Italian courts were unable to determine what happened to the money these remain suppositions today. Yet, let's take them, one by one, to see if any of the others make sense.

Personal motive: Andreotti-Calvi-Gelli-Portillo-Sindona

Some contend Sindona was involved in the bank scandal. Though he may have established the offshore Vatican banking mechanisms which made possible the scandal transactions, by the time the first deal took place in 1979 he was imprisoned by United States courts for unrelated bank fraud. A year later he was extradited to Italy and convicted of murder. He was poisoned while in prison in 1986.[5]

One might conclude Andreotti, Calvi, Gelli and Portillo were in it for the money. After all, these men formed a coalition dedicated to maintaining a rich and poor society in Europe and Latin America.

The P2-Opus Dei-Ambrosiano coalition was not only a wealthy financial organization, it was a powerful political force, as the courts have proved, suppressing *revolution of the workers*—communism—in Italy and *revolution of the poor*—communism—in Latin America.

To the extent these men had been footing the bill to suppress the *revolution of the poor* in Central America in the 1970s, it makes sense they would benefit if the tab were to be picked up by investors.

Regardless, one must keep in mind these were not necessarily bad men. It depends on which side of the aisle one is on. Like their allies in the Roman Catholic Church—John Paul II, Agostino Casaroli and Giuseppe Caprio—they were champions of their side of the aisle.

They were champions in protecting the sacred canon upon which the Church had been founded—*some people are better than others and are entitled to more.* They were champions in preserving the secular canon upon which the United States had been founded—*accumulation of vast wealth by some while others starve to death because they have nothing.* They had dedicated their lives to destroying the threatening ideology of communism—*all of God's wealth is to be divided equally among all of His children.*

An American caught up in a revolution

I know, because at the time, I was one of them.

At the time of the bank scandal and the *revolution of the poor* in Central America, I was a financial officer of the world's largest packaging corporation which had vast amounts of money tied up in these war-ravaged countries. Though a devoted admirer of this man I had met in Vittorio Veneto and of his mentor Paul VI, for at least this time in my life, I was on the other side of the fence.

Paul's doctrine *Liberation Theology* had ignited the *revolution of the poor* in these tiny counties which had all but destroyed their economies. Yet, Central America remained an important market for my company's products. Whereas one had no problem getting one's products into these countries, the problem came when one tried to get one's money out. I was faced by the same banking restrictions which had been faced by those handling the scandal transactions and dealing with the same banks at the same time.

In one case, I had several million dollars tied up in a Rothschild bank in Panama. Restricted by its central bank, I was looking at upwards of a year before I would get my hands on it. Influenced by the IOR, I executed a guarantee on behalf of my 'Fortune 100' conglomerate to Rothschild and it paid me the cash up front.

My company's treasurer motioned for my dismissal—I had usurped what he considered his exclusive authority. My secretary saved me. She researched the company's charter which held any corporate officer could execute a guarantee. I was off the hook

Regardless, as the *revolution of the poor* in Central America began to take hold after Jimmy Carter became president and cut off aid to the incumbent juntas, members of the ruling families in the war zone of Honduras, Nicaragua, Guatemala and El Salvador sought refuge in Costa Rica, Panama and the United States.

I recall meeting with the owner of a large company in El Salvador in a Miami hi-rise. Two guards with automatic weapons flanked its entrance. Another accompanied me on the elevator which opened directly into a penthouse apartment. The man was on life support transferred along with him from a hospital the day before where bullets had been extracted from his stomach.

I recall my morning joggings on the grounds of my San Jose hotel accompanied by an armed guard. I had chosen Costa Rica as a base of operations because it bordered the distressed countries, yet, had a mystique of relative safety about it. Also, much of my company's money was tied up in the central banks of Costa Rica and Panama—which countries restricted money intended to leave those countries during the economic uncertainty brought on by the revolution taking place just beyond their borders.

Regardless, it was this experience—a year later when the bank scandal broke in the press—I questioned why Ambrosiano would have deposited the money in banks of ghost affiliates in Panama City if it had intended it to ever leave Central America.

It made sense to me that it established a branch in Lima after its assets had been frozen in Nicaragua upon the overthrow of Somoza. Yet, it made no sense when the Lima Ambrosiano branch deposited the money in the Vatican bank which, in turn, transferred it back to Panama which money flow was restricted by its central bank.

From Lima, it could have transferred the money to any bank in the world. If it sought a safe haven from foreign interests its Nassau branch would have been the perfect choice.

Why transfer it back to Central America where central banks, from time to time, would freeze or delay the flow of funds out of the region for periods up to a year. The only reason would be the money was never intended to leave Central America.

I was reminded of Marcinkus' reply to my question where the $1.3 billion had gone? *"You don't run money through war-ravaged parts of the world unless you intend it remain there."*

Peaceful demonstrations

370

Although relatively safe in Costa Rica, I was reminded there was no such thing as safety in Central America when three bullets took down an associate in a drive-by shooting as we walked into the Playboy Club one evening in downtown San Jose. Then there was the time I ignored warnings not to go into El Salvador.

The Lear Jet taxied onto the runway to security rarely afforded presidents—a dozen guards in full military gear with automatic weapons. The trip to the plant—the road lined with armed guards I could see and many more, I guessed, I could not see—the driver on the radio, in ongoing dialogue with roadside guards, making a half-dozen detours en route to avoid ambush.

The giant plant loomed up out of the forest more like an ancient fortress rather than the state-of-the-art manufacturing facility it was. Yet, its turrets did not hold medieval men with bows and arrows, but many more guards with machine guns.

I wondered why Paul and John Paul had not followed the model of Gandhi's peaceful demonstrations which had been so successful in India. This had also worked for them in Italy where free elections had given rise to communism in the polls.

I was puzzled why they would cast these tiny countries into havoc and revolution which over the years would cost thousands of lives when one had the option of peaceful protest.

I got the answer on my first evening in El Salvador as I enjoyed a hundred-dollar-a-plate dinner in an upscale restaurant with my Salvadorian hosts. When we were about to leave, the waiter showed up with bags containing what we had left on our plates. I motioned him, 'No.' He tucked one into my hand anyway.

We came down the steps from the restaurant to be greeted by a dozen or so half-naked children. I don't recall if any one of them had all his or her limbs. At least one of them could not see.

We threw the bags into the mud in the midst of them. They went at it like vultures tearing the bags apart and clawing at rice and beans mixed with the mud in the street with bare hands—those who had hands. It reminded me of Luciani's words, *"Christ picked me up from the mud in the street and gave me to you."*

It was then I realized decades of peaceful demonstrations had brought nothing but an occasional burst of gunfire and starving children in the mud of the streets. It was then I realized where Paul

371

and John Paul were coming from. In a land ruled by self-serving juntas demonstrations was not a viable alternative.

Paul and John Paul knew their actions would cost lives, lots of lives. The thousand children who starved to death each day in this tiny isthmus caught up between the world's great oceans gnawed at their conscience each moment they delayed.

The money bought the conclave votes

In the search as to how the same constituency of cardinals elected a liberal in one election and few weeks later elected a conservative, we came to the conclusion Karol Wojtyla could not have possibly traded off ecclesiastical concessions for them. We know this because the contraception doctrine from which the cardinals in third world countries sought relief has never been repealed or even modified. This gives us the supposition he could have bought the votes with the only other thing that buys votes—money—the $1.3 billion.

This is consistent with the money disappearing in Latin America where most of them lived. It is also consistent with the timetable of the transactions which began shortly after John Paul II was elected.

These were mostly conservative third world cardinals who held the doctrine banning contraception to be philosophically sound, yet, objected to it because of the poverty and starvation it was generating among their congregations. They had voted for Luciani in the first election because he was the most likely to repeal it.

If they were offered huge sums of money to annihilate much of the poverty the ban on contraception caused, they could hold to their conviction the ban on contraception was sound and yet minimize its downside--poverty. They would have their cake and eat it too.

Giuseppe Caprio, as Secretary/Treasurer of the Patrimony of the Holy See, controlled the purse strings of the papacy. From a banking perspective he was the only person in the Vatican who could make it work. Caprio's relationship with Calvi—the only person outside the Vatican who could make it work—went back a decade to the time Caprio had brought Calvi's associate Sindona into his fold.

From this prospective that the bank scandal had been a part of the Genoa meeting makes sense. Yet, it makes no sense forty cardinals could have been approached to sell their votes for cash, without one of them raising the alarm. We will leave this one for the dreamers.

Solidarity

The theory the money went to Solidarity is perpetuated by the same people who claim the scandal took place under Paul VI. As if to say, Paul ripped off the investors, put it in the bank for a few years, and the Polish Pope spent it when he came along.

These people do not know their history—the time events took place. By the time Solidarity was conceived, the overwhelming weight of scandal transactions had already taken place. Though they were unable to determine what happened to the money, the Italian courts did determine 'when' and 'where' it disappeared.

I have said this before, but because it is paramount to what we are talking about here, I will say it again.

During the period in which the scandal took place—1979-81—central banks in Nicaragua, El Salvador, Guatemala, Honduras and even the neighboring countries of Costa Rica and Panama often froze or at the least slowed the flow of funds out of these countries. Even if one eventually got one's money out, its value was often significantly deflated by skyrocketing inflation rates. If the revolutionaries took control, as in Nicaragua, depending on who you were, you ran the risk of losing all your money.

Central America was the last place anyone would risk running money through a bank. You could get the money into any of these countries but getting it out of them was entirely a different matter.

"A funny thing happened on the way to the conclave..."

In our analysis of the conclaves of 1978, in the second conclave Wojtyla would have had to gain about 40 votes which had been cast for Luciani in the first conclave because he was the most likely to repeal *Humane Vitae,* the ban on contraception. Thirty-eight third world cardinals participated in the 1978 conclaves.

This raises two questions: Why did they vote for Wojtyla in the second conclave when they knew he would never repeal it?

Why would twenty Latin American cardinals and eighteen others from third world countries vote for a liberal in one election and just a few weeks later vote for a conservative?

In Chapter 11 *'How a Pope is Elected'* we determined Karol Wojtyla, like Albino Luciani before him and Joseph Ratzinger after him, won on the first day of their conclaves. To obscure the lobbying, nominating, politicking and tallying of votes that goes on before the conclave opened, Wojtyla's election, like that of his successor Joseph Ratzinger, was announced on the second day.

Yet, with one hundred and eleven cardinals to choose from, what made Wojtyla the overwhelming choice of the second conclave? What was it about this man that made him so attractive to the others in the second conclave whereas he may not have been a factor at all, or at best gained less than a third of the votes, in the first conclave?

Under Paul, *Liberation Theology* had been merely a matter of principle. To the cardinals in the first election it was not much more than talk and wishful thinking. In his short reign, John Paul I had made it much more than just talk and wishful thinking.

Whereas Paul had waged his war on poverty from the pulpit, John Paul had made it clear he would wage it on the battlefield. He would feed them food rather than faith. To the voting cardinals in Latin America and those in Africa and other third world countries, Paul's encyclical had suddenly changed from being merely a matter of wishful thinking to being a matter of their own survival.

Consider the events which followed the conclaves of 1978.

Although hundreds of priests and nuns and even a few bishops supported and fought for and even gave their lives for *Liberation Theology* in the war-ravaged countries of Central America, after John Paul's death, with the exception of Lorscheider of Brazil, none of the Latin American cardinals or, for that matter, African cardinals ever spoke out in favor of it. In fact, most of them spoke strongly out against *Liberation Theology*. There is a reason for this.

They lived in mansions and were a part of the elite themselves. They dined on fine cuts of meat and caviar and wine together with the wealthy whose influence had made them bishops and ultimately cardinals—the wealthy families of Latin America were at the time the largest contributors to the Church. They did not want war.

If revolutionaries were successful in overthrowing their ruthless dictators in Central America it would drive a wave of uncontrollable uprisings in the Condor nations of South America—Argentina, Brazil, Chile, Uruguay, Paraguay, Bolivia, Ecuador and Peru—at the time, all countries ruled by extreme *right wing* military dictators.

In the second conclave, these cardinals were offered candidates like Benelli, Colombo and Suenens. Like Luciani, they would go after the dictators of Latin America. Like Luciani, they would dig up the *Historic Compromise* which had been buried with Aldo Moro. They would turn Italy and perhaps all of Europe into turmoil.

They could not take another chance on another liberal who might threaten the capitalistic foundations their world was based on. They could not take another chance with another liberal who thought the movement toward the *left*—toward Christ—was going too slowly.

In the first conclave *Humane Vitae*—Paul's doctrine the ban on contraception—had been the issue. In the second conclave another of Paul's doctrines had suddenly risen to the top.

Communism - Liberation Theology - feed them food rather than faith

This is what made a man, who may not have been a factor in the first conclave, the overwhelming choice in the second conclave.

The word 'communism' struck fear into the hearts of the voting cardinals, just as it struck fear into the hearts of Americans who had supported the Nixon/Kissinger terrorization of the Italian people and the Reagan/Bush terrorization of the poor in Central America. They didn't care if it was the will of the people. To them, confused by what was going on in the Soviet Union, all communism was bad.

What's more, communism in the Soviet Union had risen up as the ally of atheism. The Vietnam War—the war between Catholicism and Atheism—had made communism synonymous with atheism. Atheism—meant the end of their world. They would lose their jobs.

Karol Wojtyla had spent his life fighting communism. Poland was at the frontline of the cold war—capitalism vs. communism. Of all the cardinals, he was by far the best qualified to defeat this demon which had raised its ugly head under John Paul I—feed them food rather than faith—communism. No one else came close.

They voted for the man most likely to respond to Kissinger's plea, *"Domination by Moscow is not the issue. Communist control of Italy and Central America is the issue... It would have terrible consequences for the United States and it is today the number one threat to its national security and must be dealt with accordingly."*[6]

They voted for the man most likely to maintain the status quo— pheasant under glass and swirls of *Latour* at their dinner tables while a thousand miniature caskets were lowered into the ground each day.

We have answered the question: *How is it possible the same cardinals elected a liberal in one election and just a few weeks later elected a conservative?* Communism had raised its ugly head.

The $1.3 billion did not fill the pockets of the civil principals in the scandal. Neither did it go to Solidarity nor to buy the votes in the second conclave of 1978. We have, by process of elimination.

The war in Central America

On January 1 1969, in a private audience attended by priests and nuns from Central America, Paul VI first mentioned *"Liberation Theology."*[8] Thus began the struggle for the poor.

For the first time, priests and nuns, backed by Paul's encyclical and driven by their own compassion for children starving to death while the rich dined on fine cuisine and exceptional wines, began to lead the poor of Central America into a better world.

In the late twentieth century, when the war in Central America ended, although few had reached notoriety, nine hundred priests and nuns had died carrying out Paul's edict, many of them bearing arms and leading militias to bring about a more just society.

Yet, back in 1969, as the poor in Central America took up rifles against their ruthless dictators, Richard Nixon, a republican—*a rich and poor society*—became president of the United States. He reacted immediately and sent hundreds of millions of dollars and planes and tanks and guns and bullets to mow the insurgents down.

The United States took on the role of supporting ruthless dictators against the poor who were struggling to achieve free elections and a just society. The United States, which prides itself as the epitome of democracy, allied itself against those struggling for democracy.

Yet, Paul would live to see another event occur that would give his cause renewed hope. A few years later in 1977, Jimmy Carter, a democrat—*a redistribution of wealth society*—became president.

It was Carter's election which caused *right wing* elements in the Vatican to draft the plan which led to the bank scandal. If Carter were to cut off support to the dictators, Central America would fall to communism—archenemy of the Roman Catholic Church.

Nicaragua, A week after taking office, Carter cut off military aid to the Somoza regime citing human rights violations.

In 1979, the Sandinista Liberation Front, a socialist/communist party which had grown up out of Paul's *Liberation Theology,* overthrew the Somoza dictatorship. Under Carter, the United States was the first nation to recognize the new government.

Contras, On the heels of the Sandinista takeover, the CIA-Opus Dei-P2-Ambrosiano coalition organized the Contras to overthrow the Sandinistas and return Nicaragua to a rich and poor society.

Though the CIA by-passed Carter's order and funneled some funds through Ambrosiano to the Contras, the bulk of the money came from other sources including from investors whose money disappeared in Central America and exploded in the Vatican bank scandal. As already pointed out, the first transfers from the Vatican bank to the Ambrosiano branches to Panamanian ghost affiliates occurred in May 1979—the exact time the Contras were organized.

El Salvador, The Sandinistas' success in Nicaragua had given the people of El Salvador renewed hope. The revolutionaries began to tip the scales against the regime which had ruled for centuries.

On March 29, 1980, Oscar Romero was gunned down with an American made bullet as he spoke a sermon calling for the CIA's death squads to cease terrorizing the Salvadorian people.

On the heels of Romero's assassination, the FMLN emerged, an umbrella sheltering five socialist-communist groups struggling for human rights. All-out civil war broke out broke out.

Guatemala, As early as 1951, Juan Jose Arbenz—*a redistribution of wealth society*—was elected by the will of the people. In 1954, under Eisenhower—*a rich and poor society*—the CIA implemented Operation WASHTUB planting a Soviet arms cache in Nicaragua to falsely claim Guatemalan ties to the Soviets. Arbenz was replaced by the Eisenhower administration with a military junta which it suffered under for three decades. In 1978, in a fraudulent election, General Romeo Garcia assumed power giving birth to two parallel guerrilla groups, the Organization of the People in Arms and the Guerrilla Army of the Poor. In 1979, Carter cut off financial and military assistance to the Garcia regime. Revolutionaries—until then restrained by the militia government—moved toward democracy.

Honduras, the military dictator Policarpo Paz Garcia provided safe haven to the Contras which together with the CIA set up the terrorist group Battalion 3-16. Honduras remains in poverty today.

Panama, except for economic impact, Panama was insulated from the revolution by American presence—nineteen military bases. Yet, during the period of the scandal—1978-1982—its central bank often slowed monies flowing out of the country for up to one year.

Costa Rica, enjoyed relative economic and political stability compared to its neighbors. Yet, like neighboring Panama, during the period of the bank scandal transactions 1979-1982, its central bank froze monies flowing out of the country for periods of up to a year.

Lillian Carter, the American president's mother visited Paul in his last days at Castel Gandolfo. I can't help but thinking he asked her to convey his appreciation for what her son was doing to bring an end to an everyday event in this tiny isthmus caught up between great oceans—a thousand miniature caskets lowered into the ground.

The Reagan-Bush Contra War

As 1981 dawned, the region was on a path to free elections and a just society. Contras' funds had been cut off by Carter in the United States and Italian court investigations of Vatican banking activities in Central America had cut off Contras' funds from the Vatican.

Then an event occurred which would be the Contras' salvation. Reagan—*a rich and poor society*—took over the White House.

Reagan and Bush chose Honduras as a base for their Contra war. They established an air base at Soto Cano equipping it with a vast battery of military power including planes, helicopters, tanks, jeeps, automatic weapons and ammunition. What's more, it was turned into a state-of-the-art training base for the Contras' death squads.

In identical fashion as had the Nixon administration employed CIA's *Operation Gladio* to carry on terrorist activities in Italy and frame the *Red Brigades* to turn the mindset of the Italian people against communism in the 1970s, the Reagan-Bush administration commissioned CIA's *Battalion 3-16* to carry out terrorist activities in Guatemala, El Salvador, Nicaragua and Honduras cleverly planned to frame the *Sandinistas* and turn the mindset of the people against the Sandinistas and communism in the 1980s.

CIA's *Battalion 3-16,* in conjunction with the Contras, carried on widespread bombings, kidnappings, rape and murder of civilians.

In 1982, the Guatemalan guerrilla groups joined in coalition with Salvadoran guerrillas (FMLN) and Nicaraguan guerrillas (FSLN) in a war against the United States. Reagan-Bush escalated the war raising their requests in Congress from millions to tens of billions.

Though there were hundreds of kidnappings, rapes and murders of innocent people including children, few attracted attention.

In 1980, four nuns flew from Nicaragua to El Salvador to help guerillas. They were brutally raped and murdered. Fingers pointed to the guerillas. This misconception drew congressional support for the Reagan-Bush Contra war until late 1982 when five Salvadorian soldiers trained in *Battalion 3-16* were convicted of the crime.

Though a tiny part of the atrocities, the incident caught fire in the press and turned world opinion against United States intervention.

At about the same time, Reagan-Bush began to lose their voice in congress. Though they continued to hold an edge in the senate, the house drifted overwhelmingly toward the democrats. Late in 1982, congress cut off funds for the Reagan-Bush Contra war.

Reagan appealed to the Pope who, as the most influential man in Catholicism, could do what bullets and bombs could not do.

Early in 1983, John Paul II toured Central America.

He told the people to stop supporting the revolutionaries. The revolution came to a halt as if one had turned off a water faucet.

Perhaps, nothing demonstrates more clearly what the CIA-Opus Dei-P2-Ambrosiano coalition was looking at when John Paul I made overtures that he did not oppose the revolutionaries, but he would encourage them to bring about a more equitable society. Had he lived another month to address the Puebla Conference, the United States would have been dealing with a half-dozen min-Cubas in its backyard. The reason slow poisoning was not an option in his case.

Regardless, on returning to Rome, John Paul II defrocked dozens of priests and nuns who had supported the revolutionaries. Although his visit brought a temporary lull to the revolution, within a year the people woke up and the revolution began to take hold once more.

Yet, communism had already taken hold in Nicaragua where the Sandinistas had come to power. Reagan and Bush, terrified it would spread to other countries and bring an end to poverty in Central America, took drastic measures to fund their Contra war. In 1985, in a CIA covert operation, they secretly sold arms to Iran and diverted the proceeds to the Contras—the Iran-Contra Affair.

Promoters of the Contras' reign of terror in Central America:

When and where the $1.3 billion went

'Offshore banks' *Nordeurop* and *Manic* were themselves ghost companies operating within Europe. Conversely, the Panamanian banks involved in the scheme were innocent bystanders which later cooperated with Italian courts. That most of the money was drawn in cash or wired to other Central American banks and then drawn down in cash the courts were unable to determine what happened to it.

At the risk of redundancy, there are some dates one must consider when one determines what happened to the $1.3 billion.

April 1979, Sandinistas begin to take hold and Somoza flees Nicaragua – Contras emerge to maintain a rich and poor society. Carter refuses to support the Contras.
May 9, 1979, the 1st scandal transaction - $3million 'loan' to Bellatrix in Panama.
October 11, 1979, Sandinistas seize Ambrosiano branch in Nicaragua which up to this point has deposited $378 million in the APSA/IOR which, in turn, had been transferred to Panama banks as 'loans' to Panamanian ghost companies—Contras.
October 17, 1979, the new Lima branch's 1st transaction. It deposits $134 million in APSA/IOR which loans it to *United Trading Company* of Panama—Contras.
September 1, 1980, up to this point the Vatican had loaned $1.192 billion of the $1.285 billion to ghost companies in Panama and Europe.
September 1980, Polish Solidarity is first conceived, operational by end of 1981.
January 1981, Reagan becomes president. Congress begins to finance the Contras.
March 17, 1981, Licio Gelli's villa is raided and Roberto Calvi is brought to trial.
June 10, 1981, the last bank scandal transaction takes place.
June 1981, the USA airbase in Honduras supporting the Contras is operational

During the lengthy Calvi trial, directors of the Nicaraguan and Lima branches holding unsecured notes became uneasy. The IOR issued a *letter of comfort* claiming it owned the ghost companies.

Banco Ambrosiano Andino, Lima, Peru   September 1, 1981
Ambrosiano Group Banco Comercial, Managua, Nicaragua

We directly or indirectly control:

Manic S.A. Luxembourg, Astolfine S.A. Panama, Nordeurop Liechtenstein, United Trading Corporation, Panama, Erin S. A. Panama, Bellatrix S.A. Panama, Belrose S.A. Panama, Starfield S.A. Panama
We acknowledge the indebtedness of these companies to you as of June 10, 1981.

Luigi Mennini   Pellegrino De Stroebel   Institute of Religious Works

That the letter was signed by officers Mennini and De Stroebel, and not by Marcinkus, demonstrates the conspiracy—the end use of the money—was known only to those at the very top of the Vatican Empire: John Paul II, Casaroli, Caprio and Marcinkus.

Had Mennini and De Stroebel known of the plot, they would have never signed the letter. Marcinkus eventually denied its terms.

Because those within the Vatican were never brought to trial, the courts had to reconstruct the money flow by working backwards from the banks the APSA/IOR had transferred the money to. [8]

Ambrosiano Italy (investors)	$1,285 million ($15 billion in today's $)
	↓
Ambrosiano Nicaragua	$378
Ambrosiano Lima	$907
	↓
Vatican bank — APSA/IOR	$1,285
	↓
Astolfine S.A. Panama	70
United Trading Company Panama	217
Erin S.A Panama	104
Bellatrix S.A. Panama	117
Belrose S.A. Panama	64
Starfield S.A. Panama	92
Fisalma S.A. Panama	61
Other Panamanian ghost companies (8)	97
Sub-total Panama	$822 million to the Contras
Manic S.A. Luxembourg	92
Nordeurop S.A. Liechtenstein	371
Sub-total Europe	$463 million to buy arms for Contras

In the end investors recovered sixty percent of their investments. $215 million was recovered from ghost companies mostly Manic and Nordeurop, $241 million from the Vatican and the balance from liquidation of unrelated Ambrosiano assets. [12]

Because the accounts were brought down in cash, the courts were unable to determine what happened to it. Yet, the most logical conclusion one can come to is that which disappeared in Central America went directly to the Contras and that which disappeared in Europe went to buy arms for the Contras from European sources. Had all the money gone to Panamanian banks it would have been subject to the same central banking restrictions placed on all money flowing out of the region—the reason why a part of the money was 'loaned' to European 'ghosts.' It is reasonable to believe a few dollars in the late stages may have been funneled to Solidarity.

The Great Vatican Bank Scandal began as *The Vatican-Contra Affair* in the fall of 1978—a plot to suppress the *revolution of the poor* in Central America. The closer one is to the ground, the more vulnerable one is to vendors of the supernatural. The closer one is to death, the more vulnerable one is to vendors of the supernatural. The Roman Catholic Church is the *Wal-Mart of the Supernatural World.*

Why John Paul ordered the audit of the Vatican bank?

Albino Luciani had a strong background in finance and banking. Like Marcinkus, he knew you can't run the Church on Hail Marys.

At Belluno, as vicar general, he had been responsible for finance and administration of the diocese. He had for those years worked as chief financial officer of the diocese interfacing with its banks.

When he inherited the bankrupt diocese of Vittorio Veneto, he took control of its banking bringing the diocese to solvency and in time to prosperity. During his tenure there, he chaired each of the parish banks, often riding to them on bicycles.

Likewise, in Venice, he took over Banca Cattolica del Veneto.

When elected to the papacy, he took over APSA/IOR. In taking over a bank the first thing one does is order an audit. Benelli headed up the audit not only because of his skilled banking background but because, in the near term, he would become secretary of state—the position to which all Vatican banking activities reported at the time.

Had John Paul not ordered an audit of the Vatican bank it would have been out of character for him, so I don't really have to answer the question: Why John Paul ordered the audit of the Vatican bank?

Yet, I will give you the results of the audit he ordered.

The Vagnozzi Report disclosed the IOR was operating at a $40 million deficit and had been guaranteeing Ambrosiano contracts and clearing Ambrosiano funds into international markets by-passing the Bank of Italy for rich commissions—operations legal at the time.

The Vagnozzi dossier, the courts and all that history has recorded clearly established the bank scandal—the swindling of investors out of $1.3 billion—began and ended under the reign of John Paul II.

The only deal guaranteed by IOR tried by the courts in the Ambrosiano collapse was its 'guarantee' of the $1.3 billion swindled from investors. The $241 million went entirely to these investors.

No other obligation of the Vatican was proved by courts which investigated the Ambrosiano downfall. A few guarantees the IOR had made under Paul VI which failed had already surfaced and been satisfied by the Vatican by the time Luciani was elected.

To the extent the sale of shares of the Catholic Bank of Italy at low prices to Ambrosiano in the seventies overvalued Ambrosiano shares, it would have been a part of the overall $3.5 billion 'black hole' in Ambrosiano. But, again, it had nothing to do with *The Vatican Bank Scandal*—the swindling of $1.3 billion from investors.

Yet, even in this case, the audit did not tell Luciani anything he did not already know. His signature executing the contract of the Ambrosiano acquisition of the Banca Cattolica del Veneto in 1971—the largest of these transactions—attests he sanctioned the deal—the bank was owned by the Venice archdiocese and not by the Vatican.

One could say the providential coincidence of a democrat in the Vatican and a democrat in the White House—the powers of money and influence required to enact *a redistribution of wealth society* in Central America—may have cost John Paul his life.

Yet, one is smoking funny cigarettes when one says John Paul was murdered because the audit he ordered threatened to uncover a bank scandal which had not yet occurred.

I say the proceeds of *The Great Vatican Bank Scandal* went to the Contras. The timing of Carter's presidency and the timing of the transactions match the rising of the Contras to a tee—1978-1981.

Is it mere coincidence all these champions of a redistribution of wealth society—Aldo Moro, Paul VI, John Paul and scores of others we have talked of—died of natural causes at the only moment in world history communism happened to have been taking hold in Europe and Latin America as the will of the people? I don't think so.

I have said this with much more than mere supposition.

All of the known facts point to this conclusion. One does not have to be an expert in international banking and finance to know this. One has only to use the intelligence one has been gifted with and apply a bit of common sense. *"One does not run one's money through war ravaged regions of the world unless one intends it remain there."* Paul Marcinkus first said it. We have proved it.

What's more, in my case, I know because I was there.

I woke up in my hotel room to the shouting in the streets in Guatemala City on the morning Jimmy Carter became President of the United States. I was standing in the boss's office on Shippan Point on Long Island Sound being charged with the task to figure out a way to get my company's money out of Central American banks on the day John Paul I lay on a catafalque in St. Clementine Chapel. I was enjoying lunch in San Jose when word came Oscar Romero's blood had been splattered on the altar in neighboring El Salvador. I was sound asleep in my bed in Panama City the night four nuns of the Maryknoll order were raped and murdered in Nicaragua. I was there in the lamplight of the evening in San Salvador when a dozen half-naked, half-limbed, starving children scrambled at the rice and beans mixed with the mud of the street.

Where was the rest of the world when all this horror I have spoken of here was tucked stealthy into the inner pages of papers? On their terraces sipping coffee and reading the comics and sports sections of the morning edition? In church listening to their emissary from Rome campaign for Reagan and Bush?

Yes, dropping their five-dollar bills into the poor box to support heartless men of a Vatican regime with their bellies filled and nestled comfy in their feather beds with pillows of down each night. While, on the other side of the world, a thousand miniature caskets waited silently in the dark for the coming of the dawn.

Yet, we have come to the end of the day. What do we have?

The Great Vatican Bank Scandal was just one more tug-of-war between those on the *left* who think Christ is what the good bishop of Vittorio Veneto once told me He is *"What is in this for others"* and those on the *right* who are convinced Christ is nothing more than '*A piece of bread in a cup.*'

1 *TIME-Europe* 82-84
2 *NY Times* 10 Jun 86
3 *Washington Post* 22 Jul 80
4 *New York Times* 4 Dec 86 *Iran-Contra Affair*
5 *Washington Post* 27 Mar 86 *Wikipedia Michele Sindona*
6 *TIME* 26 Apr 76 *What if Communists Win a Role?*
7 *La Osservatore Romano* 2 Jan 69 *Liberation Theology*
8 *TIME-Europe* 82-83 *Wall Street Journal* 27 Apr 87 *La Stampa* 6 Sep 85 *La Repubblica* 2 Jan 84
Ansbacher vs. Ambrosiano Irish Supreme Court 1987, *Latour vs. Ambrosiano* Paris 1985, etc.

Chapter 36

The Ides of March

1978 Poverty Summit, Vittorio Veneto

It was the middle of March nineteen hundred seventy-eight.

Halfway up the mountainside the ancient castle loomed out over the sprawling village of Vittorio Veneto.

Ghostly clouds swirled about its surviving towers forming a silent marquis, hinting of the shrouded happenings going on beneath them. Yet, they could not foretell the horror of what was about to come.

Thirty-three men surrounded by thirty-three angels. Each one in Byzantine fashion, each one in individual color, each one bearing a shield with coat-of-arms, each one armed with a weapon of medieval times, each one topped off with a golden halo, each one standing in a carved mahogany panel. Each one watching, each one listening...

The enormous clock ticked so loudly it bellowed each passing moment in time. So much so, each of the room's occupants answered in unison with a twitch each time it marked a spot in time.

The Poverty Summit

Here in the foothills of the great Dolomite Mountains, for three days and three nights, had been clustered together the leaders of the Marxist movement in the western world.

There were those whose congregations were starving to death in the wake of the rich and poor society imposed upon them and there were others who just wanted to help.

A bit of what had happened in the Russia Revolution.

In 1918, Lenin's Bolshevik Party was defeated by the Peasant Party in a free election—the will of the people. Unfortunately, it was the will of uneducated people. His objective was to achieve a more equitable society in an organized manner by progressively increased taxation of the rich; he would force the rich to give the poor equal opportunity, not only in food and shelter, but in education, to enable each of them to make his or her utmost contribution back to society.

However, the opposition Peasant Party offered a much better deal to the poverty stricken masses: a turnkey Marxist society in which the government seized all property and divided it among the poor—a free ride. Thus, motion pictures of war-torn Russia—*War and Peace* and *Doctor Zhivago*—depict mansions being divided into apartments for the poor. Lenin, losing the election, took control via military force; we all know what happened after that.

Yet, we are speaking here of another kind of communism. One which had already captured the vote in Italy and was poking its nose into the impoverished nations of Central America and other parts of the world as the clouds swirled about the towers of Vittorio Veneto.

One is speaking of a free democratic communist society driven by the will of the people—one that forces the rich to help the poor.

One is not speaking here of a society which foregoes a free enterprise system and simply divides up the pie equally. One is speaking of a society which affords each child an equal opportunity to make his or her maximum contribution back to society.

The primates of world poverty

There were thirty-three in all scattered about the immense room.

There was Valerian Gracias, Archbishop of Bombay and Primate of India. Gracias, or the 'Reincarnation of Gandhi' as he was often called, was determined to succeed where his namesake had failed.

In recent years, Gracias had risen as an enemy of the capitalistic world imposed upon him. Although he had reservations concerning contraception, he was the great ally of Luciani concerning the pill.

"It would be a godsend to the teeming masses of our country"[1] he once reasoned with Mother Teresa who was rigidly opposed to any form of contraception—she didn't care how much poverty and starvation overpopulation wrought despite she spent her life trying to minimize the damage it brought.

Cardinal Yu Pin, Primate of China, protectorate of five hundred million peasants who were starving to death sat in front of a huge fireplace trying to keep warm.

He peered up at an aging oil painting of Christ throwing the money makers out of the Temple—golden coins splashing down out of its ornate frame. Its artist, centuries removed from this room, depicting the goings on within it to a tee—rid the world of greed.

Chatting with him was Cardinal Delargey.

As archbishop of the stately province of Wellington he oversaw the impoverished islands of the South Pacific. It was no surprise the two were together here at Vittorio Veneto as they were often seen together in the public eye. They were the best of friends.

With them was Cardinal Trinh Nhu Khue, Primate of Eastern Asia—overseer of Korea, Vietnam, Cambodia and other mainland countries which had borne the brunt of the Vatican's war against atheism. Buddhist countries cast into decades of suffering and death by Pius XII and just now emerging from the horrors of war.

Off to one side, Cardinal Boleshaw Filipiak of Gniezno, Poland sat pensively gazing out of the only window in the room. He peered across the seemingly endless span of Vittorio Veneto and wondered how it had come about.

During the World War, it had been two villages—the site of the bloodiest struggle of all. Near the Austrian border, the village to the north was in the Axis ranks, the one to the south in the Allied ranks. Brother fought against brother. When all was said and done, one in ten was alive. To symbolize peace, the villages were united as a single municipality and named it Vittorio Veneto—Veneto Victory.

Though he had no official title to say so, the primate of poverty in Eastern Europe thought back three-and-a-half decades before.

During the war Filipiak had been leader of the Polish resistance. When Karol Wojtyla had risen in the Nazi ranks to quartermaster of the Solvay Chemical plant at Krakow, he approached Wojtyla that he might divert supplies to the resistance. Wojtyla refused. A few days later, Filipiak was arrested and spent the rest of the war in a Nazi prison camp, lucky to have escaped with his life. Although he had no proof, it remained his conviction Wojtyla had turned him in.[2]

After the war, he rose up as the leader of the movement against Wojtyla's effort to retain the fragments of *fascism* the allies had not yet taken from him—segregation. Wojtyla tabbed him a communist. The nametag froze Filipiak in his tracks. As a result, Poland was the last European country to admit blacks into its population. He had lost that one; but he was determined he would not lose this one.

In the eastern bloc of European nations, millions of born-out-of-wedlock children remained confined to streets and sewers. Filipiak would bring about *a society that affords each of them an equal opportunity to earn his or her fair share of the pie—communism.*

So severe was the rivalry between Wojtyla and Filipiak, John Paul II struck Filipiak's record from the Catholic Encyclopedia, the official record of the Roman Catholic Church. Filipiak is the only twentieth century cardinal not mentioned in the volume.

At the far end of the vast room, Metropolitan Nikodim and Oscar Romero sat at a massive desk. Off by themselves, they were deeply immersed in their own bit of intrigue.

What is known today—not known at the time—the youthful leader of the Marxist movement within the Orthodox Church was a secret agent for the KGB—the Soviet Union's counterpart of the CIA. So much so, his every move was tracked by the CIA. He had spent much of the trip from Leningrad looking over his shoulder.

Though the effort to bring Christ/Marx ideology into society *"Sell all thou hast and give to the poor"* had met with autocracy in the Soviet Union, he was determined a *redistribution of wealth culture* could succeed in a free democratic society.

Romero, Archbishop of El Salvador, was witness to the epitome of a rich and poor society; his people were literally dying in poverty. Like Gandhi, before him, at first he thought he could bring an end to oppression via peaceful protest backed up by the teachings of Christ.

It had been a year since he found out it didn't work. Immediately after Paul had made him Archbishop of San Salvador a long line of priest and nun assassinations followed. Within a few months, among dozens of others, his dear friends Fathers Rutilio Grande Garcia and Alfonso Grande Oviedo had been cut down by death squad bullets.

Shortly after Oviedo's death, he abandoned peaceful protests and spoke out in support of the guerillas and, many times, pointed his finger at the CIA for assassinations of priests and nuns.

One might suspect Romero sought Nikodim's intercession with the Soviets for arms assistance for revolutionaries operating in El Salvador and neighboring Nicaragua. One will never know.

Nevertheless, the primates of the world pockets of poverty were gathered together. Not, for the first time, for they had been here before, and would be here again. At least, that is what they thought.

What's that? Africa? We all know what goes on there or maybe we don't want to know what goes on there. Regardless, you're right, Cardinal Bernardin Gantin, Primate of Africa, was not there.

There was a reason he was not there. He was an enemy of Paul's Liberation Theology—the reason all the others were there. He did not believe in revolution. He did not believe society could be driven by people helping other people. He believed society could only be driven by cash. He did not believe Christ is *"What is in this for others."* He was convinced Christ was a piece of bread in a cup.

Yet, it could be he didn't want to give up his palace in Benin or his posh apartments in Paris and Rome. One will never know.

The politicians

Enrico Berlinguer, leader of the Italian Communist Party was gathered together with the communist mayors of Italy's largest metropolises, Giulio Argan of Rome and Vittorio Korach of Milan. With them sharing a white marble coffee table, was Aldo Moro.

Off to one side, Cardinal Giocomo Violardo knelt at a prayer station in a darkened corner of the huge room lightened only by the flickering of candles.

He thought back a few years to the time he had caused an uproar when he had been caught distributing Holy Communion to a group of Protestants and Communists. He explained to his adversaries, *"This is what Communion is all about—Communism—Christ."*[3]

Regardless, Paul answered the demands of Curia cardinals for his excommunication by making Giocomo Secretary for the Discipline of the Sacraments and at the same time made him a cardinal.[4]

One would wonder what the Secretary for the Discipline of the Sacraments does. Not much. Paul filled in his time as the Vatican's chief lobbyist in the Italian Parliament. Other than Paul, the astute lawyer was the closest person in the room to Aldo Moro. He was looking forward to the upcoming Thursday morning when Moro would move communist ministers into control of Parliament.

Giocomo was not a lobbyist in the common sense of the term. He didn't his spend his time wining and dining politicians in classy restaurants or working hotel lobbies. He lobbied them the same way all preachers lobby their prey—from the pulpit.

When a particular bill was on the table, Moro would furnish Giocomo with a list of Parliamentary members together with where they lived. The local parish would be privileged to have a Vatican cardinal give the Sunday sermon— Giocomo would cleverly lean his message toward the issue at hand and win over the votes.

389

It was fortunate he was praying to his God. He was about to meet Him. His body would be found beneath a stairway in a dark corner of the Palace of the Holy Office on that coming Friday morning; as the Vatican explained, *"In his seventies, the cardinal undoubtedly stumbled and slipped over the balustrade late last evening."*[5]

Moro would never learn of the loss of his dear friend. He would never be privileged to give the eulogy at the funeral of Cardinal Giocomo Violardo. By the time Giocomo lay in his coffin, Moro, himself, had already been kidnapped and readied for his own coffin.

The ringleaders

Eight men were gathered on the other side of the room.

As leader of its largest church, Paul was the most influential man on the planet. Yet, he sat at the head of the table nervously wiggling his toes in his shoes. He seemed more immersed in himself than what was going on around him. Yet, he was much more concerned with the order of the day than he was with his impending doom.

Cardinal Egidio Vagnozzi, Prefect of Economic Affairs of the Holy See, sat next to Paul as he held the purse strings of Paul's war on poverty—the Vatican bank reported to his office. One cannot fight a war—particularly a war on poverty—without money.

To Paul's other side sat his legal counsel Cardinal Pericle Felici, Prefect of the Tribunal of the Holy See, and next to Felici was the man who was always next to Felici—Cardinal Giovanni Benelli. The two were bounded together in a driving cause to destroy Opus Dei, the clandestine cult which ruled the opposing force in the Church.

Albino Luciani sat chatting in French, so fluent one would never believe he had rarely traveled outside of Italy. His audience was Leon Joseph Suenens. Suenens? Who's he?

Suenens was the leader of human fairness in the Church.

When John XXIII had created a second party in the College of Cardinals, which for a thousand years had known only one party, he gave it a leader. He explained when he named Suenens a cardinal, *"He will open the window and let in the fresh air."*[6]

John XXIII, Paul VI and John Paul I had been fluent in French.

It was no mystery in John's case, as he had spent much of his ministry in France. It was no mystery in Paul's case either, as he had the French cardinal Jean Villot at his side. But, how did Luciani, who rarely traveled outside Italy, become so fluent in French?

The reason was Cardinal Suenens. Scarcely a day would go by in his twenty years as a bishop and as a cardinal Luciani would not pick up the phone and run an issue or two by the Belgian cardinal. This was also true of both John and Paul. Scarcely a day would go by they would not pick up the phone and ask Suenens' advice.

When Luciani rose to the papacy he was fluent in Italian, English, French and Spanish and could converse with limitation in Russian, German, Chinese, Portuguese and a few African dialects.

Pericle Felici had served as apostolic nuncio to Africa and Giovanni Benelli had served as apostolic nuncio to western Africa and Albino Luciani had run missionary operations in Africa for many years. Even though its primate was not one of those scattered about the room, Africa was well represented here at the summit.

Cardinal Colombo of Milan and Cardinal Villot, who had set up the summit, rounded out those at the top.

The bystanders

There were, of course, the eavesdroppers.

There was the host, Antonia Cunial, presiding bishop of Vittorio Veneto. Then there was my friend Jack, the only person without rank other than a dozen interpreters and aides strategically placed here and there throughout the great room.

So there were some snitches in the room and my friend Jack was one of them, lest I could not bring you this accounting. There may have also been some snitches in the room that eventually caused the common dream of these men to fade into obscurity.

There were thirty-three in all.

Thirty-three men surrounded by thirty-three angels. Each one in Byzantine fashion, each one in individual color, each one bearing a shield with coat-of-arms, each one armed with a weapon of medieval times, each one topped off with a golden halo, each one standing in a carved mahogany panel. Each one watching, each one listening...

Early the next morning, a few ran off to Belluno and Venice to catch planes, while the others stayed on for the day.

Wine at the corner-wedge café

On the afternoon of March 13, 1978, fifteen men sat around a table in a sidewalk café in the mountain village of Vittorio Veneto in northern Italy. In casual clothes they went unnoticed though one was the reigning Pontiff, and the others his Secretary of State, his Chief Counsel, the Patriarch of Venice, the Archbishop of Gniezno, the Archbishop of Florence, the Metropolitan of Leningrad, the Primates of China, India, Eastern Asia, Eastern Europe and the South Pacific. Next to the Curia Cardinal Violardo was the man who picked up the check, Aldo Moro. Yes, there was one more, my friend Jack.

It was the composition of these men that was the great enemy of Opus Dei, the clandestine cult which sought to control the papacy and the moral pulse of the world. More so, it was the great enemy of the capitalistic world led by the United States. They left at four o'clock and Aldo reserved the table *"for this time next year."*

On the morning of March 13, 1979, Benelli and Felici awoke. They had decided not to travel to Vittorio Veneto that day. After all, all the others were dead. Unaware of their impending doom, they, too, were as good as dead.

So what do we have?

We Have the remarkable coincidence Cardinal Gantin, the only primate of a world pocket of poverty to survive would spend the rest of his days annihilating Paul's concept of Liberation Theology.

We have the remarkable coincidence the boy Luciani and the boy Rotov had a common upbringing by atheist fathers, Luciani having once made the acquaintance of Rotov's father.

We have the remarkable coincidence the youthful leader of the Russian Orthodox Church was the first foreign dignitary granted an audience with John Paul I and dropped dead at his feet.

We have the remarkable coincidence Yu Pin who would have locked up the election for Luciani dropped dead at Paul's funeral

We have the remarkable coincidence the unexplained deaths of Paul VI, John Paul I and Jean Villot in rapid consecutive order made possible the rise to the papacy of John Paul II, Agostino Casaroli and Giuseppe Caprio to the most powerful positions in the Church.

We have the remarkable coincidence two of these had free access to each of these victims the night they died.

We have the remarkable coincidence Karol Wojtyla's long time adversary Cardinal Boleslaw Filipiak died of undisclosed causes the day before the conclave that elected the Polish Pope opened.

We have the remarkable coincidence Aldo Moro was abducted and subsequently murdered on the very morning he was scheduled to move communist ministers into control of Parliament.

We have the remarkable coincidence Paul's 'voice' in the Italian Parliament, Giocomo Violardo, was murdered on the same day.

We have the remarkable coincidence Egidio Vagnozzi was found dead on his apartment floor while in the midst of the bank audit.

We have the remarkable coincidence John Paul's proclamation, *"It is the inalienable right of no man to accumulate wealth beyond the necessary while other men starve to death because they have nothing,"* was followed immediately by his sudden death.

We have the remarkable coincidence of eleven people who could have known of the Vatican bank scandal transactions, only four were alive when the case was tried in the Italian courts and they happened to be the four ranking men in the Roman Catholic Church.

We have the remarkable coincidence the timing of the money flow from the Vatican to Central America paralleled precisely the time of the rising of the Contras during the Carter administration.

We have the remarkable occurrence the same cardinals elected a liberal in one election and elected a conservative the next election.

We have the toll,

September 5, 1968	Pasquale Amedore	blunt object
March 16, 1978	Aldo Moro	kidnapped
March 16, 1978	Cardinal Violardo	fell over banister
May 9, 1978	Aldo Moro	shot to death
August 6, 1978	Paul VI	arsenic poison ([1])
August 11, 1978	Cardinal Yu Pin	lethal poison
August, 17, 1978	Cardinal Suenens	attempt on life
August 17, 1978	Cardinal Benelli	attempt on life
September 5, 1978	Archbishop Nikodim	cyanide
September 11, 1978	Cardinal Gracias	arsenic poison ([1])
September 21, 1978	Cardinal Suenens	attempt on life
September 27, 1978	Edoardo Calo	fell off terrace
September 29, 1978	John Paul I	lethal injection
September 30, 1978	John Champney	hit-and-run

October 14, 1978	Cardinal Filipiak	arsenic poison ([1])
November 27, 1978	Cardinal Trinh-Khue	arsenic poison ([1])
January 29, 1979	Cardinal Delargey	arsenic poison ([1])
March 13, 1979	Jean Villot	arsenic poison ([1])
March 29, 1979	Carmine Pecorelli	shot to death
March 24, 1980	Archbishop Romero	shot to death
December 26, 1980	Cardinal Vagnozzi	never disclosed
March 22, 1982	Cardinal Felici	poison wine
June 17, 1982	Roberto Calvi	hanging
June 17, 1982	Teresa Corrocher	fell out window
September 12, 1982	Giuseppe Dellacha	fell out window
June 9, 1983	Michel Sindona	poisoned
October 26, 1982	Cardinal Benelli	Vatican order
June 17, 1984	Sister Vincenza Taffarel	unknown
March 18, 1996	Cardinal Suenens	unknown
May 4, 1998	Alois Estermann	shot to death
May 4, 1998	Gladys Meza Romero	shot to death
May 4, 1998	Cedric Tornay	shot to death
February 20, 2005	Archbishop Marcinkus	not disclosed
?	Avro Manhattan	?

([1]) death consistent with-not proved. Four cardinals, not mentioned in this book, also died in 1978-1979. To the best of the author's knowledge they died of natural causes. Their average age 77 as compared with the average of those above of 56.

Currently under investigation by a criminology class in an America university:

Cardinal Delargey

Perhaps, the most puzzling death of the time was that of Cardinal Delargey of Wellington. So much so, rumors spread requiring books written to explain it. Some of these influenced by the Church claim his deterioration was so dramatic whispers of cancer in its final stages and other maladies were widespread in the 1978 conclaves, *"He looked dreadful...wasted away to skin and bones...it was obvious he was in the final stages of cancer in the first conclave...many were surprised when he showed up alive at the second conclave..."*

1978 conclave picture album

The most proliferate of these claims is that Delargey suffered from melanoma which spread rapidly to stomach cancer.

This supposition is based on his visit to an outpatient clinic in a Wellington hospital in September 1978 in which he had a mole removed from his shoulder. The hospital confirms the mole benign which established clearly Delargey did not suffer from melanoma or any other kind of skin cancer at the time.

When confined to the Auckland hospital in December, doctors were unable to diagnose his condition. It was that severe restrictions were placed on visitors and the diocese refused to disclose the nature of his illness which triggered rumors.[1] Those closest to him who felt they had the right to visit him were turned away.

His death certificate states *'inoperable adenocarcinoma of stomach area.'* The Church has often—as clear in the case of the thirty-three day pope—influenced what goes on a death certificate in cases in which the dying process is clandestine in nature and shielded from the public—a practice facilitated in a Catholic hospital. Delargey died in the Sisters of Mercy Mater Misericordiae Hospital.

By chance, the identical wording *'inoperable adenocarcinoma of stomach area'* also appears on the death certificates of Valerian Gracias and Trinh Nhu Khue other eastern cardinals who fell victim to the 1978 conclaves. Gracias died in a Catholic hospital in Bombay and Khue died in a Catholic hospital in Hanoi.

Delargey had been the closest confidant of Cardinal Yu Pin and the loudest voice calling for an autopsy when the Grand Chancellor of Eastern Affairs keeled over at Paul's funeral. He had occupied the adjoining room to Yu Pin on the ground floor of St. Damascus the night before Yu Pin dropped dead.

Villot tells the story of the progressive Delargey's visit to the papal apartment after Luciani was elected. He asked, *"We are good men. Why is it we have so many enemies?"* John Paul didn't hesitate, *"We were born before our time."*

1 *Auckland Independent* 30 Jan 79; in the late stages his illness was reported as 'grave.'

Avro Manhattan

This photo of Avro Manhattan was taken in November 1990 two weeks before his death. It accompanied a leak the renowned historian was in the process of writing a book linking the CIA to the deaths of Aldo Moro, Paul VI, John Paul and others.

Prime Minister Andreotti's disclosure in November 1990 of his involvement with the CIA and Operation Gladio in covert operations intended to terrorize the Italian population and turn its mindset against communism in the seventies, together with Judge Casson's findings earlier the same year and other developments of the time, gave great credence to what until then had been not much more than Manhattan's suspicions.

Murder in the Vatican is the book Avro Manhattan was writing when he met a sudden death.

We have one more for the road.

1 *Maharashtra Times* 22 Apr 78 or search Internet "Valerian Gracias contraception'
2 The scene of the leader of the Polish Resistance, Boleshaw Filipiak, pleading with Karol Wojtyla, quartermaster of a German supply depot, to divert supplies to the resistance, is depicted in the 2005 CBS film starring Jon Voight, *The Man Who Would Be Pope*.
3 *L'Osservatore Romano* 5 Jan 65
4 Cardinal Giocomo Violardo *Catholic Encyclopedia 2nd Edition*
5 *L Osservatore Romano* 18 Mar 78
6 *La Repubblica* 20 Mar 62

Chapter 37

The Murder of Cardinal Suenens

When John Paul II rose to power, he ordered a costly renovation of the retreat at Castel Gandolfo, going so far as to add a majestic swimming pool for his personal enjoyment—an about-face from his predecessor who had threatened to sell off the opulent estate.

When he was elected, the IOR had a deficit of forty million dollars. Had it had a surplus instead of a deficit, his spending would have gone unnoticed. But, because the 'bank' operated at a deficit, it brought harsh criticism of the new pope's irresponsible spending.

Among the critics was Cardinal Suenens, *"In order for one to see what has happened here, one must first understand the function of the IOR. It is not a bank at all in the common sense of the word. One can see this clearly in its title, 'The Institute for Religious Works.'*

"The IOR is a clearing house for funds that have been raised for the poor by charitable orders of the Church. By quite a margin, its largest single client is Mother Teresa whose order ministers to the poor and dying in the slums of Calcutta and other impoverished cities of the world. It also serves as a depository for Peter's Pence— funds raised from rich parishes to support the lavish lifestyle of the papal household. From a banking perspective, it is a depository—an account—in The Patrimony of the Holy See—the Vatican bank.

"Because Peter's Pence was insufficient to support the Pope's extravagant spending, the money for his swimming pool and other improvements to the Papal Palace and the Castel Gandolfo came from funds raised by Mother Teresa and others like her intended to help children suffering from starvation and illness in the world. Also, it is not pastorally correct of His Holiness to use these funds to pay for expensive vacations at luxurious resorts reserved for the rich and famous. Also, it is morally wrong to pay Vatican cardinals huge salaries out of these same funds intended for the poor."[1]

Suenens referred to an eighteen percent pay raise for Vatican cardinals the Pope had announced immediately after his election. *"It is almost as if it had been a part of the deal"*[2] was whispered in pubs by disgruntled Romans an Italian was not chosen.

He was wrong about the vacations. Mother Teresa didn't pay for them. They were paid for by his friend Licio Gelli. This is attested to in that most of them took place at the opulent Ovindoli Ski Lodge in the Italian Abruzzi region. Gelli owned the resort.[3]

Bodyguards

A few weeks after a section of a frieze fell and killed a visiting French bishop in Brussels and Cardinals Suenens and Benelli had narrowly escaped death when a chip of a frieze fell from a Vatican building, there was another incident. Suenens' secretary threw him to the ground to avoid an onrushing car in Brussels. The hospital reported the cardinal suffered a mild concussion in the mishap.[4]

There is nothing in the record to prove any of these incidents were indeed attempts on his life. Yet, it was obvious the cardinal, himself, sensed he was in danger as he was never seen again in public without two young priests who, if not for their garb, could be easily mistaken for soccer players—clearly serving as bodyguards.

As a precaution, he moved his office from the first floor of his residence in Brussels to the third floor. An unnecessary move, as a few weeks after the last failed attempt, John Paul II removed him as Primate of Belgium. No longer with pastoral influence, Leon Joseph Suenens seemed as good as dead.

Yet, he was not quite dead. He continued an assault from the *left*. Yet, with some minor exceptions concerning the rights of women in the Church, he had little success. Every now and then, he would gain notoriety, at times in Europe and, at other times, in the United States.

In his bid for reelection, Ronald Reagan made a commitment to the *Christian right* leader Jerry Falwell that he would use his veto power to ban funding of AIDS research, something he did do three times during his presidency. On the campaign trail with Falwell, in a heartless remark, Reagan, citing the homosexual link to AIDS, told a television audience, *"They live like that, let them die like that."*[5]

From Brussels, Suenens lashed out at Reagan, *'...Barbarian.'*[6]

1986, Elizabeth Taylor led celebrities in an event raising millions to establish AIDS research.[7]

Suenens attended the Hollywood Bowl event. *"When the Gods of Washington fail us,"* he told the reporter, *"we can always count on the Gods of Hollywood to bail us out."*[8]

397

On the tenth anniversary of his friend's death, Suenens spoke of Luciani, *"Heroes are those who dream dreams and are willing to pay the price to make them come true, for you and for me."*[9]

The following year, Bernardin Gantin reprimanded the bishop Jacques Gaillot for having sanctioned the union of a homosexual couple who were facing imminent death from AIDS, *"The French bishop will cease advancing repulsive practices in society."*[10]

Suenens criticized Gantin's action, *"I feel my duty to remind the African cardinal when Jesus said 'Love thy neighbor as thyself,' He meant* all *thy neighbors."*[11] A few years later, Gantin removed Gaillot from his bishopric for preaching *Liberation Theology.*

Gaillot said of his demise, *"I had a dream to be able to accompany the poor, the excluded, the distressed...to be able to show my indignation at destitution, injustice and famine...without fear of the guillotine..."*[12]

Regardless, Suenens' vision for the Church, his vision for the world, was so vast it would have required Vatican III to bring it about. Vatican II—the equivalent of World War II in the Church— opened the door to change, Vatican III—the equivalent of World War III in the Church—would have been required to bring it about.

Suenens was the man, the force, behind John XXIII, Paul VI and John Paul I, the three popes of the twentieth century who allowed their conscience to overrule the evils in their scripture—the three popes of the twentieth century who had brought the elevator of human justice to the fiftieth floor of the one hundred story building of righteousness. But, it has remained there since—their successors choosing to lock it there forevermore.

Cardinal Leon Joseph Suenens was scheduled to speak at John Carroll University in Cleveland. Disturbed, John Paul II was loading the College of Cardinals with conservatives, Suenens, who had once, together with Luciani, championed the ill-fated cause to remove the election of the Pope from the College of Cardinals to the Synod of Bishops, was about to call on the Vatican to remove the authority to appoint bishops from the Pope to the Synod of Bishops.

A draft of the speech he never made was found in his typewriter. A housemaid innocently released it to a *Sun Times* reporter. *"...One can see what I say here, very vividly. If, in the case of the United States, the President were allowed to appoint the members of Congress, he would then have the power of a dictator. He could load the Congress entirely with those who share his own convictions, democrats or republicans, and thereby muster the vote to render his own appointment invincible. But believe me in what I have to say here today, a plane with only one wing can fly in only one direction, and, that direction is very decidedly down!"* [13]

Suenens died very much as his prodigy Albino Luciani had died. American newspapers reported, *"Vibrant and on the job to the end...Suenens...the Architect of Twentieth Century Catholicism...the chief negotiator of Vatican II...was found sitting up in bed wearing his reading glasses...Upright in his hands was clutched a book... The bed lamp was on and the window next to his bed was wide open.*

The book was his own book, one he had written years before. The book was ...Day by Day. It was opened to page fifty-six.

His eyes were open and they seemed to be fixed on a phrase at the bottom of the page, 'Let us all look around us with new eyes. A whole world of discovery will open up before us!'

It seemed Suenens was editing his bestseller for republishing.

In the margin of the opposite page were scribbled the words, 'Always look forward, never look back!'" [14]

The great man had left his mark in time. John XXIII, Paul VI and the little boy Albino Luciani had left their mark in time. Disciples of Lacordaire *"Have an opinion and do something about it!"* [15]

The record is there for all time. It is there for men and women of good conscience to soak up.

1 *Le Soir Brussels* 2 May 79

2 *La Stampa* 2 Nov 78

3 *A Life with Karol* Cardinal Stanislaw Dziwisz - *IL Messaggero* 23 Jan 07.

4 *La Tribune de Bruxelles* 12 Dec 83

5 *CBS News* 12 Sep 83 *

6 *La Tribune de Bruxelles* 17 Sep 83

7 The author's short story *The Queen of Theology* in his book *'Let's All Get Behind the Pope'* also published as *'The Reincarnation of Albino Luciani'* recounts Elizabeth Taylor's struggle for AIDS

8 *Los Angeles Times* 26 Mar 86

9 *Philadelphia Inquirer* 29 Sep 88

10 *La Repubblica* 22 Nov 88

11 *Philadelphia Inquirer* 25 Nov 88

12 *Voice of the Desert* Feb 95

13 *Sun Times* 21 Mar 96

14 A composite of the *New York Times – Boston Globe – Cleveland Sun Times – Washington Post –* 19 Mar 96. Five months after his death the Vatican cited Suenens died of thrombosis – embolism

13 Reprinted from Albino Luciani's book *Illustrissimi* 1976

* In 2003, a documentary was censored by major television channels because it included this clip.

Chapter 38

"...by the grace of God."

"*...John Paul was able to retain his papers upright in his hands by the grace of God.*" The Vatican, October 10, 1978[1]

Bullshit!

There are tens of thousands of words in *'Murder in the Vatican.'* Whereas, alone, any one of them might lose its voice in court, I am reasonably certain, if taken en masse to the tribunal, they will stand the test of time.

As we have demonstrated, the press is immensely more reliable than witnesses of motive who want to make him out to be whatever serves their political purposes. Yet, as it comes from different sides of the aisle, even the press can be less than reliable in determining the true cloth of a man, particularly one as controversial as this man.

Although it is not possible to reconstruct precisely the man he truly was, hopefully, we have come close to what a pope should be.

Likewise, the press is more reliable in the case of murder. That is, the reports as they first appear immediately following events before the clergy and fiction writers get their fingers on them. The reason references herein are mostly from the first reportings of events. You will not find Effortil, digitalis or anticoagulants in any of them.

Yet, what we have set forth does not necessarily, in every case, prove murder. Still, most of the surviving evidence suggests murder. These people died of mysterious circumstances which have never been satisfactorily explained and the Vatican has repeatedly refused to take actions normally prudent under the laws of nations.

In cases where murder was suspect, the Vatican repeatedly denied independent autopsy, which, in itself, could have prevented rumors. In cases where murder was apparent, the Vatican denied independent investigation which could have solved the crimes.

In the case of the Swiss Guard murders, the Vatican had nothing to lose and everything to gain by taking Scotland Yard up on its offer to investigate the murders. Why would one not want to know who killed these three, one of which was the closest person to the sitting Pontiff. Why didn't John Paul II overrule Cardinal Sodano and take Scotland Yard up on its offer? Why would he have not wanted to know who had murdered the most precious person to have ever come into his life? Could it be an investigation would have traced Estermann to have been the rookie guard assigned to the palace the night of John Paul's death? One will never know.

All we do know is he died suddenly at the age of 65 when he appeared to be, and medical records proved him to be, in exceptional health. We know one thing more. Many people wanted him dead.

Some claim the weight of the papacy killed him.

There have survived scores of pictures and films of his papacy. It is a rare spot in time to find a glimpse of him not smiling, laughing and joking—the reason he is remembered as the smiling pope.

Albino Luciani was having the time of his life. One does not die of stress when one is having a good time.

He died short of his genetic promise.

He lost a grandmother in the 1918 flu and his other grandparents and his father lived into their eighties and nineties.[2] Heart disease was not a factor in any of their deaths.[3] His mother died of cancer at 74[4] at a time life expectancy was twenty years short of what it is today. His full-blood siblings[5] lived into their nineties, his brother dying at 91 and his sister, today in her nineties, can read this book.

'Luciani was a doctrinal conservative. He didn't care how much suffering doctrine imposed on the everyday lives of innocent people.'
You will hear this from those who want to destroy ecclesiastical motive for murder. You will hear this from those who think there is something holy about depriving others of equal rights under the laws of nations. You will hear this from those who seek his canonization in a conservative church. For this reason his family and some others who knew him will deny anything of a controversial nature he may have said or done—particularly his compassion for homosexuals in a homophobic church—unreliable witnesses to his true testament.[6]

Nothing strikes closer to the truth of the ecclesiastical Luciani than his first words to his newly acquired congregation in Venice February 8, 1970, *"Today science has developed tremendously and purified our knowledge from thousands of defects in our religious knowledge of the past. Our religious knowledge has to cleanse itself of these falsehoods which science has exposed, which were not, anyway, a part of the true authentic Christian revelation—the glory of the Church will not be judged in its worship of mythical specters of the past, nor its magnificent buildings and ritual, but in its efforts to realize fraternal union among people. I mean all people."*[7]

Yet, what is really important of this man is not his life on earth, not the things that are said of him, not even the lingering mystery of his death. Like any God, or for that matter, like any man, all that counts is what he left behind, *"It is the inalienable right of no man to accumulate wealth beyond the necessary while other men starve to death because they have nothing."*[8]

Notices in newspapers around the globe the day he was elected seemed uncoordinated. They said all kinds of things.

Because it was part of the Associated Press release, there was a small clipping which appeared in all of the world's newspapers.[9]

> He once said: "The true treasures of the church are the poor, the little ones to be helped not merely with occasional alms but in a way they can be promoted."

Slipped into the inner pages, for the most part it went unnoticed. It had been extracted from something he had said as a cardinal two years earlier, *"The Church's real treasurers are the poor, the little ones, who should not be helped by means of mere occasional alms but by a society which insures the opportunity of each little one to make his or her fullest contribution. Charity is like sandbags placed against onrushing waters, it will never stem the tide..."*[10]

Charity is an excuse for compassion in a selfish society. One can amass wealth beyond one's wildest dreams and drop one's pennies into the poor box. Charity does not exist in a communist society.

Albino Luciani was convinced the coalition of capitalism and charity could not work. The world had poverty written all over it.

He would force the rich to help the poor. He once told the nun Vincenza, *"When I preach compassion for the poor, they call me a saint. When I do something about it, they call me a communist."*[11]

Abhorred by what was taking place in the Soviet Union, he was encouraged by the success of what had already taken place in Italy which had drawn the wrath of Henry Kissinger, *"I believe the advent of communism in these (Italy and Spain) European countries is likely to result in a sequence of events in which other European countries will move in the same direction... the Communist Party has emerged*

402

as an effective vehicle for developing jobs and providing education for the common people and this endangers our free capitalistic society... If communism takes hold in Italy, NATO would collapse and the United States would be dangerously isolated..."[12]

Insofar as *Murder in the Vatican* presents compelling evidence linking prominent Italian and American statesmen to the murders of Aldo Moro, Paul VI, John Paul I and other leaders of the Marxist movement in the free world, the author reminds the reader, it was the sworn duty of these men, imposed upon them by the laws of their nations, to head off what they viewed as a dangerous slide to the *left.*

Luciani was hopeful the ideology of a free democratic-communist society once established in Italy and Europe would spread across the pond to the Americas. He would demolish the driving force behind poverty in third world countries with the 'pill.' He would create a society based on the principle—his principle, *"What is important is not how many children are born, but that every child that is born has an equal opportunity at a good and healthy life."*[13]

Finish

Whereas they do not all support my case, I have presented all the events of the time—thousands of them—in chronological order.

It is the strategy of writers to leave most of them out and present only those that support one's suppositions and even those out of order. It puts the reader at a disadvantage to the writer's conclusions. Like a shell game with a thousand shells and a half-dozen peanuts, mesmerize the reader and he'll believe most anything you tell him.

I have taken the time to put them in historical order for a reason. Though I am reasonably certain the conclusions I have set forth are sound, I am only one mind. Yet, it may be, it will take many minds, many investigations, to carry this game to its end.

Hopefully, the day is not far off, someone with great analytical skills, a modern day Hercule Poirot, will score the winning goal.

Aside from stories of his young life which are my direct witness, I have said nothing here that has not been said before, either in the press or in the writings of this good man. All that is to my credit is that for the first time the full record has been brought together in one place, *"Twentieth century capitalism as it was jointly embraced by the Vatican and the United States and those caught up in it."*[14]

So we have walked with him, and we have talked with him, in the woods, together with Pinocchio and the Cat and the Fox and the Poodle Medoro. Yet, I feel I have said poorly what Albino Luciani could have said so much better. Still, the important thing is not that I have written, but that you have listened.

Now, take it with you. Carry it with you to the ends of the earth. That what he dreamed of, those things he fought for, those things he willed to be, will come to be, for each of them, and for me, and for you, and for all humanity.

I wonder? I often wonder?
If I will still be around...when the ball goes into the net!

George Lucien Gregoire

I want to thank those who have taken the time to review my book on the Internet and in journals and those I have met along the way that made it possible.

All inquiries responded to:
George Lucien Gregoire
University of Maryland
38 South Paca Street, # 403
Baltimore Maryland 21201
Vatican@att.net (1) 410 625 9741

Preview author's books on: www.johnpaul1.org

1 *Vatican Radio* 11 Oct 78. Vatican corrected release of circumstances of John Paul I's death
2 Source: tombstones and cemetery records.
3 Heart disease is a genetic impairment in which the liver cannot discharge excess cholesterol.
4 There is confusion concerning his mother. No birth certificate exists. Baptismal certificate seems to read 1874 which supports age at death 74. Marriage certificate seems to read '1879' which supports age at death '69.' The confusion is between the handwritten '4' and the '9.'
5 A brother Federico did not survive infancy.
6 Those seeking his sainthood are particularly denial of any compassion he had for homosexuals as they depend on the most homophobic pope in history—Benedict XVI—for his elevation.
7 *Il Gazzettino* 9 Feb 70. *Messaggero Mestre* 9 Feb 70. The quote was subsequently published by *The Times* and many other world newspapers. That he used the word *'thousands'* instead of *'many'* demonstrates the depth he must have gone to in analyzing religion vs. science – religion vs. the truth.
8 Film clip of JP saying this is on you-tube. Link is on homepage of www.johnpaul1.org
9 Clipping is from *The Evening Bulletin* 29 Sep 78. The phrase appears in all newspapers of the time
10 *Messaggero Mestre* 22 Jan 76
11 *Veneto Nostro* 17 Sep 67
12 *Covet Action Quarterly* Washington DC No. 49, summer 94
13 *La Repubblica* 2 Aug 78 Luciani's on artificial insemination.
14 T. Frances Elliott's review of *Murder in the Vatican, The Times*

Appendix

The Vatican Deception

Shortly after John Paul's interment in the crypt beneath St. Peter's Basilica, there began a program by the Vatican intended to create two misconceptions, 1) Albino Luciani had been, all of his life, a strict conservative—to destroy the ecclesiastical motive for murder, and, 2) he was on the brink of death when elected to the papacy—to support its supposition he died of natural causes.

The conservative Luciani

Teams of workers showed up at Belluno, Vittorio Veneto and Venice scouring through his writings, sermons and press releases destroying anything controversial he said or did. Original documents were removed and replaced with forgeries to 'prove' he took positions the exact opposite of what he actually stood for.

The objective was to create a man who had spent his life on his knees and ignored the humane issues of his day; to change his image from the progressive he had been to the conservative the Vatican wants him to be remembered as.

In 1984, David Yallop proved the case for murder.
Under John Paul II, the Vatican reacted quickly to Yallop's book.
The Curia drafted a twenty-thousand word biographical brief—the equivalent of the largest chapter in this book. I call it *The Vatican Deception.*
The objective was to create a man who had been on the brink of death from the time he stepped out of the womb until that fateful morning he woke up reading his papers held upright in his hands with his glasses halfway down on his nose.
"When he was born the midwife baptized him immediately because he was so frail, she feared he would die...Within a year of his ordination, his health, never good, broke down and he was taken to the sanatorium, a very ill man, he was expected to die...He recovered, but many times more, he again and again spent many months in and out of sanatoriums and hospitals..."
It goes on, *"...After the war, he was confined for six months in a sanatorium for what was believed to be tuberculosis and turned out to be pneumonia..."*
TB is a slow-progressing condition symptomatic of weight and energy loss and coughing of blood. Pneumonia is a rapidly progressing deadly upper respiratory condition most often symptomatic of coughing up green or yellow phlegm and high fever. Unless arrested quickly it kills in the short term. Whereas it is possible to misdiagnosed one for the other, hospital tests will quickly disclose the error.
To survive for six months with pneumonia would be more than a medical miracle. Regardless, what the Vatican has successfully accomplished here is to translate his three day stay in a Belluno hospital for bronchitis in 1947 into six months in an unnamed sanatorium. You go to a sanatorium for tuberculosis or other highly contagious disease. You go to a hospital for pneumonia.
Whereas, it is true, he had once been taken to a sanatorium, it occurred when

405

he was twenty-three in 1935. His illness had been misdiagnosed as tuberculosis. He was released in a few days after clearing up a bout with bronchitis.

He mentioned this experience to me as he had been scared to death he had TB. He had been thankful it had not occurred a year earlier when he was still in the seminary. He prided himself that from the time he entered elementary school in 1917 until he graduated from the seminary in 1935, he had never missed a day. By divine providence, his tonsils and adenoids had cropped up in summer break.

Regardless, penicillin was discovered in 1928 and became the wonder drug of the thirties. During the war the antibiotic streptomycin was developed and in 1944 it was successfully implemented. TB was no longer an automatic death sentence.

Yet, I guess, in this case, I must do more than tell you he told me this. I must prove it. I call on witness of the man himself. In his 1976 book *Illustrissimi*, Luciani speaks of his sole time in a sanatorium in his letter to Saint Therese.

> I remembered this when they took me, ill, to the sana-
> torium, at a time when penicillin and antibiotics had not
> yet been invented, and so the patient had to expect
> death, more or less immediate.
> I was ashamed at feeling a bit of fear. "Thérèse, at

He had been a remarkably healthy child attested to by his perfect attendance record at school and dozens of photos that have survived showing nothing other than one of impeccable health, even those taken at the time of his 'sanatorium' stay.

1935

Regardless, in an ongoing assault, *The Vatican Deception* speaks of Luciani as being in such fragile condition, from the beginning to the end of his days, as if each breath would be his last. One is kept in constant suspense throughout the narrative wondering if he will make it to the end of the script.

It establishes the 'fact' he spent ten days in the Stella Maris Institute on the Lido a month before he was elected—a 'fact' which was later disclaimed by Luciani's doctor Dr. Da Ros and by the Stella Maris Institute itself.[1]

Consistent with its master plan, *The Vatican Deception* paints him out to be a man who spent his life on his knees talking to statues and ignoring the issues of his day. It idolizes his devout mother and ignores his atheist father. It carries its deception into his papacy cleverly editing out anything controversial he had to say.

The Vatican Deception was published in Catholic countries in 1985 through religious orders under various titles—authors unnamed to mask its source—an anonymous priest in Italy, an anonymous monk in France, an anonymous Jesuit in Brazil, an anonymous missionary in India, an anonymous nun in the states…

Scores of 'biographies' published by members of religious orders have since been sourced from this document the reason they paint him out to have been on the brink of death from the time he came out of the womb and he never did anything to help those whose everyday lives were oppressed by doctrine.

This is what makes members of religious orders poor historians. They blot out those things that don't fit their own fascist convictions. Though I do not entirely agree with their conclusions, the true historians of the Church have been men like Avro Manhattan, David Yallop and John Cornwell, who recorded the truth.

His medical history

He had four minor operations—tonsils at eleven, adenoids at fifteen, gallstones at fifty-two and hemorrhoids the same year. Tonsils and adenoids were routine for children at the time. All-in-all, nothing unusual for a man of sixty-five.

He had been hospitalized four other times.

In 1935, he was taken to a sanatorium for what was misdiagnosed as TB and turned out to be bronchitis. He was released within a week.

In 1945, he was confined overnight in a Belluno hospital for bronchitis

In 1947, he was confined for three days in the same hospital for bronchitis.

In 1975, he spent a night in a Mestre clinic for an eye problem. His viscosity tested as normal and the condition was corrected with mild medication.

The bronchitis never reoccurred. After the war, he became an avid mountain climber and later a runner, which activities build a powerful respiratory system.

We have covered them all, as he told the world the day he was installed.[2]

> He talked of love and hunger and of the sick to the audience of over 10,000. Conveying his love to the ailing, the 65-year-old healthy-looking pontiff said: "The pope has been hospitalized eight times and has had four operations."

The Vatican Deception was augmented by the Vatican collaboration with John Cornwell to write his book in 1987 and by the Lorenzi video of 'pain' after a decade of silence tempered only by his own testimony, *"As a Don Orione monk, I have taken a vow of allegiance to the sitting pontiff. I do anything I am told."*[3]

Today, one can add the Vatican's production of multi-million dollar satirical documentaries depicting Albino Luciani's lifelong struggle against death.

I have always been puzzled why those who have doubt of what I have to say go to the Vatican and its tributaries and clergy to verify what I have to say. I have taken the time to provide more than five hundred direct sources for what I have to say. These are available in libraries and, to an extent, on the Internet.

Cornwell ran into this same problem. In 1987, he was engaged by the Vatican to write *A Thief in the Night* to discredit Yallop's *In God's Name*.

Many ate it up, despite Cornwell was on the Vatican 'payroll' so to speak.

Ironically, a few years later, the same thing would happen to Cornwell.

In 2000, he presented powerful evidence in his book *Hitler's Pope* Pius XII knew of the plight of the Jews during the war and did nothing to help them.

In 2005, David Dalin wrote his book *The Myth of Hitler's Pope* claiming Pius had done much to help the Jews. Though Cornwell clearly had the facts, many ate it up because Dalin is a Rabbi—he is the independent 'expert' so to speak.

Or could it be, somewhere along the way, David Dalin was offered a full professorship at Ave Maria University? He is on the Vatican payroll. Fools!

1 *Il Giornale Andrea Tornelli* 27 Sep 03
2 *The Evening Bulletin* 29 Sep 78
3 *A Thief in the Night* John Cornwell. See film clip www.johnpaul1.org

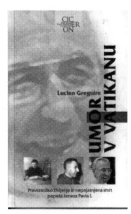

Slovenia: www.ciceron.si*   Albino Luciani = White Light   Forgive me for the cover,
                                                              the Devil made me do it

* *Murder in the Vatican* is available in some foreign languages, French and Italian in 2011.

White Light Dark Night, A theological expansion of the biog included in *Murder in the Vatican*. Readers who have read the 2010 edition of *Murder in the Vatican* are advised not to buy *White Light* as they have already read most of it. *White Light* has its own site **www.JohnPaulI.org**.

Let's All Get Behind the Pope includes 44 short stories in which the author recreates little known incidents in the lives of Albino Luciani and other famous people which caused them to rise up as champions of human justice—see sample story on the following page. Included are the author's award winning short stories: *The Violin Bow*—the story of a student of the Peabody Conservatory of Music and a violin bow, and *The Icicle That Would Not Fall*—an old man sacrifices his life to save a young boy. Also included is the 110 page novella *The Reincarnation of Albino Luciani* also published as *In Search of the Human Soul* and *End of Faith* in which the reincarnated Luciani in the voice of ten year old boy defines the human soul— based on Luciani's doctoral thesis, *The Origin of the Human Soul...*

www.amazon.com   www.amazon.co.uk   www.barnesandnoble.com
www.authorhouse.com   Ask for at any bookstore worldwide

Bookstores: returnability is guaranteed by Ingram worldwide
Bookstores best discount UK and USA: bkorders@authorhouse.com 888 280 7715

Preview author's books: www.johnpaul1.org   www.murderinthevatican.com
Meaningful hardcover or paperback books make lasting gifts
Contact author for questions and signed copies: vatican@att.net   (1) 410 625 9741

The following is a representative story reprinted from *Let's All Get Behind the Pope:* scores of little known incidents in the lives of Albino Luciani and other famous people which caused them to rise up as champions of human justice—forty-four stories in all plus the novella *The Reincarnation of Albino Luciani*—in the voice of a ten year old boy Albino searches for his soul.

I Want to Learn to Count

"Never be afraid to stand up for what is right, whether your adversary be your parent, your teacher, your peer, your politician, your preacher, your constitution, or even your God!" [1]

Albino Luciani

"One, two, three, four, five, six...?" her little brother stopped. He looked around the room as if someone had hidden the next number behind the chair, under the rug, perhaps, in the closet?

He started up again, "One, two three, four, five, six, seven..."

The little boy seemed lost. He tried again, "One, two, three, four, five, six, seven, eight, nine...?" He stopped again.

His eyes searched along the floor, glanced up to the ceiling. He found it under the dust in the corner, "...ten!" he beamed.

Susan told her mother, "I, too, want to learn how to count!"

Her mother laughed, "No. Girls don't have to know how to count."

The blackboard had three panels. Each day one of them would change. The big one in the middle, the one reserved for the lesson of the day.

The *Pledge of Alliance* was written on the one on the left, as if by this time one could not have possibly learned it by heart.

I pledge allegiance to the flag of the United States of America, and to the republic for which it stands, one nation under God, indivisible, with liberty and justice for all.

The *Ten Commandments* were listed on the one on the right. As if by this time one could not have possibly learned them by heart.

I am the one and only God, bow down and adore me.
Thou shalt have no graven images before thee.
Thou shalt not take my name in vain
Thou shalt keep the Sabbath
Honor thy mother and father
Thou shall not kill
Thou shall not commit adultery
Thou shalt not steal
Thou shalt not bare false witness
Thou shalt not desire to take from thy neighbor his property,
    including his house, his wife, his slaves, his ox, his ass.

Ichabod Falwell was an old wrinkled up prune with chalk dust wedged into its fingernails. He scrubbed yesterday's lesson off the center panel as a mixed-bag of ragged and dressed up boys and girls pushed and shoved their way boisterously into the one-room schoolhouse behind him.

He picked up a piece of chalk and wrote on the center panel,

The Minutemen

What those brave young lads at Concord
took those first bullets for

He rapped his stick. The chatter and clamor stuttered to an end.

He pointed to the left panel.

The children stood up and clasped their hearts and droned to an old flag which seemed to have fought the war itself.

The master struck his pointer toward the panel on the right.

They droned again, this time to the board itself. Not one of them had made it his or her responsibility to learn them by heart.

The wrinkled up old prune spread out his arm toward the center panel. "Today we are going to talk about the Minutemen. We are going to talk about those brave young lads at Concord. What they took those first bullets for in the spring of 1775?"

Susan raised her hand and stood up.

The old man was disturbed, "Why didn't you go before class?"

She interrupted the snickers, "It's not that. It's something else." She hesitated as if to gather the courage, "I want to learn to count."

The class broke into a frenzy. The old man laughed, "You don't have to learn to count. You are a girl.

"Sit down." he ordered. She hesitated a bit and sat down.

The old prune with chalk dust wedged into its fingernails turned to the class, "Let's get back to the business of the day. What those brave young lads took those first bullets for in the spring of 1775?"

Susan stood up again. This time she didn't wait for the okay. "That's what I'm talking about. What those brave young lads took those first bullets for in the spring of 1775?"

"Nonsense!" The old man, frustrated by the girl's persistence, repeated, this time at full volume, "Sit down!"

The little girl held her ground, "You don't understand. I have the right to learn how to count."

This time the class didn't laugh. It had never asked itself why boys were taught how to count, and girls were not taught how to count. If nothing else, its silence demanded an explanation.

The old prune with chalk dust wedged into its fingernails frowned, "You're wrong. You don't have the right to learn how to count. There is no reason for you to know how to count for you are not among the counters. You are among the counted.

"See, here," he pointed and read the Tenth Commandment aloud, *'Thou shalt not desire to take from thy neighbor his property, including his house, his wife, his slaves, his ox, his ass.'*[2]

"Only a man counts his property, his money, his slaves, his sheep, his cows, his chickens, his ox, his wife, his children and all else he owns.

"According to Almighty God under whom our great nation has been built, according to its constitution, like other animals you are mere property. Being property you cannot own property. Having no property to count, you have no reason to learn how to count."

Susan didn't blink an eye, "I am not an animal. I am a human being." The boys doubled up laughing. The girls looked up at her as if they had just come back from the dead.

The old prune with chalk dust wedged into its fingernails closed his case. "Not according to God, not according to the facts." He pointed once more to the Tenth Commandment. The boys giggled. The girls accepted their fate. It was obvious to each of them Susan was in over her head.

The old prune with chalk dust wedged into its fingernails glanced around the room. With the exception of his adversary, it was clear he had convinced the lighter sex of their role in life. He had done a masterful job of presenting the facts. He had won his case. He had removed the question mark from each of their stares. On top of it all, he had made a fool of this

411

impudent little girl. "Now let's get on with the business of the day. What those brave young lads took those first bullets for in the spring of 1775?"

Susan was not quite finished, "That's not what it says."

"It is exactly what it says." The old man pointed again and read, *"Thou shalt not desire to take from thy neighbor his property, including his house, his wife, his slaves, his ox, his ass.'"* [2]

Taking up his chalk he underlined '*his property*' → '*his wife*' inserting an arrow between the phrases.

"Not there, over here."

The little girl pointed to the *Pledge of Allegiance*. With a defiant smile she demolished his case, the case of this old prune with chalk dust wedged into its fingernails. Susan read, *"...liberty and justice for all!"*

Her classmates looked to their master for an explanation. He answered their unasked question, "My mistake," the frustrated old prune chuckled. Taking up the chalk, he added the word '*men.*'

Standing back, he read, *"'...liberty and justice for all men!'* Yes, that's better" he announced to the class, "This is what those brave lads took those first bullets for in the spring of 1775!"

The little girl kept the thought to herself. "This is not what those brave young lads took those first bullets for in the spring of 1775. They took those first bullets so that I, too, can learn how to count.

"Furthermore, I am going to learn how to count.

"What's more, I am going to make it possible for all those little girls who come after me to be able to learn how to count.

"I am going to change Ichabod Falwell's blackboard back to what those brave lads took those first bullets for in the spring of 1775, '*...liberty and justice for all!'*"

———

Until the mid-20th century, there were virtually no women engineers in the United States, engineering requiring a strong aptitude in mathematics.

On April 9, 1775, British troops fired on Minutemen at Concord. Two fell dead and four others were wounded by '*the shot heard round the world.*'

Susan B. Anthony was a precocious child having learned to read and write at age three. In 1826, when she was six years old, a teacher refused to teach her arithmetic because of her gender. That night, Susan announced to her family she was going to learn how to count so that all little girls who would come after her would have the same right to learn how to count.

Her father, a cotton manufacturer and abolitionist, groomed her into the human rights activist she became—one dedicated to women's rights, particularly as they concerned themselves with custody rights of their own children. She would change the definition of 'woman' from 'property' to 'human being' which, in turn, changed the definition of marriage; marriage would no longer be a barter between one man and another—a maiden for a cow—but the decision of two people who are in love.

412

The Author

on his first trip to Vittorio Veneto

Born in New England, *George Lucien Gregoire* completed his undergraduate and graduate work in Massachusetts schools.

He spent his military years in U.S. Army Intelligence in Italy and the Arctic and his professional career as an officer of American and European corporations.

He was an American industrialist operating in Central America dealing with the same banks the Vatican was involved with when the Vatican bank scandal and revolution he speaks of in this book took place.

For a time, a national figure in cooperative education, he has served on boards of secondary schools and universities. He is the founding trustee of charitable organizations, many providing education to impaired children.

Gregoire made the acquaintance of John Paul in the sixties when the Pope—as a little known bishop of a remote mountain province in northern Italy—was involved in the priest-worker revolution which eventually gave rise to the success of the communist and socialist parties in the polls.

"This chalice contains one hundred and twenty-two of the world's most pristine diamonds. Do you really think this is what Christ meant by his Church?"

John Paul I, 4th audience 27 Sep 78

Author contact info is on page 404

Author's other books see pages 408-412